Dispatches of Milanese Ambassadors, 1450–1483

prepared by

Paul Murray Kendall & Vincent Ilardi

DISPATCHES

with Related Documents of Milanese Ambassadors in FRANCE and BURGUNDY,

1450 – 1483

OHIO UNIVERSITY PRESS

VOLUME TWO: 1460-1461

EDITED WITH TRANSLATIONS BY

Paul M. Kendall and Vincent Ilardi

 ATHENS·OHIO·1971

Copyright © 1970 by Ohio University Press
Library of Congress Catalog Card Number: 68–20933
International Standard Book Number: 8214–0082–7
All rights reserved
Printed in the United States of America

CONTENTS

ILLUSTRATIONS

INTRODUCTION

Unlike the documents of Volume I, 1450–60, those of the present volume cover a span of but eleven months, from late August of 1460 to late July of 1461, and are mainly concerned with two affairs of state.

The first is the negotiation, followed by the renegotiation, of a treaty linking the Duke of Milan and Louis, Dauphin of France, a refugee from his father, dwelling at Genappe in Brabant under the protection of his uncle-by-marriage, Philip, Duke of Burgundy, peer of France and independent ruler of the Low Countries. The second affair concerns the development of relations among the Duke of Milan, the Dauphin, the Duke of Burgundy, and the Yorkists in England, a development aimed at countering French intervention in Italy, in the form of the Angevin occupation of Genoa and invasion of the Kingdom of Naples, and the menace of a French attack upon the Duke of Burgundy.

The first document in the volume, dated August 27, 1460, sets forth the Duke of Milan's instructions to his envoy, Prospero da Camogli, on the eve of Prospero's departure to negotiate a treaty with the Dauphin. The last document, of July 20, 21, 1461, is a dispatch written by Prospero about four days before the Dauphin received the news of the death of his father on July 22 that made him King Louis XI. The Milanese dispatches of the next five years—from July 22, 1461 to

the arrival in France in the latter part of March, 1466, of the tidings of the death of Francesco Sforza, March 8—have been published in four volumes by B. de Mandrot (and, for the fourth volume, C. Samaran). The succeeding volumes of this edition, encompassing Milanese documents for France and Burgundy, 1466–83, will each, like the present volume, cover a comparatively brief time span, the documentation being very rich.

After spending less than a month at the delphinal court, September-October, 1460, Prospero da Camogli returned to Milan with the Treaty of Genappe signed by the Dauphin. It embodied the alliance which had been worked out between Francesco Sforza and envoys of the Dauphin, except that Louis had insisted upon the inclusion in the treaty, as an adherent of his to be rescued by Milan, of Giacomo di Valperga, ex-chancellor of Savoy whose estates the Duke of Savoy had just seized by force. Sforza duly ratified the treaty, but sent Prospero back to Genappe in January of 1461 with instructions to persuade the Dauphin to exclude Valperga from the document, an operation that occupied Prospero for months but which was finally resolved by direct negotiations between Louis and Sforza. In the course of recounting the progress of his mission, Prospero gives an unrivaled picture of the character and of the methods of diplomacy of the Dauphin; he offers information not elsewhere recorded about the Dauphin's court and about the Dauphin's prickly relations with the Duke of Burgundy and ambiguous relations with his father, Charles VII. The dispatches of the Milanese ambassador also yield valuable insights into the explosive situation at the court of Burgundy which he visited—the slackness of the Duke's government, the position of the Duke's favorites, Antoine and Jean de Croy, the feud between the brothers de Croy and the Duke's heir Charles, Count of Charolais. Prospero likewise describes a ceremonious assembly of the Burgundian Order of the Golden Fleece, and sketches lively vignettes of courtly life and ambassadorial difficulties in the mid fifteenth century.

The other principal matter of these dispatches and instructions,

Milanese-Delphinal-Burgundian-English relations, is perhaps even more significant, and presents a much wider scope of diplomatic activity, though the accession of the Dauphin to the throne of France brought the movement to an abrupt end. This diplomatic campaign can be seen as a fledgling effort to apply the Italian political system of shifting combinations of states within the framework of the League of Italy— a rudimentary "balance of power" concept—to the large, less sensitively organized political spaces north of the Alps. For the first time, the remote island of England became a factor in the designs of an Italian statesman, Francesco Sforza. The somewhat bizarre instrument of this diplomacy was a diminutive papal legate, and protégé of Sforza, Francesco Coppini (see below, p. xxii). Through him, ties already established between the Yorkist Earl of Warwick (the future "Kingmaker"), Captain of Calais, and the Dauphin and the Duke of Burgundy were rapidly strengthened, and by the same agency and the Dauphin's helping hand Sforza and the Yorkists were brought into a promising rapport.

From the latter half of 1460, the Duke of Milan had been hoping for a Yorkist attack on France. In the spring of 1461, as an answer to Angevin successes in the Kingdom of Naples, the support accorded by Charles VII to the Lancastrians, and the efforts of the anti-Burgundian party at Charles VII's court to push the King into war with the Dauphin's protector, there appeared the possibility of a treaty of amity, or at least a close understanding, among the powers thus threatened—Milan, Burgundy, England. The central figure of the design, Dauphin Louis, though he nurtured the semblance of a league against France and lent ear to Yorkist talk of a cross-Channel invasion, did not encourage Sforza to ally with Burgundy or with England—a league which could prove most inconvenient when he himself became the ruler of France.[1] No other contemporary source presents so vivid a

---

[1] For a study of the Dauphin's life and his political maneuvering during 1460–61, see P. M. Kendall, *Louis XI,* New York and London, 1971; for details of the conflict between Lancaster and York, 1460–61, see P. M. Kendall, *Warwick the Kingmaker,* New York and London, 1957.

week-by-week, and sometimes almost day-by-day, picture of the turmoil of news and rumor stirring the Low Countries and the see-sawing hopes and fears of the Dauphin and his uncle during the time that the Yorkists and Lancastrians, in the crowded months from December, 1460, to April, 1461, struggled for the mastery of England.

Thus the diplomacy reflected in this volume foreshadows the coalitions and counter-coalitions that would begin, following the French invasion of Italy of 1494, to give expression to the dynastic ambitions and nationalist rivalries of the sixteenth and later centuries.

Prospero Schiaffino da Camogli, commonly known as de Camulis or Camulio, takes his name from his birthplace, Camogli, an enchanting fishing village perched on the hills overlooking the Ligurian Sea some twenty-five kilometers south of Genoa. The Schiaffino, like many other prominent families of Camogli, had long been active in the turbulent politics of the Genoese Republic, and Prospero himself had taken part as a partisan of the Adorno and the Spinola clans against the Campofregoso, who had wrestled the Dogeship from the Adorno in the late 1440s. Little is known about this early period of Prospero's life except that late in 1455 he was involved in the negotiation of an agreement among the Adorno, the Spinola, and the Fieschi clans seeking to unseat Doge Pietro Campofregoso, as a result of which in the following year he was sent by the Spinola to Milan to obtain aid from the Duke.[2] It is possible that he may have performed some service for Sforza before his capture of Milan, but it was only in November of 1456, probably in the course of the above mission, that Prospero was made a member of the ducal household at the monthly salary of 30 florins at 32 imperial pennies per florin.[3]

---

[2] Giovanni del Carretto, Marquess of Finale, to Sforza, Finale, Oct. 28, 1455 and Prospero to Sforza, Lerma, Dec. 8, 1455, *Genova*, cart. 410; Prospero to Cicco Simonetta, Lerma, Sept. 3, 1456 and Famiglia Spinola to Cicco, Genoa, Sept. 17, 1456, *ibid.*, cart. 411.

[3] Sforza to *Maestri delle entrate*, Milan, Nov. 9, 1456, *Reg. Missive* 15, fol. 379r. Two writers, who have pieced together much of Prospero's biographical data, date

Prospero's first diplomatic missions deal with Genoese affairs, in which he was an acknowledged expert. In April of 1457 he was sent on a circular embassy to Bernardo de Villamarina (Aragonese Admiral blockading Genoa), Giovanni Filippo Fieschi, and to Florence, Siena, Rome, and Naples, one of the principal objectives of which was to coordinate Milanese and Neapolitan efforts with the Genoese exiles in order to prevent French occupation of the city.[4] In October of the following year he was dispatched to the exiles in a vain effort to reconcile them with the former Doge, Pietro Campofregoso, and promote a united front for the expulsion of the French.[5] In 1459 he accompanied the Duke to the Congress of Mantua. From 1457 to the eve of his departure on his first mission to the Dauphin, he was given intermittently the task of settling a dispute which had arisen among the sons and heirs of Orlando Pallavicino (d. 1457), in the course of which he was accused by them of having falsified their account books—a charge from which Prospero never appears to have sufficiently cleared himself.[6]

---

his service for Sforza some years earlier. C. Braggio, "Giacomo Bracelli e l'umanesimo dei Liguri al suo tempo," *Atti della Società Ligure di Storia Patria,* XXIII(1890), 84, citing a letter (1478) by Antonio Ivani, a humanist unfriendly to Prospero, claims that he had entered Sforza's service before 1450. F. Gabotto, "Un nuovo contributo alla storia dell'umanesimo ligure," *ibid.,* XXIV(1892), 36, 187, argues for 1451 on the basis of a misdated letter. The wording of the letters cited in the preceding note makes it clear, however, that as of 1455 he was eager to serve the Duke, although he may have been in contact with him before that time. Moreover when he was discharged in 1467, he claimed to have served the Sforza for eleven years [see below, n. 11].

[4] Instructions for Prospero, Milan, April 21, 1457, BN, *Fonds Italien,* Cod. 1587, fols. 166r–175v, and Prospero to Sforza, Casciano, Apr. 23, 1457 and Serravalle, Apr. 27, 1457, *Genova,* cart. 412. Prospero left Milan on Apr. 21 and returned on July 16, as it appears in an account of his extraordinary expenses, dated July 21, 1457 [*Reg. Missive* 15, fol. 407r].

[5] See Sforza's instructions for Lancelotto de' Bossi, Milan, Dec. 2, 1458, *Francia,* cart. 524; Prospero to Bartolomeo da Recanati, Serravalle, Dec. 11, [1458], and Castelletto, Dec. 14, 1458, *Genova,* cart. 412; cf. Nunziante, XIX(1894), 64, n. 2, 70–71, n. 1.

[6] Prospero had first been sent to Busseto, the stronghold of the Pallavicino, to in-

His embroilment with these powerful and troublesome feudal lords, mention of which is made in these dispatches, may have played a part in his eventual estrangement from Cicco Simonetta whose son, Antonio, was related by marriage to the Pallavicino. By the time of his departure for Genappe, Prospero had created powerful enemies at court who did not hesitate to compromise the success of his mission by leaking important information to the Dauphin. These indiscretions, and the long periods of silence from Milan, poisoned his relations with the Dauphin who finally bypassed him and sent his own envoys to Milan to conclude the negotiations.[7] Left without instructions, the ambassador was given leave by the new King and was back in Milan by September 21, 1461. He carried with him a memorandum by Coppini outlining Louis' new radical demands as well as the Legate's letters to the Duke praising his diligence and ability, and suggesting that he be sent first to brief Pius II and then redispatched to France with the new Milanese ambassadors.[8]

Prospero, however, was never sent back to France. After a short

---

vestigate their dispute on Aug. 25, 1457 [*Reg. Missive* 39, fol. 45v]. Much of this register deals with this interminable question and with Prospero's efforts to settle it. The last letter by the Duke to Prospero on this matter is dated June 27, 1460, fol. 455r. For an undated accusation by Giovanni Manfredo Pallavicino that Prospero had falsified the books, and for Prospero's reply, also undated, denying the charge and accusing the *confidenti* of the Pallavicino family of the misdeed, see *Fondo Famiglie*, cart. 40. Prospero's reply was published and misdated (1451) by Gabotto, "Un nuovo contributo," doc. II, 187–90.

[7] In a dispatch from Rheims, Aug. 17, 1461 [*Francia*, cart. 526; Gabotto, "Un nuovo contributo," 205–06], Prospero complained that for the last two and one-half months he had received no communication from the Duke, and that Milanese messengers had ignored him altogether. Moreover he lamented that he could not support himself and the other eight persons in his entourage with the 40 ducats he had received since his departure, and consequently he had been forced to incur a debt of approximately 300 crowns. Cf. Prospero to Sforza, Paris, Sept. 5, 1461, *Francia*, cart. 526; Mandrot, I, 59–63.

[8] Coppini to Sforza, Paris, Sept. 4 and 6, 1461, Mandrot, I, 54–59, 63–67. That Prospero was back in Milan by Sept. 21, is gathered from a letter by Sforza to Ottone del Carretto, Milan, Sept. 21, 1461, *Roma*, cart. 51. Mandrot, I, 75–80, errs in attributing to Prospero a dispatch written from Tours on Oct. 15, 1461.

mission to Florence and Rome to brief Cosimo de' Medici and Pius on the attitude of Louis XI towards Italian affairs, and another to the Pope in the following year, he returned to Milan to begin a period of disappointment and relative obscurity.[9] He continued to serve as secretary and member of the ducal household, but it seems that he was never employed in an important capacity. Following Louis XI's infeudation of Genoa in favor of the Duke (Dec. 1463), Prospero sought to play a leading role in its acquisition from Doge Paolo Campofregoso, and thus secure an important post in that region which he had craved for so long, but Sforza deliberately kept him out of the negotiations and subsequent military operations.[10] Finally, on Feb. 8, 1467, he was discharged and apparently expelled from Milanese territory following an accusation by Giovanni Simonetta and possibly others that he wanted to become *Signore* of Genoa. Thereupon he repaired to Florence where he sought in vain to secure a position with Piero de' Medici.[11]

---

[9] Prospero left for Florence and Rome on Oct. 7 [Sforza to Ottone del Carretto, Milan, Oct. 12, 1461, *Roma,* cart. 51], and arrived in Rome on the 22nd [Ottone and Prospero to Sforza, Rome, Oct. 23, 1461, *ibid.,* cart. 51]. He planned to leave Rome on Nov. 3 after having made an excellent impression on the Pope [Ottone to Sforza, Rome, Nov. 2, 1461, *ibid.,* cart. 52]. For his second mission to Pius in July of 1462, see below, n. 27.

[10] Prospero had urged the Duke to infiltrate secretly a body of troops into the city and then coordinate with them an attack from the outside, so that he would be able to capture Genoa without the aid of the troublesome exiles. He offered to make the necessary preparations himself. See Prospero to Sforza, [Milan, March 2, 1464], *Genova,* cart. 418. In reply to a complaint by Prospero's friend, Antonio de Montaldo, that Sforza held Prospero in "poca stima," Corrado da Fogliano, the Duke's brother, argued unconvincingly that on the contrary both he and the Duke repeatedly consulted him on Genoese affairs and that Sforza treated him as "carnal fratello." [Corrado da Fogliano], to Antonio de Montaldo, Savona, Feb. 23, 1464, *ibid.,* cart. 417.

[11] Prospero to Bianca Maria, Florence, Apr. 15, 1467, and Bologna [?], Sept. 23, 1467, *Firenze,* cart. 273 and *Autografi,* cart. 118, fasc. 4, respectively. In these letters Prospero demanded a trial to clear his name, his reinstatement to his position as secretary, and the settlement of his claims regarding the expenditure of personal funds during eleven years of continuous and faithful service for the Sforza. He also denied that he had plotted with Genoese exiles against Milan. He

With his expulsion from the Duchy, Prospero began a most un-happy period pursuing alternately a conciliatory and threatening policy towards the Sforza and particularly Cicco Simonetta, to whom he at-tributed all his misfortunes. By 1469 he had taken holy orders and secured the post of councilor to the Emperor for whom he executed various diplomatic missions.[12] In the 1470s he passed to the service of Sixtus IV, who employed him for a mission to Scotland (1477), follow-ing which he was made Bishop of Caithness in that kingdom (May 25, 1478).[13] Returning from Scotland, he was detained at Chiavari (May 1477) by Milanese officials and sent to Milan for interrogation on his anti-Sforza activities particularly among the Genoese exiles.[14] Freed a

---

signed the letters, "Prosper de Medicis Camulis," though he had no connection with the Medici family. See Nicodemo da Pontremoli to Bianca Maria and Gale-azzo Maria, Florence, Apr. 21, 1467, *Firenze,* cart. 273.

[12] Prospero, however, was not happy either with the troublesome state of affairs in Germany or with the barbarous customs he found there, and once again sought in vain a position with Piero de' Medici [Prospero to Sagramoro da Rimini, Krein-burgh, Nov. 12, 1469, *Firenze,* cart. 277]. From Venice he sent a message to Gale-azzo Maria and Cicco Simonetta signifying that despite the injustices suffered at Milan, he was still willing to serve both [1469, "beginning of July," *Autografi,* cart. 118, fasc. 4]. The following year, through his brother Liberio, he sent two Turkish horses as a gift to Galeazzo Maria [Giorgio de Annono to Galeazzo Maria, Parma, Nov. 26, 1470, *ibid.,* cart. 118]. On his activity in Germany, see also F. Cusin, "I rapporti tra la Lombardia e l'Impero dalla morte di Francesco Sforza all'avvento di Lodovico il Moro (1466–1480)," *Annali della R. Università degli Studi Economici e Commerciali di Trieste* VI(1934), 313–14, n. 6.

[13] C. Eubel, *Hierarchia catholica medii aevi,* reprinted ed. (Padua, 1960), II, 122.

[14] Giovanni Simonetta brushed aside Prospero's claim that he was traveling as an ambassador of the King of Scotland, "il quale se pò dire in culo mundi," and that he styled himself councilor of Louis XI, and ordered the officials to send him to Milan under a vigilant escort "essendo stato apto inimico di questo Stato ad Roma, dalo Imperatore e dove s'é trovato et dinovo ad Zenoa" [G. Simonetta to Giovanni del Conte and Amurato Torelli, Savignano, May 6, 1477, *Autografi,* cart. 118, fasc. 4]. It is significant that Simonetta does not mention Prospero in his biography of Francesco Sforza. For Prospero's intrigues with Genoese exiles, see Cicco Simonetta to Prospero, [Milan, 1476?], *Fondo Famiglie,* cart. 40, pub-lished by Gabotto, "Un nuovo contributo," doc. XVIII, 211–14; the Bishop of

few months later,[15] he was sent by Sixtus IV and King Ferrante on a mission to Switzerland, the Archduke Sigismund of Austria, and the Emperor to arrange an alliance against Milan.[16] The Emperor charged him with another mission to the Swiss and Louis XI presumably against Milan.[17] This was probably Prospero's last diplomatic role. No documents have been found to shed light on his last years until his death in 1484.

Likewise little is known about Prospero's literary activity, which surely suffered because of his frequent peregrinations and constant involvement in political affairs. His correspondence with his brother-in-law, Pier Candido Decembrio, and other humanists shows him to be a bibliophile more than a writer. At least no work written by him has come to light. His private letters and certain of his dispatches are written in a horrible scrawl and are characterized by numerous circumlocutions and vague expressions, the product, it seems, of a quick but disorganized mind overflowing with plans and ideas set down in haste. There is no doubt that his blunt language, his indiscreet behavior,

---

Parma and Ziliolo Oldoino to Bona and Giangaleazzo Sforza, Rome, Jan. 1, 1477, *Roma,* cart. 83.

[15] Pressure by Prospero's brother and sister, and probably by other influential people, including Sixtus IV, played a part in his release. See Gabotto, "Un nuovo contributo," 43–44, and docs. XX–XXI, 215–17, and "Una supplica degli uomini di S. Stefano di Genova per Prospero da Camogli (10 maggio 1477)," *Giornale storico e letterario della Liguria,* III(1902), 137–40.

[16] Prospero's efforts in Austria and Germany were frustrated by the Milanese ambassador who called him "fonticho di puza" [Pietro Paolo Pegius to Bona and Giangaleazzo Sforza, Unada, Feb. 6, 1479 and Innsbruck, Feb. 12, 1479, *Alemagna,* cart. 573].

[17] In order to foil Prospero's mission to Louis XI, the Milanese ambassador in Austria urged Cicco Simonetta to inform his colleague at the French court that Prospero had warned the Emperor that the King did not keep his word, and had urged him to employ Swiss mercenaries in order to prevent their serving France. [P. P. Pegius] to [Cicco], Gratz, Apr. 22, [1479], *Alemagna,* cart. 573. While in France, Prospero appealed to Louis XI to press the Sforza to satisfy his claims [Giovanni Andrea Cagnola to Bona and Giangaleazzo Sforza, Tours, Sept. 9, 1479, *Francia,* cart. 544].

and his quarrelsome spirit earned him the enmity of influential people and played a considerable role in his personal misfortunes. His contemporaries portray him well versed in astrology, through which, however, he was not able to chart a more successful course.

Equally controversial was Francesco Coppini, Bishop of Terni, whose letters from France are included in this volume only because they are intimately connected with Prospero's mission, which the Bishop aided in every possible way in his role as a secret agent for the Duke of Milan. Although Coppini claimed, probably rhetorically, that he was a servant and follower of Francesco Sforza from his infancy, the first documented official contact between the two men occurred in October of 1457 when he was sent by Calixtus III to the Duchy of Milan to collect the tenth for the projected crusade against the Turks.[18] In February 1459 Coppini passed through Milan to discuss again the matter of the tenth on his way as *referendarium et oratorem* to Henry VI, having been charged by Pius II to help settle the Lancastrian-Yorkist conflict and secure royal representation at the Congress of Mantua.[19] It is probable that at this encounter the Duke enlisted the Bishop's support on behalf of Milanese interests which favored a Yorkist victory, equally dear to the Dauphin and the Duke of Burgundy, over the Lancastrian party backed by Charles VII. Whether there was an actual understanding or not, this is the way Coppini behaved subsequently with the hope of gratifying Sforza, through whose offices he hoped to obtain a cardinal's hat.

---

[18] Ottone del Carretto to Sforza, Rome, Sept. 22 and Oct. 2, 1457, *Roma,* cart. 46; cf. Sforza to Coppini, Milan, Sept. 14, 1457, *Reg. Missive* 29, fol. 381ᵛ, and Sforza's proclamation of Apr. 1, 1458 allowing Coppini's deputy, Friar Antonio Panormitano de Santoro, to collect the tenth [*Frammenti Reg. Ducali-Missive,* cart. 2].
[19] Coppini's credentials for Henry VI are dated Jan. 7, 1459 [Rymer, *Foedera,* XI, 419], and for Sforza, Jan. 14, 1459 [*Roma,* cart. 48]. He had an audience with the Duke on or before Feb. 24 [Sforza to Ottone del Carretto, Milan, Feb. 24, 1459, and Coppini to Pius II, Milan, Feb. 24, 1459, *Roma,* cart. 48]. That he already was thoroughly devoted to Sforza is revealed by the fact that the Duke referred to him as "persona digna et molto nostra."

The Bishop arrived in England in the spring of 1459, and was able to secure the appointment of two low-ranking royal envoys to the Congress of Mantua, but his efforts to heal the Lancastrian-Yorkist feud failed partly through the opposition of the Lancastrians, who may have already suspected his partiality towards their enemies.[20] Rebuffed in his efforts, in the early spring of the following year Coppini withdrew to the Low Countries where he joined Warwick and other Yorkist leaders, who had taken refuge at Calais after their setbeck at Ludford, Oct. 12, 1459. In June 1460 he recrossed the Channel with the Yorkist party, now openly arrayed on their side, and played a self-proclaimed leading part in the events which by autumn had given the Yorkists control of England. With the defeat and death of the Duke of York at Wakefield (Dec. 30, 1460) and the advance of the Lancastrian army southward, the Bishop suddenly decided—whether with or without Warwick's approval is uncertain—that a change in scene was in order. He sailed from England about two weeks before the second battle of St. Albans was fought (Feb. 17), and landed in Holland on February 10, and then made his way to Bruges. Here he met Prospero da Camogli with whom he proceeded to cooperate in the effort to cement a closer alliance among the Dauphin, Philip the Good, and the Yorkists, who had finally triumphed at Towton (March 29).

Throughout these eventful months Coppini had kept Sforza fully informed of his plans, for the success of which he desired the secret approval of the Pope and his elevation to the cardinalate with consequent conferment of full legatine powers. Contrary to what he wrote later in his *Commentaries,* Pius was cognizant of and approved the

---

[20] For Coppini's activity in England, see particularly C. L. Scofield, *The Life and Reign of Edward the Fourth, King of England and of France, and Lord of Ireland* (London, 1923), I, 71ff., and CSPM, I, IX–XX, 20–105, which publishes most of his correspondence in translation. Pius II, *Commentaries,* Books III, VII, and XI gives a biased account against the Bishop. Cf. A. Gottlob, "Des Nuntius Franz Coppini Anteil an der Entthronung des Königs Heinrich VI und seine Verurteilung bei römischen Curie," *Deutsche Zeitschrift für Geschichtswissenshaft,* IV(1890), 75–111.

activity of his Bishop (though perhaps unaware at this time of all the scandalous details) and gave him the full status of a legate *de latere* (Oct. 9, 1460), a dignity normally reserved for cardinals, but refused to promote him owing to opposition in the Curia.[21] Coppini's subsequent unauthorized approach to the Dauphin in reference to the abolition of the Pragmatic Sanction, however, angered the Pope who recalled him to Rome unless he was needed by the new Legate, Jean Jouffroy, dispatched to France on this delicate mission.[22] Pius had also become irritated by Coppini's equally unwarranted discussions with Louis XI on Italian affairs, which revealed that the new King was demanding a radical change in the foreign policy of both the papacy and Milan— an about-face which the Pontiff deemed incredible and attributed to the Bishop's ambition to meddle in great affairs of state in order to secure his advancement. Despite the assurances of Prospero da Camogli and of the Duke that Coppini had in no way misrepresented the King's position, and had intervened in the discussions only at the request of the ambassador, Pius remained of the opinion that the Bishop's "state-

---

[21] The exceptional character of Coppini's elevation to the status of a Legate *de latere* has been noted by G. L. Lesage, "La titulature des envoyés pontificaux sous Pie II (1458–1464)," *École Française de Rome. Mélanges d'archeologie et d'histoire,* LVIII(1941–46), 219–20, 231. In response to Yorkist and Milanese requests for the Bishop's promotion, the Pope replied that although he was pleased with the Legate's accomplishments, he was reluctant to press for his elevation because some cardinals believed that he had exaggerated his accomplishments in order to gain the red hat [Ottone del Carretto to Sforza, Rome, Feb. 22, 1461, *Roma,* cart. 50]. A month later the Duke recommended that Coppini be given the Archbishopric of Florence, then vacant, if it had been decided to grant it to a non-Florentine [Sforza to Ottone, Milan, Mar. 20, 1461, *ibid.,* cart. 50]. This request was repeated the following year [Sforza to Ottone, Milan, Mar. 14, 1462, *ibid.,* cart. 53].

[22] Jouffroy, Bishop of Arras, was appointed "nuntium cum potestate legati de latere," for France, England, Scotland, and Burgundy on Aug. 20, 1461. For Jouffroy's role in these negotiations, see C. Lucius, *Pius II und Ludwig XI von Frankreich, 1461–1462* (Heidelberg, 1913), 27 ff.; C. Fierville, *Le Cardinal Jean Jouffroy et son temps (1412–1473)* (Coutances, 1874), 109 ff.; and Pastor, *Storia,* II, 101 ff.

ments about the kingdom of Sicily represented his own ideas, not the King's." [23]

Coppini's return to Rome in February 1462 after another unsuccessful mission to England to arrange an accommodation between Edward IV and Louis XI, undertaken at Jouffroy's request with subsequent papal approval, was an unhappy one. He returned as an agent of Edward IV, who also granted him an annuity and the privilege for his nephews to include a white rose in their coat of arms.[24] On his passing through Milan, Sforza made him a member of his *Consiglio Segreto,* gave him a pension, and recommended him in the highest terms to Pius, expressing the hope that the Pope would disregard all accusations against him and reward him for his services to serve as an example to others.[25] This powerful support, however, was negated by accusations from his enemies—French elements at the Curia, including Cardinal Jouffroy—that instead of promoting peace Coppini had incited war in England, had raised the standard of the Church against the Lancastrians, and had been guilty of scandalous simony. But the most serious offense in the eyes of the Pope was his alleged encouragement of Louis XI to prosecute the Angevin claims to the Kingdom of Naples.[26] In

---

[23] Pius II, *Commentaries,* B. VII, 509. Cf. Ottone del Carretto to Sforza, Tivoli, Oct. 3, 1461, *Roma,* cart. 51. Both Prospero da Camogli and Sforza praised the Legate's work and tried to dispel this view, soon to be proved erroneous [Sforza to Ottone, Milan, Oct. 12, 1461, and Ottone and Prospero to Sforza, Rome, Oct. 23, 24, 29, 1461, all in *Roma,* cart. 51]. It is interesting to note that according to the ambassadors' reports, Pius at this time had become convinced of the accuracy of Coppini's statements in reference to Louis XI's position!

[24] Scofield, *Edward the Fourth,* I, 214–15.

[25] Sforza to Ottone del Carretto, Milan, Feb. 22, 1462, *Roma,* cart. 52. Coppini was appointed to the *Consiglio Segreto* on the same date [Santoro, 6].

[26] Pius' earlier suspicions about the Bishop's role in the King's abrupt change of policy were confirmed by a letter from Jouffroy in which it was alleged that Coppini had led Louis XI to believe that both the Pope and Sforza would be willing to further French territorial ambitions in Italy, especially with respect to the Kingdom of Naples [Ottone del Carretto to Sforza, Rome, Jan. 27, 1462, *Roma,* cart. 52]. Coppini believed that this false accusation was the major cause of his ruin; for the rest he admitted that he had overstepped his authority, but he

the winter of 1462, the Bishop was confined to Castel Sant'Angelo, secretly tried, and found guilty of gross misconduct. Despite last minute appeals by Sforza, delivered by Prospero da Camogli himself and others,[27] he was deprived of his bishopric, but was allowed to enter the Benedictine Order as a simple monk in the monastery of S. Paolo fuori le mura in Rome assuming the name of Ignatius. He died a year later having "made a better monk than Bishop," according to Pius.[28]

Described by contemporaries as being of small stature and not particularly striking in appearance, but spirited, quick witted, and eloquent, Coppini burned with the same flame of ambition that consumed his colleague and partner in misfortune, Prospero da Camogli. His letters show the same vividness of expression, self-praise, and bombastic style and are written in the hurried hand of one who is impatient to set down his ideas. Their downfall can be attributed both to their want of discretion and moderation, and to the change in political climate which cast a shadow over their achievements.

NOTE TO THE READER

Beginning with this volume, italics will be used to indicate passages in cipher.

---

vehemently denied that he had stolen 70,000 ducats in Church funds, as was charged, pointing out that he remained poor, with fatherless nephews to support, after twenty-five years of service to the Church [Coppini to Sforza, [Castel Sant'Angelo], July 10, 1462, *Roma,* cart. 53].

[27] See Sforza's instructions to Prospero, Milan, July 24, 1462, *Siena,* cart. 262; Sforza to the Cardinal of Pavia, Milan, Nov. 10, 1462, and to Ottone del Carretto, Milan, Nov. 12, 1462, *Roma,* cart. 53 and *Siena,* cart. 263, respectively.

[28] *Commentaries,* B. XI, 703. It is not certain whether Coppini died in Rome or in the monastery of S. Benedetto in Mantua, where he planned to go in June of 1463 [Ignatius to Sforza, ex Monastero S. Pauli de Urbe, June 1, 1463, *Roma,* cart. 55].

ABBREVIATIONS

ASF	Archivio di Stato di Firenze
ASM	Archivio di Stato di Milano
B.	Busta
Cart.	Cartella
C. C.	Chancery Copy or Copies
D.	Domino
F.	Filza
Ill.mo	Illustrissimo
Mag.tia, Mag.co	Magnificentia, Magnifico
Mons., Mons.re	Monsignore
N. S.	Nostro Signore
Orig.	Original
Paris, BN	Paris, Bibliothèque Nationale
Reg.	Register
Ser.mo	Serenissimo
S., Sig.re, S.re	Signore
Sig.ria, S.ria	Signoria
S. M., S. M.tà	Sua Maestà
S. Sig.ria, S. S.ria	Sua Signoria
S. S.tà	Sua Santità
V. E., V. Ex.tia	Vostra Excellentia
V. P.	Vostra Paternità
V. S., V. Sig.ria, V. S.ria	Vostra Signoria

Beaucourt, G. du Fresne de., *Histoire de Charles VII*. 6 vols. Paris, 1881–91 [Beaucourt].

Charavay, E., ed., *Letters de Louis XI*. Vol. I. Paris, 1883 [Lettres, I].

Chastellain, G., *Oeuvres*, ed. Kervyn de Lettenhove. 8 vols. Brussels, 1863–66 [Chastellain].

Desjardins, A., *Négociations diplomatiques de la France avec la Toscane. Documents recueillis par Giuseppe Canestrini*. Vol. I. Paris, 1859 [Desjardins].

Hinds, A. B., ed., *Calendar of State Papers and Manuscripts Existing in the Archives and Collections of Milan*. Vol. I, 1385–1618. London, 1912 [CSPM].

Lecoy de la Marche, A., *Le Roi René. Sa vie, son administration, ses travaux artistiques et littéraires*. 2 vols. Paris, 1875 [Lecoy de la Marche].

Mandrot, Bernard de., *Dépêches des ambassadeurs milanais en France sous Louis XI et François Sforza*. 4 vols. Paris, 1916–23 [Mandrot].

Mathieu d'Escouchy, *Chronique*, ed. G. du Fresne de Beaucourt. 3 vols. Paris, 1863–64 [Escouchy].

Nunziante, E., "I primi anni di Ferdinando d'Aragona e l'invasione di Giovanni d'Angiò," *Arch. storico per le province napoletane*, XVII (1892), 299–357, 564–86, 731–79; XVIII(1893), 3–40, 205–46, 411–62, 561–620; XIX(1894), 37–96, 300–53, 417–44, 595–658; XX(1895), 206–64, 442–516; XXI(1896), 265–99, 494–532; XXII(1897), 47–64, 204–40; XXIII(1898), 144–210 [Nunziante].

Pastor, Ludovico von., *Storia dei Papi dalla fine del Medio Evo*. New Italian translation by A. Mercati. Vol. I. Rome, 1958 [Pastor, *Storia*].

Perret, P. M., *Histoire des relations de la France avec Venise du XIIIe siècle a l'avènement de Charles VIII*. 2 vols. Paris, 1896 [Perret].

Pius II, *The Commentaries of Pius II*, Translation by F. A. Gragg, with an introduction and notes by L. C. Gabel, *Smith College Studies in History*, Book I, XXII(1936–37); Books II–III, XXV(1939–40);

Books IV–V, XXX(1947); Books VI–IX, XXXV(1951); Books
X–XIII, XLIII(1957) [Pius II, *Commentaries*].

Santoro, C., *Gli Uffici del Dominio sforzesco (1450–1500)*. Milan, 1948
[Santoro].

Simonetta, G., *Rerum gestarum Francisci Sfortiae commentarii,* ed. G.
Soranzo in L. Muratori, *RR. II. SS.,* XXI, pt. II. Bologna, 1932–59
[Simonetta].

The documents published in this volume have been taken from
the following series, most of which have already been described in
the Introduction to Volume I.

Milan, *Archivio di Stato*
  1. *Potenze Estere: Francia,* cart. 525–526; *Borgogna,* cart. 514;
     Inghilterra e Scozia, cart. 566.
  2. *Trattati,* cart. 1528.
  3. *Autografi,* cart. 51. This anachronistic collection is composed
     of autograph letters (some of which are not) by rulers and other
     prominent individuals in all fields of endeavor. Fasc. 6 of this
     cartella contains two dispatches by Francesco Coppini which
     properly belong in the *Potenze Estere* series.
  4. *Sommari,* cart. 1560. This series contains summaries of dispatches
     by Milanese ambassadors, intercepted dispatches of other powers,
     reports by spies, and various other confidential communications
     about activities in other states. Fasc. 2 of this *cartella* contains
     summaries of Prospero da Camogli's dispatches of which only
     two have not survived in the original: one of April 9, 1461 is
     cited in doc. 90, n. 2; the other of June [6?], 1461 has been
     included in this volume, doc. 114.
Paris, Bibliothèque Nationale
  1. *Fonds Italien,* Cod. 1588, 1595.
  2. *Fonds Latin,* Cod. 10133. This codex of 491 folios contains Fran-
     cesco Sforza's ratification of the Treaty of Genappe (July 24,

1461) as part of a collection of documents regarding Franco-Milanese relations for the period August 26, 1460 to September 27, 1494. Few supporting documents dating from 1451 onwards are also included. Partly written by Cicco Simonetta, and compiled under his direction for Duke Galeazzo Maria Sforza, the codex was continued by others after Simonetta's death (1480).[29]

[29] For a detailed description of this codex, its history and contents, see P. M. Perret, "Le manuscrit de Cicco Simonetta" (Manuscrit Latin 10133 de la Bibliothèque Nationale) *Notices et extraits de manuscrits de la Bibliothèque Nationale,* XXXIV, pt. 1 (1891), 323–63.

DISPATCHES

Prospero, we want you to go to the most serene and excellent lord Dauphin of Vienne, first son of the Most Christian King of France, etc., and, after the greetings and compliments you will extend on our behalf, you will express our devotion to his excellency and offer—as unreservedly and reverently as is fitting and as you know to be our intention etc.—our state, person, powers and whatever we have in the world.

Then you will say that, as a result of the negotiations Giacomo di Valperga[2] and Gaston,[3] the Dauphin's squire, have carried on with us here, we have agreed with them on a certain pact[4] between his excellency and us; but it has seemed to us fitting, for the greater honor of his excellency, to send to him for the concluding and sealing of the said agreement, according to the terms reached with Giacomo and Gaston. Since his excellency understands our attitude and our sincerity, we have made the agreement with all the deferences to his wishes and with all the genuine commitments on our part that were possible, as by word of mouth you will explain at length. We believe that no difficulties can be made about the treaty proposals that you bring because they are all designed for the glory and exaltation of the Dauphin's state. Therefore make every effort to conclude and seal quickly and take your departure, and also to understand clearly the attitude, disposition, and thoughts of the Dauphin and to learn everything you can so that you re-

54·*Instructions of the* DUKE OF MILAN

to PROSPERO DA CAMOGLI[1]

Francia, cart. 525. Orig.; BN, Fonds Italien, Cod. 1588, fols. 318r–319r. Minute

Prospero, volimo che te transferisse allo Ser.mo et Ex.mo Sig.re Mon.re Delphino de Vienna, primogenito del Christianissimo Re de Franza etc., et poy le visitacione et commendacione gli faray per nostra parte, gli diray la nostra optima disposicione verso la Ex.tia Soa, offerendo lo Stato, persona, facultate et quello habiamo al mondo, tanto largamente et con quella reverentia che se rechiede et che tu say é nostra intencione etc.

Deinde diray che la pratica havuta con Nuy qui per D. Iacomo de Valperga[2] et Guaston[3] suo scudero, havemo con loro rasonato certo apuntamento[4] fra la Ex.tia Soa et Nuy, et ne é parso per più honore della Soa Ex.tia mandare ad essa et là fare concludere et sigillare dicto apuntamento, secondo la substancia havemo praticata et rasonata con loro; et perché intenda la Soa Ex.tia l'animo et sincerità nostra, havemo firmate le cose con quella reverentia et realità ne é stato possibile, como a boca poray largamente exponere; et credemo ad quello tu porti non sia da fare alcuna difficultà, perchè tutte sono cose accomodate al Stato, laude et gloria et exaltacione soa. Però te sforza presto concludere et sigillare et venire via, sfforzandote [sic] de intendere ben la mente, disposicione et penseri suoy et tutto quello te sia possibile, perché tu vegni informatissimo dela mente soa et de tutte le cose dellà.

S'el te fosse facto difficultà circa lo numero dele gente del subsidio,

turn fully informed about his attitude and about all things there.

If, however, some difficulty should be made about the number of troops to be sent in aid—namely that whereas we are offering 3,000 horse and 1,000 foot, his excellency is committed to 4,000 horse and 2,000 archers—we say that we have established this difference for the honor and glory of his serenity, for our rank and power cannot compare with his. However, though we do not believe any such difficulty can arise, if he wishes the troops committed by each party to be equal in number, we are content that the matter be so concluded; and you will say that you have been ordered by us to do as his lordship commands—it being understood, however, that you will not go beyond the substance of the agreed proposals.

In addition, you will bear the letter of credence to the most illustrious lord, the Duke of Burgundy; and you will extend greetings to his excellency before and after the conclusion of the treaty, at whatever time and in whatever way the Dauphin will be pleased to order. When you speak with the Duke you will express such warm and reverent sentiments as seem appropriate, offering to his lordship both our state and our person etc. in such large terms as you think best. You can also greet and compliment the illustrious Duke of Clèves, if you happen to meet him, and my lord [Jean] de Croy.

Item: in case you encounter such difficulty that you cannot conclude—which we do not believe—we wish you in that case to send by our courier immediate word to us, written in cipher, of the difficulty and await our reply. Be sure to explain clearly—not confusedly—the reasons and motives for the difficulty, and also inform us fully of the state and situation of the Dauphin and of the Duke of Burgundy and of the affairs of England and of France, in as much detail as possible, and also of everything else you learn there, etc.

Item: in the event that you conclude the treaty, when it is concluded we wish you to inform us at once by the courier, whom you will send as soon as you have sealed the document, letting us know what day you concluded and what day you will depart and on what day you ex-

cioé dove offerimo aiutare de III^m cavalli et mile fanti, et la Ex.tia Soa
IIII^m cavalli et II^m arcieri, dicimo che l'havemo posto per honore et
gloria della Ser.tà Soa, perché el facto suo non ha comparatione con lo
nostro. Però non credemo gli sia facto difficultà; pur quando volesse
che lo numero delle gente hinc inde fosse equale, siamo contenti faci et
concludi como vole la Ser.tà Soa, dicendo che tu hay comandamento et
ordine da Nuy fare como vole et comanda la S.a Soa, intendendo però
non passi la substancia del facto.^a

Insuper portaray la littera de credenza ad lo Ill.mo Mon.re Duca de
Bergogna, et parlaray et visitaray la Ex.tia Soa prima e dapoy facta la
conclusione, et participaray con la S. Soa, prout et quemadmodum
piacerà et te ordinarà esso Mon.re Delphino; et quando gli parlaray
diray quelle affectionate et reverente parole te parerà, offerendo alla
S.Soa et lo Stato, et la persona etc., tanto largamente, quanto te parerà;
cossì poray salutare et confortare lo Illustre Duca de Clevi, se a luy te
abbatesse, et Mon.re de Crovi.

Item volimo, in caso te fosse facta tali difficultà che non potesse
concludere, quod non credimus, che eo casu mandi subito da Nuy le
difficultà, scritte in cifra, per lo nostro cavallaro, et aspecti la nostra
resposta; ma sforzati scrivere chiaro, et non confuso, et le rasone et
casone, evisandone integramente del Stato et condicione d'esso Mon.re
Delphin et Mon.re de Bergogna, et dele cose de Inglittera et de Franza
tanto particularmente, quanto sia possibile, et cossì de ogni altra cosa
che tu sentiray dellà etc.

Item, casu che tu concludi, facta la conclusione, volimo d'essa ne
avisi subito per lo cavallaro, quale mandàray immediate che haveray
sigillato, avisandone del dì haveray concluso, et del dì che te partiray, et
del dì credi essere qua da Nuy, et cossì dele cose soprascritte tutte.

Vogli li capituli et contracto sia facto per mano de notaro et possa^b
sottoscripti per man propria de Mon.re Delphino etc.; et retornato che

---

a. Crossed out in the minute: de quanto porti instrupto et per li capituli et per questa
instructione.
b. Read: poscia.

pect to arrive here in our presence, and also inform us about all the matters above written.

You will request that the articles and contract be drawn up by the hand of a notary and then signed in the Dauphin's own hand etc.; and when, on your return, you have made your report by word of mouth, you will then make a summary of it in writing; and that report and this instruction and the other writings you will give to Cicco our secretary.

Cicco [Simonetta]

HISTORICAL NOTES

1. See Introduction, p. xvi. Prospero's powers of Aug. 26, 1460 [*Trattati,* cart. 1528, orig.; *Francia,* cart. 525; BN, *Fonds Italien,* Cod. 1595, fol. 211r–211v and *Fonds Latin,* Cod. 10133, fol. 21r–21v], valid for six months, designated him "nuncium, mandatarium et procuratorem" armed with "plenissimum et amplissimum mandatum" to negotiate and conclude the alliance with the Dauphin, but not Charles VII. Letters of credence, dated Milan, Aug. 27, 1460 [*Francia,* cart 525; *Lettres,* I, 323–24], were issued to Prospero for the Dauphin, the Duke of Burgundy, the Duke of Clèves, and Jean de Croy. A passport (*littere passus*) was issued on the same day to Prospero and his retinue of six horses [*Francia,* cart. 525].

2. See doc. 55, n. 1, p. 18.

3. Gaston du Lyon, the Dauphin's councilor, chamberlain, chief equerry, and carver [See Vol. I, doc. 40, n. 1, p. 268].

4. This is the schema of the treaty of alliance between the Dauphin and Sforza negotiated at Milan [See Appendix, doc. I, p. 455].

saray et facta la relacion ad boca, la faray ancora sub compendio in scritto, et quella una con questa instructione et l'altre scripture daray ad Cicho, nostro Secretario.

Cichus [Simonetta]

I did not arrive here, and have my first audience with the Dauphin, until the twenty-third of the past month, because his lordship was in Brussels, a city of the Duke of Burgundy, and his lordship did not want the treaty to be negotiated anywhere else but here. I could not, indeed, describe to Your Lordship his kindness and benignity *and the good welcome he gave me and how* frankly and freely *he declares himself ready to do everything possible for Your Lordship's welfare.*

For *his lordship has discoursed to me concerning his present situation and his* aims *and plans,* all *of which,* he says, *are based on Your Lordship and the Duke of Burgundy. With the Duke,* for example, *relations with England have been settled, as Your Lordship will be informed by others* or *by me. With Your Lordship, though, there remain those same three matters on which decision has been in the past deferred,* about which he insisted on making a great fuss; *because his lordship desired* to specify in the treaty *that Messer Giacomo di Valperga*[1] be protected and defended *by Your Lordship*—and so much does he take this to heart that he said *he would make every treaty stipulation more favorable to you* if you agreed to it. I, on the one hand, kept in mind that *I must not exceed the terms of my commission,* but, on the other, I thought it wise not to displease him, he being who he is and being also most beneficently disposed toward you.

55·PROSPERO DA CAMOGLI *to the*

DUKE ·OF MILAN

Francia, cart. 525. Orig.[a]

Io iunxi qui a 23 del presente[b] *dal conspecto de questo Delfino et*
non atanti [sic], *perchè la Signoria Sua era a Burcelle, citade del Duca*
de Bergogna, et non parse a Sua Signoria che alibi che qui se trattasse
de la intelligentia. Io non potria, perdio, renarrar a la S. V. la humanità
et benignità *sua et le bone acoglense et quanto* francamenti et liberamenti *se fa inanti a tutto quanto he da far per ben de la S. V.*. Nam *la*
S. Sua mha narrato et fatto un discurso de suo stato, intentione *et*
designi, quali tutti dice haver *fundati in V. S. et Duca de Bergogna,*
sichè *con el Duca de Bergogna se he posto in forma le cose de Anglia,*
come per altre aut *per me la S. V. intenderà; con la V. S. el havia de*
usato quelle tre cose, alias protracte, etiam in le quale gli hè stato da
desbater assay, *perchè la S. Sua voleva* specificare omnino *che meser*
Iacobo de Valperga[1] sia protecto et defenso *da la V. S.;* et intanto lo ha
in animo, che diceva voler *miglorar ogni condition a la S. V.* pur che
cossì fusse, et io era riguardo da l'un canto de [non] *passar commission,*

---

a. The key for the cipher used by Prospero in 1460 lacks a few symbols referring to
persons and places. The meaning of these symbols has been derived from the three deciphered Chancery copies accompanying the original dispatch. The last paragraph,
which is intended for Cicco Simonetta, is not in the original dispatch but appears at the
end of one of the Chancery's copies. Its somewhat garbled character, and its slightly
different orthography, suggest that it also was originally written in cipher.
b. Read: passato.

Today, however, thank God, I spoke to him in such a way that *we have remained in accord: he is content that the treaty take the form already settled upon,* and that I return to *Your Lordship* with all speed *in order to inform you of all matters and of his most beneficent attitude toward Your Lordship.* He wanted me without fail to write this to Your Excellency and to beg you in God's name not to be less willing *to favor the Dauphin* at this time—for he will more appreciate a small thing now than a very great one when he *becomes King of France* —*than you favor King Ferrante,* about whom, for Your Excellency's information, he speaks most kindly and hence in the opposite way about the *Duke of Calabria.* The Dauphin also hopes that you will not be less willing to favor *Messer Giacomo* [di Valperga] *than you formerly were to favor the Count of Regana.*[2]

Although I am not well informed on the subject, I replied, however, that if *Your Lordship supports King Ferrante, it is because that King is a member of the League* [of Italy] *and the Pope,* who is head of the *league,* so commands, and, in the same way, that *count* is bound by ties of gratitude to *Your Lordship;* whereas these conditions are lacking in the case of *Messer Giacomo.*

The Dauphin says, however, that, *Your Lordship being most wise,* he hopes, and wants to believe and hold it certain, that you would do a greater thing than this for him, though there could be nothing more pleasing to him now—and indeed, he says, he would rather risk his *succession to the Crown of France* than abandon Valperga.

He begs Your Lordship, then, to please him in this matter in whatever way seems best, he mentioning that an agreement might be negotiated or that the matter might be placed under the jurisdiction of the *papal Rota,* since *the Pope* is the head of *the League of Italy,* or that some better way be worked out, at least for a period of *six months* within which he hopes *to dispose of matters here* in such a way that if his enterprise flourishes, *he could do very well indeed.* At this point he told me that if *Your Lordship would like Genoa, Asti, and Vercelli* and indeed anything else in *Italy,* he will be content and indeed will always

da l'altro non me pareva de descontentarlo, essendo quello che hè et benissimo hedificato; pur hoggi, gratia a Dio, gli ho ditto tanto che *siamo rimasti d'acordio che l'è contento si facia in forma data* et che io me ne ritorni *a la V. S.* presto presto [sic] *per darli aviso de tutte le cose et de la bonissima mente sua verso la V. S.,* et ha voluto che omnino io scrivi questo a V. Ex.tia et la preghi che per Dio, non sia a V. Ex.tia manco caro *far per el Delfino* in questo tempo ch'el apreria più una cosa picola che alias quando *serà Re de Franza* una grandissima, *quanto la S.V.* [Per] *Re Ferrando,* del quale per aviso de V. Ex.tia el dice benignissimamente, et cossì lo contrario del *Duca de Calabria,* nè manco caro lo dicto *messer Iacobo quanto fu alias lo conte de Regana*[2]; al che, benchè io non sia ben informato, pur resposi che se *V. S. fa per Re Ferrando, el hè in liga et el Papa,* che he patron de la *liga,* lo commanda et cossì quello *conte* havia obligo de reconoscentia a la *V. S.,* li quali respecti mancano in *meser Iacobo;* pur el dice che *la S. V. hè sapientissima et* spera et vole creder et esser certo faria maior cosa che questa, ma che non se gli ne porria far niuna più grata cum sit ch'el seria più tosto apto ad impignar la *sucession del Regno* che abandonarlo, et ideo prega V. S.ria gli vogla compiacer de questo per quello modo parerà a quella megliore, ricordando la via de qualche trattamento de compositione aut che la cosa se conosca de iuri in *rota del Papa,* posteaquam *el Papa* hé lo superior de *la liga de Italia,* aut per quello altro più meglore, saltim fin a *sei meisi,* infra li quali el spera de *messedar de le cose de qua* grande et quibus vigentibus, se poria *far del ben assai.* Et qui mha ditto che se *la S. V. vorà Zenoa, Ast et Vercelli* et cossì ogni altra cosa in *Italia,* serà contento et hè contento sempre che piacia a *la S. V.;* al che non ho voluto responder, nè acertarmene più specificamenti non sapendo nè volendo saper plus quam oportet saper. Ben ho rengratiato *el Delfino* quanto mhè stato possibile in generali et me respose replicando multe raxon, perchè *ogni augumento de V. S.* gli deba esser più grato che s'el fusse suo proprio, et quando *el sii Re de Franza* dice che V. S.ria se ne faza bon capitale et fermo concepto, se *le presupona* vostro proprio. Et qui mha ditto *de alti et grandi raxonamenti* et, perdio, monstra uno grandis-

be willing to satisfy *Your Lordship*. To this I did not wish to reply nor to press for further details, since I do not know nor wish to know more than it is proper for me to know.

However, I thanked *the Dauphin* in general as warmly as possible, and he made me a long reply, repeating his arguments. He declared that *every augmentation of Your Lordship's state* would be more pleasing to him than if it were his own, and he says that when *he is King of France,* Your Lordship will be able to make capital of the situation if *you will but take it for granted* that he is your devoted supporter. At this point he spoke to me of *lofty aims and grand designs,* and indeed he shows the most intense *desire to achieve every height,* for the attaining of which ambitions he is counting on the aid of *Your Lordship,* whom he praises highly in his every sentence and every discourse, saying that, on his word, when he is *King of France,* he will so vigorously forward your affairs that *you will have no difficulty seeing the result.* I believe, indeed, that Your Lordship has made a good bargain.

Your Lordship is much indebted to *the Dauphin's officers for their praise of Your Lordship.*

The Dauphin is sending an ambassador to the Pope[3] *in order to obtain a judgment against the Duke of Savoy,* and he desires Your Lordship's good offices in the matter; also, *the Duke of Burgundy* is sending *two* [ambassadors][4] *to the Duke of Savoy at the instances of the Dauphin, whom the Duke honors* extravagantly *and whose every wish he obeys.*

I have been to offer my respects to *the Duke of Burgundy;*[5] he wished to pay me *the same honors that Your Lordship does to Burgundian ambassadors,* but I made a courteous refusal and went *to see him privately.* He made me a gracious welcome and very kindly thanks Your Lordship for your splendid treatment of his subjects, concerning which, for Your Excellency's information, there is in this country great and glorious report. *The Duke* also makes grand offers of service to Your Lordship. I likewise paid my respects to the *Duke of Clèves.*

simo sentimento *et animo ad ogni sublimitate,* in le quale el spera assay
in *la S. V.,* la quale el commenda in omni verbo et sermone summamenti, dicendo che in fede sua, quando el sia *Re de Franza,* ch'el se farà
tanto inanti che *veda V. S.,* la quale credo, perdio, harà fatto bona mer-
catantia; et ha grande debito V. S.ria a *li servitori del Delfino, perchè
referen* affectionatissimamenti de *V. S.. El Delfino manda al Papa un
ambassator*[3] *per obtener contra el Duca de Savoya* cose iuste et desydera bon adritio et favor de *V. S.;* etiam *el Duca de Bergogna* manda
dui [ambassatori] [4] *al Duca de Savoya ad instantia del Delfino, il quale
Duca de Bergogna honora* extremementi *el Delfino et fa tutto quello
vole et Delfino.*

Io son stato a visitar *el Duca de Bergogna,*[5] el quale me haria voluto
render *del honor fa la V. S. a li suoi;* il che ho recusato honestamenti et
son andato a far *la visitation secreta;* [me] ha fatto gratiosa acoglensa
et multo humanamenti rengratia V. Ex.tia de le bone demonstratione
fatte a li suoi, de le quale per adviso de V. Ex.tia in questo paise hè
grande et gloriosa fama, et cossì se offerì *el Duca de Bergogna* grata-
menti a V. Ex.tia. Il simile ho fatto al *Duca de Clevi. Meser Iohan de
Crovi* non gli era; lo fratello hè il tuto con *lo Duca de Bergogna* et hè
de grandissima reputatione. El me mandò a recheder secretamenti ch'io
volesse andar a star in casa sua, et me volse far conviti et solemnitate,
quale tutte con bona pace et supportation de Sua S.ria ho evitato; et hè
remasto contento. Me strinsi in uno ragionamento con lui per *scrutar
et meglo intender diverse cose,* precipue *de la fede tra el Delfino et el
Duca de Bergogna et del stato de Anglia,* et me satisfece a la prima parte
optimamenti; a la secunda, me disse come *li cavalli et arceri de Anglia
a martio eran per passar in Franza et ch'el Duca de Iorch et Conte de
Varvich sonno signori del Re de Ingliterra et Anglia, et* mha ditto tutti
li origini de quelle cose che seria longo scriver. Spero *sabato proximo
partir de qui ben expedito et, Deo duce, de brevi esser da la V. S..
Farimo la via de Basula* et da lì in antea quella che havemo *fatto al
venir qui.* Io non mi sento però ben sano, tamen farò quanto et quello
me serà possibile. Insuper adviso V. S.ria ch'el *Delfino* mha ditto che

13

Jean, Lord of Croy [and of Chimay] was not with *the Duke.* His brother [Antoine, Count of Porcien] who is everything with the Duke of Burgundy and enjoys the highest reputation, sent secretly to request me to lodge in his house and wished to offer me banquets and stately entertainment, all of which I avoided with the kind assent and good will of his lordship, who remained satisfied.

I sought in a conversation with him to *inquire into and better understand a number of matters,* especially *the relationship between the Dauphin and the Duke of Burgundy and the situation in England.* He clarified the first subject perfectly. Concerning the second he told me that *English men of arms and archers were to pass into France this coming March and that the Duke of York and the Earl of Warwick rule the English King and England,* and he explained to me the origins of the present situation in England, which would take long to write.

I hope *to leave here Saturday next with mission accomplished and, God willing, to be with Your Lordship shortly. We will go by way of Bâle* and from there will follow the same road that we *took in coming here.* Though I am not feeling very well, I will journey as quickly as I can.

In addition, I inform Your Lordship that *the Dauphin* has told me that *the Venetians are negotiating intensely*[6] with the King of France; he also says that it is to *Your Lordship's* interest that *the government of the Duke of Savoy* be reconstituted and *Lord Giacomo be maintained and so he recommends Giacomo most earnestly to Your Lordship. In the meanwhile the treaty is being drawn up, and,* since the Dauphin strongly *favors secrecy, it will not be notarized—that,* furthermore, not being the custom here—but *will be signed in the Dauphin's own hand and sealed.*

I recommend myself humbly to Your Lordship, whom God keep in happy state.

I write briefly to Your Lordship because it would take infinity to report all the arguments and modes of procedure I have had *to make*

Venetiani tenen grande pratica[6] *col Re de Franza* et che etiam tocca al interesse de *V. S.* che *la casa de Savoya* se reforme et ch'el ditto *messer Iacobo sia conservato et sic lo racomanda stretissimamenti a V.S.. Lo contratto se transcrive interim et, perchè el Delfino multo lauda la secretansa, non serà per man de notaro, perchè* etiam qui non se sole usare, sed *serà sottoscritto de man propria del Delfino et sigillato.* Me racomando humiliter a la Ex.tia V., che Dio conservi in felice stato.

Io scrivo breve a la V. S., perchè infinito seria scriver tutti li rasonamenti et li modi he stato necessario *servare, attento quanto el Delfino ven libero et vuole* identidem *dal compagno* et, trovandomi io *ligato per la commissione,* mhè stato necessario *in generali tenerlo ben edificato verso la S. V.,* maxime che pur gli hè *stato de li contraria,* como de tutto *aviserò la S. V..* Insuper *el Duca de Bergogna et el Delfino mostrano odio al Re Renato et grande, et mostrano che gli seria caro la S. V. gli tolesse Zenoa; et el Delfino dice* deliberar omnino *a questo primo tempo o per via de inteligentia con el Re de Franza o per* [. . .]*[c] de mettersi a recuperar la autorità, a lui devuta in lo Regno de Franza,* et cossì veneria a mancar *favora al Re Renato.*

[To Cicco Simonetta]

Io ho facto la recommandatione vostra al Delfino et holo trovato molto ben edificato in contrario; non so se procede aut da relatione de Petro da Pusterla[7] aut perchè questi amano fenochy et in vuy non è, aut perchè li messi del Delfin, quilli del Re Renato praticaria con vuy et perciò, ch'el Delfin è de natura liberissima, el me l'ha dicto chiaro et a tuto ho resposto et satisfacto et bene, in modo che resta contentissimo de vuy; et heri me domandò molto studiosamente de vuy et vostra barba et tute le conditione vostre et me disse cossì: Io son certo che Cicho ami el Duca de Milano sopra tutto et, che vedendo che io dispono deinceps amarlo como mi proprio, son certo ch'el me vorà bene et voglio fargli qualche demonstratione; et se tu vedi de qua cose per le quale se gli posse com-

---

c. Unintelligible cipher.

use of, seeing how freely the Dauphin speaks and that he wants whomever he is talking with to speak freely too. Consequently, since I *am restricted by my commission,* I have had to speak *in generalities in order to keep him well disposed toward Your Lordship,* especially since there have been *disagreements and difficulties,* about which *I will* fully *inform Your Lordship.*

In addition, *the Duke of Burgundy and the Dauphin show hate toward King René, great hate; they indicate that they would be happy for Your Lordship to take Genoa from him, and the Dauphin says* he has decided at all costs *in this coming spring, either by way of coming to an agreement with the King of France or by* [other means?], *to devote himself to recovering the position of authority which rightfully belongs to him in the realm of France.* In that case, *King René would be left without support.*

[To Cicco Simonetta] I have paid your respects to the Dauphin and have found him very well disposed toward you. As for the contrary attitude, I don't know whether it proceeds from reports by Pietro de Pusterla[7] or from the fact that people love deceitful flattery and there is none of that in you. . . . Since the Dauphin is by nature very free in his speaking he told me this directly, and I replied to everything and well satisfied him so that he remains most pleased with you. Yesterday he asked me in detail about you, about your uncle, and about all your circumstances, and said this to me: "I am certain that Cicco loves the Duke of Milan above all and, since he sees that I, in turn, am disposed to love the Duke as myself, I am certain that he will love me also. I want to give him some demonstration of my affection for him, and if you see here something that would please him, I will happily give it to him"—and he made quite a point about giving you a present, intended, I am certain, as a token of esteem, but he has wished that there be written precisely these words, viz: he knows that, Count Gasparo[8] and Pietro de Pusterla being Ghibelline, the Duke of Savoy has recourse to them, and that the sooner, therefore, his agents have recourse to you

piacer, io le farò voluntere et fecene specificatione de farvi un presente, et cossì son certo farà in pignis amoris, sed l'ha voluto che io ve scriva ad unguem queste parole infra videlicet: che sa lo C. Gasparo[8] con Petro da Pusterla esser ghibelini et che a lor non[d] ha recorso Duca de Savoya et che più tosto li soy hanno recorso a vuy che non sete nè ghelfo, nè ghibelino; et ideo ve prega vogliati havere lo facto de D. Iacomo Valperga recomandato.[9]

---

d. Read: ne.

since you are neither Guelf nor Ghibelline. He likewise begs you to favor Giacomo di Valperga's cause.[9]

HISTORICAL NOTES

1. Doctor of Law, Count of Masino, and member of an ancient noble family of Piedmont, Giacomo di Valperga had become chancellor of the Duchy of Savoy in November of 1452 apparently through the influence of his protector, the Dauphin. Having excited the jealousy and opposition of Savoyard nobles and the Cipriotes, favorites of the Duchess, all led by his rival for the chancellorship, Marquess Antonio di Romagnano, Giacomo was forced to flee Savoy late in 1456 and seek refuge with the Dauphin. His flight led to the accusation that he had plotted in 1452 to surrender the town of Vercelli to Francesco Sforza for which he was tried and condemned in absentia to the confiscation of his lands (May 28, 1459), despite Sforza's denial of the incident and the intervention of the Emperor to whom Giacomo had appealed for justice. In June of the following year, the Duke of Savoy initiated active preparations to carry out the sentence against Giacomo, who at this time is believed to have taken refuge in the Abbey of Chiaravalle, near Piacenza, under the protection of the Duke of Milan [L. Cibrario, *Jacopo Valperga di Masino e Filippo di Savoia. Triste episodio del secolo XV* (Turin, 1866), 11–23; F. Gabotto, *Lo Stato sabaudo da Amedeo VIII ad Emanuele Filiberto,* vol. I (1451–1467) (Turin, 1892), 22, 39–41, 50–55; L. Marini, *Savoiardi e Piemontesi nello Stato sabaudo (1418–1601),* vol. I, 1418–1536 (Rome, 1962), 71–72, 114–15].

2. Unidentified.

3. The Dauphin sent Baude Meurin, a secretary, and Jean Philippe, a member of his household, to Florence and to the Pope to protest against the Duke of Savoy's confiscation of Valperga's property and also against Savoy's failure to pay the arrears of dowry he owed the Dauphin for his daughter Charlotte, the Dauphin's wife [*Lettres,* I, 313; 344–47; and see doc. 68, p. 113].

4. This mission, composed of Anthune, Jean Boudault, and Jean Meurin, left on Oct. 12, 1460 [Beaucourt, VI, 307, n. 5] and arrived at the Savoyard court on Nov. 22 to champion Valperga's cause and press for the pay-

ment of Charlotte's dowry [A. Maletta to Sforza, Carignano, Nov. 26, 1460, *Savoia,* cart. 480].

5. On Sept. 29, 1460, the Duke of Burgundy wrote to Sforza that he had received his letter of credence for Prospero [*Borgogna,* cart. 514].

6. On July 6, 1460, Charles VII gave instructions to his envoy, Galois de Rougé (later replaced by Nicolas Petit, Galois having died on route), who was accompanied by Guy de Brilhac, Jean de Rouville, and Jean d'Etampes, representing respectively the Duke of Orléans, the Duke of Britanny, and the Count of Angoulême, to consult first the Duke of Modena and then go to Venice for the purpose of contracting an alliance designed to dethrone Sforza and install the Duke of Orléans at Milan with the aid of French troops. They were also to discuss the feasibility of calling a church council to consider measures both against the Turks and Pius II. Following the expected victory, Venice was to obtain Cremona and the confirmation of its possession of the Bresciano and the Bergamasco; the Duke of Modena was to gain Parma and the *condottiere,* Giacomo Piccinino, Piacenza, if he agreed to fight for the allies. The envoys arrived at Ferrara by Sept. 25 and by the 30th Sforza had already been informed of the scope of their mission by the Mantuan and Estense ambassadors at Milan, Vincenzo della Scalona and Ugolotto Facino respectively [Vincenzo della Scalona to the Marquess of Mantua, Milan, Sept. 27, 30, and Oct. 2, 1460, A. S. Mantova, *Carteggio-Milano,* B. 1621]. The ambassadors reached Venice on Sept. 29 and on Oct. 11 received a reply in which the Venetian *Signoria* reaffirmed its neutrality [Beaucourt, VI, 302–03; Perret, I, 345–55].

7. Able *condottiere* and diplomat under Filippo Maria Visconti, later one of the leaders of the Ambrosian Republic, he finally entered the service of Francesco Sforza, who employed him in several diplomatic missions including one to Louis XI in November 1461 [Mandrot, I, 86, n. 1]. On Jan. 3, 1477 he became a member of the *Consiglio Segreto* [Santoro, 13], and as one of the leaders of the Ghibelline faction opposed to Cicco Simonetta, he was instrumental in the latter's downfall and subsequent execution (1480). As this document suggests, the emnity between the two was already evident at this time.

8. Gaspare da Vimercate, an experienced *condottiere,* had taken a leading role in Francesco Sforza's entry in Milan (1450). In 1464 he was in charge

of the occupation of Genoa by Milanese forces [A. Sorbelli, *Francesco Sforza a Genova (1458–1466)* (Bologna, 1901), 140–52], and a year later he was one of the leaders of the Milanese contingent sent by the Duke to aid Louis XI during the war of the Public Weal. [P. Ghinzoni, "Spedizione sforzesca in Francia (1465–1466)," *Arch. storico lombardo,* Ser. II, VII (1890), 314–45.]

9. Apparently the Dauphin had received reports about anti-French feelings held at this time by Cicco Simonetta for which the secretary had been mildly but unmistakably rebuked a year earlier by the Duchess of Milan, whose pro-French sympathies are well known [Vincenzo della Scalona to the Marquess of Mantua, Milan, Apr. 20, 1459, A. S. Mantova, *Carteggio-Milano,* B. 1620].

I do not know whether Martin, Your Excellency's courier, has returned safely, because we have heard that he was molested on the road.
By Martin I sent a letter to Your Excellency reporting that on that day[1]
the Dauphin and I reached agreement to conclude on all points, as contained in the draft, and accordingly he gave me a signed carte blanche.

After that *the Dauphin* raised some objections which caused him
to change his views, and it was necessary to thrash the matter out again
point by point. I therefore remained in great anxiety of mind for six
days. As things stood, it was impossible for me to prevent the treaty
from being altered, nor was *the Dauphin* willing for me to send any
word to Your Excellency; and so, for some reasons[2] that I will explain
to Your Excellency, I thought it best to accept the treaty. Thus have we
concluded—and yet, though I think the conditions are more favorable
to Your Excellency than those of the original draft, still, because of the
care an agent must take not to exceed his commission, I have had inserted in the treaty[3] that Your Excellency is given the right of confirming it or not within a period of two months.

I want to believe, therefore, that, with the grace of God, Your Excellency will be very much pleased with what has been done; and if you
confirm the treaty you can be sure that, if he has sworn as a *prince*
should swear, then it is to be believed that he will be entirely one with

56·PROSPERO DA CAMOGLI *to the*

DUKE OF MILAN

Francia, cart. 525. Orig.

Io non so se Martin, cavalaro de V. Ex.tia, sia retornato a salvamento, perché pur per camino havimo inteso ch'el havia havuto qualche molestia. Per lo dicto Martino io scriveva a V. Ex.tia come a quello dì[1] io era remasto d'acordio de fermar cum *el Delfino,* in omnibus et per omnia, come se conteneva in la scrittura, et cossì me havia mandato una carta bianca suttoscritta de man sua. Doppoi sonno intervenuti al dicto *Delfino* alcuni respecti per li quali el mutoe proposito, et fu necessario de passo in passo argumentare etc. Et cossì stetti in grande anxietà de animo 6 dì. Or non mi fu possibile far che la cosa staesse iuxta lo ordine, né volse *el Delfino* che io daesse adviso alcun a V. Ex.tia; et cossì, per alcuni respecti[2] che dirò a V. Ex.tia, me parse bene fermar et cossì havemo concluso et per ben, che me pare la cosa stia in meglor conditione per la Ex.tia V. Pur per lo riguardo debe haver uno servitore a non passar commissione, io ho facto metter in la scriptura[3] che V. Ex.tia habea tempo doi misi et arbitrio de confermar o non. Voglio perciò creder, cum la gratia de Dio, V. Ex.tia se contenterà assai de quello che hé facto et cossì confermando può esser certa, se la promissa cum sacramento de uno *Principe* se debe creder, che *el Delfino* serà io[. . .][a] unum et idem cum *la V. S.ria;* et cossì m'ha imposto che

---

a. There follow two cipher symbols, one of which has no meaning and the other does not appear in the key.

you. *The Dauphin* has, in fact, insisted on my assuring *Your Excellency* that he will think and act for you as for himself, as I will more fully inform Your Excellency if God brings me safely to you, to whom humbly I always recommend myself.

I have arrived here at this point with my companion,[4] and we have been twenty-five days on the road because *the Dauphin* ordered us to take this route, and, by heaven, we have passed safely, God be praised, through many dangers resulting from the warfare here and the strangeness of the country.

Sunday evening[5] I hope to be with Your Excellency. My companion has the treaty with him and has divers commissions to perform in Italy, all of them to be accomplished with the good offices of Your Excellency, whom God keep in happiness.

[On the back] In all haste and faithfully, because it is urgent, [forward this] through the Referendary of Como to the magnificent Lord Cicco.

HISTORICAL NOTES

1. i. e. Oct. 2. See preceding doc. 55.

2. Among these *respecti* there may have been one which Prospero revealed to the Mantuan ambassador at Milan; namely, that Charles VII and the Dauphin *together* were conducting secret negotiations with Venice against Sforza [Vincenzo della Scalona to the Marquess of Mantua, Milan, Nov. 6, 1460, A. S. Mantova, *Carteggio-Milano*, B. 1621].

3. The Dauphin's letters patent of Oct. 6, 1460 [Appendix, doc. II, p. 462], which constituted the treaty of alliance between the two rulers.

4. Baude Meurin, the Dauphin's emissary to the Duke.

5. In a letter to Sforza [Genappe, Oct. 7, 1460, *Francia*, cart. 525; *Lettres*, I, 129–30], in which the Dauphin announced Prospero's departure and recommended again Valperga's affairs to the Duke, there is a Chancery's notation at the bottom indicating that the ambassador arrived at Milan on "Sunday, Nov. 1." Sunday, however, fell on Nov. 2.

acerti V. Ex.tia ch'el penserà et farà cossì per quella, como per si medesmo, como da me più a pleno intenderà V. Ex.tia, se Dio me conduce
salvo a quella, ala qual humiliter semper me racomando.

Io sum iuncto qui in questo puncto cum lo compagno,[4] et siamo
stati dì 25 in camino perché *el Delfino* n'ha commandato la via; et,
perdio, havemo passato a salvamento, Dio laudato, multi pericoli per le
guerre et straniesse del paese. Dominica[5] a sera spero de esser da la
Ex.tia V. Lo compagno ha la scriptura lui et ha diverse commissione in
Italia, tutte cum adricio de V. Ex.tia, che Dio conservi feliciter.

[A tergo]: Cito, cito, cito per D. Referendarium Comi in manibus
M.ci D. Cichi fideliter, quia importat.

After the Most Serene Lord the Dauphin, his lord and master, Gaston loves Your Lordship above all the other lords of the world, as much for the humaneness, prudence, brilliance of mind, and generosity that he recognizes in Your Lordship as for the infinite honors and favors he has received from Your Excellency and from your court, for which he will always consider himself most deeply obligated to Your Lordship. He is therefore at present very much upset, seeing the honor of the Dauphin to be greatly compromised, not without blame to Your Excellency, and he wishes to recapitulate for Your Excellency what has happened regarding this matter so that it can be more effectively considered. Hence, fearing that because of his speaking so much about it and because of the language difference, Your Lordship does not perfectly understand the whole affair, he has decided to put this memorandum in writing; and he begs Your Lordship kindly to give him counsel and to take it all in good part, because he intends it in good part and to a good end and not otherwise, and more for the welfare, honor, and advantage of Your Excellency and of your state and descendants, all things considered, than for the welfare of my lord the Dauphin.

First, says Gaston, he came to Your Excellency with letters of credence[1] from my lord the Dauphin and with the latter's instructions; and Your Lordship, having heard his relation and the instructions,

57 · MEMORANDUM OF GASTON DU LYON

to the DUKE OF MILAN

Francia, cart. 525. Two copies

Perché Gascon il quale apresso al Serenissimo Mons.re el Dalphino, suo Signore et Maestro, ama Vostra Sig.ria sopra tutti li Signori del mondo tanto per la humanità, prudentia, animosità et liberalità che cognosce in essa Vostra Sig.ria, quanto per infiniti honori et beneficii recevuti da Vostra Ex.tia et da li vostri, per li quali sempre se reputarà obligatissimo ad essa Vostra Sig.ria, se ritrova al presente in molti affanni; vedando [sic] l'honore del prefato Mons.re essere grandemente gravato, non senza carico de Vostra Ex.tia; vogliando luy recitare con Vostra Ex.tia le cose passate in questa materia, adciò se possa più commodamente fargli pensiero; dubitando per longo parlare et diversitate de sua lingua Vostra Sig.ria non intenda perfectamente il tutto, ha deliberato fare questo memoriale in scripto, supplicando Vostra Sig.ria se digni ben avisarlo et prendere tutto in bona parte, perché luy in bona parte et ad bon fine lo prende et non altramente et più per bene, honore et commodo de Vostra Ex.tia et de vostro Stato et posteritate, che per lo bene de Mons.re, il tutto considerato.

Primo dice esso Gascon che venne da Vostra Ex.tia con littere de credenza[1] de Mons.re et cum sua instructione, et Vostra Sig.ria intese sua relatione etiam la instructione et fece Vostra Sig.ria la risposta ad bocha, quale ad sua richiesta fo reducta in scripto[2] et mandata per lo fratello[3] al prefato Monsig.re, per la quale intendendo che Vostra Ex.tia

made reply verbally, which at Gaston's request was put in writing[2] and dispatched by the brother of Gaston[3] to my lord the Dauphin. He thus learned that Your Excellency had replied graciously to all the points. However, since, on the subject of recovering Dauphiné at the present time, Your Lordship mentioned some aspects, on account of which the enterprise seemed to him difficult, the Dauphin dismissed and put aside that item. On the subject of the Duke of Savoy, Your Lordship replied frankly, without using ambiguous terms nor instancing articles or league [of Italy], that everything His Lordship requests and thinks should be done regarding the two matters Your Lordship would do readily and with good will, of which matters one was concerning the marriage and the other concerning the government of Savoy. As for the government of Savoy, Your Lordship at that time named Messer Giacomo di Valperga and Messer Luigi Bolleri[4] as being the best qualified and also as being your friends. On this reply of yours, which my lord the Dauphin accepted as firm and settled, he based his willingness to help and defend Messer Giacomo, hoping that aid from you would not be lacking; and out of trust in Your Lordship, and with no other assistance, he undertook to defend Messer Giacomo—because his excellency, being far off and deprived of his rule and dominion, had no means for this defense save by way of Your Excellency. In regard to the marriage, when the Dauphin received your reply he took such steps, by letters, instructions, and messengers sent to the Duke and Duchess of Savoy to break off the negotiations etc., that the matter has remained in a good state; and my lord the Dauphin willingly set aside any regard for the displeasure of his close relatives at his not discharging his obligation and insisting on the conclusion of the negotiations already begun.[5]

Then the Dauphin sent back Gaston's brother and Baude Meurin with the mandate[6] for Messer Giacomo di Valperga and Gaston to conclude negotiations [with the Duke of Milan], and he also wrote additional letters of credence with new instructions. After Gaston related his credence, Your Lordship said, among other things, that you wished to have the enemies of the Dauphin's friends for your enemies and his

haviva respoxo gratiosamente ad tutte le parte; dunde perché alla parte
de recuperare al presente lo Delphinato Vostra Sig.ria allegò alcune occasione, et li pariva difficile, esso Monsig.re ha demissa et posta da
canto questa parte; et alla parte del Duca de Savoya, alla quale respon-
dessino franchamente senza usare termino dubioso nì allegationi de capituli nì de lighe, che tutto quello ve richiederà Sua Sig.ria et parirà che
debiati fare in l'una materia et l'altra Vostra Sig.ria lo farà volunteri et
de bona voglia; le quali materie una era del matrimonio et l'altra del
governio de Savoya. Et per lo governio de Savoya Vostra Sig.ria nominò
extunc Misser Iacomo de Valperga et Misser Aluyse Bolere[4] per più
sufficienti et vostri amici. Per questa tale vostra resposta, quale esso
Monsig.re accetò per ferma et salda, fece Monsig.re suo fundamento
di volere adiutare et deffendére el dicto Misser Iacomo, sperando esso
Monsig.re che vostro subsidio non mancheria; et ad fidutia de Vostra
Sig.ria ha interpreso de defendere Misser Iacomo et non per altro conforto, perché essendo Sua Ex.tia in parte longinqua, et tratto de Sua
Sig.ria et dominio, non haveva modo ad questa defensione salvo per
medio de Vostra Ex.tia. Et alla parte del matrimonio, come esso
Monsig.re intexe vostra resposta et deliberatione, fece tal provisione
per sue littere, instructione et messi mandadi da Monsig.re et Madama
de Savoya che interrope le pratiche etc., per modo che la cosa é remasta
in bon termine; et non ha voluto havere respetto esso Monsig.re ad
displicere ad soy proximi parenti per fare suo debito et per venire alla
conclusione delle pratiche principiate.[5]

Apresso remandò Monsg.re lo fratello de Gascon et Bandizon con
lo mandato[6] in persona de Misser Iacomo predecto de Valperga et
d'esso Gascon per concludere le dicte pratiche, et così scripse altre littere de credenza con altre instructione; et facendo esso Gascon la relatione de sua credenza, Vostra Sig.ria inter le altre parte li disse che
voliva havere li inimici deli amici de Monsig.re per suoy inimici et lí
amici per amici, et che tutto quello che Vostra Sig.ria potesse fare con
suo honore in deffensione de Misser Iacomo lo voleva fare. Et in quella
relatione disse luy ad Vostra Ex.tia, como Monsig.re li haviva scripto

friends for friends and that everything that Your Lordship could do in defense of Messer Giacomo, your honor saved, you would do. In the course of his relation Gaston said to Your Excellency that the Dauphin had ordered him to send his brother and some of his servants, named by the Dauphin, to the castle of Masino[7] but that he had left his brother at Trecate,[8] not wishing to send him to Masino until Your Excellency had been informed. To this Your Lordship replied that you did not want Gaston's brother to go alone.

After his brother had entered Masino with the abovementioned members of Gaston's household[9] and Gaston had then requested aid, Your Excellency allowed him sixteen cuirassiers of the illustrious Sforza's[10] company and twelve cuirassiers of the magnificent Count Pedro's[11] company, who received from Gaston 200 ducats. As they were about to ride off, Your Lordship had them stopped, hoping that by way of your ambassadors the trouble could be alleviated; and to the Duke of Savoy was sent Filippo da Tortona,[12] who accomplished very little—all this notwithstanding the fact that Gaston had said to Your Lordship that such a mission, unless military aid were provided, would do little.

At this time there arrived Jeannot de Sainte Camelle[13] with further letters of credence from my lord the Dauphin, who commended to Your Lordship [the safeguarding of] his honor and the defense of Messer Giacomo; and Your Lordship replied that you wished to do everything possible, your honor saved; and it was then decided to send Messer Gerardo de' Colli[14] to the Duke of Savoy. In the presence of Gaston, Jean du Fou,[15] Jeannot de Sainte Camelle, and some others, Messer Gerardo was given a very strongly worded commission by Your Excellency, to the effect that if my lord of Savoy will not willingly come to an agreement, he will be made to come to it. In fact, however, Messer Gerardo accomplished little.

Some days later, as Baude Meurin was about to depart [for the Dauphin's court] in the company of Prospero [da Camogli], Your Lordship said that you wanted to aid Messer Giacomo in every way possible but that there were the articles of the peace [i.e. the League of

che mandasse suo fratello et alcuni di suoy servitori nominati in el castello de Maxino,[7] et como l'haviva lassato suo fratello ad Trechà,[8] et che non l'haviva voluto mandare che prima Vostra Ex.tia non fusse avisata, et la Vostra Sig.ria li respose che non voliva che suo fratello andasse solo.

Da poy che suo fratello fo intrato in Maxino con li dicti famigli,[9] instando esso Gascon de havere subsidio, Vostra Ex.tia gli concesse coraze XVI dela Compagnia del Ill. Sforza[10] et coraze XII della Compagnia del Mag.co Conte Pedro,[11] li quali haveno da luy ducati ducento; et essendo aviati per cavalcare, Vostra Sig.ria li fece soprasedere, sperando che per via de vostri ambassatori le cose se mitigasseno; et fu mandato Filippo, Tertonexe,[12] da Mon.re de Savoya, il quale fece molto poco fructo, non obstante che lo dicto Gascon dicesse ad Vostra Sig.ria che l'ambassata farebe poco senza le gente d'arme.

In questo tempo zonse Zanotto da Sancta Camella[13] con altre littere de credenza de Monsig.re, il quale reccomandava ad Vostra Sig.ria lo suo honore et la diffensione de Misser Iacomo; et Vostra Sig.ria respose de volere fare tutto quello fusse possibile con vostro honore, et tunc fo deliberato de mandare Misser Gerardo Collo[14] da Mon.re de Savoya, allo quale fo dato per Vostra Ex.tia, in presentia de esso Gascon, de Zoane du Fo,[15] de Zanotto de Sancta Camella et de alcuni altri, commissione molto gagliarda con dire se Mon.re de Savoya non vegnirà allo accordio voluntieri che gli vegnirà per forza, il quale Misser Gerardo fece poco in substantia.

Et dapoy qualche zorni, essendo Bandizon in termino de partirse in compagnia de Prospero, essa Vostra Sig.ria disse di volere adiutare Misser Iacomo de tutto quello fare se potesse, allegando li capituli dela pace etc., et fu remandato da Monsig.re de Savoya il dicto Misser Gerardo Collo.[16]

Dallì ad octo dì dapoi la partita di Bandizon et de Prospero, deffendendosi ancora quelli che erano per Misser Iacomo, Zoane du Fo et Zanotto de Sancta Camella, deliberano de retornare da Monsig.re;[17] et in la sua partita, ultra molte bone parole usate per Vostra Sig.ria, non

31

Italy], and Messer Gerardo de' Colli was sent back to my lord of Savoy.[16]

Then eight days after the departure of Baude Meurin and Prospero, the adherents of Messer Giacomo still putting up a defense, Jean du Fou and Jeannot de Sainte Camelle decided to return to my lord the Dauphin.[17] At their leave-taking Your Lordship, in addition to warm expressions of good will, said that you could not, without being guilty of breaking the articles of the peace, send enough men to raise the sieges but that you would send a good company of foot, trusty and experienced soldiers, for the defense of Messer Giacomo's fortresses and that, furthermore, you would again dispatch an ambassador to my lord of Savoy. It was in these circumstances that Jean du Fou and Jeannot de Sainte Camelle took their leave, and this was the reason that my lord the Dauphin did not, for so long a time, send another messenger, being certain that Your Lordship had dispatched sufficient troops to save Messer Giacomo's fortresses.

As soon as Jean du Fou and Jeannot de Sainte Camelle had departed, Antonello d'Alagno[18] was dispatched with a band of foot, who were very well paid by Your Lordship; but, learning on the road that Roppolo had been lost, they had no mind to go farther and returned directly; and since, given this instance of fidelity, Gaston made no further provision, Vestigné was lost.[19]

A few days after the loss of Vestigné, Your Lordship decided that another detachment of loyal foot soldiers should be dispatched for the safeguarding of the castle of Masino, a company of about twelve well paid through the agency of Boschino.[20] In traveling by night through the region of Bianzé,[21] they became fearful of going farther and so returned, saying that they had been attacked and wounded—which was not true—and thus was lost the town of Masino.

After these had turned back, from the castle of Masino there arrived Frachasso,[22] sent to secure aid. Gaston gave him money for a company of twelve, who would not go beyond Candia,[23] and in fact took to their heels; of whom one came to Boschino and said that he and others had

possando Vostra Sig.ria senza carico de contrafare alli capituli dela pace mandare tanta gente che levasseno lo campo, disse de mandargli una compagnia de fanti boni, fidati et apti alla defensione dele forteze de Misser Iacomo, et in ultra de mandare ancora uno ambassatore da Mon.re de Savoya; et con questo se partireno dicti Zoane du Fo et Zanotto de Sancta Camella, et questa fu la casone perché Monsig.re stette molto tempo che non mandò altro messo, credendo certamente che Vostra Sig.ria li havesse mandato gente in bastanza per conservare le dicte forteze.

Incontinenti loro partiti fu mandato Antonello D'Alagno[18] con una frotta de fanti a pede, quali furono per Vostra Sig.ria molto ben pagati; et perché inteseno per camino che Roppolo era perduto non haveno animo de passare, et retornareno indreto, et ad fiducia de questi esso Gascon non fece altra provisione et per questo fo perduto Vestigna.[19]

Fra pochi zorni, dapoy la perdita de Vestigna, Vostra Sig.ria deliberò fussero mandati alcuni altri fanti fidati per la guardia del castello de Maxino; et forono ben pagati per mane de Boschino[20] circa XII compagni, li quali caminando de nocte per la campagna de Bianza,[21] se dubitarono de passare più ultra et se ne retornareno dicendo che erano stati assaltati et ferriti [sic]: che non fu vero, et per quello fu perduta la villa de Maxino.

Retornati questi indreto, zonse dal castello de Maxino, Frachasso,[22] mandato per havere subsidio; esso Gascon li dedi dinari per XII compagni, li quali non volseno passare tutti Candia,[23] anzi fuzirono, deli quali venne uno da Boschino che li disse como luy et alcuni altri erano fuziti, salvo quattro compagni che intrarono con Frachasso nel castello de Maxino; et questo fu tutto lo conforto et soccorso che have suo fratello et li altri che erano nel dicto castello; et cognoscendo esso Gascon che questo era poco subsidio, dubitando de quello che é intervenuto, con grande instantia et prece supplicò Vostra Sig.ria se dignasse havere reccomandato l'honore de Monsig.re, et che o per via de subsidio o per altra via, tenesse modo de intertenire et conservare lo dicto castello; non

fled, save four of the troop who with Frachasso entered the castle of Masino. And this was all the support and help that was given Gaston's brother and the others in the castle. Gaston, realizing that this was but feeble aid and fearing what has, indeed, since happened, urgently solicited Your Lordship to have the kindness to safeguard the honor of my lord the Dauphin by taking measures, in the form of outright help or otherwise, to conserve the castle of Masino so that it could hold out at least until you had news from my lord through Baude Meurin or Prospero or in some other way. Nonetheless no further provision was made, except to send Iob[24] to my lord of Savoy, Iob accomplishing no more than if he had not gone; and so through negligence the castle of Masino was lost,[25] with great injury to the honor of my lord—for Your Lordship well understands how much honor is affected in such a case. Then, a few days after the loss of the castle of Masino, Your Lordship learned, from a letter of Prospero,[26] what in part Prospero had accomplished in his negotiations with my lord.

Some days later, on the return of Baude Meurin and Prospero,[27] Your Lordship was informed how extremely well disposed to you my lord was—not so much by Prospero's report as by the tenor of the treaty itself.[28] Your Lordship then spoke most warmly and emphatically of taking great steps to restore my lord's honor, especially by sending to Lord Guglielmo [of Montferrat] to see if he would undertake the mission, etc. If he were unwilling to do so, Your Lordship said you would provide money for such troops as would be necessary, these to be commanded by Gaston or others, on behalf of my lord. In addition Your Lordship decided to make approaches to the heirs or executors of the late Messer Luigi Bolleri or to others, in order to provide secure bases for these troops. Since then, however, Your Lordship has shown yourself very cool toward these undertakings.

Taking into account this whole situation, Your Lordship must therefore consider and weigh, on the one hand, both what advantage there is in defending Messer Giacomo and what injury to my lord's honor will otherwise result, and, on the other, what good will, generos-

se perdesse almancho finché havesse novelle da Monsig.re o per Bandizon overo per Prospero o altramente. Nondimanco non fu facta altra provisione, salvo de mandare Iop[24] da Mon.re de Savoya, che tanto fece come non li fusse andato, et così per negligentia é perduto lo dicto castello[25] in gran mancamento de honore de Monsig.re, como Vostra Sig.ria ben comprehende quanto importa de honore in simile caso.

Dapoy la perdita del dicto castello de Maxino de pochi dì, Vostra Sig.ria have littere[26] da Prospero, per le quale intese parte de quello era facto per lo dicto Prospero con Monsig.re.

Et post aliquos dies sono retornati Bandizon et Prospero,[27] dal quale Prospero Vostra Sig.ria ha inteso la bona et optima dispositione de Monsig.re et non tanto per sua relatione, quanto per lo effecto dela scriptura;[28] dunde Vostra Sig.ria ha facto de bono, alto et grande parlare in volere fare cose assay per restaurare l'honore de Monsig.re, et spetialmente de mandare dal S.re Gulielmo ad praticare s'el voliva prendere lo carico etc., et quando esso non lo acceptasse, Vostra Sig.ria era contenta de pagare le gente d'arme necessarie con questo che esso Gascon o altri per Monsig.re facesse la conducta; et ancora più ultra Vostra S. avisava per havere loghi de retratta, de fare praticare con li heredi ho governatori de quondam Misser Aluyse Bolero e con altri, et dapoy se é monstrata Vostra Signoria in questi facti molto freda.

Siché recogliando tutte queste cose, Vostra Sig.ria de' bene consyderare et ballanzare tanto lo termino servato in questo caso dela deffensione de Misser Iacomo, che tutto redunda in carico del honore de Monsig.re, quanto la bona dispositione et liberalitade et grande offerte et mazore effecto che Monsig.re ha demonstrato verso Vostra Ex.tia che là unde Vostra Sig.ria se offeriva et obligava ad Sua Ex.tia, esso Monsig.re per sua innata clementia et humanità ha voluto de propria voglia et suo animoso instincto obligarse ad Vostra Sig.ria et ad vostra posteritate; et ultra de questo ha voluto pigliare la deffensione del Stato vostro et de vostri contra ogni Signore et parente, adcioché dal canto suo non restasse che questa intelligentia havesse loco et Vostra Sig.ria ben pò comprehendere quanto habia ad importare questa parte.

ity, great offers and even greater performance my lord has shown toward Your Excellency—to such an extent that, whereas Your Lordship was obligating himself to his excellency, my Lord has wished of his own volition, out of his innate clemency and humaneness and ardent feeling, to obligate himself, in return, to Your Lordship and your posterity, and, in addition, has wished to pledge himself to defend your state and your House against any lord, even if a relative; so that on his side there would be no impediment to concluding this treaty, and Your Lordship can well understand how important this is to you.

Since, then, the matter has developed as indicated above and since my lord's honor has been put in such a situation—though by so many letters, instructions, and messengers Your Lordship was requested to safeguard it—Gaston begs Your Lordship kindly to decide on the most effective and quickest way of saving, or redeeming, my lord's honor and of keeping the promises you made in writing or by verbal reply, and also to bear in mind what kind of person my lord is—not one to be led by words or pretensions or fictions, he himself having come to the making of this treaty so generously and frankly. Also, Your Lordship, who is versed in all the affairs of the world, should not lend ear to those who perhaps do not understand the matter—and who, if they do understand it, would be greatly displeased by such friendship and alliance. Finally, will Your Excellency kindly deign to counsel Gaston as to how he can make his report to the Dauphin in such a way as to preserve his honor and yet cast the least blame upon Your Lordship, Gaston wishing to do the office of faithful servant to his lord and also of entire friend and servant to Your Lordship—in which matter may God counsel you and keep you in prosperous and blessed state.

If perchance it will appear to Your Lordship that there is error in this memorandum, because something is exaggerated or otherwise departs from truth, will Your Lordship kindly cancel that part; and in case the memorandum is accurate, as Gaston without doubt believes it to be, he humbly begs Your Excellency to make such response and give him such final answer, and that briefly, that he can return to the Dau-

Essendo adunque, Ill.mo S.re, le cose passate in tal forma, como é sopradicto, et conducto l'honore de Monsig.re in tal stato, il quale per tante littere, instructione et messi é stato ad Vostra Sig.ria reccomandato, supplica esso Gascon se digna Vostra Sig.ria ben avisare del modo più proprio et breve de salvare o emendare l'honore de Monsig.re, et di servare la promessa et parola vostra, quale per risposta é in scripto mandata, et ben considerare la qualità de la persona de Monsig.re, quale non é da essere conducto per parole nì per ambitione nì per fictione, essendo Sua Ex.tia venuto ad questo facto tanto liberamente et franchamente; et anche non debbe Vostra Sig.ria, quale é experientia de tutte le cose del mondo, ponere orechie a persuasione de quegli che forse non intendeno, et se intendeno, seriano forte displicente de tanta amicicia et intelligentia; et ultra se digna Vostra Ex.tia de consigliare esso Gascon in che modo possa fare soa relatione ad Monsig.re ad suo honore et ad manco carico de Vostra Sig.ria, volendo luy fare l'officio de fidele servitore de suo Sig.re et de prefecto [sic] amico et servitore de Vostra Sig.ria, la quale Dio consiglia in questo caso et conserva in prospero et votivo stato.

Et se per aventura parirà ad Vostra Sig.ria che in questa scriptura sia deffecto de essere scripto più o altramente che la verità, se digna Vostra Sig.ria de cancellare quelle parte; et al caso che la scriptura sia vera, como esso Gascon crede senza dubio, supplica humelmente che Vostra Ex.tia se digna fare tale responsa et tale spazamento et breve che esso Gascon possa retornare da Monsig.re ad vostro honore et ad vostro profecto[a] et ad contentamento de Monsig.re.

Esso Gascon ha deliberato, non apparendo altro, de non perdere più tempo in questo facto, perché serà presto compito l'anno che s'é partito da Monsig.re.

Die dominico ultimo novembris 1460. Responsum oretenus eidem Gasconi ad omnia suprascripta particulatim in aula .C. per D. Thomam Reatinum, Petrum de Pusterla, Cichum et Prosperum Camulium etc.[b]

---

a. Read: profitto.
b. This paragraph is missing from one copy.

phin, to your honor and profit and to the contentment of the Dauphin.

Gaston has decided, if nothing else comes up, to lose no more time in this matter, because it will soon be a year since he departed from my lord the Dauphin.

Sunday, November 30, 1460. Verbal response to Gaston, item by item, concerning all the matters written above, made in the council chamber by Tomasso da Rieti, Pietro de Pusterla, Cicco [Simonetta], and Prospero da Camogli.

HISTORICAL NOTES

1. Dated Dec. 12, 1459. See Vol. I, doc. 40, n. 1, p. 268.

2. The Duke's reply, dated March 10, 1460, was published in Vol. I, doc. 40, pp. 267.

3. Raymond, a man of arms in the Dauphin's household guard [*Lettres,* I, 292–93].

4. Luigi Bolleri, a Piedmontese baron, lord of Centallo and Demonte and ally of Sforza.

5. At least since 1455 the Dauphin had attempted to arrange a marriage between Sforza's eldest son, Galeazzo Maria, and the Duke of Savoy's eldest daughter, Maria [The Dauphin to Sforza, Valence, Feb. 20, 1455, *Lettres,* I, 68–69]. Galeazzo Maria, however, was already betrothed to Susanna Gonzaga, and later (1457) to her sister, Dorotea, both daughters of the Marquess of Mantua, and Maria of Savoy herself had been betrothed to Sforza's second son, Filippo Maria. Since the marriage between Maria of Savoy and Filippo Maria did not take place, it appears that in 1460 there were plans at the Savoyard court, probably instigated by the Dauphin, to have Galeazzo Maria break his engagement with Dorotea and marry Maria of Savoy [S. Davari, "Il matrimonio di Dorotea Gonzaga con Galeazzo Maria Sforza," *Giornale ligustico,* XVI (1889), 377, n. 2; cf. Bartolomeo Mascha to the Marchioness of Mantua, Pavia, Dec. 11, 1460, A. S. Mantova, *Carteggio-Milano* B. 1621]. This document suggests that the Duke of Milan opposed these plans.

6. Dated at Genappe, June 3, 1460 and received at Milan on July 1 [*Francia,* cart. 525; *Lettres,* I, 120–22].

7. Masino, Valperga's castle.

8. Trecate, near Novara in Piedmont.

9. The Dauphin had dispatched some 60 men of arms to defend the castle of Masino which, in the absence of Giacomo di Valperga, was held by his wife, Violante [Cibrario, *Jacopo Valperga,* 23; Gabotto, *Lo Stato sabaudo,* I, 53].

10. Sforza Secondo, natural son of the Duke.

11. Count Pietro dal Verme.

12. On May 13, 1460 [*Reg. Missive* 44, fol. 249r], Sfora had accredited to Gaston Filippo da Tortona, who was being sent on this mission to the Savoyard court. After jousting in Milan on Sunday, Apr. 27 [see Vol. I, doc. 40, n. 1, p. 268], topping the list of the contestants [*Potenze Sovrane,* cart. 1483; cf. Vincenzo della Scalona to the Marquess of Mantua, Milan, Apr. 27, 1460, A. S. Mantova, *Carteggio-Milano,* B. 1621], Gaston had left for the Savoyard court during the first part of May, for on May 10 Sforza investigated a complaint that his officials had mistreated him the "other day" at Novara, and also sent him a horse as a gift [Sforza to P. Caimi, *referendarius* of Novara, Milan, May 10, 1460, *Reg. Missive* 48, fol. 159r]. Gaston acknowledged receipt of the gift from Moncalieri on June 7 [*Lettres,* I, 369–70, n. 6]. The Duke had announced Gaston's departure for the Dauphin's court on May 15 [*Francia,* cart. 525; *Lettres,* I, 322], but it is clear from this document that the envoy did not return to Genappe. He probably lingered in Savoy until he received his new powers [see above, n. 6] to conclude the treaty with the Duke, in the pursuit of which he was authorized on June 25 by the Dauphin to receive 100 crowns a month [*Lettres,* I, 304–05].

13. On July 28, 1460 [*Francia,* cart. 525], the Dauphin accredited to Sforza, Jeannot de Sainte Camelle, a member of his household, to discuss means for the defense of Valperga's lands threatened by the Duke of Savoy.

14. Gerardo de' Colli had already been sent on this first mission to the Savoyard court where he arrived on July 18 [Colli to Sforza, Carignano, July 21, 1460, *Savoia,* cart. 480]; i.e. ten days before Jeannot's letter of credence had been issued [see above, n. 13]. The envoy found that the Duke of Savoy, influenced by Antonio di Romagnano, remained adamant in his aggressive posture towards Valperga claiming that Gaston du Lyon, through forged letters, was manufacturing the Dauphin's interest in the defense of the former chancellor, a charge denied by Sforza [Sforza to Colli, Milan, July 26, 1460,

39

ibid., cart. 480]. In addition the Duke requested Colli to recall the Milanese troops from Masino, as he had been instructed to do by the Duke of Milan, who alleged that these troops had gone to that castle against his orders [Colli to Sforza, Carignano, Aug. 1, 1460, *ibid.,* cart. 513].

15. Jean du Fou, equerry and cup-bearer to the Dauphin [*Lettres,* I, 308].

16. On Aug. 21, 1460 Colli arrived at the Savoyard court on his second mission [Colli to Sforza, Carignano, Aug. 27, 1460, *Savoia,* cart. 480]. The Duke of Savoy refused to see him for several days, and finally informed him that it was too late to reach an accord because his troops had already captured Valperga's possessions of Roppolo and Vestigné, and were besieging the castle of Masino itself [Colli to Sforza, Carignano, Sept. 15, 1460, *ibid.,* cart. 480]. The ambassador planned to leave for Milan on Sept. 22 [Colli to Sforza, Carignano, Sept. 21, 1460, *ibid.,* cart. 480].

17. On Sept. 5, 1460, Sforza notified the Dauphin that Jeannot de Sainte Camelle was returning to Genappe [*Reg. Missive* 44, fol. 295r]. It appears, therefore, that Meurin and Prospero da Camogli left Milan for the Dauphin's court on Aug. 28. Gaston du Lyon remained at Milan awaiting the results of Prospero's mission, while Valperga left for Genappe some time in September [Vincenzo della Scalona to the Marquess of Mantua, Milan, Sept. 30, 1460, A. S. Mantova, *Carteggio-Milano,* B. 1621].

40

18. Milanese *condottiere*.

19. For the loss of Roppolo and Vestigné, see above, n. 16.

20. Unable to identify him.

21. Bianzé, near Vercelli.

22. Gaspare Sanseverino, called "Fracasso," son of the renowned Milanese *condottiere*, Roberto Sanseverino [C. H. Clough, "Caterina Sforza, Gasparo Sanseverino e Il Cortegiano del Castiglione," *Atti e Memorie della Deputazione di Storia Patria per le province di Romagna,* New Ser., XV–XVI (1963–65), 224 ff.].

23. A locality near Casale Monferrato.

24. Iob de Palazzo, a member of Sforza's household.

25. Violante di Valperga surrendered the castle of Masino to the Duke of Savoy's men on Oct. 12, 1460 [Gabotto, *Lo Stato sabaudo,* I, 57].

26. The dispatch of Oct. 2 [doc. 55, p. 9], receipt of which was acknowledged by Sforza in a letter to the Dauphin [Milan, Oct. 23, 1460, *Francia,* cart. 525; *Lettres,* I, 330–31]. In this letter the Duke thanked the Dauphin for the conclusion of the negotiations, and notified him that upon Prospero's return he would send another ambassador presumably to reside at the Dauphin's court.

27. Nov. 2, 1460 [see doc. 56, n. 5, p. 24].

28. i.e., the treaty.

Reply and justification etc. in regard to the points raised in the instructions of the Honorable Baude de Meurin, secretary and ambassador of the Dauphin.

We have diligently studied what by Gaston [du Lyon] and Baude, on behalf of the Dauphin, has been explained,[1] and what also by Prospero has been reported, and we have understood the Dauphin's complete good will. We do not know how we can possibly express the thanks we owe to his serenity, he having embraced with such benevolence and benignity us and our affairs. However, we can but attempt, with that capacity which God has granted us, not to be unappreciative of so ample a beneficence. But because the exposition of the aforesaid contains many divisions and parts, we are summarizing our conclusions under certain heads that will include the whole, namely: first, the three appointments[2] sent by Gaston to his serenity; second, the business of Giacomo di Valperga; third, the generosity his highness has shown for us and our affairs; fourth, the mission of Baude de Meurin and what, regarding this, we have to do.

Concerning the three appointments we reply as follows. We have well in mind that, in the event of the death of the King his father, we promised, and gave in writing to Gaston, that we would expend all our force and power for the conquest and stabilizing of his lordship's state

58 · *Memorandum of the* DUKE OF MILAN

to the DAUPHIN

Francia, cart. 525. Minute

Resposta et iustificatione facte etc. ale parte se contengano in l'instructione del Spectabile Baldizon Morin, secretario et ambassatore del Ser.mo Mon.re Delphin.

Havemo inteso dilligentemente quanto per Guastone et Baldizon per parte del Serenissimo Mon.re el Delfin de Viena ne é stato exposto,[1] et quanto ancora per Prospero nostro secretario ne é stato referito, et cognosciuta la soa optima dispositione. Non sapemo ad che modo possiamo alla Soa Serenità debite et condecente gratie rendere, havendo Nuy et le nostre cose con tanta benivolentia et benignità abrazate; pur ne sforzaremo con quelle facultate che Dio ne ha concedute non essere de tanto et si amplo beneficio scognoscenti. Ma perché le expositione deli sopradicti contengano molte distinctione et partiti, Nuy ne prendremo alcune conclusione che sarano el summario de tutte, cioé li tre appuntamenti[2] mandati alla Ser.tà Soa da Guaston; secundo, el facto de D. Iacomo Valperga; tercio, la liberalità usata da Soa Celsitudine verso Nuy et nostre cose; quarto, la imposicione che ha el soprascritto Baldo et quanto Nuy circa ciò havemo ad fare.

Alla prima parte dunque deli appuntamenti respondemo cossì: che Nuy molto bene havemo ad memoria che venendo el caso dela morte del S. Re suo padre promettemo et detemo in scritto ad Guaston che Nuy metteressemo tutta nostra forza et possanza per la conquesta et

—item, regarding Dauphiné, as is contained in the said appointments.

Item: similarly, regarding the matter of the government of Savoy, we say that we will do everything possible to satisfy the will of my lord the Dauphin; but we did not intend this promise to mean going to war with the Duke of Savoy, who is, after all, the father-in-law of his lordship. And therefore we always take for granted that his lordship would prefer to bring about the reformation of that state by other means than force. In addition, the Duke is a member of our League of Italy, on which account our using force against Savoy would directly and expressly contravene the articles of that League. For us to do so would not, we are certain, be pleasing to my lord the Dauphin, because first of all, such an act would impugn our honor, which we have always prized more than life itself; and second, because, leaving aside that it would give reason for the Duke of Savoy to put himself in the embrace of the King of France, or of the Venetians, this act would cause all the members of the League justly to take arms against us.

Similarly we reply, concerning the matter of Giacomo di Valperga of whom in the aforesaid appointments no mention was made, that at that time no such matter was even spoken of. Notwithstanding this, we, knowing that my lord has the matter much at heart, secretly aided Valperga with money and troops and alerted the mounted men of our son Sforza and those of Count Pietro dal Verme to send them in Valperga's behalf, under the pretense that they were not our soldiers. But it then seemed best not to dispatch them because Masino was well supplied and, with winter threatening, the siege of Masino would have to be raised. Thus we refrained from sending these mounted troops, it seeming to us that the footsoldiers would be more useful.

In addition we dispatched many different embassies to the Duke of Savoy, not only to express our displeasure at the undoing of Lord Giacomo but also to remind the Duke that perpetrating such an injury to my lord Dauphin would be remembered in due time and could result in the Duke's destruction, adding other menaces as well.

Item: we want my lord to know that some of the men we provided

stabilimento del Stato de Soa Sig.ria; item del facto del Delfinato, como in dicti appuntamenti se contene.

Item et similiter del facto del governo de Savoya, dicemmo che operaressemo tutto quello che ad Nuy fosse possibile per satisfare alla voluntà del sopradicto Mon.re Delfino; et questo non intendevamo con rompere guerra al Duca de Savoya, quale hé pur socero de Sua S.ria. Et per questo sempre acettemo che Sua S.ria cum li modi, più tosto che cum le forse [sic], dovesse etc. voler la reformatione del Stato. Et ultra é membro dela nostra Liga de Italia, perché seria de directo contravenire expressamente alli capituli d'essa Liga, la quale cosa semo certi non piaceria ad dicto Mon.re, perché saria primamente mancamento al nostro honore, quale havimo sempre preciato più che la propria vita; secondo, che lassamo stare che haveressemo data casone al Duca de Savoya butarse in le brace della M.tà del Re de Franza, o de Veneciani, ma tutta la Liga haria iustamente prese l'arme contra de Nuy.

Similiter respondemo al facto de D. Iacomo de Valperga, del quale nelli predicti appuntamenti non fo facta mentione alcuna, però che in quelli tempi non si parlava de cotale cosa; ma questo non obstante, sentendo Nuy che questa cosa era molto al core de dicto Mon.re, lo havemo subvenuto secretamente de dinari et de fantarie, et havevamo messo in puncto li cavalli de nostro figliolo Sforza et quelli del Conte Petro dal Verme per mandarli in suo socorso, sotto specie che non fosseno nostri soldati; ma parse poy[a] per lo meglio non andasseno, perché Masino era ben fornito, et che instando lo inverno el campo bisognava levarse; et cossì restamo Nuy de mandarli, parendo li fanti fossero più utili.

Insuper havemo mandato più diverse ambassarie al Duca de Savoya non solamente ad dire quanta displacencia havemo Nuy dela desfactione de D. Iacomo, ma etiam ad recordarli che facendo questa iniuria al dicto Monsignor Dalfino se ne recordaria a loco e a tempo che ne porria seguire la desfaction soa et più altre parole minatorie.

Item volimo che dicto Mon.re sapia che alcuni di nostri provi-

---

a. Crossed out: ad Guaston et a D. Iacomo soprascritti.

for Valperga, who were captured while serving him and then hanged by the Duke of Savoy, were made to confess that it was we who sent them to attack him. The Duke, having had these confessions drawn up in legal form, then sent them to the King of France[3] and to the Venetians in order to accuse us.[4]

But, above all we are eager that my lord the Dauphin understand the outrageous treatment meted out to our troops who were at Masino. Some were taken prisoner, others tortured and held long in prison wounded. His lordship can therefore imagine how many men would go there willingly, seeing that those there were hanged by enemies and ordered tortured by their friends. Had Lord Giacomo and his brother[5] treated well those who went to aid them, not only from among our troops but from all Lombardy there would have gone so many in such a war that they would perhaps have given the Duke of Savoy a bad year.

HISTORICAL NOTES

1. On Dec. 6, 1460 [*Francia,* cart. 525], Gaston du Lyon wrote to Cicco Simonetta, from his residence in the "Hospitio Puthei" in Milan, that the day before he had received from the Dauphin new letters and certain "avisi" which he wanted Sforza to know before the conclusion of his mission scheduled for that day. The nature of these "avisi" is not known.

2. See the Memorandum of the Duke of Milan to Gaston du Lyon, March 10, 1460, published in Vol. I, doc. 40, p. 267.

3. In response to an appeal by the Duke of Savoy, Charles VII had written to Sforza [St. Jean D'Angely, July 26, 1460, *Francia,* cart. 525] asking him not to aid Valperga. Sforza replied on Aug. 22 [*ibid.,* cart. 525] that he had attempted by means of diplomatic missions to reconcile Valperga with the Duke of Savoy, but had refused to give him military support. He admitted, however, that some of his soldiers had fought of their own will for the former chancellor. He invited the King to send an impartial observer to Italy to investigate this matter as well as his alleged military support of King Ferrante and his supposed intrigues against royal authority at Genoa. He also

46

sionati, quali sonno stati presi nelli servicii de Messer Iacomo et poy dal Duca de Savoya impicati, sonno stati facti confessare che Nuy gli havimo mandati alle soe offese et facto sopra ciò processo, quale ha poy mandato et alla M.tà del Re de Franza[3] et ad Venetia per dare carico ad Nuy.[4]

Ma sopra tutto havimo caro ch'el prelibato Mon.re intenda li extranei portamenti[b] usati verso le nostre gente che erano ad Masino, deli quali ne son stati alcuni presi, altri curlati et tenuti lungamente in preson feriti; siché pensi Soa Celsitudine chi gli doveva andare volenteri, essendo da inimici apicati et dali amici preficet, curlati, che se D. Iacomo et suo fratello[5] havesseno facta bona compagnia ad quilli che andavano alli loro favori, non solamente di nostri soldati, ma de tutta Lumbardia gli ne sarianno andati tanti a tal guerra che haveriano forse dato al Duca de Savoya el male anno.

took the precaution of sending a copy of his reply by special courier to Raoulin Regnault, a royal equerry, urging him to make certain the King read his letter [Sforza to Regnault, Milan, Aug. 26, 1460, *ibid.,* cart. 525]. The King replied on Sept. 24, 1460 [*ibid.,* cart. 525; published by Beacourt, VI, 493–94 with wrong date of Sept. 23], seeming to accept the Duke's assurances.

4. Upon reading the confessions of the captured Milanese soldiers, the Venetian *Signoria* sent to Sforza a special emissary, Fra Simonetto della Barba, to remonstrate that the Duke's behavior was contrary to the terms of the Italian League. According to the Mantuan ambassador at Milan, pressure from Charles VII and Venice, and the arrival of the French ambassadors in Italy [see doc. 55, n. 6, p. 19], induced Sforza to cancel plans to send additional troops in support of Valperga [Vincenzo della Scalona to the Marquess of Mantua, Sept. 19 and 30, A. S. Mantova, *Carteggio-Milano,* B. 1621].

5. Ludovico Valperga.

---

b. Crossed out: de D. Iacomo et de li soy che hanno.

Prospero, his most illustrious and excellent lordship the Dauphin, having sent back his secretary[2] with the documents you know about, and in addition we having seen from the secretary's instructions the reaction of his lordship to the propositions you discussed with him, we have drawn up a reply in our justification, as you will see by the copy[3] of those responses, which memorandum we wish you, in the conversation you have with the Dauphin, to follow as the rule and guide in such speaking and discussion as you happen to engage in.

In the treaty negotiated through you and ratified[4] by us, there is included the affair of Messer Giacomo di Valperga, whose situation, as we have had you clearly informed, has so deteriorated that it no longer corresponds to what is required in the treaty, and thus, through the failure of others, the treaty article has been rendered impossible of accomplishment because Valperga had lost his possessions before we received your letters, nor had we received word of what you had concluded with the Dauphin. His loss, then, occurred through no fault or failure of ours, given the circumstances it was necessary to bear in mind etc. and given also what touches upon the Dauphin's honor in regard to Savoyard affairs, namely that his proceedings in those affairs appear entirely justified.

Having that reverence that we have for his most illustrious

59 · *Instructions of the* DUKE OF MILAN

to PROSPERO DA CAMOGLI[1]

Francia, cart. 525. Two minutes[a]

Prospero, perché lo Ill.mo et Ex.mo Monsignore lo Delphin ne ha remandato el suo Secretario[2] con quella scrittura che tu say, et oltra havimo veduto per l'instructione a luy data per quante et quali rasone se move Soa Ill.ma Signoria ad quello de che tu hay conferto con quella, ad quale tutte rasone havimo facto respondere per nostra iustificacione, como tu vederay per la copia[3] de quelle resposte, quale volimo, in li rasonamenti te accaderano, siano norma et regula del tuo parlare et argumentacione che te accaderan.

Attento che in quella scrittura contracta per ti et ratificata[4] per Nuy gli é el facto de Messer Iacomo Valperga, quale, como te havimo facto chiaramente intendere, é descaduto del grado che se rechiede in essa scriptura et per defecto de altri reducta ad impossibile per esserse perduti suoy beni inanti che havessemo recevute toe littere, né havuto aviso de quanto havevi concluso con lo prefato Ill.mo et Exellen.mo Sig.re et non per alcuna colpa, né defecto nostro, attenti li respecti ne bisognava havere etc. per supplemento de quanto reguarda l'honore d'esso Mon.re in li facti de Savoya, che ne pareno tutti iusti dal canto d'esso Mon.re; et havendo Nuy quella reverentia che havemo ad Soa Ill.ma Sig.ria, ve-

---

a. One of the minutes, signed by Cicco Simonetta, has served as the text. The other is identical except that the last four paragraphs follow in different order and it has the important addition given below.

lordship, we undertook, in the name of God, to make provision for these matters, and, as you know, by two means. First, we sent the embassy to persuade the Duke of Savoy to reconcile himself to the Dauphin and to reform his government in a way that would be pleasing to his illustrious lordship. On this mission we sent the honorable knight and doctor, Lord Alberico Maletta,[5] our trusty and honored councilor, in whose representations we had great hope because of his authority, his prudence, his mastery of the art of diplomacy, and the great credit he enjoys at the court of Savoy. However, he returned with the answer of which Gaston and you have been informed, on which account we do not repeat it to you here.

Second, by way of force, to lord Guglielmo[6] we recently sent, as Gaston and you know, Pietro da Gallarate,[7] who is devoted to us and is also an intimate adherent of his, to urge him to undertake the mission, pointing out to him all appropriate reasons for so doing. This we did because it seemed to us that lord Guglielmo's services would provide a more effective, expeditious, and suitable way of giving military aid to Valperga than any other. Pietro, however, has returned a negative reply, as Gaston and you know, and we saw no other way of being able, from our quarter, to make provision for the matter, in the manner required, because of the stringent obligations to which we have subscribed with all the powers of Italy and with the Duke of Savoy. These obligations have been demonstrated to Gaston,[8] and you have been given a summary of them, so that you can inform the Dauphin in what way we are obligated to and leagued with the Duke of Savoy and with all the other powers of Italy. Therefore his lordship will want to examine and understand this matter thoroughly; for our person, our sons, our state, and all that we have in the world are dedicated to fulfilling every commandment and wish of his lordship. We leave to him, then, counseling us about the way which we must take, because we are certain that, on account of his magnanimity, clemency, and prudence, he will give the kind of counsel he would wish to be given, in return, by his lordship in a similar case. However, you will finally say, as we have

nemo in nome de Dio ad provedere dal canto nostro in quelle cose et
como tu say per le doe vie; cioé per mandare l'ambassata et dire, et per-
suadere lo Illustre S. Duca de Savoya ad reconciliarse con esso Monsig.re
et reformarse in modo che sia grato ad Soa Ill.ma Sig.ria, gli mandassemo el Spectabile Cavalero et Doctore D. Alberico Maleta,[5] nostro fido
et honorato Consigliero, in la chuy opera speravamo assay per l'auctorità
et prudentia soa et che ha grande noticia de tutti li modi apti etc. et che
ha grande credito in quella Corte; el quale é retornato con quella resposta et expedision che lo dicto Gaston et tu seti informati, per el che
non te ne replicamo qui altro.

Al modo della forza, in questi dì proximi, como el dicto Gaston et
tu sapeti, Nuy havemo mandato al S. Guilielmo[6] Petro de Galerate,[7]
nostro fidelissimo et suo strecto et acceptissimo, per confortarlo et ac-
cenderlo ad questo facto, recordandoli tutte le rasone opportune; et
questo fecemo, parendone esso S. Guilielmo lo più apto modo et la più
expedita et conveniente via ad questo facto che niuno altro. El quale
Petro é retornato con la resposta del non, como dicto Gaston et tu sapeti,
per el che Nuy non vedemo per altra via de gente del canto de qua
possere provedere ad questa materia, como saria bisogno, per respecto
alle strecte obligacione che Nuy havemo con tutte le potencie de Italia
et con esso Sig.re Duca de Savoya, le quale havimo facto monstrare al
dicto Gaston,[8] et ad ti ne havimo facto dare lo extracto ad ciò che possi
informare lo prefato Ex.mo Mon.re lo Dalphin in che modo Nuy siamo
obligati et ligati con lo dicto Sig.re Duca de Savoya et con tutte l'altre
potentie de Italia. Ergo la Sig.ria Soa vogli molto ben intendere et exa-
minare questo, perché essendo la persona nostra, li figlioli nostri et lo
Stato et tutto quello havimo al mondo dedicato ad ogni commanda-
mento et voluntà della Soa Sig.ria, essa ne ha ad consigliare del modo
che Nuy havimo ad servare, perché siamo certi per soa magnanimità et
clementia et prudentia ne darà quello consiglio che ella voria fosse dato
reciproce ad essa Soa Sig.ria in simile caso; et nondimeno finaliter diray,
como havimo dicto ad Gastone, che Nuy siamo contenti adaptando la
Sig.ria Soa lo modo dele gente, con lo dinaro fare quella spesa in la

told Gaston, that we are willing, if his lordship arranges a way of providing troops, to defray such part of the expenses as his lordship will decide and such as we offered to pay Lord Guglielmo, as you have been informed by us by word of mouth.

Having ordained what we explained to you above, so that it is clearly understood what we are able to do, for our part in upholding the Dauphin's honor, in defense of which the Dauphin is seeking and intends to make provision, we wish you to return to his most illustrious lordship and express our devotion to him with all humility, reverence, and offers of service possible. See to it that, in every way you think best and with all care and diligence, you so proceed that the Dauphin is satisfied with our offers, as above—given that we cannot act in a direct way for reasons aforementioned—and remains kindly disposed and of good will toward us and ours and our state. You will be sure to explain to him that, truly, were it not for the great respect it is necessary to observe for the League of Italy, especially at present in such upheaval of minds and affairs, we would in person with all our force and ability dispose ourselves to carry out his every wish.

As for the most kind regard for our state which his lordship expressed to you and the offer he made you regarding the three towns[9] etc., we wish you to thank his excellency with all the power of eloquence you can summon in this world.

To the most illustrious and most excellent lord [Philip], Duke of Burgundy, you will say, having offered what appropriate greetings and expressions of regard seem best to you, that because of his excellency's great reputation throughout the world as well as because of the personal friendship and fraternal feeling that existed between his excellency and the late Duke Filippo,[10] our father and predecessor, we—although not equal to our predecessors—nevertheless consider ourselves the happy heir of that friendship; and in all reverence, love, affection and deed possible to us, we are disposed, for our part, to conserve that relationship. You will therefore give full assurances to his lordship that he can make capital, as if his own, of all our resources, our state, and

gente che la Sig.ria Soa ordinarà et che Nuy facemo al presente nel
S. Guilielmo, como tu sey informato da Nuy ad boca.[b]

Siché, havendo Nuy ordinato quello che te dicemo de sopra, che ne
pare quello possiamo fare Nuy dal canto nostro in supplemento del
honore, al che cerca et intende esso Ill.mo Mon.re provedere, volimo
che tu retorni da Soa Ill.ma Sig.ria et ad quella ne recomandi con tutte
le humilitate et reverentie et offerte che te sarà may possibile; et guarda
per tutte quelle vie te parerà, con ogni studio et diligentia procurare
con Soa Ill.ma S. se contenti de quello che offerimo utsupra, attento che
per via directa non la possiamo fare per li respecti utsupra, et resti in lo
suo humanissimo et bon proposto verso Nuy et nostri et nostro Stato; et
tu gli dighi ad ogni modo che in vero se non fosse lo grande respecto é
necessario havere ad la Liga de Italia, maxime al presente in tanta su-
blevacione de animi et movimenti de cose, Nuy in persona con ogni
nostro sforzo et ingenio se metteressemo ad ogni executione che gli
piacesse.

Alla parte del respecto che te ha monstrato tanto gratiosamente
havere Soa Ill.ma S. al nostro Stato, et la offerta te ha facta de quelle tre
terre[9] etc., vogliamo regratii Soa Excel.tia quanto may più poray et saperay in questo mondo.

Al Illustrissimo et Excellentissimo Signore Duca de Bergogna, con
quelle convenientie te parerà et recommandatione et salutatione, diray
che oltra la grande reputatione dela Soa Ex.tia per tutto el mondo,
etiam per la privata amicicia et fraternità che Soa Ex.tia ha havuto con
lo Ill.mo quondam Sig.re Duca Filippo[10] nostro padre et precessore,
Nuy, quantunque non equali alli nostri predecessori, tamen se repu-
tamo boni heredi de quella amicicia et con tutte le reverentie, caritate,
affectione et operacione a Nuy possibile disponemo dal canto nostro
conservarsele; et in questo certificaray largamente Soa Sig.ria che ogni
nostra possibilità et lo Stato et de quanto habiamo, Soa Sig.ria se ne pò
fare capitale, como de cosa propria; et con questa fede recoremo da

---

b. In the left hand margin of the other minute: fiorini XI^m ad soldi LIIII° pro fiorino.

whatever we possess. It is with this pledge that we have recourse to him.

You will then proceed to narrate the affairs and negotiations that we have with his most serene lordship, the Dauphin, as formerly the Dauphin urged you to tell the Duke of Burgundy on our behalf. You will also tell the Duke how much we lament finding ourselves bound by these links to the League and Peace in Italy, because we cannot, without bringing grave charges upon us, do otherwise nor more than we are doing. Since, then, we know his excellency to be most prudent, kindhearted and honorable, we beg him to understand this situation and the condition of affairs as herein explained, and to give us his counsel. We add that whatever we can do, in a completely honorable way, we are disposed to do for the Dauphin, to whom it has seemed right for us to dedicate ourselves, our sons, our state, and all that is ours etc. Inform us diligently of the replies made by the Duke of Burgundy and also by my lord [Antoine or John] of Croy; and as far as you deem is operative and useful in the negotiations, having regard for the instructions we have given you, you will follow his counsels and directions etc.

To [Richard,] Duke of York, you will say just about the same things that we tell you, here above, to say to the Duke of Burgundy, such as regard the reminder of the ancient friendship etc. and our disposition.

To the Earl of Warwick, after commending his prowess and valor, you will express how happy we shall always be to do him pleasure.

With the Duke and the Earl you will share our negotiation with my lord the Dauphin, speaking to the extent and in the way that the Dauphin will order you—doing so for the purpose of disposing them to act well in our matter for thereon depend many things etc.

To the Legate[11] you will express our entire pleasure with what he has been doing and the prudence he has shown in these matters, for which not only King Ferrante and we are obligated but all Italy as well—all those in Italy, that is, who have the right attitude. Here you will inquire closely and attentively about the situation in England, about how matters stand and whether the Yorkists will cross [the

quella, alla quale tu proseguiray de narare queste cose et tractamenti che havemo con lo prefato Ser.mo Mon.re, como altra volta te conforta Soa Sig.ria che tu gli dicesi da parte nostra; et cossì gli diray como Nuy ne dolemo grandemente trovarne in questi vinculi de Liga et Pace in Italia, perché senza nostro grande carico non possemo fare altro né più de quello faciamo; tamen, perché sapiamo la Soa Ex.tia prudentissima et affectionatissima et honestissima etc., la pregamo che ella vogli ben intendere questa materia et lo grado et stato dele cose hinc inde presentate et sporgene suo consiglio, cum sit che de quanto may possiamo honestissimamente fare, siamo disposti verso lo prefato Mon.re, al quale se paremo essere dedicati Nuy, li nostri figlioli, lo nostro Stato et ogni nostra cosa etc. Et de quanto te responderà Soa Sig.ria et cossì Mon.re de Crovi, darane aviso diligentemente, et per quello te sarà possibile et utile alla materia iusta l'ordini che tu hay da Nuy, metti ad loco suoy consigli et adrici etc.

Al Duca de Iorch diray etiam quasi quello medesmo te dicemo qui de sopra da dire al Duca de Bergogna quanto specta alla recordacione dela amcicia antiqua etc. et disposicione nostra.

Et al Conte de Varvich, commendando la virtù et valorosità soa, diray quanto haverimo sempre grato farli piacere.

Et con luy et l'altro participaray del tractamento nostro con Mon.re lo Dalphin, dicendo in questo quanto et como te ordinarà Soa Sig.ria ad utilitatem de disponerli ad bene prosequendum, perché ibi pendunt multa etc.

Al Legato[11] diray como Nuy siamo tanto contenti quanto dire se possa del opera et bona prudentia che el ha operato in quele cose delle quale se ne trova non solamente Re Ferdinando et Nuy obligati, sed tutta Italia de quelli che habiano voglia de ben vivere; et qui gli domandaray strectamente et con bona attencione del grado de Ingliterra, et in che stato siano quelle cose, et sonno per passare aut non, et con che fundamenti etc., et de tutto ne daray aviso diligenter.

Con Mon.re lo Delphin diray dele ambassate[12] de Franza venute in Italia per opera del Duca de Bretagna; et qui vederay de dolertene con

Channel] or not, and with what supports, and concerning all this you will diligently send word.

With my lord the Dauphin you will speak about the embassies from France[12] that have come into Italy at the instigation of [Francis II,] Duke of Brittany; and here you will be sure to complain about them to his lordship and to discover, by what openings the Dauphin gives you and others you are able to devise, the proceedings and aims of these embassies. We will consider it most acceptable if, through the Dauphin, they can be hampered—not so much out of any fear that we have as from our desire never to have any contention with the House of France, especially since we bear it true affection and reverence.

If his lordship accepts the treaty document ratified and subscribed by us, you must solicit to have his ratification and reconfirmation in proper form. If it is possible to remove from the treaty the article regarding lord Giacomo, we will be pleased. For it does not fit into the alliance, which is perpetual, and the Valperga affair is of a nature that, reduced to a formal obligation, it subjects us to charges and gives him little help; and what is really needful we are disposed to do to the best of our ability, as is said, and this should suffice him.

In all the matters that you have to negotiate with the Dauphin, we wish you to work with Gaston and share all proceedings with him and follow his opinion and counsel, he being one who because of his capacities, loyalty and devotion is highly favored by the Dauphin and most friendly toward us. We are completely certain that he will as lovingly and faithfully deal with our business as he does with the Dauphin's and that he will do as we ourselves would do if we were there in person.

Item: we wish you to inform yourself of the titles and status of the barons and courtiers of the Dauphin and of the Duke of Burgundy and also of the cities in those regions; and bring this information in writing with you on your return.

About going to England you will do what seems best to the Dauphin, taking from his lordship the guide-lines for what you have to do there. When you arrive in England, you will first go straight to the

Soa Sig.ria, et vede per quelle vie te darà Soa Sig. ria et per altre ad ti possibile, intendere li processi et fundamenti de tale ambassate, et se per via de Soa Sig.ria se potesse restringnere [sic] Nuy lo haveremo acceptissimo, non tanto per timore che habiamo, quanto che per nostro desyderio seria de non havere may contencione alcuna con la Casa de Franza, maxime perché gli portamo bona affectione et reverentia.

Siché, acceptando Soa Sig.ria la scritta della intelligentia ratificata et sottoscritta per Nuy, haveray ad solicitare de havere la ratificatione et reconfirmatione de quella in opportuna forma; et possendone tore via la specification de D. Iacomo, lo haveremo grato, perché é non ben al proposto dela dicta Liga, che é perpetua, et item lo facto d'esso D. Iacomo é de natura che in scripti ad Nuy dà carico et ad luy zova poco, et li bisognano facti, al che Nuy siamo disposti fare con effecto pro posse nostro, como é dicto, et gli debbe bastare.

Tandem volimo che in tutte le cose che tu haveray ad fare et agitare con lo prefato Ill.mo Mon.re Dalphino te debii intendere con el M.co Gastone et sempre in ogni cosa participare con luy et seguire el suo parere et consiglio, como quello che per la soa virtù, fede et devotione é gratissimo et acceptissimo al prefato Ser.mo Mon.re et amicissimo ad Nuy; et siamo certissimi che amorevelmente et fidelmente tractarà le nostre facende, como quelle del prefato Mon.re, et ch'el farà como faressemo Nuy stessi, se personalmente gli fossemo.

Item volimo te informi del titulo deli baroni et cortesani del Ser.mo Mon.re Delphin et de quelli del S. Duca de Bergogna, et cossì delle comunità dellà; et nelo porti in scritto alla toa retornata.

De l'andata de Ingliterra ne faray quanto parerà al prefato Mon.re Delphin, et togliendo dala Soa Sig.ria la norma de quello che tu haveray ad fare; quando saray là faray capo primo ad Mon.re lo Legato, et da luy prenderay l'informatione necessarie etc.; et con questi adricii te presentaray dalla M.tà del dicto Sig.re Re et l'altri principi, como é dicto de sopra.

Cichus

Legate and secure all information necessary from him etc. Thus informed, you will present yourself to His Majesty the King and the other princes, as is said above.

Cicco

HISTORICAL NOTES

1. In two letters of Dec. 23, 1460 [*Francia,* cart. 525; *Lettres,* I, 333–35], Sforza announced to the Dauphin the impending departure of Prospero and Gaston du Lyon. Letters of credence were issued on the same date to Prospero for the Duke of Burgundy, the Duke of Clèves, Antoine and Jean de Croy, the King of England, the Duke of York, the Papal Legate, Francesco Coppini, and the Count [sic] of Warwick. On Dec. [23?], 1460 [Reg. Ducale 160, pp. 308–09], the Duke issued passports to Prospero traveling with twenty horses; to Baude Meurin with six horses; and to Gaston with twenty persons. Meurin was bound for Florence, the papal court, and Venice to complain about the intransigence of the Duke of Savoy [see doc. 55, n. 3, p. 18], a mission which was strongly supported by Sforza [Sforza to Pius II and to the *Signoria* of Florence, Milan, Jan. 8, 1461, *Roma,* cart. 49]. Prospero and Gaston left Milan on Dec. 25 [see doc. 64, p. 81].

2. Baude Meurin, who had brought the Treaty of Genappe to be ratified by Sforza [see doc. 56, p. 23].

3. See preceding doc. 58.

4. The record of the ratification of the Treaty of Genappe, dated at Milan, Dec. 6, 1460 [*Francia,* cart. 525; *Lettres,* I, 331–32], lists several dignitaries present at the ceremony, including the Marquess of Mantua and Galeazzo Maria Sforza as well as Prospero and Gaston, all sworn to secrecy. The instrument of ratification, signed the same day [Appendix, doc. III, pp. 467–69], expressed reservations in reference to the reinstatement of Valperga to his possessions.

5. Maletta arrived at the Savoyard court on Nov. 25, three days after the arrival of the Burgundian ambassadors [Maletta to Sforza, Carignano, Nov. 26, 1460, *Savoia,* cart. 480]. He found the Duke of Savoy obdurate both with

58

respect to Charlotte's dowry and to the reinstatement of Valperga; thereupon the ambassador scheduled his departure for Dec. 4 [Maletta to Sforza, Carignano, Nov. 27 and Turin, Dec. 3, 1460, *ibid.,* cart. 480; the first dispatch was published in *Lettres,* I, 335–36]. Maletta, formerly Professor of Law at the University of Pavia, member of the *Consiglio Segreto* since 1455 and an experienced diplomat, later (1463–65) was Milanese ambassador to Louis XI [E. Lazzeroni, "Il Consiglio Segreto o Senato sforzesco," *Atti e memorie del Terzo Congresso Storico Lombardo* (Milan, 1939), 114, n. 76; Mandrot, I, 306–08, n. 1].

6. Brother of the Marquess Giovanni di Monferrato.

7. Pietro da Gallarate, ducal councilor and diplomat, who later (1466) was sent on a mission to Louis XI [Mandrot, I, 26, n. 3]. In 1477 he became a member of the *Consiglio Segreto* [Santoro, 14].

8. In an undated memorandum, Gaston had argued that the Duke of Savoy had not been included in the Peace of Lodi and in the Italian League, or if he had been included, he had not ratified the pertinent instruments. Sforza replied on Dec. 8, 1460 [*Francia,* cart. 525; *Savoia,* cart. 480; *Trattati,* cart. 1528; all copies preceded by Gaston's memorandum]that the Duke of Savoy had indeed been included in both treaties as an "adherent and ally" of the Republic of Venice, and also was so designated by King Alfonso of Naples in the instrument of the League, all of which was subsequently ratified by Savoy. Moreover the Duke pointed out that he was bound by a separate peace treaty and a marriage alliance with Savoy, negotiated in 1454 by Giacomo di Valperga himself, and shortly after ratified by Duke Ludovico of Savoy.

9. The Dauphin had signified to Prospero [see doc. 55, p. 11] that he would be happy to see Sforza in possession of Genoa, Asti, and Vercelli.

10. Filippo Maria Visconti, Duke of Milan (1412–47), and Sforza's father-in-law.

11. Francesco Coppini, Bishop of Terni and papal legate in France [see Introduction, p. xxii]. As a result of Warwick's victory over the Lancastrians, July 10, 1460, at Northampton, where Henry VI was captured, and the subsequent return of the Duke of York from Ireland, the Yorkists had formed a government in London, with which Coppini, who had given his blessing to the Yorkist cause, enjoyed high favor.

12. See doc. 55, n. 6, p. 19.

Since your departure there have been few occurrences in these parts to be taken into account. However, of those that seem worthy of the Dauphin's notice we herewith inform you. Count Iacomo,[1] after he left the field to put his troops in barracks, went to Aquila[2] to secure money and was there for a few days. However, he left without money, malcontent, and went to Ortona,[3] where he was given quarters for himself. The Pope's troops[4] and ours, which were opposing Count Iacomo, have withdrawn to barracks in those towns in the neighborhood of Rome. In the Kingdom of Naples, His Majesty King Ferrante has been prospering for quite some time now and continues to prosper and many of the barons of the kingdom have been reduced to His Majesty's obedience, as especially the whole House of Sanseverino,[5] and others continue to submit. The Prince of Taranto[6] has withdrawn to his lands; Duke John[7] is in Apulia; and the Prince of Rossano[8] is at Sessa. King Ferrante in all ways follows up his good fortune so that there is no doubt that His Majesty will conquer and obtain that Kingdom, to the great enhancing of his reputation.

We also have letters from Catalonia reporting that His Majesty [John II,] King of Aragon, on December 2 arrested the Prince of Navarre his son,[9] and has put him in prison. In what relates to the Prince of Navarre, however, we believe that the region where you are may

60 · *The* DUKE OF MILAN *to*

PROSPERO DA CAMOGLI

Francia, cart. 525. Minute

Dopo la tua partita sono occorse poche cose alle bande de qua da farne stima, pur de quelle che ne parono digne della noticia delo Ill.mo Mon.re Dalphino te ne daremo aviso. Lo Conte Iacomo,[1] dopo che se levò per andare alle stantie, se ne andò ad l'Aquila[2] per havere li dinari et gli é stato alcuni dì; et tandem se n'é partito senza dinari et mal contento et andato ad Ortona,[3] dove gli é deputata la stantia della persona sua. Le gente[4] del Papa et nostre, ch'erano al opposito d'esso Conte Iacomo, sono andate alle stantie in quelle terre circumvicine ad Roma. In lo Reame, la M.tà del Re Ferrando ha prosperato da parichii dì in qua, et prospera tutta via; et sono redutti alla obedientia de Sua M.tà parichii de quelli Baroni del Reame, et in spetialità tutta la Casa de Sansverino[5] [sic], et tutta via se ne reducono delli altri. Lo Principe de Taranto[6] é redutto in le terre sue, lo Duca Iohanne[7] é in Puglie et lo Principe de Rossano[8] é ad Sessa, et lo prefato S. Re Ferrando tutta via proseque la prosperità sua, in modo che non é dubio che la M.tà Sua vincerà et obtenirà quello Reame con sua grande reputatione. Havemo ancora littere de Cathellonia come la M.tà del Re de Ragona a dì doy del mese proximo passato destenne el Principe de Navarra[9] suo figliolo, et l'ha misso in presone; crediamo però che de questa parte del Principe de Navarra se ne sia havuto dale bande dellà più presto noticia, che non se é de qua; pur niente demeno, de tutto tu daray opportuna noticia al

have received word before we did. Nonetheless you will give due notices to the Dauphin of everything; and similarly we charge you to keep us informed of occurences there, in England and in all the other countries thereabouts.

HISTORICAL NOTES

1. Giacomo Piccinino, renowned *condottiere,* who in the spring of the previous year had invaded the Abruzzo region of the Kingdom of Naples in support of Duke John of Anjou against King Ferrante [Nunziante, XIX (1894), 625 ff.].

2. Leading city in the Abruzzo which on Jan. 6, 1460 had joined the Angevin cause and where Piccinino had hoped to receive money from Duke John [*ibid.,* XIX, 421].

3. A town on the Adriatic coast of the Abruzzo.

4. The contingent of troops sent by Pius II and Sforza to bar Piccinino's advance in the Kingdom of Naples.

5. Roberto Sanseverino, Count of S. Severino and Marsico, later (1463) Prince of Salerno, who after Ferrante's defeat at Sarno (July 7, 1460) joined the Angevin camp but returned to the King's fold in December of that year [B. C. de Frede, "Roberto Sanseverino Principe di Salerno," *Rassegna storica salernitana,* XII (1952), 13-17].

6. Giovanni Antonio del Balzo Orsini, Prince of Taranto and feudal lord of about half of the Kingdom of Naples, had promoted the Angevin invasion

prelibato Mon.re Dalphino, caricandote che similmente tu ce avisi delle occurrentie dele bande dellà, tanto de Ingliterra, quanto de ogni altro paise dellà.

[A. Squittieri, "Un barone napoletano del 400. Giovanni Antonio del Balzo Orsini, Principe di Taranto," *Rinascenza salentina,* VII (1939), 154 ff.].

7. Duke John had failed to exploit his victory at Sarno and now had gone to Puglia, penniless and scarcely supported by the Prince of Taranto [Nunziante, XXI (1896), 274 ff.].

8. Marino Marzano, Duke of Sessa and Prince of Rossano, another leading promoter of the Angevin invasion.

9. Don Carlos, first son of John II of Aragon and his first wife, Blanche d'Evreux, Queen of Navarre (d. 1441), had for several years opposed his father's plans to by-pass him for the succession in favor of his half-brother, Fernando, son of John's second wife, Juana Enriquez. The King arrested Don Carlos at Lerida on Dec. 2, 1460, but freed him and recognized his rights to the succession in the following June under the threat of a Catalan revolt. The Prince died three months later [G. Desdevises du Dézert, *Don Carlos d'Aragon, Prince de Viane, Étude sur l'Espagne du nord au XVe siècle* (Paris, 1889), 262–390; cf. J. Vicens Vives, "Trayectoria mediterránea del Principe de Viana (1458–1461)," *Principe de Viana, XI* (1950), 234–50].

63

I have just now learned that this most illustrious prince is sending
the present messenger to our most illustrious lord for a falcon that he
desires to have, and since I did not know about this sooner, I could not
write earlier, and cannot now write in such haste, either to his Lordship
or to my Lady, the Duchess, or to the others to whom it would be
pertinent to write about the subject. Nevertheless I have thought it good
to write this to Your Magnificence, whom I beg to communicate concerning the matter with his Lordship, my Lady, and the others who
are concerned in this business.

We, viz, my companion [Gaston du Lyon] and I, arrived here
eight days ago, but not in this town nor in the presence of the Dauphin,
because he had secluded himself over a period of days for certain religious observance, as is his custom. Thus it was yesterday that I was here
received with good will and great kindness and was given a thousand
thousand thanks for the treatment Gaston enjoyed. I inform his Lordship that Gaston and all his company perpetually preach the goodness
and glorious greatness of his Excellency, and Gaston has even surpassed
himself in what, most devotedly, he says and does for the good of your
cause.

However, he has encountered some obstacles, raised by certain opposing interests—among which is *Giacomo di Valperga,* although he

61·PROSPERO DA CAMOGLI *to*

CICCO SIMONETTA

Francia, cart. 525. Orig.

In questo puncto ho sentito come questo Ill.mo Principe manda il presente messo dal nostro Ill.mo S.re per uno ocello ch'el desydera de havere, et non havendolo saputto più presto, in tanta subitessa non posso scriver né al S.re, né a Madona, né a li altri a chi perteneria scriver de la materia. Tamen m'hé paruto utrumque scriver questa a V. M.cia, quale prego ne facia communication cum la Ex.tia del S.re, de Madona et de li altri cum chi se hé agitato questa facienda.

Noi, videlicet lo compagno et io, iunxemo qui octo dì fa, sed non in questa terra, né a la presentia del Ill.mo Monsignor, per certi dì ch'el ha havuto in reguardo per religione sua consuetudinaria; anci heri io fui qui receputo de bon vulto et grande benignità cum mille milia rengratiamenti de lo trattamento fatto al M.co Gascon; advisando la Ex.tia del S.re che lui et tutti li suoi sonno perpetui predicatori dela bontà et inclita virtù de Sua Ex.tia, et lo dicto Gascon fin a che se passa optimamenti et devotissimamenti al ben dela cosa. Pur gli hé deli obstaculi per certi contrarii, inter li quali, licet a me dica il contrario, *D. Iacomo Valperga* lavora per vie coperte straniamenti, confortano *el Delfin* a strengersi cum *el Re de Franza,* et me par la cosa ale strette. Pur *Gascon* me dice de certo ch'el fatto andrà bene, et ch'el confida rumpir lo argumento a chi deturba la opera nostra. Item *el Delfin* heri m'ha ditto che, audito li riguardi che gli ho ditto deli inconvenienti

tells me the contrary, who is working hostilely by hidden ways. These men are urging the Dalphin to tie himself to the *King of France,* and it seems to me to be a near thing. *Gaston,* however, tells me for certain that our business will go well and that he is confident he can get the better of those who are giving us trouble.

Item, *the Dauphin* yesterday told me that, having heard the points I made concerning the difficulties that could result if *the Duke of Savoy* is antagonized, he thinks that it would be better for him to refrain from making *war* on *the Duke of Savoy* and rather attempt to reform the *Duke's government* by *sending embassies to the Duke*—and here he noted that working through *Guiottino*[1] [de Nores] would be best, and in other things also he has given me good hope.

I have decided, however, neither to write nor to dispatch Martin[2] unless I have something assured to report.

The Dauphin sent to France my lord of Beauvoir,[3] who is, along with Gaston, his most trusted follower, as formerly I told his Lordship, and Beauvoir was received with the greatest favor by the King and with the highest honors by the court; but on account of the absence of [............] Charles, Count of Maine, negotiations have been delayed, so I have been told. According to what I have learned here from the common report of those intimate with the Dauphin, if the Dauphin comes to terms with his father through the mediation of *Charles, Count of Maine,* it is to be feared that the *Duke of Lorraine* [King René, Maine's brother] will find favor.

I am sure that from England you have had news of what has happened there. The Queen [Margaret of Anjou] raised an army against the Duke of York and took the city of York, a fine town. The Duke of Somerset [Henry Beaufort] favors her. The Duke of York went against the Queen with many troops and it seemed to the King [Henry VI] and to the Earl of Warwick [Richard Neville] that the expedition of the Duke of York, who was accompanied by Warwick's father and two of Warwick's brothers,[4] was of sufficient strength to defeat the Queen. And so the Duke of York set forth.

1461

DOCUMENT 62. PROSPERO DA CAMOGLI TO THE DUKE OF MILAN. GENAPPE, 6 FEBRUARY, 1461. DAMAGED.

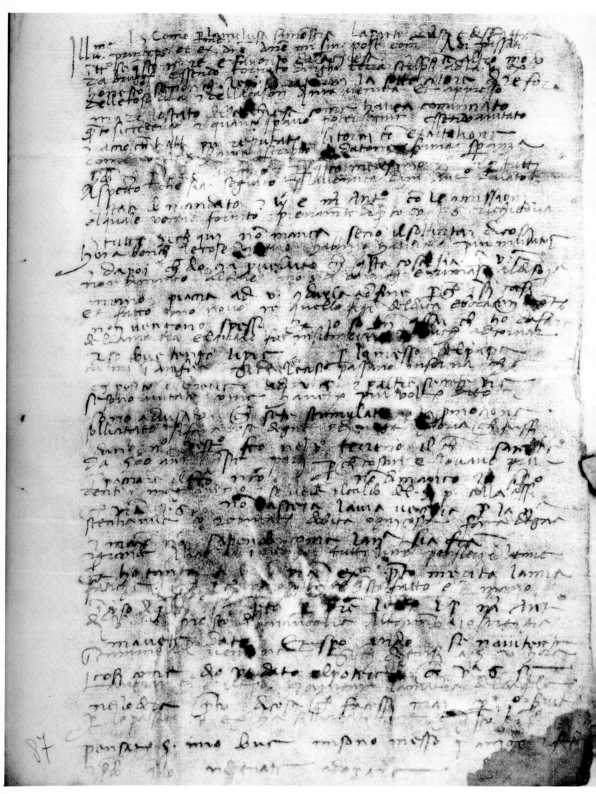

DOCUMENT 93. FRANCESCO COPPINI TO THE DUKE OF MILAN. MALINES, 17 APRIL, 1461.
THE DARKER LINES WERE WRITTEN IN SYMPATHETIC INK.

PORTRAIT OF FRANCESCO SFORZA ATTRIBUTED TO FRANCESCO BONSIGNORI, PROBABLY A COPY
OF A LOST PORTRAIT BY ANDREA MANTEGNA PAINTED LATER THAN THE DATE SHOWN, 1455.
COURTESY OF THE NATIONAL GALLERY OF ART, WASHINGTON, D.C., WIDENER COLLECTION.

VESCOV. DI TRENTO

Cles
Cavalese
Bellur
Feltre
Ceneda

Bellinzona
Sondrio
Tione
Riva
Trento
Schio
Bassano
Treviso

Bellagio
Como
Lecco
Bergamo
Brescia
Vicenza
Dolo

Aosta
Gallarate
Milano
Crema
Peschiera
Padova
Este

Chambery
Moutiers
Masserano
Biella
Novara
Lodi
Cremona
Mantova
Rovigo

S. Jean
Vercelli
Trino
Mortara
Pavia
Casale
Piacenza
Correggio
E. FERRA

Susa
Rivoli
Chivasso
Casale
Parma
Ferrara

Torino
MARCH. DI
Alessandria
Reggio
Modena

Carmagnola
Asti
Tortona
Bologna

Saluzzo
MARCH.
DI
SALUZZO
Acqui
Pontremoli
Imola
Faenza
Forli

Cuneo
MONFERR.
Savona
GENOVA
Genova
Chiavari
Sarzana
Pistoia
Fiesole

Tenda
Ceva
Finale
Levanto
Lucca
Siena
Bibbiena

Albenga
Porto
Pisano
Pisa
REP. FLORENTINA
Firenze
Arezzo

Oneglia
I. GORGONA
Volterra
Cort
Peru

Nizza
Ventimiglia
Monaco
I. CAPRAIA
Donoratico
Siena
REP. DI
SIENA
Chiusi

C. CORSO
Massa
Piombino
Drvieto
Bolser

MAR
LIGURE
S. Fior
Bastia
ELBA
Grosseto
Soana
iterbo
Castro

Calvi
I. DI PIANOSA
Sutri

Sagona
Corte
Aleria
I. DI
MONTECRISTO
I. DEL
GIGLIO

CORSICA
Ajaccio
Civitavecchia

S. Lucia
MARE TIRRENO

Porto Vecchio

Bonifacio

C. TESTA

I. ASINARA

Porto Torres

REGNO DI
SARDEGNA
(ALL'ARAGONA)

Cagliari

MARE MEDITERR

Cartography by Norman Clark Adams

Courtesy of Fondazione Treccani degli Alfieri per la storia di Milano.

1.	Principato di Monaco	8.	Dominio dei Pallavicino
2.	Principato di Oneglia	9.	Principato di Correggio
3.	Marchesato di Finale	10.	Contea della Mirandola
4.	Domino dei Malaspina	11.	Marchesato de Mantova
5	Contea d'Asti	12.	Republica de Lucca
6.	Principato di Masserano	13.	Contea di S. ta Fiora
7.	Contea di Guastalla	14.	Principato degli Appiani
		15.	Republica di San Marino

0   50   100   150

CHILOMETRI

Trieste

VEGLIA

CHERSO

I.ARBI

I.LUSSINO

Zara

REPUBLICA DI VENEZIA

MARE ADRIATICO

LUNGA

Sebenico

Spalato

Illia
Ancona

I. BRAZZA

I. LESINA

I. LISSA

I.CURZOLA

I. MELEDA

I. LACOSTA

Macerata

Fermo

Ascoli

mo

Pescara

Pescara

L'Aquila

Chieti

Avezzano

Sulmona

I. TREMITI

Termoli

Vieste

Castel di Sangro

REGNO

Sora

STATO DELLA CHIESA

Boiano

Lucera

Foggia

Siponto

Cassino

Volturno

Piedimonte

Bovino

Troia

Trani

Bari

erracina

Teano

Benevento

STATO DELLA CHIESA

Ascoli

Ofanto

Canne

Conversano

Monopoli

Gaeta

Capua

Caserta

Melfi

Aversa

Nola

Avellino

Napoli

DI

Salerno

NAPOLI

Catanzaro

MARE

IONIO

Palermo

Messina

Reggio

Melito

REGNO DI SICILIA
(ALL'ARAGONA)

Catania

Terranova

Siracusa

0

Pius II (1405–1464). Marble bust (1463) by Paolo Romano. Vatican, Appartamenti Borgia. Photo: Alinari.

VIEW OF CAMOGLI, BIRTHPLACE OF PROSPERO SCHIAFFINO. PHOTO: ALINARI.

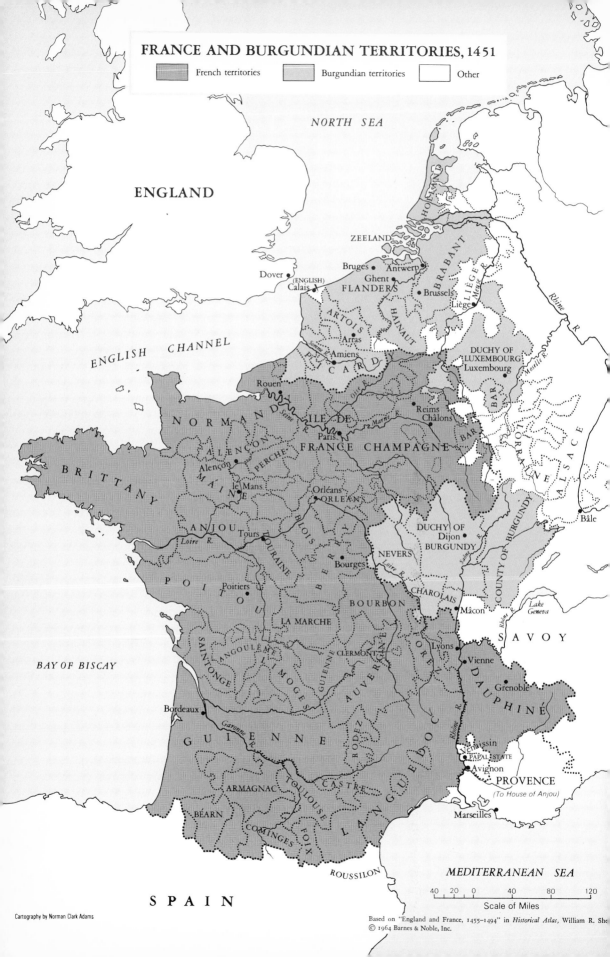

FRANCE AND BURGUNDIAN TERRITORIES, 1451

French territories   Burgundian territories   Other

NORTH SEA

ENGLAND

HOLLAND

ZEELAND

Bruges · Antwerp
Ghent · · Brussels
FLANDERS
BRABANT · LIÈGE
Liège
Meuse R.
Rhine R.

Dover ·
(ENGLISH)
Calais
ARTOIS
Arras ·
HAINAUT
DUCHY OF
LUXEMBOURG
Luxembourg
Moselle R.

ENGLISH CHANNEL

Somme R. · Amiens
PICARD Y
Oise R.
BAR
LORRAINE
ALSACE

Rouen ·
NORMANDY
Seine R.
ILE-DE-
FRANCE
Paris ·
Marne R.
CHAMPAGNE
Reims ·
Châlons
BAR

Alençon
ALENÇON
PERCHE
le Mans ·
MAINE
Orléans ·
ORLÉANS
DUCHY OF
Dijon ·
BURGUNDY
Bâle ·

BRITTANY

ANJOU
Loire R.
Tours ·
TOURAINE
BLOIS
BERRY
Bourges ·
NEVERS
Loire R.
COUNTY OF BURGUNDY
Saône R.

BAY OF BISCAY

POITOU
Poitiers ·
LA MARCHE
BOURBON
CHAROLAIS
Mâcon ·
Lake
Geneva

SAINTONGE
ANGOULÈME
LIMOGES
GUIENNE
CLERMONT
AUVERGNE
FOREZ
Lyons ·
Vienne ·
Rhône R.
SAVOY

Bordeaux ·
Garonne R.
GUIENNE
RODEZ
LANGUEDOC
Grenoble ·
DAUPHINÉ

ARMAGNAC
TOULOUSE
CASTRE
Chaissin
PAPAL STATE
Avignon ·
PROVENCE
(To House of Anjou)

BÉARN
COMINGES
FOIX
Marseilles ·

ROUSSILON

MEDITERRANEAN SEA

SPAIN

40 20 0   40   80   120
Scale of Miles

Cartography by Norman Clark Adams

Based on "England and France, 1455–1494" in *Historical Atlas*, William R. She
© 1964 Barnes & Noble, Inc.

porrian seguire a chi exasperasse *el Duca di Savoya,* el gli pare che meglo sii contenerse da far *guerra* al ditto *Duca de Savoya,* ymo tentar de transformar el *Stato* per *ambasserie;* et qui ricorda che la via de *Guiotin*[1] seria optima, et in ceteris m'ha dato bona speransa. Pur io non delibero de scriver, né de mandar Martin[2] nisi in re certa. Questo Ill.mo Principe ha mandato Monsignor de Broval,[3] che hé il più fido ch'el habia equale a Gascon como altra volta dissi al S.re, et hé ditto Monsignor de Broval dal Re suo padre, recepto in grandissime carezze dal Re et extremi honori da li cortesiani, ma per la absentia de [........ .....][a] *D. Hiucine Karlandagar* lo tractamento et apuntamento de le cose si ritarda, secondo m'hé dicto, et per quello che ho inteso qui da voce comune de tutti questi intimi, facendosi le cose per man de *D. Hiucine Karlandagar* hé da dubitar ch'el non si favorisca *el Duca de Lothoringia.*

De Anglia sum certo si à le novelle de là di quanto hé seguito. A questi dì proximi la Regina fece exercito contra lo Duca de Iorch et preise Iorch, che hé bona cità. Lo Duch de Sumbresseth hé in suo favore; et lo Duch de Iorch andò contra a la Regina cum multa gente d'arme et parse al Rei et lo Conte de Varvich che bastasse la cavalcata del dicto Duch de Iorch et del padre de epso Conte de Varvich cum doi de suoi figloli fratelli[4] de epso Conte et cossì andò. Et gli intervenne quello che sole accader a chi per prepotentia dispretia lo inimico: furon conflicti et morto il Duch de Iorch, suo figlolo, lo padre del Conte de Varvich et li doi figloli, et cossì interfecti homini da XII[m] in XVI[m], et poi in altre bataglole morti multi altri quorum numerus incertus. Ma intendiasi ch'el va a miglara. His auditis lo Rei monstrò grande commovimento quantunque lo Duch de Iorch pare esser stato morto più per odio de haver affectato il Regno che per altro; et hé deliberato ch'el Conte de Varvich vadi a vindicar tanta iniuria et hé andato cum combatenti chi dice LX[m], chi dice più. La cosa sta in cymbalis, per il che

---

a. There are two or three words crossed out which are illegible and appear to be attempts to write in cipher. They are followed by the cipher symbol for Hiucine Karlandagar.

There then happened what usually happens to one who out of arrogant overconfidence scorns his enemy. Battle was joined [at Wakefield, Dec. 30], and the Duke of York, his son [Edmund], the Earl of Warwick's father [Richard Neville, Earl of Salisbury], and Warwick's two brothers [one, Sir Thomas Neville] were killed, as were from 12 to 16,000 of the combatants. In later battles many others have perished. The figures are uncertain but it is understood that the number of the dead reaches thousands.

On hearing the news of the battle, the King appeared to be greatly moved—although the Duke of York seems to have perished rather because of the hatred his aiming at the throne aroused than for any other reason—and it has been decided that the Earl of Warwick should avenge this outrage. He has set forth with his troops—some say 60,000; some say more.

Things stand in the balance, on which account *the Dauphin* believes that I should not, for the present, think of doing anything in England and that, likewise, I should not now approach the *Duke of Burgundy; for* my Lord of Charolais, the Duke's son, has laid deadly accusations against my lord of Croy [Antoine]. The Duke has ordered him to present his case against Croy before the ducal council, and so Charolais has formulated eight or twelve charges, all important ones. Since he is the Duke's only son and is a headstrong young man and since Croy is a dearly beloved servant of the Duke, the quarrel between them has caused a great division in the court. However, within fifteen days both the *English* and the *Burgundian* situations will be resolved, and *the Dauphin* thinks that I should await these outcomes so that I will then know how to shape my plans.

I tend to believe that if *the Earl of Warwick* conquers, *the Dauphin* will exact a high price for an accord with the *King of France*.[5] Should it turn out otherwise, if *the Dauphin* can perhaps secure a guarantee of *peace* [from Charles VII] for the *Duke of Burgundy,* he will come to terms with the *King of France;* for I have just now been told that if *the*

pare *al Delfin* che io non deba pensare per lo presente de bisognar alcuna cosa in Anglia, et similiter a parte del *Duca de Bergogna; nam* Monsignor de l'Herloes, figlolo de lo Ill.mo S. Duca de Bergogna, ha havuto contra de Monsignor de Crovi parole mortale et ha comandato el padre di mandarli contra per via del Consiglo, et cossì gli ha formato capitulo 8 vel 12 contra, importanti; siché lui per essere figlolo unico et volenteroso, l'altro per esser servitore caro et ancorato, tengono quella Corte in grandi balanci. Pur XV dì daran sententia et de *Anglia* et de *Bergogna,* et pare al *Delfin* che io aspecti questi exiti per saper come adriciar lo intento. Io sum in qualche opinione che se *el Conte de Varvich* vince, *el Delfin* se venderà caro *al Re de Franza.*[5] Cum autem aliter cadet, forse che s'el possa metter *el Duca de Bergogna* in securessa *de la pace, la pace dal Delfin al Re de Franza* harà loco; nam fin de mò m'hé ditto che volendosi el *Duca de Bergogna alargar, dal Duca de Bergogna*[b] reharà lo suo et de le altre cose.

Del camino nostro et de le glacie de Rhino et periculi de quelle crudesse barbaresche de Germani non ho spacio per lo presente a recitar; Deo gratias se siamo qui. Et quanto per me, io acerto V. M.cia che forse delibererò più tosto de esser in periculo per la bona via, che stentar in tanti barbarissmi [sic] como ho fatto tre volte et non sine periculo. Prego V. M.cia lega questa et me faci qualche resposta destesa per lo messo presente, nec spernamur hec, perché la natura de le cose nostre me par lo patisca. Me racommando humiliter ala Ex.tia del S.re et ala M. V., bono nostro patre.

---

b. Manifestly a ciphering error for Delfin.

Duke of Burgundy is willing *to go that far* the Dauphin will repay all that he owes him and do other things for him too.

About our journey and the icy Rhine and perils and the barbarous crudities of the Germans I have no space at present to give you an account. Thank God, we are here, and as for me, I inform Your Magnificence that I will perhaps decide rather to be in danger on the good route than to endure such barbarities as I have thrice done, and not without danger.

I beg Your Magnificence to read this and send me a detailed reply by the present messenger; and do not scorn to do so, for it seems to me that the nature of our affairs demands it. I recommend myself humbly to his Lordship and to Your Magnificence, our good father.

HISTORICAL NOTES

1. Guiottino de Nores, leading Cyprian favorite of the Duchess of Savoy, Anne of Cyprus.

2. The courier.

3. Jean de Montespédon, called "Houaste," First Chamberlain to the Dauphin [*Lettres,* I, 134].

4. By one brother only, Thomas, but also by York's second son, Edmund.

5. Charles VII favored Margaret of Anjou and the Lancastrians, while the Dauphin was hoping for an understanding with the Yorkists that would prevent any hostile move by his father.

Yesterday, on learning that the present messenger was suddenly on the point of departing—because of the matter pertaining to birds, which are flying animals[1]—and not being able to persuade him to remain until I had fulfilled my duty of making a report, I wrote to the Magnificent Cicco about what had happened up to yesterday. Then, having found more to write about, I was thankful that the messenger remained here until today—which he did because of the usual delays that occur in the dispatching of such people and for no other reason— so that I could have the opportunity of adding this note to Your Excellency.

To summarize briefly how things have gone up to now—according, not to what I know for certain, but to what by conjecture I can perceive—*the Dauphin* is content with those elements of the treaty which pertain to his desires and wishes and his own interests; and, in particular, in regard to *the Duke of Savoy,* he agrees that *Your Lordship should not make war* but accomplish whatever possible through Your Lordship's ambassadors; and he recommends that you work through *Guiottino* [de Nores] because he knows him to be entirely opposed to the present government *of the Duke of Savoy.*

There remains the business of *Giacomo di Valperga. The Dauphin,* because of the nature of the case and the matter of his honor, shows

62·PROSPERO DA CAMOGLI *to the*

DUKE OF MILAN

Francia, cart. 525. Orig.

Heri, intendendo dela partensa del presente messo multo sub [ito], [come?] accade in le cose pertinente ali ocelli che sonno animal volante,[1] non possendo far demorar lo messo avanti io satisfacesse al officio mio in lo scriver, scripsi al M.co D. Cicho la substantia de quanto hera su[cesso] a li dì hesterno. Doppoi, essendomi accaduto più ultra, ho havuto de gratia la demora del ditto messo fin ad anchoi, quale hè stata per le solite dilatione che accadeno in la expedition de simile gente et non per altro; sichè m'hè stato grato haver spacio de subiunger questa ala Ex. V.

La summa summaria conclusione de quello accade ala materia fin a chi secundo posso non acertare, sed per coniectura comprehender, hè che *el Delfin* se contenta de quanto parten a suoi desyderii et appetiti et particularità, specialità verso *el Duca de Savoya* che non per via de *guerra,* sed per *pratica de li ambassadori la V. S.ria* faci le operatione possibile. Et in questo ricorda la via de *Guittin,* perchè sa lo animo suo contrariissimo al presente *stato del Duca de Savoya.* Resta il fatto de *D. Iacobo Valperga,* el quale, attento lo caso et quello pare per [l'honore] del *Delfin,* epso *Delfin* monstra pur multo desyderar ch'el sii contento epso *D. Iacobo.* Et qui vorria che tutti quelli *dinari* che ho arbitrio fussero del ditto *D. Iacobo,* s'el se ne contenta. Io ho resposto che non sum mandato a *D. Iacobo,* sed al *Delfin* et che *la S.ria V.* per suo honor,

great desire that *Giacomo* be satisfied and would like all the *money* that I am empowered to offer, to be given directly to *Giacomo,* if he is content with the amount. I replied that I had not been sent to *Giacomo* but *to the Dauphin* and that *Your Lordship,* out of regard for the Dauphin's honor, would rather, if he were able, do a great thing for *the Dauphin* than a small one for Giacomo, because *Your Lordship* has no obligation *to compensate Giacomo for losses that he has brought upon himself* and that cannot be laid to the charge of the *Dauphin* and the *Duke of Milan.* So the affair stands up to now.

For Your Lordship's information, I was told—and by conjecture I perceived and then sufficiently investigated the matter to be certain— that the *Marquess of Montferrat's* brother [Guglielmo] has sent a letter here attacking *Your Lordship.* First, he says that I, although I claim *to be empowered to offer* only *12,000 am* actually *empowered to offer 100,000* [florins]. Then, he says *the Dauphin should have well in mind that Italians are adept at making empty promises.* This letter has greatly prejudiced our business. However, I will send fuller information by Martin.

A letter that has come here reports that ambassadors have left Savoy to go to the King of France to propose a marriage between the firstborn son of the Prince of Piedmont, son of the Duke of Savoy, and the daughter of the Duke of Orléans,[2] the which negotiation is evidently aimed at strengthening the [Italian] claims of the Duke of Orléans and of others on this side of the Alps who make much of their rights and pretensions.

I recommend myself to Your Excellency, begging you to consider this letter, since I have little time to write, as a supplement to the one I yesterday wrote to Messer Cicco, and if possible please give me some reply concerning the situation. I remain most ready to fulfill your commands.

più tosto faria ogni grande cosa, possendo, per *el Delfin,* che una picola per *D. Iacobo,* perchè non specta a *V. S.ria pagar li danni che se ha facto sensa culpa del Delfin et del Duca de Milano.* Sichè la cosa sta cossì fin a qui.

Ma adciochè la S. V. sii advertita, io sum acertato, et per coniectura ho inteso et poi sum tanto andato cercando, che sum chiaro ch'el fratello del *Marchese de Monferrato* ha scritto qui una littera in carrico de *V. S.ria,* primum dicendo che io, quantunque non monstrerò *arbitrio* salvo de *dodecimmilia, ho* commissione *de centomilia;* item che *el Delfin riguarde ben che bone parole se da in Italia,* il che fa grande nocumento ala cosa. Tamen per Martino vederò de scriver più ad plenum.

Qui hè littere como ambassatori [erano partiti] de Savoya per andar ala M.tà del Rei a operar si facia parentato da uno figlolo primogenito del Principe, figlolo del Duca de Savoya, in la figlola del Duca de Orliens,[2] il che par che tenda assai per li dritti in che pretendeno lo dicto Duca de Orliens et altri de qua da monti, che fan grande stima de dritti et spectative, etc. Me racommando ala Ex. V., supplicandoli prenda questa cum quella che heri scripsi a Messer Cicho in supplemento de quello posso far, havendo il tempo scarso, et si possibile est per questo proposito me faci qualche resposta. In mandata paratissimus. Raptissime.

HISTORICAL NOTES

1. Apparently Prospero is making a joke out of the fact that the messenger bore a request from the Dauphin for a falcon [see preceding doc. 61].

2. i.e. between Filiberto, son of Amedeo, Prince of Piedmont, and Mary, four-year-old daughter of Duke Charles of Orléans, who later in the year was promised in marriage to Pierre de Bourbon, Sire de Beaujeu [Mandrot, I, 78, n. 1].

Some days ago by a merchant's courier we received your letter written from London on January 9, a letter of the Earl of Warwick, and also one from Antonio della Torre[2] written from Sandwich on January 24, by which we have been informed about the battle and its outcome.[3] The news has caused us the greatest displeasure for every possible reason, since any disaster in that quarter has a disastrous effect here. As soon as we received Your Lordship's letters and those addressed to the Pope, we forwarded the latter with all speed to Rome. In support of your elevation [to the Cardinalate] we have written appropriate letters, and what by our efforts we can do to aid you, we will do as zealously as we would for our own brother; for we know how much you love us and we cordially return the feeling. We expect from day to day the arrival of Antonio della Torre and also the reply from Rome, after which we will send you such word as the situation requires.

We write you thus briefly so that Your Paternity may know that we have received your letters, that we have taken appropriate steps, and that we have the highest regard for your concerns and the warmest interest in your advancement. We then beg you, and charge you, as earnestly as we can, that in the meanwhile you will employ all your wits and abilities on working to restore the situation there and in giving effective direction to affairs, so that that kingdom may remain in peace

63 · *The* DUKE OF MILAN *to*

FRANCESCO COPPINI[1]

Inghilterra e Scozia, cart. 566. Minute

Ali dì passati per uno corero de mercadanti recevessemo vostre littere date ad Londra ali VIIII° del passato et cossì havessimo littere del illustre. Conte de Veroich, etiam littere de D. Antonio dalla Torre[2] date ad Sandonico ad XXIIII del dicto mese, et per quelle inteso el caso del conflicto como é passato;[3] ne havimo havuto displicencia grandissima per ogni respecto consyderato che ogni sinistro dal canto de là vene ad redondare sinistro dal canto de qua. Subito che havemo le littere dela S. V. et cossì l'altre se drizavano in corte de Roma alla S.tà de nostro S., volantissime le mandassemo et per la exaltacione vostra havimo scritto opportunamente et quello che per opera nostra ve porimo zovare tanto farimo per vuy quanto facessemo per nostro fratello proprio, perché sapiamo quanto ne amate et nuy versa vice ve amamo cordialmente. Expectamo de dì in dì la venuta del dicto D. Antonio et cossì la resposta de Roma; poy ve avisaremo quanto bisognarà. Questa solo ve scriviamo perché la P.V. intenda che havemo havute le littere et la provisione havimo facto et la nostra bona et optima disposicione in le facende vostre et per l'honore vostro, pregandovi et caricandovi quanto a nuy é possibile, che in questo mezo vogliati usare ogni vostro incegno et industria per adaptare et recuperare le cose dellà et drizarle alla bona via; siché quello Regno resti in pacifico dela M.tà del Re, perché dal canto della S.tà de nostro S. siamo certi non se gli mancarà

under His Majesty the King [Henry VI]. We are certain that, as far as the Pope is concerned, His Holiness will provide timely support for your cause, and we will not fail to do what we can in influencing King Henry, according as we learn from you what should be done—but it will be necessary for us to have more frequent information about what is happening there. We hope that through your intelligence and your great ability the situation in England will be effectively dealt with.

We inform you that His Majesty King Ferrante's cause is prospering and in every way his affairs go better so that we hope that this summer, with divine favor, final victory will be his.

HISTORICAL NOTES

1. See Introduction, pp. xxii–xxvi.

2. An emissary of the Earl of Warwick, about to journey to Milan and to the Curia.

3. Battle of Wakefield, Dec. 30, 1460 [see doc. 61, p. 67].

de favore opportuno et nuy non gli mancaramo di solicitudine presso Soa S.tà, secondo da vuy intenderimo el bisogno, ma saria necessario ne tenesti avisato più spesso delle cose como succedano. Speramo che mediante l'animosità et virtute vostre le cose dellà se debiano drizare alla bona via, avisandove che la M.tà del Re Ferrando é in bona prosperità delle cose soe et tutta via procede de bene in meglio, per modo speramo questa estate habia ad obtenire integra victoria mediante la divina gratia.

On the sixth of the present month I dispatched to *Your Lordship,* by a member of *the Dauphin's* household, a brief letter,[1] not having time to recount at greater length the pertinent details of my journey up to that point. The day before I had hurriedly written a letter[2] to *Cicco,* from which *Your Lordship* could learn something, and now I write more fully.

For greater safety I will repeat what I wrote the previous time. We arrived here on the third of the month, because I had to remain in the neighborhood for three days while *the Dauphin* devoted himself to religious observances; and so, because of hindrances and extortions by those barbarians, we have been forty days on the road. By heaven, though I am always ready to obey *Your Lordship's* commands, I would rather go by way of *France* and take some risk than endure the bestiality of the Germans, who are so barbarous that they have no knowledge of the names of princes nor of civilized behavior. Then we made our way by boat, 340 miles and more, from Strasbourg to Cologne, on the Rhine, the ice on which had, fortunately for us, broken up the day before. The inhabitants of the region told us that they had not been in such danger since 1435; for from Mainz to Cologne there are 108 localities, and there has not been a town nor a castle, however well walled, that has not had walls leveled by the ice, and in many places it was

64 · PROSPERO DA CAMOGLI *to the*

DUKE OF MILAN

Francia, cart. 525. Orig.

Ali dì sei del presente, per uno famiglo del *Delfin,* scripsi a *V. S.ria* sutto[1] brevità non havendo tempo aconcio per scriver più desteso quanto perteneva al render raxon de me fin a lì. Haveva lo dì avanti ut potui raptim scritto un'altra[2] a *D. Cicho* per la quale *V. S.ria* potesse esser advisata de qualcosa, hora per questa più diffuso. Et per più secureza replicherò quello scripsi l'altro dì. Noi iunxemo ali tre del mese, perché me fu necessario demorar qui presso tri dì quali *el Delfin* haveva in religione; et cossì siamo stati in camin dì 40 per impacii havemo hauto in multe extorsione de quelli barbari. Et per Dio quanto per me presuposito sempre de obedir quanto *V. S.ria* comanderà, io vorria più tosto andar per *Franza* cum qualche periculo, che per quella inhumanità de Todeschi apud quos tanta barbaries est, ut principum nomina et humanitatem non intelligunt. Et ultra havemo navigato da Trasburgo a Colonia milia 340 in più per lo Rheno, quale havia de uno dì avanti per nostra ventura scopiato le glacie, che dicono li paisani che dal 35 in qua non hanno sentito tanto periculo. Nam sonno da Magonoa a Colonia terre cento octo, che non hé stata città, né castello sì ben murato, ch'el Rheno non habia equato le mure de la glacia e a multe terre hé stato necessario apriri le porte et recever la furia dele glacie del fiume, ne diruerent et prostrarent muros; né altra nave ha navigato per Rheno quelli dì excepto la nostra; pur gratia a Dio siamo iuncti salvi per

necessary to open the gates and receive the fury of the river-ice lest the walls be demolished; and no other ship navigated the Rhine that day except ours. Thank God, however, we journeyed safely both by water and land. This I write only to satisfy any one who might marvel at our delay in arriving.

I was received here with the accustomed kindness and benignity of this prince. Indeed, I was overwhelmed, and I therefore asked, and also made the request through others, that he please not treat me so grandly. I was not, however, successful and I can but lament that this splendid courtesy is wasted, especially on me who take no pleasure in such display. But Gaston [du Lyon] and his men speak so highly of Your Lordship that this prince, who would like to repay your hospitality, feels that what he does fails even to approach what Your Lordship does for his emissaries.

For company I have been given the viscount, brother of Gaston, and the honorable François Royer and his brother.[3] I will try to bring about some moderation of my expenses. Concerning other happenings I will in further letters inform Your Lordship, to whom I humbly recommend myself.

In addition I inform Your Excellency that, because of their scarcity here and because of the war in England, I fear it will be difficult to accomplish, as to horses, what Your Lordship ordered me. However, I have made what arrangement was possible in the direction of Brittany. It is true that Jean, Bastard of Armagnac, Marshal of Dauphiné, has a bay horse with white-spotted mane and forehead, which is reputed the flower of the horses here and which he could sell for 500 crowns. The horse is not much taller than the grey lyard that Gaston had at Milan. I have wished, out of duty, to inform Your Excellency of this, to whom I always humbly recommend myself. Since, I have learned that it will be very difficult to secure the aforesaid horse at any price. I recommend myself humbly to Your Excellency, whom God prosper.

aqua et per terra. Questo scrivo volunteri a satisfaction de chi se meravi-
glassi dela dimora. Io fui receputo qui in la solita humanità et benignità de questo Principe, et per Dio me confundo et ho domandato et
fatto domandar de gratia non si faciano tante demonstratione, nec ob-
tinui et dolemi che hé liberalità consumpta, maxime in me chi sono
alieno da tali apparati. Ma il M.co Gascon et li suoi predican tanto de
V. S. che a questo Principe, chi vorria vencer, non par iunger ala minima parte de quello fa V. S.ria verso li suoi. In compagnia m'hé dato il
Vesconte, fratello de Gascon et il Sp.le Francesco Roero et suo fratello.[3]
Io me sforcerò de obtener qualche temperamento ala spesa. De aliis
contingentibus per altre littere adviserò V. S.ria, ala quale humiliter me
recomando.

Insuper aviso V. Ex.tia come qui per la penuria, né in Angliterra
per le guerre, dubito serà fatica a dare modo ali cavalli de che me havea
imposto V. Ex.tia, pur ho ordinato quello hé stato possibile de verso
Brittannia. El hé vero che el M.co Cavallero D. Iohanne Batardo de
Armignaco, Marescalco del Delphinato, n'ha uno qui baio con le crine
learde e faciuto davante, el quale hé reputato la flore deli cavalli de qui,
del quale n'ha poduto havere scudi cinquecento; non hé tropo più alto
cavallo de quello leardo grisone che havea Gascone a Milano, del che
per mio debito ho voluto V. Ex.tia sia advisata, ala quale humiliter
sempre me recomando. Post hec ho inteso che serà grande difficultà
haver per precio alcuno ditto cavallo. Io me racomando humiliter a V.
Ex.tia, che Dio feliciti.

HISTORICAL NOTES

1. See doc. 62, p. 73.
2. See doc. 61, p. 65.
3. Gaston du Lyon's brother: Raymond, a man of arms in the Dauphin's
household guard [*Lettres*, I, 292–93]; François Royer, lord of Peurin, and his
brother Philippe were members of the Dauphin's household, François later
becoming concilor and chamberlain to Louis XI and bailli of Lyons [*Lettres*, I, 283, 298, 314].

Before this one, I wrote Your Excellency three letters,[1] here enclosed. In the first I gave Your Excellency an account of our journey
and of the way this most worthy prince treats me, better and grander
treatment than is fitting for one of my unimportance. In the second I
reported what was happening in these parts. In the third I offered my
opinion on matters, because the instructions of Your Excellency ordered me to do so. This letter, which because of its importance should
be first, I have reserved for last, because there has been a scrimmage
here with more and more arguments occurring and I was awaiting
some firm conclusion of which I could inform Your Excellency so that
you would have a sound basis for your deliberations. For this reason I
think I should report, in sequence, the arguments I have had over this
business, which as briefly as possible, are these:

The first audience after my arrival was occupied with compliments
and the usual courtesies and offers of service on behalf of Your Excellency and, on the Dauphin's part, with thousands of thanks and praises
for your kindness and generosity to Gaston [du Lyon], his brother, and
his whole company. Here the Dauphin enumerated again the courtesies
you had extended to Messer Tristan,[2] Jean du Fou, Jeannot de Sainte
Camelle, and these two brothers and to every other member of his

65·PROSPERO DA CAMOGLI *to the*

DUKE OF MILAN

Francia, cart. 525. Orig.

Avanti questa ho scritto a V. Excell.a tre littere[1] pur alligate qui: la una in la quale rendo ragion a V. Ex.tia del camin nostro e del tractamento me fa questo dignissimo Principe, meglior et maior che non mi par convenir ala tenuità mia; l'altra dele novelle del paese; l'altra del apparer et ricordo mio, perché cossì me commanda la instruction de V. Ex.tia. Questa, chi per la importantia havia ad esser la prima, ho reservato in ultimo, perché qui hé stato la suffa, et intervenutogli più et più disputatione, et io aspectava qualche ferma conclusione che fusse adviso a V. Ex.tia et per consequens fundamento al ben deliberarsi. Et per questo me par debito scriver per ordine le argumentatione havute in questo facto, quale, sutto quella maior brevità hé possibile, sonno queste. Iuncto qui, la prima visitatione che io feci a questo Ser.mo Principe se passò in recommendatione et li convenienti conforti et offerte per parte de V. Ex.tia, et miglara de rengratiamenti et predicatione de vostra humanità et liberalità usata verso Gascon, suo fratello et tutti suoi. Et qui se fece repetition dele cortesie de V. Ex.tia da Messer Tristan[2] a Iohan de Uffo, Zanotto da S.ta Camella, et questi doi fratelli, et ogni altro cum grande laude de V. Ex.tia. La seconda visitatione fu in ragionar del stato de Italia et per reciproca del stato de Francia, Angliterra et questi paesi, pervenendosi poi hinc ale specialitate del bon esser de V.

household who came to Milan, and he greatly praised Your Excellency.

The second audience was spent in discussing the situation in Italy and, in turn, the situation in France, England, and neighboring countries, after which we came to the particulars of Your Excellency's flourishing state, then to the good prospects and the negotiations with which the Dauphin is at present engaged, about which I have given information in one of the letters mentioned above. In concluding this second audience, the Dauphin went no further that to say that as regards our main business, he would appoint a time and place to discuss it but that for several good reasons I should in the meantime see *Giacomo di Valperga* and talk freely with him.

I replied that I was always ready to do anything that would please his lordship, but I begged him to consider that I was not sent as an emissary to *Giacomo di Valperga* and that there were in this negotiation many particulars not suitable to discuss with anyone else except his lordship, especially not suitable to discuss with *Giacomo di Valperga,* because of his special interest in the matter etc. In consequence his lordship remained content that I should withhold from Valperga whatever seemed advisable.

No sooner did I open my interview with *Valperga* than he was insisting that he be maintained in the same position, as regards rank and property, that he held at the time Jean du Fou and Jeannot [de Sainte Camelle] left Milan to return to the Dauphin—as is stated in the *treaty*[3]—and then he began making great calculations concerning the worth of his property. I replied that that article in the *treaty* had been inserted by the *Dauphin* here and had never been ratified by *Your Lordship,* for, before the arrival of my letters from Genappe and before my return to Milan, *Valperga's* cause was already lost,[4] and through no fault of *Your Lordship.* I added that if he wished to contradict me, I was ready to make reply etc.

And so I concluded with this observation: *Your Lordship* is under no obligation concerning his lost property; on the other hand, if ever

Ex.tia, inde dele bone speranse et tractamenti de cose in che conversa al presente Sua S.ria, dal che per una de dicte littere io suplisco. La desinentia dela seconda visitation fu solum questa, che quanto specta ala substantia dela materia etc., Sua S.ria me daria hora et loco, ma che per certi boni rispecti io volessi interim trovarmi cum *D. Iacomo Valperga* et che a lui io volessi ragionar largamenti. Al che io resposi che a tutto quello che piaceva a Sua S.ria io era presto, verum tamen che io supplicava Sua S.ria a consyderar che io non era mandato a *D. Iacomo,* item che era in questo tractamento multe cose et particule chi non sonno ben conveniente a dir ad altri che a Sua S.ria, specialmenti cum *D. Iacomo,* per la particularità sua etc.; siché Soa S.ria remase contenta che io tenesse la brigla in man cum *D. Iacomo* de quello me paresse. Siché fossimo insieme, et subito intesi che *D. Iacomo* se attacava a ch'el fussi conservato in quello grado et stato che era ala partensa de dicti Iohanne de Uffo et Zannotto, come dice la scriptura de la *liga,*[3] et cossìià veniva a uno extimo deli suoi beni a grandi computi. Io resposi che quello capitulo chi era cossì scrito in la *liga* fu voluntà del *Delfino* qui, et che non fu mai ratificato per *la S.V.,* nam, ante mie littere et mio ritorno la cosa era perduta[4] non per culpa de *la S.V.;* et s'el voleva dir altramenti, che io era presto a responder etc. Et cossì gli feci questa conclusione, che *la S.V.* deli suoi beni perduti non ge ne havia obligo alcuno, ymo, che se era Principe al mondo chi gli ne fusse tenuto, era *el Delfino,* et che essendo tanto S.re et de sì grande expectatione, gli posseva piacer assai in li suoi infortunii haver sortito de acompagnar la fortuna sua cum quella del *Delfin;* et che s'el pensava ben quello pertocca a uno savio infortunato, trovaria che conservarsi la gratia de *la S.V.* gli può esser sano al stomaco. Et qui presi licentia da lui, dicendo che io seria cum *el Delfin,* a chi era adriciato etc.

Fui cum *Gascon* et gli disse quanto me pareva bisognar, dolendomi che io dovesse bisognar questa faccenda cum *D. Iacomo;* il qual *Gascon,* per adviso de *V.S.,* hé affectissimo a *V.S.,* ma intesi essergli intervenuto quello che spesso accade sensa culpa ali boni per esser ben veduti, nam me par che li boni trattamenti de *V.S.* lo habian, in la cosa de *D. Iacomo,*

there was a prince in the world who was obligated to him, it was *the Dauphin,* and since the Dauphin was who he was, a prince with grand prospects, *Valperga* could console himself in his misfortunes by reflecting that he had the good fortune of linking his destiny with the *Dauphin's,* and that if he considered well how it behooved a wise man to behave in misfortune, he would perceive that to keep the good will of Your Lordship could be the healthy thing to do. At this point I took leave of him, saying that I would see *the Dauphin,* to whom my mission was addressed etc.

I then consulted *Gaston* and told him what seemed necessary, complaining that I had to negotiate this business with *Giacomo di Valperga. Gaston,* for *Your Lordship's* information, is most devoted to *Your Lordship,* but I learned that there has happened to him what often happens, through no fault of their own, to the good because they are highly regarded—for I think that *Your Lordship's* good treatment of him has almost made him suspect, as regards the *Valperga* affair, because *the Dauphin* has forbidden him to meddle, either in word or deed, with anything pertaining *to Giacomo,* unless he speaks favorably of *Giacomo;* and so he unwillingly obeys, but for *Your Lordship* he does and solicits every possible good.

I decided therefore to investigate this business in order to see if *the Dauphin* might be harboring in his mind some unfavorable opinion of *Your Lordship,* which may lead him to leave you in the lurch etc. When I saw *the Dauphin,* I begged him, for the honor of Your Lordship and the good of our negotiations, to attend to the matter himself and not give me a tainted intermediary, and as to what concerns *Giacomo* I begged him to understand well how matters had gone for he would then find *Giacomo* to be the one to blame, not *the Dauphin* nor *Your Lordship.*

He immediately replied that he had been informed by *Gaston* and all his other emissaries that *Giacomo* had in many things acted in such a way that the entire blame could be placed on him and that if *Giacomo* were in his accustomed position, he, the Dauphin, would let

quasi posto suspecto, per modo che *el Delfin* gli ha imposto che de quanto tocca a *D. Iacomo* el non se impacie né in far, né in dirne, excepto bene, et cossì licet invitus ubedisse. Pur per *V.S.* el fa et sollicita ogni ben possibile. Ego tamen disposi de scoprir questo facto per intender se *el Delfin,* in lo animo suo, havia alcuna non bona opinione de *V.S.,* silicet [sic] che volunteri se fusse lassiato perder etc.. Et fui cum *el Delfin,* pregandolo che per honor de *V.S.* et per lo ben dela cosa, lui *Delfin* volesse intender ala materia et non darme intercessore malato; et quanto aspecta a *D. Iacomo* io pregava ch'el volesse intender ben le cose come erano andate et ch'el troveria *D. Iacomo* esser lui lo culpabile, et non *el Delfin,* né *la S.V.* Subito el me rispose ch'el era ben informato da *Gascon* et da deli altri suoi tutti che *D. Iacomo* se era in multe cose deportato per modo che la culpa se porria convincer tutta a lui; et che se *D. Iacomo* fusse in lo stato suo solito, el gli faria intender ch'el hé *terribile homo,* ma che non hé cosa di *Principe* affliger li afflicti, et per questo el havia deliberato de non metter in desputation alcuna, né la iustificatione de *V.S.* et de *Gascon,* né le culpe de *D. Iacomo,* ymo de fargli in tutte le cose bona chiera et bon trattamento s'el dovesse partir del suo Stato cum lui. Cum sit che, una volta vadi la cosa come se voglia et dica chi dir vol, che *D. Iacomo* ha perduto, et ha perduto cum carico et sutto la protection del *Delfin.*

Per il che, se ello podesse al presente recompensarlo, a retribuirlo, che in vero el faria voluntieri, si per perseguir ogni sua liberalità cum la *V.S.,* come ha fatto fin a qui, si etiam perché lui confessa esser quello solo a chi specta satisfar ditto *D. Iacomo;* ma, dappoi che al presente a lui non hé possibile, et che fin dal principio del primo contratto posto da canto ogni altra sua proprietà lui non rechedeva altro che la conservation de *D. Iacomo,* gli pareria cosa inhonestissima che epso *Delfin* dovesse far li fatti suoi et lassiar *D. Iacomo* destructo. Per tanto, amando il suo honor come fa, ha disposto, s'el dovesse ben guastar li facti suoi, guastarli più tosto che abandonar *D. Iacomo.* Ma ben gli pare che *ofendendo el Delfin, tre Duca de Lothoringia, Britannia et Orliens* per far *liga con la V.S.,* la *S.V.* non gli debe denegar questa reciproca picola.

him know that he is a *dreadful man;* but that it is not a *prince's* way to afflict the afflicted, and therefore he has decided not to argue the matter —neither the justification of *Your Lordship* and of *Gaston* nor the culpabilities of *Giacomo,* but merely to favor *Giacomo* in all matters, even if he had to become an outcast with him. And even if the truth of the matter is as alleged, no matter what anyone can say, Giacomo has been ruined and he has been ruined while his affairs were the responsibility, and he was under the protection, of the *Dauphin.*

On which account, if he could at present recompense or repay Giacomo, he would indeed do it readily, partly because he would like to continue the generosity to *Your Lordship* which he has shown up to now, partly also because he confesses that he alone is responsible for satisfying *Giacomo.* Since, however, he cannot do this at present, and since from the time the first draft of the treaty was drawn up he had put aside his own interests and requested only the preservation of *Giacomo,* it would seem to him most dishonorable that the *Dauphin* should get what he wanted and leave *Giacomo* to be destroyed. Therefore, loving his honor as he does, he has decided, even if he should ruin his prospects, to ruin them rather than abandon *Giacomo.* But it seems to him, since it is likely that *if he is thus repulsed* he will be reduced to coming to terms *with the Duke of Lorraine* [King René], *the Duke of Brittany, and the Duke of Orléans,* and *leaguing with them against Your Lordship,* that you should not deny him this small reciprocal favor.

I replied that it was true that these *three dukes* represent great and honorable names, but that if the *Dauphin* thought the matter through, he would perceive that what these dukes could accomplish against *Your Lordship* is precisely nothing. Therefore it seemed to me that the *Dauphin* should consider that *joining forces with Your Lordship* and being thus able to count on you in the future would do him more good than any harm the aforesaid dukes could do him, for they can do nothing now nor will they in the future be able to do anything.

Here I told him that he would do well to consider what the *Duke*

Al che io resposi che el era vero che quelli *tre Duca* sonno nomi grandi et degni, ma che se epso *Delfin* pensa ben il fondo, troverà che lo effecto chi deba reusir da loro per metter alcun riguardo a *V.S.* hé nullo. Per tanto che me pare epso *Delfin* habia a consyderar che fermarsi el *Stato* de *V.S.,* et posserselo metter a suo computo in futurum, gli relevarà più che cosa alcuna de che se potesse maii gravar li supradicti, cum ciò sia che né al presente fan, né in futurum sonno per far cosa alcuna. Et qui gli dissi che haria caro de intendere quanto mai haveva facto *il Duca de Orliens* quando era *in Italia* et che niuno gli dava impacio, et più cose in questo proposito. Or in summa io non lo ho mai potuto mover de schaco et me fece questa resposta: che se io haveva arbitrio de far contento *D. Iacomo,* che del resto, poi ch'el lo haveva una volta promesso, el contracteria meco a mia voluntà et designo. Io lo rengratiai et gli dissi che io havia arbitrio et possa grande, sed che non haveva commissione, salvo deli XII, et che cum supportation non me pareva honesto metter la cosa in deliberation de chi ioca de proprietà sua; adunche piacesse al *Delfin* determinar quello gli paresse honesto et consyderar chi vadi pur la cosa come si vogli, el *Stato* de *V.S.* hé cosa sua; et se *el Delfin* me dicesse cosa infra la commissione che io lo faria, quando supra la commissione uno iota che io ne adviseria *V.S.* et attenderia resposta. Et cossì, quamvis gravandosi dela impresa, acceptò de veder de redur *D. Iacomo* a quello fussi honesto et conveniente, semper dicendomi che quantunque *D. Iacomo* se tenessi fuori de quello, pareria a me che omnino lui non faria mai *liga con V.S.,* se *D. Iacomo* non era contento. Questo hé quello ho fin a qui potuto cavar, et dubito che sutto tal parlar non gli sii altro. Nam heri el mandò per me et mi condusse in loco separato et dissemi: *Prospero,* io vorria intender da te che tu me solvessi questa questione: se *el Re de Franza* mi manda in *Italia* per favorir *el Duca Iohanne* et contrariar al *Duca de Milano,* et io prendo il *partito con el Re de Franza* et facio *liga con el Duca de Milan,* chi reguarda al reverso del *Re de Franza,* come posso salvar. Al che io, cum quella modestia me fu possibile, resposi che, havendo *V.S.* lo proposito reverente al *Delfin* et disponendo pur *el Delfin* de haver a far in *Italia,* ch'el

of *Orléans* had ever accomplished when he was *in Italy,* and then nobody offered him any opposition; and I made additional observations
on the subject.

But, in sum, I was never able to budge him from his position. He
made me this reply: that, if I was empowered to satisfy *Giacomo,* for
the rest, since he had once so promised me, he would contract with me
on what terms I wished. I thanked him and told him that I had authority, and indeed broad authority, but that as regards money I was empowered only to offer 12,000 florins and that, if I might say so, I did not
think it honorable to put such a decision in the hands of one who fools
away his own property. I therefore requested the *Dauphin* to decide on
what seemed to him an honorable sum and to consider that if the matter is resolved as one could hope, the Dauphin can call *Your Lordship's
state* his own. If *the Dauphin* should name a sum within my commission, I would agree to it; if the sum were greater by an iota than my
commission allows, I would inform *Your Lordship* and await reply.

The Dauphin, though complaining of the mission, agreed to see
about reducing *Giacomo* to a sum honorable and fitting, continually
telling me, however, that *Giacomo* might well hold out for a greater
sum and that under no circumstances, it should be clear to me, would
he ever *league with Your Lordship* if *Giacomo* were not satisfied.

This is what I have, up to now, been able to extract, and I fear that
beneath such talk there may be something else. For yesterday the *Dau-
phin* sent for me and took me into a private place and said to me:
"*Prospero,* I would like you to resolve me this question. If *the King of
France* sends me *into Italy* to favor *Duke John* and oppose the *Duke of
Milan* and I take *the King's part,* and yet *have leagued myself with the
Duke of Milan,* whose interests are the opposite of the *King's,* what can
I do?"

With what humility I could command, I replied that, given *Your
Lordship's* reverent attitude toward the *Dauphin* and given the *Dauphin's* intention to play a part *in Italy,* the *Dauphin's* principal object
should be to ally himself with *Your Lordship;* for if *the King of France*

principal concepto si dovesse far *el Delfin* seria intendersi cum *V.S.,* perciò che, se *el Re de Franza* lo mettesse in questi cimbali a mal fin, per questa via el faria intender la prudentia sua. Sin autem *el Re de Franza* lo mettesse in questo a bon fine, come *el Delfin* facesse meglo, *el Re de Franza* ne resteria più contento; et che io non dubitava niente che quando *el Delfin* deliberassi pur de acceptar pertito [sic] in Italia, facendo *liga con el Duca de Milano, la S.V.,* gli faria intendere le cose facile et le difficile, cosa che, venendo cum altro proposito et solum facendo ragion ch'el suo nome facesse *inclinar* alcuni de *Italia,* che io non sapeva ben come fusse securo consiglo. Et qui gli missi lo exemplo del *Duca Iohanne* per esser adversato a *V.S.;* item, lo exemplo de li *oratori*[5] del *Re de Franza et Duca de Britannia,* quali sonno ritornati più incerti che quando andaron, et similia. Nam deli ditti *oratori el Delfin* proprio al rettorno del suo messo dal *Re de Franza,* me confirmò la incertitudine utsupra et dissemi che gli pareva quelli pensieri esser fumo. Siché el taque et intrò in altri ragionamenti familiari. Per il che, Sig.re, io sum qui in grande involuppo et da l'un canto non ho li advisi, salvo da chi piadesa meco; da l'altro la liberalità de parlar de questo paese me dissuade pensar altro che quello m'hé dicto. Interea le cose tutte me paiono ragionevele et non so che dir, salvo supplicar a V.S. per Dio se digni de advisarme et ammaystrarmi, adciò che io sapia far quello desydero supra tutto per ben operar per la S.V., ala quale quello concluderà *el Delfin* metterò per inclusa qui; et interim, non reducendosi *el Delfin* a meglor conclusione, io per non despiciar tanta cosa, chi doppoi non se porria reapiciar, starò in lo paese et mi metterò in qualche loco separato per attender resposta de V.S., in cuius mandata sum semper paratissimus.

put him in this critical situation to no good end, the *Dauphin* would, in taking part with the *Duke of Milan,* make the *King* realize his political sagacity, and if his father put him in this situation for a good purpose, namely, to test the *Dauphin's* ability to forward the interests of the *House of France,* the *King* would be the more pleased with him for his choosing *Milan.* I had no doubt at all, I continued, that if he decided to play a role in Italian affairs, *allying himself with Your Lordship* would make him see what things are easy and what difficult, for if he came into Italy as *Your Lordship's* enemy, thinking *to secure Italian support* merely by the use of his name—that, I told him, would hardly be a sound plan. At this point I gave him the example of *Duke John* ['s troubles] because of his being your adversary, and the example of the *French* and *Breton ambassadors,*[5] who returned [from Italy] more dubious than when they departed, and similar examples. For upon the return of the *Dauphin's emissary* to the *King of France,* the Dauphin himself confirmed to me the uncertainty of the aforesaid ambassadors and told me he thought French designs on Italy were but smoke. The Dauphin, saying no more on this subject, then began to talk pleasantries.

Therefore, lord, I am in great uneasiness of mind. On the one hand, I have no information save what the people here tell me; on the other, the frankness of speaking in this place dissuades me from doubting the truthfulness of what is said to me. Meanwhile, all these things seem to make sense, and I do not know what to say except to beg Your Lordship please to have the kindness to advise and instruct me so that I may know how to do what I desire above everything, namely, to work successfully for Your Lordship, to whom I will dispatch, herein enclosed, what *the Dauphin* decides. In the meantime, if *the Dauphin* does not reach a more satisfactory conclusion, I, in order not to break off such an important negotiation that afterwards perhaps could not be renewed, will remain in this region, withdrawing to another locality, in order to await the reply of Your Lordship, whose commands I stand always ready to obey.

HISTORICAL NOTES

1. The dispatches of Feb. 6, Feb. 17, and Feb. 17 with additions of Feb. 18 and 28. Despite the date, the present dispatch was evidently written on or after Feb. 28.

2. Tristan de Mainmont, who in May 1459 had been at Milan as a messenger of the Dauphin [see Vol. I, doc. 40, n. 1, p. 268].

3. i.e., as of Sept. 4, 1460 [see Appendix, doc. II, p. 462, cf. doc. 57, n. 17, p. 40].

4. See doc. 57, notes 16 and 25, pp. 40–41.

5. See doc. 55, n. 6, p. 19.

I would not be so presumptuous as to venture to give my opinion
on affairs, especially in such matters as are beyond my limited intelligence, but since Your Lordship has ordered me to do so, I will record
here what thoughts I have had concerning the object of my mission.

First: My lord, during the course of this last journey I decided to
concentrate my efforts at the first battle on securing *the Dauphin's assent that war not be made on the Duke of Savoy* but rather that the
matter be dealt with by opportune ways and means etc., as in previous
letters I have written and repeated etc.; and I was happy that *Your
Lordship* thus escaped no small a burden and a difficulty. As I see it,
however, *the Dauphin* does everything he can in order not to fail in any
generosity toward *Your Lordship;* and by how much the more he is
willing to give up his desires and his special interests and *abandon everything he has requested of Your Lordship,* by so much the more *is he
set upon* your helping *Giacomo;* and in exchange for such sacrifice of
his interests and in return for the great *promises he makes,* he thinks he
merits this act of reciprocity on your part. In his many talks with me he
instances the things that you do, the burden and *the expenditure that
you assume,* on a large scale and persistently, in behalf of *King Ferrante.* Besides, the inopportune hindrances this business has encountered and the fact that it has not been *kept private* may perhaps cause

66·PROSPERO DA CAMOGLI *to the*

DUKE OF MILAN

Francia, cart. 525. Orig.

Io non seria si presumptuoso che ardisse de far motto maxime in tale cose che sonno supra la tenuità del sentimento mio, ma perchè V. S.ria in le commissione m'ha dato me ne incarrica, io dirò qui le consyderatione me accadeno in questa materia. Primum, S. mio, in questa ultima cavalcata me parse far assai ala prima batagla da may obtener che *el Delfin se contentasse che al Duca de Savoia non si facessi guerra,* ymo che la cosa si tractassi cum li modi et tempi opportune, etc., come per altre ho scritto et per altre replico etc., et me religrai che mi pare *V. S.* esser fuori de uno non picolo carrico et affano; ma me par intender chiaramenti *el Delfin* fa tutto per non manchar dal canto suo da ogni liberalità verso *V. S.,* et quanto più el hè remesso de ogni suo appetito et sua specialità, *et quitandosi ogni sua rechesta a V. S.,* tanto più el se *incasca sul* fatto *de D. Iacobo* et in scambio de tante remissione ch'el ha fatto de sua specialità et per contra a tante *promesse chei fa,* gli pare meritar questa reciproca; et in multi suoi ragionamenti el me butta a campo la opera, lo carrico *et la spesa che fasi* largamenti et perserveratamenti *V. S. per Re Ferrando.* Preterea, essendo intervenuti li inconvenienti intempestivi che sonno intervenuti in questo fatto et per essersi la cosa tenuta mal *celata* forse suscitassone *de novi penseri a pié de alcuni* etc., più volte io ho consyderato che chi havessi potuto redur la cosa *a quitti et quitti* servandosi li animi *de la Sua S.ria et la V. S.ria* in

some folk to have new ideas etc. Many times have I thought that if this matter *could have been kept within its original limits,* with a good and honorable amity *preserved between the Dauphin and Your Lordship,* it would have been no small accomplishment[1]; but this line of thinking is now useless to me.

For, although, truly, *the Dauphin thinks* very highly *of Your Lordship* and gives every indication that no happening could alter this good disposition, the great pressures that, it seems, are brought to bear on him make me fear that it might not be possible to keep him in that *frame of mind* unless he *were already bound to you by treaty.*

For, my lord, *England* has never been so *torn by war* implacable, in which a great many veteran *men of arms* have *perished.* As a result, I believe indeed that it is folly to think that English troops will ever in our days *invade France;* but, similarly, the plan of the *Queen of England* [Margaret of Anjou] to make a *league* with the *King of France* is equally illusory because the *English* harbor a universal *hatred* toward the *French* and also because the *Queen's* principal favorite, the *Duke of Somerset* [Henry Beaufort], is intimately linked *with the Duke of Burgundy's* son [Charles, Count of Charolais]. On the other hand, *France* has never in our days been *so tranquil and so united,* and no obstacle seems to confront it except *the Dauphin,* who is, in my opinion, in the same position as was *Count Iacomo*[1] [Piccinino] *in Italy*—a man without a place. Since *the Dauphin* is most firmly determined never to go to *the King his father,* the pressures under which he is laboring will inevitably push him in one direction or another. If *the Dauphin should be able to secure from the King guarantees of peace for the Duke of Burgundy,* and thus, on receiving promises and obtaining the *lands which lie between Dauphiné and Burgundian territory,* [comes to terms with his father], he will then have to play some *role;* and since he has a *regal* mind, the greater *the role* the better it will suit him. If he should be offered an enterprise *in Italy,* I think that what with the promptings of his relatives and the *opportunities that ill-disposed people will hold out to him,* his temptations will be great; and in consequence I would fear *Your Lordship* might be subjected to anxieties of mind or a drain

bono et amichevole proposito, non seria stato puocho, ma questo argumento me si rumpe al presente. Nam, quantunque in vero *el Delfin sente de V. S.* ogni bene et monstra che mai niuno accidente lo deba destor da questo bono animo, pur lo grande peiso de cose che pareno supravenire me fa dubitare che non si porrà servar in questo *bon tesor* chi prima *non lo obliga.* Nam, Signor mio, *Anglia* non fu mai tanto *straciata de guerra* implacabile et *morti* ne sonno assai deli utili *gente d'arme,* per modo che quanto io voglo creder, che sia folia pensar che deba ali nostri dì *passar gente d'arme in Francia.* Il simile penso ben ch'el penser havria fatto la *Regina de Anglia* de far *liga* con el *Re de Franza* serà in fumo per lo *odio* universale che ha *Anglia a Franza,* et ultra perciò ch'el *Duca de Sambrecet,* chi hè il principal favor dela *Regina de Anglia,* ten multo *con lo* figlolo del *Duca de Bergogna.* Da l'altro canto *Franza* non fu mai ali nostri dì sì *quieta et unita,* et non pare essergli altro impacio salvo *el Delfin,* quale hè, a mio iudicio, come alcuna volta hè stato *in Italia el Conte Iacomo,*[1] a chi non se trovava loco; et essendo *la Sua S.ria* in fermissimo proposito de mai non andar *dal Re de Franza,* hè necessario che questo fiume habia usita, et mettendo *el Delfin con il Re de Franza in securo el Duca de Bergogna* sì, per vigor de promisse, come per obtenere *terre contigue dal Delfinato* ale *terre del Duca de Bergogna,* serà necessitato *el Delfin* a prender *partito;* et havendo lo animo *regio,* come *lo partito* serà de più impresa, serà più secundo lui; et s'el obtenesse *in Italia* io voglo creder che tra stimuli de suoi parenti, tra opportunità gli seria *sporgiuta* da male edificati, le temptation serian grande, et per consequente io dubiteria de affano de mente, o de spesa, dela qual non me par *V. S.* bisogni; cosa che s'el fussi *in liga con V. S.,* quando accadessi il bisogno io voglo creder che lui stesso essendo *Delfin* veniria *a vostri favori,* et essendo *Re,* l'autorità et *favori* seriano presti et honorevoli. Qui tuttavia se tratta, tuttavia se sollicita et non se perde tempo. Io li ho confortato de aspectar a remandar *lo ambassatore* suo *al Re de Franza* finchè si veda lo exito dal *Conte de Varvich* ala *Regina de Anglia* per haver più spacio in advisar *V. S.,* et tamen lo remanda de brevi et quantunque el m'ha resposto deliberate et conclusive quello che scrivo per la altra a V. S.ria

99

on your resources that, it seems to me, you have no desire to experience: whereas, if the *Dauphin* were leagued with *Your Lordship,* I believe that, when need arose, as *Dauphin,* he would come to *your aid,* and, as *King,* he would immediately use *his power to fulfill his obligations* honorably.

Here, every possibility is explored, every means is solicited, and no time is lost. I have urged *the Dauphin* to hold off, and to send back *his emissary to the King of France,* until the outcome of the struggle between the *Earl of Warwick* and the *English Queen* is known. This I did in order to have more time to send information to *Your Lordship,* and the *Dauphin* is indeed sending his emissary back soon. Although he has given me firm and conclusive replies, as previously I wrote to *Your Lordship,* and the matter seems to me thus *defined;* nevertheless, since, if *King Ferrante* holds his position *Your Lordship* will take one view of affairs whereas if *Duke John* and the *French* cause are established *in Italy* you might perhaps take another view, I have thought it good to go no further until I have a reply from Your Lordship.

Meanwhile I condole with *the Dauphin* over the fact that matters here have got into an impossible situation, always concluding with the statement that *Your Lordship* will be happier than anyone else in the world over any good fortune that comes to him; and I always return a quiet and soothing answer to his every reply, keeping in mind that the will and the decision of *princes* customarily proceed from God.

My lord, this is my view of affairs up to now. It may be that I do not see what I should, and I always remit everything to the judgment of *Your Lordship* and of whoever else understands these things better than I; and if I do not project my ideas to *Your Lordship* in the way that would be used by one who is more experienced, nevertheless I am trying to do my duty in informing *Your Lordship* what I think. I therefore beg you to take it in good part, as a benign prince should accept such a dispatch from an entirely loyal servant.

18 February
Postscript. I do not know whether there should be some doubt

et che la cosa me par *cassa,* tamen perciochè mantenendosi *el Re Ferrando, V. S.* haverà uno apparere et confirmandosi *in Italia el Duca Iohanne* et lo nome de *Franza* forse ne haria un altro, a me hè paruto de restar usque ad responsum de *V. S.ria.* Interim me condoglo cum *el Delfin* che le cose se mettano a l'impossibile, concludendogli semper che *V. S.* de ogni suo vero ben et augumento semper serà leta et contentissima più che persona del mondo et mi semper me acquieterò de ogni sua reposta cum sit, che ogni voluntà et deliberation de *principe* sole proceder da Dio. Signor mio, questo hè il apparer mio fin a qui in el quale porria esser che io non vedo quanto bisogna et remettendomene semper a *V. S.* et a chi meglo intende, et se io non lo sporgo a *V. S.* cum quelli modi faria uno più pratico, saltem per me pare far officio mio in advertir *V. S.* de quello sento. Sichè prego V. S.ria lo prenda in bona parte come debe uno benigno principe acceptar dal puro et fidel servo, il quale humiliter a quella se racomanda. Data Genepii die 17 februarii, mane.

Die 18 februarii

Post scripta. Io non so se deba dubitar de quello che scrivo veduta la *reposta del Delfin,* se forse questo *partirse da Teraato* venisse dal *Re de Franza et dal Duca de Britannia* per la facenda de *li ambassatori* chi *furon in Italia da Veneti* [et] *Duca de Modena.*[2] Sichè resterò per intender tutto, che pur semper me fu qualcosa suspecto il dissuadermi de andar dal *Duca de Bergogna,* perchè pur *el Duca de Bergogna* hè multo stretto del *Duca de Orliens* et so ch'el gli ha dato adviso al *Duca de Bergogna* dela venuta mia et ha hauto reposta. El può esser che questo mio pensiero sii uno sogno, perciochè per mia natura io sum multo timido, anci tratto; pur per pura fede io lo ho voluto subiunger a *V. S.,* chi sum certo intenderà ben multo meglo il tutto, et ala S. V. semper me racomando.

Die 28 februarii

Io non mando la resposta del *Re de Franza* scritta, come in la littera io scrivo a V. Ex., causa est ch'el secretario del *Delfin* non gli hè et

about what I wrote concerning the Dauphin's reply, if perchance this man who is departing from Terrato should come from the King of France and the Duke of Brittany in reference to the mission of the (French) ambassadors who visited Venice and the Duke of Modena.[2] Therefore I will remain here in order to understand all, for I was always somewhat suspicious about the Dauphin's dissuading me from going to the Duke of Burgundy because the Duke of Burgundy is very intimate with the Duke of Orléans, and I know that the Dauphin has informed the Duke of Burgundy of my presence here and has had a reply. It can be that this thought of mine is no more than a dream, for I am by nature very apprehensive and tend to read too much into things. However, out of pure loyalty I have thought it good to add this note to Your Lordship, for I am certain that you will understand everything.

28 February

I am not sending you a copy of the reply of the King of France [to the Dauphin's emissary], as previously I wrote Your Highness that I would, because the Dauphin's secretary has been absent from here for ten days and I have not been able to discover where he is. On account of his absence, the Dauphin also is not writing to Your Excellency nor to my Lady, the Duchess, nor to Count Galeazzo nor to the others to whom he said he would write. If I have further news, especially about England—it is expected that we shall hear marvels from there within ten days—I will inform Your Lordship by way of *Bruges*.

HISTORICAL NOTES

1. Count Giacomo Piccinino, who in the late 1450s had kept Italy in turmoil with his attempt to capture a *signoria* for himself.
2. See doc. 55, n. 6, p. 19.

sonno dì X ch'el hè absente et non ho possuto intender ubi sit; per il che etiam *el Delfin* non scrive ala Ex. V., nè ala Ill.ma Madona, nè alo Ill.mo S. Conte Galeaz, nè a de li altri a chi el me havia ditto de rescriver. Se altro accaderà, maxime de le cose de *Anglia,* de che se aspecta fra X dì mirabilia, io adviserò per la via de *Brugs* V. S.ria, ala quale humiliter me racomando. Data utsupra.

From a letter of mine that I dispatched to Your Magnificence by a member of *the Dauphin's* household sent there on a flying errand,[1] and from the many long letters that I am now dispatching by Martino, Your Magnificence will see the whole of the matter. Because Your Magnificence is occupied with so many affairs of great importance, I am certain that you will find tedious the number and the prolixity of my letters. I excuse myself on two counts: first, that at other times when his lordship sent me on missions, Your Magnificence wanted from me, written out in detail, everything that pertained to the business, and thus I comply; second, the road is a long one and the way to shorten the time and the mission, it seems to me, is to write everything so that the matter will be the better understood and Your Magnificence, who is discerning, will be able to put forward what particulars seem to you pertinent. As for me, I think it is pertinent for me to look into everything, and in many matters it seems to me that conjecture is no less a part of the business than information.

Will Your Magnificence please see to it that I am sent a clear reply, particularly in regard to the *money business?* I beg Your Magnificence to be clear on this matter yourself and to see that I am clear on it, for we have to do business with a man who speaks plainly and demands plain speaking in return. It is my opinion that the more quickly we settle this

67·PROSPERO DA CAMOGLI *to*

CICCO SIMONETTA

Francia, cart. 525. Orig.

Per una mia che scripsi a V. M.cia per uno famiglo del *Delfin* remandato là per cosa volatile,[1] et multe mie et longhe che scrivo al presente per Martino, V. M.cia intenderà il tutto dela cosa; et perché in
tante et altre occupation de V. M.cia sum certo ch'el numero et prolixità
de mie littere serà tedioso, io me excuso per due ragione: la una, che
alias quando il S.re me ha mandato in altri lochi V. M.cia ha voluto da
me particulariter in scritti tutto quello perteneva ale facende, et per
questo io satisfacio; l'altra, ch'el camin hé longo et lo modo de ascurtar
lo tempo et la pratica me par de scriver il tutto per esser meglo inteso;
et V. M.cia, chi hé discreta, potrà proponer quelle particule gli parerà
pertinente ala cosa. Il che, quanto a me, me pare che sia pertinente ex-
aminar tutto, cum sit che multe cose me paren consister non manco in
coniectura, quanto in quello che io scrivo; et perdio vogli V. M.cia far
ch'el mi sii risposto chiaro et inter cetera quanto specta a *dinari*. Io prego
V. M.cia chi vogla ben intender et ben far che io intenda, nam havemo
a bisognar cum persona chi parla chiaro et cossì vole per reciproca,
ricordando ben quanto per me ch'el meglor mercato chi si possi haver
de questo fatto hé far presto, perché me dubito ch'el longo tractamento
dela materia non faci trovar qualche cossa chi guasti tutto; et se si fussi
fatto cum lo bon servitore quello merita la fede et la devotion, hoc est
dirgli tutto et poi dargli la moderation scritta, et non reputar che chi va

business the better deal we shall have, for I fear that a long drawn out negotiation may turn up something that will spoil all. If the proper treatment had been given to a good servant who merits trust and devotion—namely, tell him everything and then limit him in his written instructions, and do not think that he who knows what he is doing is bound to blunder—the time which has been lost in my awaiting the response from you would have been gained and I would even have concluded my mission and returned home. However, I say the Lord's Prayer daily—i.e. "thy kingdom come, thy will be done."

For the rest, *the Dauphin* remains very much pleased with Your Magnificence, because of what you have written to him and because of what my companion [Gaston du Lyon] relates about you, for concerning myself I say no more. I suggest that to the honorable Master Jean Bourré, *the Dauphin's* first secretary, you might do well to send a handsome inkstand and some fine paper in token of fraternal benevolence, if the idea seems good to Your Magnificence, to whom I suggest it for what it is worth, and to whom I always refer my judgment and recommend myself. Genappe, 17 February, 1461

February 18

Your Magnificence will see the Dauphin's final reply, which seems to me very odd, and that part about letters that are said to have been written I do not understand. However, since I cannot take any other way except the direct one and have thus transcribed his reply word for word, I beg Your Magnificence to edit my dispatch as you think best so that it conforms to the customs of his lordship, with which I have not had much experience and so have no other recourse but to report the plain facts. I want Your Magnificence to know that *Giacomo* has been fully informed about my whole mission, and, from what I can learn, *Jean Philippe*[2] sent him the information.

This information, together with what the *Marquess of Montferrat* and his brother have written, has caused a great deal of harm, and I

securo scapucii, lo tempo chi se perde in aspectar questa resposta se seria guadagnato et io seria utrumque expeditus et in reditu. Pur io dico il pater noster quottidiano, hoc est fiat voluntas tua dummodo adveniat regnum tuum.

Ceterum el *Delfin* resta multo ben contento de V. M.cia per lo scriver vostro et per le relatione del compagno mio, nam de me non dico altro. Vi ricordo che al Spectabile Mastro Johan Borree, Secretario primo de Monsignor lo Dalfin, faresti ben a mandar qualche bello calamaro et del paper subtile in signum fraterne benivolentie s'el pare ala Ma.cia V., ala quale io lo ricordo per ben, et sempre me gli remecto et racomando. Genepie 17 februarii 1461.

Die 18

V. M.cia vederà la resposta final dela materia, la qual me par strania; et quanto parten ale littere che se dice esser state scritte, io non so intender quello parlare; pur percioché io non so andar per altro camin, che per lo dritto, io ho voluto scriver tutto de verbo ad verbum. Prego V. M.cia la sponga come gli pare che sii più conveniente ali costumi del S.re, de li quali non essendo più pratico, io me ne ricurro ala verità del fatto. Ben voglo V. M.cia intenda che *D. Iacomo* hé stato advisato ad plenum de tutta la expedition mia; et secondo intendo, hé stato *Ioan Fucip*[2] [sic], la qual cosa, cum quello ha scritto *el Marchese de Monferrato* et lo fratello, causa male assai et dubito che el *Delfin,* che mostrava andar netto, non si sii sdegnato.

Die 28

Ogni dì abunda reuma, et per quello io multiplico il scriver. Sum stato in questi dì diversimode quasi ranegato qui, et questo non, secondo intendo, per culpa de *D. Iacomo,* sed per advisi che vengono dal *Re di Franza,* da uno che sta a facende del *Delfin* a pié del *Duca de Savoya;* et havia ditto finaliter el *Delfin* de quelli *cavali* et *fanti* che sonno stati contra *D. Iacomo,* come vedeti per la littera[3] che scrivo al *Sig.re;* et

fear that the *Dauphin,* who seemingly likes plain dealing, may be offended.

February 28

Since there are new developments every day, I have to keep writing. Of late I have been in many ways an outcast here, and this, not—according to what I learn—through any fault of *Giacomo,* but because of information that has come from the *King of France,* through one who is in the process of negotiating for the *Dauphin* with the *Duke of Savoy.* The *Dauphin* has spoken finally about the *horse* and *foot* that were sent against *Giacomo,* as you will see by the letter I am writing to *his lordship.*[3] If such indeed were the case, as I cannot believe it to be, it would have been well to have told me about it so that such charges should not catch me by surprise. I inform you, in sum, that any blame that I imputed to *Giacomo* is not really his.

Item: it seems reasonable to the *Dauphin* that since he offers such advantageous terms in the treaty, he should have something in return, namely, a generous settlement in regard to *Giacomo's* demands.

I inform Your Magnificence that the *Dauphin,* in my judgment, handles great affairs with consummate intelligence and makes marvelous replies.

The Duke of Brittany and many others of the *House of France* are constantly making him offers of *money* and of anything else he wants. He always replies that it is just a case of people having nothing and claiming to possess everything, and thus ridicules such offers. If it were not for the matter of recompensing *Giacomo,* he would have dispatched my business from the first day, when I opened to him the offer etc. I therefore beg Your Magnificence to pass on the appropriate information to his lordship and to see that I am given in writing what anyone who understands as little as I do, should know and that I receive some answer concerning what I write about the *Marquess of Montferrat* and his brother.

I beg Your Magnificence to see to it yourself that my dispatches are

perdio se cossì era, come tamen non posso creder, era bene che me ne
fussi stato dato adviso, perché tali colpi non mi iungessero improvisto;
vi adviso insumma che imputation che io faci ad inculpar *D. Iacomo*
non se gli attacca. Item par ragionevole al *Delfin* che facendo tale cose
in *liga* al *Sig.re,* la cosa debia costar qualche recambio per contra, et
pargli fare uno bon mercato de quello richede *D. Iacomo.* Adviso V.
M.cia che el *Delfin,* a mio iudicio, in rebus magnis est maximi ingenii
et fa resposte mirabile. *El Duca de Britannia,* et multi altri de Casa del
Re de Franza, gli fan dele offerte assai de *dinari* et de ogni altra cosa, et
in omnibus el responde tanquam nihil habentes et omnia possidentes, et
se fa beffe de tale offere; et se non fusse per dar a *D. Iacomo,* el me haria
licentiato fin del primo dì, quando io lo havessi invitato de la offerta
etc.; perciò [?] prego V. M.cia dia li advisi opportuni al S.re et proveda
me sii scritto quanto si debe a chi intende puocho, como fo io, et quanto
specta a quello che io scrivo del *Marchese de Monferrato* et suo fratello.
Prego V. M.cia per lo officio suo vogli far che io sii tenuto secreto, et
cossì pregar il S.re che non vogli che inter alios *el Conte Gaspar,*[4] né
Petro da Pusterla ne sapiano cosa alcuna per bon rispecti che ben me
possiti intender. Me racomando a V. M.cia et al M.co D. Iohanne,[5]
vostro fratello.

kept secret and to request his lordship not to disclose their contents to, among others, *Count Gaspare*[4] nor *Pietro da Pusterla*—this for certain good reasons that you can well understand.

I recommend myself to Your Magnificence and to his magnificence, Lord Giovanni, your brother.[5]

HISTORICAL NOTES

1. i.e. to secure a falcon! [see doc. 61, p. 65].

2. Jean Philippe, a member of the Dauphin's household, who was at this time on a mission with Baude Meurin to Florence and the papal court [see doc. 68, p. 115].

3. See doc. 70.

4. Count Gaspare da Vimercate [see doc. 55, n. 8, p. 19].

5. Giovanni Simonetta, secretary and biographer of Francesco Sforza.

We have received your letters of February 6, written at Genappe, and noted what you write and also what you wrote to Cicco our secretary etc. In reply we say that we are delighted that the Dauphin has sent to request a gerfalcon,[1] and we are sending him one, with the falconer because the falconer has to train him and explain the bird's ways and customs to whoever will have him in charge. It would have given us the greatest pleasure if we had found two or three good falcons worthy of his lordship, for we would have been happy to send them to him along with this one; and we wish for you to make our excuses to his lordship, to whom you are to express our devotion as ardently as you can, making every effort to discover whether we have anything here that would please him. If there is something, send word to us and we will immediately do what you say, for truly we much desire to be able to please his serenity. You will tell him that there is no need to thank us for the way we have treated Gaston because we did very little in comparison to what we consider ourselves obligated, and desire, to do for his lordship.

We are certain that by the time you receive this you will have concluded with the Dauphin, and effectively, what you have gone there to do and will have clearly informed us by Martino. If, however, you have not concluded by the time you receive this—which we do not believe—make every effort to conclude quickly and effectively, and send a full

68 · *The* DUKE OF MILAN *to*

PROSPERO DA CAMOGLI

Francia, cart. 525. Minute

Havimo recevuto le toe littere de dì VI del presente, date in Gene-vra,[a] et per quello inteso quanto tu ne scrivi, et cossì quanto hay scritto ad Cico nostro Secretario, etc.. Respondendo dicimo che ne é stato caris-simo che quello Ser.mo Principe ne habia mandato ad domandare el girifalco,[1] et cossì gli lo mandamo una con lo falconero, perché l'habia ad uselare et insignare li modi et costumi soy ad chi l'haverà ad gov-ernare; et sarìane stato grandemente piacere, se ne fossemo trovati duy, o tre boni et digni de Soa Sig.ria, che gli l'haveressemo mandati con questo molto volenteri et de bona voglia; et volimo ne faci la scusa nostra con Soa S., alla quale ne recomanda quanto strectamente saperay et porray, sforzandote de investigare et intendere se potessimo havere de qua cosa che grata gli fosse; et ne avisi, che subito faremo quanto ne scriveray, perché invero molto desyderamo potere fare cosa grata alla Soa Serenità, alla quale diray non bisogna ne regracii del tractamento havimo facto ad Gaston, perché l'é molto poco per respecto de quello ne tegnamo obligati et desyderamo fare per quella.

Siamo certi che alla recevuta de questa haveray concluso con la Se-renità de quello S. quello perché tu sii andato là et bene, et ne haveray avisato chiaro per Martino; et pur quando non havessi conclusato alla

---

a. Read: Genepie.

and clear report, also informing us in detail about lord Giacomo di Valperga's attitude toward us and about occurrences there, in France and in Hungary; and make every effort to send full information that is as clear and accurate as possible.

Since Gaston is acting beneficently and in our favor in the business at hand, we wish—though we have received nothing new on this score —that you thank him on our behalf as profusely as is possible in this world, asking his aid in this affair, which, what with the benignity of the Dauphin and his own prudence, will be concluded, we have no doubt, in the way desired. To Gaston we are writing a brief letter[2] of thanks, remitting it to you so that you can elaborate on the subject as you think appropriate.

The honorable Baude Meurin and Jean Philippe have been to Florence and to the Holy See, where they have had gracious audience and favorable reply. They will now have left Rome and be returning to Florence in order to go to Venice; and we await word of what they will have done at Venice and what audience and reply they will have had.[3]

Concerning the business of the letter written by the brother [lord Guglielmo] of the Marquess of Montferrat—that [. . .] lord Gugielmo has reported things to our discredit—we say that you are to take all pains to get to the bottom of this matter, and then inform us in detail and clearly about the whole thing.

To the remaining items in your letter we make no response because we are awaiting Martino, through whom, we are certain, you will inform us clearly about everything; and on learning what you have to say, we will reply to what calls for an answer.

havuta de questa, che non credemo, sforzate de concludere presto et bene; et avisane de tucto chiaramente, avisandone ancora distinctamente et particularmente como se porta D. Iacomo de Valperga con Nuy et delle occurrencie dellà, de Franza et de Ungaria, sforzandote de avisarce de tutto più chiaramente che possibile te sarà et del vero.

Ch'el M.co Gaston se porti ben in la facenda et in nostro favore, benché non habiamo cosa nova, volimo lo regracii per nostra parte quanto più al mondo sii possibile, pregando Soa Magnificentia che gli piaza aiutare questo facto, quale mediante la benignità de quello Ser.mo S. et la prudentia soa, non dubitamo se reduca ad optato fine. A luy scrivemo una littera[2] breve et regratiatoria, remetendone ad ti, siché circa questo te extenderay quanto te parerà conveniente alla materia.

El Spectabile Baudizon et Iohanne Filippo sonno stati ad Firenza et ad Roma dala S.tà de Nostro S., dove hanno havuto grata audientia et bona resposta; et cossì serano mò partiti da Roma et tornano ad Firenza per andare ad Venetia, et expectamo sentire de quanto haverano operato ad Venetia, et che audientia et resposta harano havuto.[3]

Circa el facto dela littera scritta per el fratello del Marchese de Monferrato, che [. . .] [b] vogli dire al S. Guilielmo in nostro carico, dicemo che te ingegni de intendere ben questa cosa et avisane particularmente et chiaro del tutto.

Alle altre particularitate hay scritto per toe littere, non facimo altra resposta, perché expectamo Martino, per lo quale siamo certi ne avisaray chiaramente de ogni cosa, quale intese, responderemo ad quello accadrà resposta.

---

b. Illegible.

HISTORICAL NOTES

1. In replying to Louis' request for a falcon, dated Feb. 3, 1461 and received at Milan by the 24th [Vincenzo della Scalona to the Marquess of Mantua, Milan, Feb. 24, 1461, A. S. Mantova, *Carteggio-Milano,* B. 1621], Sforza expressed appreciation for the Dauphin's cordial sentiments towards him, commended the work of Gaston du Lyon, and announced that he was sending the falcon with his falconer, Facino da Felizzano [Sforza to the Dauphin, Milan, Feb. 28, 1461, *Francia,* cart. 525; *Lettres,* I, 347–49; undated passport for Facino, probably issued on the same day, in *Francia,* cart. 525].

2. Sforza to Gaston, Milan, Feb. 27, 1461 [*Francia,* cart. 525].

3. Apparently the envoys received from Pius II and Venice the same dec-laration of neutrality, with regard to the struggle between the Dauphin and the Duke of Savoy, made by the Florentine *Signoria* on Jan. 24, 1461 [*Lettres,* I, 344–47; Desjardins, I, 105–08; cf. Ottone del Carretto to Sforza, Rome, Feb. 4, 1461, *Roma,* cart. 50]. Meurin lingered in Italy until the following July [Sforza to the Dauphin, Milan, July 13, 1461, *Reg. Missive* 52, fol. 661; *Lettres,* I, 353].

Having viewed a large number of edifices in this region, I have thought it good to send some drawings of them to Your Excellency, not so that the talented Bartholomeo,[1] Your Excellency's architect, change his style nor improve it, but solely that he may see the architectural forms of other nations. For this reason I send, herein enclosed, to Your Excellency, the sketch of a town gate in these parts, derived from a design of Julius Caesar, who has left in these territories numerous glorious memorials of himself. I have taken the trouble of having another gate reproduced, which he himself constructed in a town in lower Germany which is called Julius Caesar.[2] If I learn that Your Excellency is pleased with my zeal in this sort of matter, I will not fail to make every effort, with what small ability I possess, to satisfy Your Excellency, to whom I humbly recommend myself.

HISTORICAL NOTES

1. Bartolomeo de Gadio da Cremona, Sforza's general superintendent of works (Commissario Generale sui lavori), on whom the Duke had conferred Milanese citizenship in 1458 [C. Santoro, *I registri delle lettere ducali del periodo sforzesco* (Milan, 1961), Reg. 2, N. 138].

69·PROSPERO DA CAMOGLI *to the*

DUKE OF MILAN

Francia, cart. 525. Orig.

Havendo io veduto de li edificii de questo paese assai, m'hé paruto conveniente mandarne qualche insegna a V. Ex.tia non perché l'indus-trio Bartholomeo,[1] architecto de V. Ex.tia cambi phantasya, né la cres-chi, sed solamenti adcioch'el veda li designi de altre natione. Pertanto mando qui alligato ala Ex.tia V. lo designo de una porta de villa de questo paese, retratta dala stampa de Iulio Cesare, che ha lassiato in questi paesi diverse memorie gloriose de lui. Et de un'altra ho dato cura de haver retratta, ch'el fece lui medesmo in una terra chi si domanda Iulio Cesare[2] in Alamagna bassa; in el che, se intenderò V. Ex.tia haver grato lo studio mio, etiam non mancherò in questa parte de perforsarmi in satisfar a V. Ex.tia per quello puocho che io sapia et possa, ala qual humiliter me racomando.

2. Apparently the town of Jülich on the right bank of the Ruhr River, 16 miles northeast of Aachen, whose foundation is in fact attributed by some to Julius Caesar.

After writing all the foregoing, I waited to receive a conclusive reply from the Dauphin. Today I received the reply, an *inconclusive* one, which is, word for word, as follows:

"Prospero, I have sought to reduce *Giacomo's* demands to the smallest possible sum, but in the end I could not reduce them to less than 22,000 *crowns in money and an assured annual income* of 2,000 *crowns.* Since you tell me that you are empowered to offer no more than *12,000 Rhenish florins,* I think it would take so long to reach any agreement that the best and shortest way, in my opinion, is to make no *league* at all. Indeed, considering the *Duke of Milan's* continual allegations that the *Duke of Savoy* is in the *league*—on which subject of his being or not being a member I am well informed—and considering the letters that the Duke of Milan dispatched to *Savoy* and elsewhere during the war against *Giacomo,* it might be thought by some that the *Duke* never desired, in truth, the preservation of *Giacomo.* And I might add that in comparing what the *Duke* has written with what he has said, either for not understanding the language or for whatever reason, I have never been able to distinguish his *"yes" from his "no" concerning what he was willing to do* in the matter of *Giacomo.* Yet that matter was always my principal object for reasons essential to me.

Nevertheless, notwithstanding all this, I think that *Giacomo* sets

70·PROSPERO DA CAMOGLI *to the*

DUKE OF MILAN

Francia, cart. 525. Orig.

Post omnia scripta. Aspectando io de haver conclusiva resposta, hoggi la ho hauta *disclusiva,* quale de verbo ad verbum hè questa: *Prospero,* io ho cercato de redur et restrenger *D. Iacomo* al manco che fu possibile et finalmenti io non lo posso redur a manco de *scudi vintidoamiille in dennari et una rendita certa annuale* de *scudi doemille,* et dicendomi tu non haver arbitrio de più de *florenis rheni duodecimmille,* la cosa me par tanto longa da redur, ch'el meglo et la più curta via de questo camin me par che de *liga* non se facia nulla. Et se ben per le allegation ha fatto *el Duca de Milano* continuamenti che *el Duca de Savoya* fu in *liga,* de la qual cosa quello che ne fu o non io ne sum ben informato. Item per le littere ch'el ha scritto in *Savoya* et in altre parte durante la guerra de *D. Iacomo,* altri volesse imputar ch'el *Duca de Milano* non habi mai voluto da vero la conservation de *D. Iacomo* et io me poteria attacar qui che recolendo li scritti del *Duca de Milano* cum le parole, o per non intendere la lingua, o perchè se sia mai non se hè possuto intender *nè il si, nè il no, data* [sic] *sua voluntà* in lo fatto de *D. Iacomo,* il qual semper fu il mio principal obiecto per cause necessarie ad me. Tamen non obstante tutte queste cose a me pare che *D. Iacomo* se metta troppo alto; et perciochè sii andata la cosa come si voglia, *D. Iacomo* hè *misero* per me. A me par che specti mi farlo contento, cossì de beni come de suo bon voler. Et in vero se io havesse al

too high a price on himself; but things having turned out as they have, *Giacomo* is *wretched* because of me, and I think that it is up to me to satisfy him, as regards both material compensation and his morale. In truth, if I now had the wherewithal I would be as generous toward the *Duke of Milan* in this, on my word, as I have been in other things; and I am ashamed to speak of such a matter because I am truly the one responsible. Since at present I cannot compensate him by giving him *money* nor by restoring his property, at least I will satisfy him in the best way I can, namely by placing his interests before mine; and since it is not my nature ever to abandon one who puts himself in my protection, nor will my honor permit me to do well for myself while one who is *wretched* because of me remains *in desperate straits,* I will put aside the advantages, great and honorable ones, I indeed believe, that I would gain by *leaguing myself with the Duke* of Milan. Never will there come a time, however, that I do not consider myself obligated to the *Duke of Milan* for the honor he has done me in his princely treatment of my emissaries.

"I remind him, by the way, that the *Duke of Savoy* is so ill that perhaps *he will not see Easter,* and since, at his death, *my brother-in-law* [Amedée, the Duke's heir] *will be Duke of Savoy, neither Madame* [Anne of Cyprus, Duchess of Savoy] *nor the Cyprians will have any authority.* More could now be accomplished, therefore, in *reconstituting* the government of *Savoy* and in providing for *Giacomo,* by means of a *league* including appropriate compensation [between the Duke of Milan and myself] than at any other time or by any other means."

Your Lordship may be sure that he did not *refrain from using all sorts of quibbles* and that no reply or *argument of mine in your defense* had *any effect;* hence it has not been possible to get him to reduce his demands to a lower figure than the foregoing. Therefore, if *Your Lordship* for any reason *thinks it good to pursue the matter, it might be possible to bring Giacomo to an accord with Your Lordship whereby he would consent to accept some compensation in Valperga.* I made no mention of the possibility, however, nor do I assert that it can be accom-

presente de che, io seria cossì libero verso *el Duca de Milano* in questo, come sum stato in le altre cose per mia fede. Et mi vergogno de parlar de tal materia perchè io sum lo vero debitore. Et perciò che al presente io non lo posso pagarlo [sic] de *argento,* nè de refacimento del suo, al manco lo satisferò del mio proprio, hoc est che per lui io preponerò la sua specialità a la mia; et poi che mia natura hè de non abandonar mai chi se mette in mia protectione, nè la honestà patisse che io facessi li facti mei et che uno chi sia *misero* per me resti *desperato,* io lasserò da canto la utilità mia, la qual credo ben seria grande et honorevel de guadagnar per la *liga* el *Duca de Milano.* Non serà perciò mai che io non me gli reputi obligato per lo honore m'ha fatto in le careze de li mei. Ben gli ricordo che el *Duca de Savoya* hè in termine de malatia che forse non *vederà Pasca* [sic] et perciò che tunc *mio cognato serà Duca de Savoya, nè Madama, nè Ciprani haran loco alcuno.* Al presente faria maiore operation in la *reformation* et lo fatto de *D. Iacomo* per via de *liga* cum li trattamenti opportuni che per niun altro nè tempo, nè modo. Può esser certa *V. S.* che non hè *mancato* de quello und'el *spuciò;* me serva nè resposta a vostra *iustificatione,* nè de debatimento, a la *adaptatione* de la cosa, he [sic] mai se hè potuto redur infra quello se dice de supra. Sichè, se per alcun respecto *parerà a la V. S. attender a la facenda, el se potria forse veder de condur D. Iacomo da la S. V. cum lo contrato facto, lo qual fusse in Valparga in che se reducesse a qualche contentamento.* Ma io non ho parlato, nè affermo ch'el si possi fare, perchè dubito de altro, come scrivo in la littera de li recordi. Nam, poso la dicta resposta, sentendo *el Delfin* che io spaciava il cavalaro, mandò *Francisco Roer* da me a dirmi che questa cosa gli par de tanta difficultà che cum littere ella non si possi scusar, significandomi per cigni che gli seria grato che *io me ne retornasse* da *V. S.* Al che resposi che ho in mandatis da *V. S.* de scriver in prima et dar li advisi a *V. S.* de quanto accada che facia difficultà a *liga,* ma che se *el Delfin* reputa che la dimora de uno *ambassatore* del *Duca de Milano* gli sia nociva in aliquo, che io me retrarò in qualche loco da parte e cossì farò, finchè habbi resposta da *V. S.,* certificando el *Delfino* ch'el non ha parente, nè amico al

plished, for I fear other things, as I write in the letter recording my opinions.

After he had made this reply, *the Dauphin,* knowing that I was dispatching a courier, sent *François Royer* to tell me that the business seemed to him so difficult it could not possibly be settled by letters; and he hinted that he wanted *me to return* to *Your Lordship.* I made answer that I had been instructed by *Your Lordship* to let you know, before doing anything else, about any difficulty that might arise in concluding the *treaty,* but that if *the Dauphin* thought that the continued sojourn of an *ambassador* of the *Duke of Milan* were in any way harmful to him, I would withdraw to another locality—as I will do, until I hear from *Your Lordship.* I assured him that he has neither relative nor friend in the world who rejoices more in his true prosperity than the *Duke of Milan* and that, whatever happens, he can always call upon your resources as if they were his own. Thus did I answer, in accordance with what *Your Lordship,* in a special letter, instructed me to do in such a case and for the reasons I give you in the letter recording my opinions.

Item: in order to investigate whether some other meaning lies beneath the *Dauphin's* words, I will make no move until I hear from *Your Lordship,* to whom I humbly recommend myself. In addition, since the road is long and time is short and pressing because of the way things happen here, I have thought it good to send also to *Your Lordship* an account of a further conversation I have had with the *Dauphin.* For from the time I [almost] dispatched the courier on the nineteenth of this month up to now,[1] I have been uncertain about my not having allowed him to depart. According to what I have been told by Gaston— and I really do not know whether to believe it for I have handled matters with kid gloves—*Giacomo* is the one who is seeking to have me sent away, persuading the *Dauphin* that *Your Lordship* is disposed to concede much more than I have indicated, and throwing out many remarks in the same vein—such as, that if I *am given my dismissal* one of two things is bound to happen: either I will make further offers

mondo chi sia semper per esser più contento del vero ben suo, come el *Duca de Milano,* et che cadi la cosa come si vogla, semper del *Duca de Milano,* la *S.ria Soa* se ne potrà far capital come di cosa propria, et cossì per quello me comette in tal caso per littera special la *S. V.,* come sonno per li respecti scrivo in la littera de li recordi. Item per scrutar se altro iace sutto queste parole, io suprastarò fin a resposta de V. S.ria, a la qual humiliter me racomando.

Preterea, essendo il camin longo et il tempo breve et acuto per quello accade de qua, el m'hè paruto de scriver a *V. S.* etiam questo ultimo ragionamento havuto con il *Delfin.* Nam da l'expedition del cavalaro, che io feci a li 19 del presente,[1] fin a qui, sum stato tenuto suspeso de non lassiar andar il cavalaro, et secundo sum stato advisato da *Gascon* et non so ben che creder, perchè io me governo satis dulciter in causa, hè che *D. Iacomo* hè quello chi cerca che io me parti de qui, persuadendo a il *Delfin* che *V. S.* hè disposta de multo più che io non mi lassio. Et multe altre cose iacta in questo proposito, che se io *sum licentiato* non falirà una de le due cose, o vero che avanti che io me despici *dal contrato* io usirò più avanti, o vero che quando io serò *da la V. S.,* la *S. V.* manderà altri chi seran più gratiosi in la cosa de *D. Iacomo,* et cossì se sonno perduti questi puochi dì. Or hoggi in questa hora siamo, el *Delfin et Prospero,* stati al quatenus da solo a solo *et el Delfin m'ha ditto: Prospero,* io ho voluto operar ogni mio studio in che *D. Iacomo* se reduca ad admanco, non perchè non me para ch'el merita assai più, sed perciò che merita da me et non da altri, io vorria ch'el si contentasse al presente de quello perchè cum mia honestà io me possesse ben strenger de *liga con el Duca de Milano,* ma doppoi ch'el non si vol contentar, io non ne posso più, ma Dio sa lo bon voler mio et io vorria che franchamenti tu me dicessi il tutto. Io gli domandai licentia de dir franchamenti, come servitore per suo bene, et non come *ambassatore* per ben del mio Sig.re, perchè come *ambassatore,* io credeva haver ditto il tutto. Et cossì, quamvis sutto più longhe parole, io gli feci intender ch'el hè due cose in le quale se contengono tutte le actione humane, honestà et utilità, si fattamenti coniuncte per natura et per ragion insieme, che

before abandoning *the mission* or, once I have returned to *Your Lordship, Your Lordship* will send other emissaries who will be more amenable in settling the *Giacomo* business. This is how the last few days have been lost.

Now today, within this hour, we have been, the *Dauphin and I,* alone together, *and the Dauphin said to me:* "*Prospero,* I have sought in every way possible to persuade *Giacomo* to accept a lower figure, not because I do not think he merits very much more but because he merits it from me and not from others. I would like him for the moment to be satisfied with this so that with honor I could bind myself in a *league with the Duke of Milan,* but since he refused to be thus satisfied, I can do no more. But God knows my good will in the matter, and I would like you to tell me frankly how you see the whole situation."

I asked leave to speak freely, as a servant concerned only for his welfare and not as *an ambassador* concerned for the welfare of my master, because, as *an ambassador* I believed I had said everything I could say. And so—though speaking at greater length than I here report—I gave him to understand that there are two categories into which all human actions fall, honor and self-interest, so intimately joined by nature and by reason that they cannot be separated one from the other. If, I told him, I might use his life as an example, it seemed to me that his lordship had so much adhered to honor in defending this one and that one etc. that he had deprived himself of many great and grand advantages, like his sequestering himself from his father, who is indeed the sovereign of Christendom, and thus losing his position in the world and having to depend on others for succor etc. And it grieved me to see at present that because of advices from the *Marquess of Montferrat* and his brother—who in the past have played the *Dauphin* false and who think to excuse themselves by casting blame upon others—that is, because of falsities intruded by others, and because of such a one as *Giacomo,* his lordship should be put in the position of failing to league himself perpetually with *Your Lordship* and your state. Although *Your Lordship* would always be his to call upon, still because of many cir-

non si possono divider l'una da l'altra; et che, facendo io uno discurso de sua vita, me pareva che Sua S.ria se fusse tanto adherita su l'honestà per defender questo et quello etc., ch'el se era privato de multe grande et alte utilitate, come de sequestrarsi dal padre, che hè pur lo soprano de christianità et perder del suo stato et redursi a sucurso de altri etc.; et che me doleva al presente veder che per advisatione del *Marchese de Monferrato* et suo fratello, chi una volta se sonno dehonestati cum el *Delfin* et, cum incarricar altri, se voleno excusare. Item per errori introducti de altri et per uno tale, come *D. Iacomo,* el mettessi Sua S.ria a partito de non ingagiarsi in perpetuum la *V. S.* et il vostro Stato, quamvis perciò semper era *V. S.* per esser suo, ma che per respecto a multi casi, che me pareva posser intervenir, io faceva grande differentia de esser obligato per *liga,* ad esser ben disposto per voluntà etc. et che, come desyderoso del comun ben de le parte, io sapeva recordare che per ben de Sua S.ria et per utile de *D. Iacomo* era prender quello che io offero et venir al effecto etc. Et multe altre argumentatione gli feci a questo proposito, che serian longhe al scriver. La resposta fu questa: ch'el me confessava esser vero che quando ben per despecto d'epso *Delfin V. S.* havesse lassiato *perder D. Iacomo,* era tante le bone demonstratione fatte in altre cose, ch'el ve era obligato; confessava item esser vero che per defensar questo et quello gli erano accaduti de mali assai, ma che, per esser figlolo de principe et chi spera de esser principe, gli hè semper paruto più debito far cossì per honestà, che altramenti per utilità. Et qui me fece una commemoration che cossì come el hè apto a defender per bona voluntà ognun chi se mette in lui, identidem el seria apto a remunerar; per il che, quantunche il *Duca de Bergogna* antiquamenti haveva receputo tutte le grandesse sue de la casa del *Re de Franza,*[2] del che el me fece una, a mio parere, saggia historia, et che quasi per qualche ragione el fa al *Delfin* tante cortesie, tamen ch'el non haverà mai epso *Delfin* havuto denaro dal *Duca de Bergogna,* ch'el non renda semper ch'el possi et statim de li primi; et che quando ben el descadesse el *Delfin* da li provedimenti del *Duca de Bergogna,* semper che epso *Delfin* se vorrà lassar etiam dextramenti manesare dal *Re de Franza,* gli basterà

cumstances that, it seemed to me, could occur, I made a sharp differen-
tiation between being obligated by *treaty* and being moved by good will
etc. Being desirous of the good of both parties, I could say that it would
be for the welfare of his lordship and advantageous to *Giacomo* for his
lordship to accept the terms I was offering and conclude the treaty etc.
And I put to him on this subject many other arguments, that would
take long to write.

His reply was this: he confessed to me it was true that even if in
scorn of the *Dauphin Your Lordship* had *let Giacomo be ruined,* such
was your display of good will in other things you did that he felt himself obligated to you. He confessed it was also true that for his defending this one and that one many tribulations had fallen upon him but
that since he is the son of a prince and hopes to be a prince himself he
has always thought he should act thus in accordance with honor rather
than in accordance with self-interest. Here he gave me a reminder that
just as from good will he is quick to defend anyone who puts himself
under his protection, so would he likewise be quick to return favors
done him. For example, though the *Duke of Burgundy* in times past
had received all his greatness from the *House of France*[2]—concerning
which the *Dauphin* unfolded what was, in my opinion, a very learned
history—and that for good reason, as it were, he treats the *Dauphin* so
courteously, nevertheless the Dauphin will never take money from the
Duke that he will not repay, to the best of his ability and as soon as he
can. If the *Dauphin* should lose the support of the *Duke of Burgundy*
whenever the [Duke] is willing to let himself be cleverly brought to
terms by the *King of France*—even then the *Dauphin's* will to live will
suffice him. At this point he told me many things in the same vein
which were manifestly intended to let me see that his least concern is
money and that his greatest concern is to work for those who put their
hopes in him. He then repeated everything he had previously said about
Giacomo, as I reported in my letters, and about his obligation and what
seems to him the right thing to do since *Giacomo* is wretched and it is
the duty of every prince to raise the afflicted.

lo animo de viver. Et qui me disse multe cose a proposito che fusse
manifestamenti per inteso che lo menor pensamento ch'el habia hè li
denari et lo maior hè far per chi spera in lui, confirmandomi qui tutto
quello che io scrivo, epso *Delfin* alias havermi ditto de *D. Iacomo* et del
debito che gli ha, et del respecto che gli par dovergli havere, essendo in
miseria et pertenendo ad ogni principe sublevar li afflicti. Et per questo
mi confutò tutte le raxone scritte a iustificatione de *V. S.* per la perdita
sua, dicendomi apertamenti non posser creder che tale resposte siano
procedute da *V. S.*, come indicente, ymo vero se condolse gravamenti
che de *auxilia, et el et*[a] ben, de *V. S.* sian stati a la *destructione* de
D. Iacomo. Et qui me affermò la *Sua S.ria* in sua fede haver lo adviso
da altri che da *D. Iacomo*, et me disse che gli eran stati de quelli de
messer *Tiber* [*to,*] *et Sanseverin*, et lo *nepote de Boschino*[3] *cum provi-
sionati cinquanta*, et che non bisognava puncto dir che se la *V. S.* havesse voluto cum pocha spesa et manco carrico, se seria *sostenuto D. Iacomo;* et ch'el haria creduto che saltim in una cosa tanto picola la *V. S.*
non dovessi haver havuto manco rispecto a lui come à de quelli chi,
quando seran ben grandissimi, non seran equali a lui, etiam in la mini-
messa unde hè al presente. Et qui me disse il mondo de parole et argumenti gaglardi et stranii che tutti m'hè paruto scriver a la *V. S.* per adviso etc. Reducendosi perciò la *Sua S.ria*, che non obstante tutte queste
cose, per rispecto de servar sua parola, el era contento de far *liga* a mio
modo et designo, se io facesse contento *D. Iacomo*. Et quanto a la parte
del *Marchese de Monferrato* et suo fratello, lui intendeva multo ben che
l'era vero quello che ho ditto, tamen che lui non ha havuto in vero altre
littere, salvo che gli han mandato a dir *che de bone parole hè bon mercato* etc., et che pur cum le altre cose dicte de supra el se ne crede qualche parte. La conclusion fu che io me retrovasse cum *D. Iacomo* et cossì
ho fatto et debatuto assai cum lui quanto gli tocca apresso a la perdita
de suoi beni conservarsi la gratia de *V. S.* et chiaritogli che quanto la
resposta del *Delfin* hè significativa de grande bon animo che gli porta

---

a. Probably an error in ciphering; et should read sa.

Thus, in regard to *Valperga's* losses, he confuted all my arguments in justification of *Your Lordship,* telling me openly he could not believe such replies came from you for they were beneath you and at the same time complaining bitterly that from the *Duke of Burgundy* and, he knows well, from *Your Lordship* has proceeded the *destruction* of *Giacomo.* Here *his lordship* affirmed, on his honor, that he had received the information not from *Giacomo* but from others; and he told me that there had been involved in that destruction troops of Messire *Tiberto* [Brandolini], [Roberto de] *Sanseverino* and *fifty soldiers of Boschino's nephew.*[3] Further, it was not even necessary to point out that, if *Your Lordship* had wished it, *Giacomo could have been sustained* with little expense and no difficulty; and he would have thought, at least in a matter so small, that *Your Lordship* should not have had less respect for him than for those who at their greatest could not be equal to him even at his least, as he is now. And here he gave me a world of words and arguments, vehement and heated. All of this I have thought good to report to *Your Lordship* for your information etc.

His lordship finally summed up his attitude thus: notwithstanding all that he had said, in order to keep his word he was content to conclude a *treaty* on my terms if I satisfied *Giacomo.* As for the *Marquess of Montferrat* and his brother, he understood very well that what I said about them was true, but in fact he had not had communications from them, save that they had sent word that *the only bargain he is getting is flattering words* etc.; and that as for the other things they had said, he believes only a part of them. His conclusion was that I should have another interview with *Giacomo.*

So have I done. I argued at length with him that the loss of his goods rendered it all the more important for him to conserve the favor of *Your Lordship* and made clear to him that since the *Dauphin's* reply signifies the high favor in which he stands, the more will *Your Lordship* hold him responsible if the league should not, on his account, be negotiated. Here he talked at enormous length, not without tears, about

el *Delfin,* tanto più gli hè de carrico a piè de *V. S.* quando per lui man-
chassi etc. Et qui dicto il mondo de parole et ragionamenti, il qual
D. Iacomo, non sensa lachrime, me disse multi de suoi infortunii et car-
richi de *moglier,* figloli, lo prothonotario,[4] figlole, amici destructi, et
multe cose che accadeno a li destructi, pregandomi assai ch'io volessi
ben pensar su quello che si può et non si può dir de *V. S.* et far lo ben
de *V. S.,* hoc est che per picola cosa non si perdesse la grande; et tandem, debatuto assai, havemo priso termine de esser io cum el *Delfin,*
perchè semper gli ho ditto ch'el mi grava del suo caso, ma che, non
havendone altra commissione, io harò recorso al *Delfin* et epso *D. Iacomo* potrà far come gli parerà il meglo. Die II martii.

Ill.mo Sig.re mio, io prego Dio chi me dii bona gratia de dar bon
fin al mio scriver, ma V. Ex. può comprhender quanti butti bisogna al
spenger la nave a l'aqua. Io sum stato hoggi a gravarme cum el *Delfin*
che io non posso più sensa mio carrico retener lo presente messo et pregar la *Sua S.ria* chi vogli havermi per excusato, se io non me apuncto
cum *D. Iacomo;* primum, che non me par honor del *Duca de Milano;*
secundo, che non ho commissione alcuna; tertio, che io vorria posser
iuvar cum honestà a *D. Iacomo,* et qui cum honestà non posso se non
nocerli; per il che, perdio, piacia a la *S.ria Sua* determinar da si stesso
questa cosa et farme una resposta chi me para resposta da *Delfin,* monstrando che io reputo tutte le response m'ha fatto una arte et uno scricio
quale prendo perciò semper in bona parte, et tandem deliberatamenti el
m'ha resposto ut infra: *Prospero,* nè el *Duca de Milano* non se debe
meraviglar, nè tu gravarte, se io ho dato longa a questo fatto, perchè
procede da bon mio animo a la materia, et fin a chi non me sum saputo
deliberar unde inclinar, strengendomi da l'un canto la vergogna de non
posser proseguir in questa cosa picola la liberalità mia verso el *Duca de
Milano,* come ho fatto in li *articuli maiori;* da l'altra parte io non posso
lassiar *D. Iacomo,* nè posso io al presente *provedergli,* nè debe parer mo-
lesto ad alcuno se io ho tanti respecti a *D. Iacomo,* perchè el mi conven
haver qui più consyderatione che forsi tu non pensi. Primamenti voglo

131

his many misfortunes: the tribulations of his *wife,* his sons, the pro-thonotary,[4] daughters; friends ruined and many things that befall those ruined friends. He insistently begged me that I should think care-fully about what can and cannot be said about *Your Lordship* and what is for *Your Lordship's* good—namely, that for a small thing you should not lose a great one. Having argued at length, we concluded on the note of my seeing the *Dauphin* again, for I have constantly reminded him that though I sympathize with his misfortune, I am empowered to negotiate only with the *Dauphin,* and therefore *Giacomo* can do as he thinks best. March 2

My most illustrious lord, I pray God give me the good grace to bring this letter successfully to an end, but Your Excellency can under-stand how much work it takes to launch the ship. I have been today to complain to the *Dauphin* that I can no longer, without incurring blame, retain the present courier and to beg *his lordship* to hold me excused for not coming to an agreement with *Giacomo:* first, because it does not seem to me to accord with your honor; second, because I have no commission to deal with him; third, that I would like to be able honorably to aid *Giacomo* but that as things stand here I can, in all honesty, only do him harm. I therefore asked his lordship please to decide this matter himself and make me an answer that seems a genuine reply from the *Dauphin*—thus indicating that I consider all the replies he has hitherto made, to be artful maneuvering, which, for all that, I always take in good part.

Then, speaking with deliberation, he replied as follows:

"*Prospero,* neither should the *Duke of Milan* marvel nor you com-plain if I have given long consideration to this business, for it proceeds from my good will. Up to now I have not been able to make up my mind which side to take, being pressed, on the one hand, by the shame of not being able to continue in this small matter the generosity toward the *Duke of Milan* that I exercised in the *more important clauses of the treaty;* on the other hand, I cannot abandon *Giacomo* but neither can I at present *provide for him.* It should, by the way, give offense to no one

che tu sappii che in casa del *Re de Franza* el hè multo[b] *reputato et amato,* et quando el se ne andassi al *Re de Franza,* non te dubitar ch'el seria *restituito* et cum honore, et non gli mancheria le intercessione del *Duca de Orliens figlo et D. Huicine Karlandagar;* et se tu credessi che *D. Iacomo* fusse lui quello chi contenda del *suo viver,* io te adviso ch'el hè *parente* del *Duca de Bergogna,* il qual non gli lasseria manchar cosa alcuna, se io non fusse chi per honor mio non voglo; et m'ha narrato el *Delfin* la *genologia del parentato* etc., perchè, dice el *Delfin,* a me hè necessario havergli multi rispecti et essendo *destructo* per me et [......] [c] *refacto* per altri, *povero* per me et *pasciuto per altri,* tu poi pensar che carrico et vilipendio me seria questo. Ma doppoi che tu me strengi, io te dirò uno fin ultimo de questa materia: *a me pare che a quello se haverà a bisognar così del Duca de Savoya, come de D. Iacomo, quelli dodecimillia sian puochi, come te farò intender chiaramenti doppoi, et serà necessario sian più, in el che nondemeno io me restrengerò quanto serà possibile, perchè, per nostra Dona, in mio uso non voglo ne resti uno, et se io prenderò partito con el Re de Franza, farimo tanti beni, gratia a Dio, che ognun de nui serà contento, se non habbi per certo che a quello bisogna in queste facende gli anderà de questi et de l'altri che mi serà necessario trovar;* et ultra, a me par che non si possi a manco de dare a la *dona et famigla* de *D. Iacomo* uno qualche *castello* vicino a suo *fradelo,*[5] chi hè *cavaler* de *Rhode,* dal quale serà dato provedimenti et fatto visitatione come in tali grado se convien, et una provisione mensuale de *ducati cento* finchè a li fatti suoi Dio metta remedio; et a me pareria bon la *rocha* d'Aracio, quale, secundo m'hè ditto, ha in pigno per III[m] floreni *Carlo Cacheran.*[6] Nam, ad ogni modo, se vegno mai *in Italia,* io farò ch'el saperà che hè de servirme, et perchè tu me hai ditto questi dì in li ragionamenti nostri che se l'ha fatto come homo del *Duca de Savoya* et non del *Duca de Milano,* et in

---

b. There follows a word crossed out and illegible, probably an error in ciphering the following three words.

c. Six cipher symbols which do not appear in the key and were not deciphered in C. C. They may have no meaning and were used here to render more difficult any effort to break the cipher.

that I have such regard for *Giacomo,* for I have to take more things into account than perhaps you realize. First, I want you to know that in the household of the *King of France* he is highly *reputed and loved,* and if he should go to the *King of France,* you need have no doubt that he would *secure restitution,* and with honor, and he would not lack the good offices of the *Duke of Orléans* and of *Charles, Count of Maine.* If you think that *Giacomo* is one who has to make *his own way in the world,* I can tell you that he is *related* to the *Duke of Burgundy,* who would not allow him to want for anything, but, out of honor, I do not wish the Duke to help him." At this point the *Dauphin* recounted *Giacomo's genealogy.*

"Therefore," he then continued, "I have had to take many things into consideration. *If Giacomo were ruined* through me and *restored* by others, *impoverished* through me and *nurtured by others,* you can realize what disgrace and dishonor would be heaped on me.

"However, since you press me to do so, I will give you my final answer. *I think that for what has to be done, regarding the Duke of Savoy and also regarding Giacomo, those 12,000 Rhenish florins you offer are insufficient, as in a moment I will make you see clearly. A greater sum is necessary, but I will keep it as small as possible, for, by Our Lady, I have no wish to retain a single florin for myself. If I come to terms with the King of France, we will, thank God, secure so many benefits, the Duke and I, that each of us will be content. If not, he may be sure that to meet the requirements of this Valperga business, there will go to Giacomo not only the sums I am asking of the Duke but additional sums that I will have to find.*

"In addition, one cannot do less, I think, than to give to *Giacomo's wife and family* some *castle* in the neighborhood of *Giacomo's* brother,[5] who is a *Knight* of *Rhodes.* The family should also be provided with a household and treated socially as befits their rank and receive a monthly pension of *one hundred ducats,* until God remedies their affairs. I think an appropriate castle would be the *fortress* of Araco, which, I am told, *Carlo Cacherano*[6] has mortgaged for 3,000

nomine Dei, io lo castigherò lui et lo frattello, come homini del *Duca de Savoya* et non del *Duca de Milano;* et se quella *rocha* non si può, se ne trovi qualche altra circumvicina et de tal decentia et qualità. Nè bisogna che tu me alleghi tanti rispecti de *liga* de *Italia,* perchè el *Duca de Savoya* non gli hè, et questo, come più volte te ho ditto, io conforteria cascun a non contenderlo meco, perchè ne sum più informato che tu non te credi, et ultra intendo perciò che facendo *liga, el Duca de Milano* me deba aitar cum tutti li modi *non gueriali al'opera de la transformation de lo Stato del Duca de Savoya.* Sichè provedendo ti al *logiamento* ut supra et a qualche più de XII ut supra, et che io intenda *el Duca de Milano* disposto a darmi *el Duca de Savoya* per *ambassatore* a la dicta *transformation,* sum contento che ordini *la liga* come pare a te, et come tu farai meglo per *lo Duca de Milano,* io serò più contento. Et faci raxon *el Duca de Milano* de far queste cose a me proprio, chi me par non dever esser existimato de manco come *el Re Ferrando,* nè manco posser iuvar lui et *suoi figloli;* et sum certo *la S.ria Sua* deba consyderar che pur io merito in *liga* qualche reciproca et che gli parerà bon mercato che io me contenti de questa picola, et se lui *ha voluto che io salvi lo suo honor in non voler chei rumpi guerra cum el Duca de Savoya, etiam el debe voler salvar si fattamenti lo honor mio, che io non perdi li amici et la reputatione.* Et quando non gli paia, o non possi far ut supra, basterà a me che da me non mancha, che mai non ho cercato, nè rechesto altro, nè me si potrà imputar de la legeressa de *Franza,* perchè non ho mai mutato proposito, nè mai lo muterò, salvo de ben in meglo,[d] possendo far per el *Duca de Milano;* et per puro adviso *de Vostra Excelentia, a D. Iacomo proprio serà redutto avanti questa* [con]*cluxion in fiorin Rheni* 18 *millia et in una rendita de uno castello de ducati* 600 *et le provision mensuale de* 100, *aut ver che gli fussi pagato el tertii* [sic] *de quello ha perdudo; a quale particularitate io non ho resposto, semper dicendo che io non ho ad far cum lui salvo bene, et quando el domande* [sic] *dal Duca de Milano alcuna cosa che ho da responder talmenti che*

---

d. Ben in meglo . . . puro adviso: these words were transcribed from C. C. because they are torn off the original.

florins—for if ever I come *into Italy* I will see to it that *Cacherano* knows that he is to serve me, and since you told me in a recent conversation that he has acted like the *Duke of Savoy's* man and not the *Duke of Milan's* man, in the name of God I will castigate him and his brother both, for being the *Duke of Savoy's* men. If that *fortress* cannot be had, one nearby should be found, of comparable worth and dignity.

"Nor need you keep bringing up the *league* of *Italy,* for the *Duke of Savoy* is not a member of it. I know this, and, as I have said to you many times, I urge everyone not to argue with me about it for I am better informed than you think; and besides, it is my understanding that if the *treaty* is concluded the *Duke of Milan* is to aid me in every way, *except by resort to war, in effecting the transformation of the state of Savoy.*

"Therefore, if you arrange for the *lodging* of *Giacomo's* family and for something more than 12,000 florins, as I have indicated, and providing that I am correct in thinking the *Duke of Milan* agreeable to my effecting, by *diplomacy, the transformation of the Savoyard state,* I am content that you draw up *the treaty* as seems best to you, and the better terms you make for the *Duke of Milan* the happier I will be. *The Duke* certainly has reason to do these things in my behalf, for I do not believe he should esteem me less than he esteems *King Ferrante* nor think me less able to aid him and *his sons* than *King Ferrante* is; and I am certain *his lordship* should consider that I merit, in this *treaty,* some reciprocity and should think he has a good bargain in my being satisfied with this little thing. If *the Duke has wanted me to save his honor by not requiring him to make war on the Duke of Savoy, so should he be as willing to save my honor in not asking me to lose friends and reputation.* If, however, he does not think it good to do, or he cannot do, as I have requested, it will suffice me that negotiations have not broken down on my account, since I have neither sought nor requested anything else; nor can 'French fickleness' be imputed to me because I have never changed my mind—nor will I ever change it, except for being able to do more and more for the *Duke of Milan.*"

*forsi el deveria refar a V. S., al che el Delfin non ha voluto se vegna,
confessando epso D. Iacomo non haver da far cum Vostra Excelentia
salvo ogni bene et confessando epso Monsignor Delfin esser lui lo debi-
tor et non el Duca de Milano, item admonendome ch'el tempo et la
miseria de D. Iacomo non rechede per honor se gli facia excepto cortesia et bon vulto.* Sichè Signor, V. Ex. può intender *questa facenda* et
deliberarsi *al sì aut lo non.* Nam in lo redur al manco io ne spero puocho, perchè etiam hoggi, die 3 martii, gli ho dato un'altra batagla et
non si move de proposito, ymo gli par haver declinato assai in tutte le
altre cose et in questa quanto se può. Tamen non desisterò de quanto
mi serà possibile et ne adviserò *per la via da Brugs* V. Ex.tia, a la qual
me racomando humiliter. Genepii, die 4 martii 1461.

I inform *Your Excellency*, however, *that for Giacomo himself the demands will be reduced, before the Dauphin makes his final answer, to 18,000 Rhenish florins and the provision of a castle worth 600 ducats a year and the monthly pension of 100 ducats, or else the payment of a sum equal to a third of what he has lost.*

To this detailed demand I have made no reply, except to keep repeating that all I can do is wish Giacomo well and that if he asks anything of the Duke of Milan, such must be my answer; so that perhaps he should apply to Your Lordship, though the Dauphin has not wanted him to do so since Giacomo confesses to have had nothing but good from Your Excellency and the Dauphin admits that he, and not the Duke of Milan, is the one obligated to Giacomo. Still, I wonder if the general situation and Giacomo's wretchedness do not suggest that, purely for honor, he be accorded a courtesy and a good turn. In sum, Your Excellency can now understand *the whole matter* and can decide *"yes" or "no";* for I have little hope that Giacomo will lower his terms, since today also, March 3, I gave him another battle but he could not be budged, he feeling that he has had great losses in all other matters and in this one cannot afford to lose more. Nevertheless I will not cease to do everything that I can, and, *by way of Bruges*, I will send word to Your Excellency, to whom I recommend myself.

HISTORICAL NOTES

1. Prospero meant to write "passato"; however, from docs. 73 and 79, pp. 146 and 182, it appears that the ambassador dispatched no letters until March 4, on which date he sent off all those written since Feb. 6.

2. Philip the Good was the grandson of Philip the Bold, created Duke of Burgundy by his father, King John, and wedded, through the good offices of his brother, Charles V, to the heiress of the County of Flanders.

3. Tiberto Brandolini and Roberto di Simonetto Sanseverino, Count of Caiazzo, both Milanese *condottieri,* the latter not to be confused with the

Neapolitan baron of the same name. The nephew of Boschino cannot be identified.

4. His son, Giovanni or Zanetto. In an effort to please Giacomo di Valperga and the Dauphin, Sforza pressed the Pope to appoint Giovanni Prior of the Church of San Andrea in Turin despite the opposition of the Duke of Savoy [Ottone del Carretto to Sforza, Rome, May 12, 1461 and Sforza to Ottone, Milan, June 22 and July 21, 1461, *Roma,* cart. 50 and 51 respectively].

5. Ludovico di Valperga, Lord of Roppolo, Dorzano, etc. in Piedmont.

6. Carlo Cacherano, Lord of Cocconato and friend of the Duke of Milan, who at this time controlled the fortress of Arazzo near Asti.

There are here at the Dauphin's court two especially important men: one is my lord of Montauban,[1] *who, because he is devoted to the Duke of Brittany and because his mother is a descendant of the late lord Bernabò etc., is entirely against our league; the other is* the magnificent knight John, Bastard of Armagnac, Marshal of Dauphiné, who *out of despite and respect etc.* [i.e. as a rival of Montauban's and therefore favoring what Montauban opposes] has behaved very well indeed toward me. I have thought good to provide this information for Your Excellency so that, if you think it a good idea, you can send him [i.e. the Bastard] a special letter of thanks—I always remitting myself, however, to Your Excellency's judgment. There is also the honorable Soffroy Allemand, lord of Châteauneuf, cousin of Guillaume de Mugnon, who, they tell me, sings the praises of Your Excellency, to whom I humbly recommend myself.

HISTORICAL NOTE

1. Jean de Montauban, son of Guillaume de Montauban and Bona Visconti, great-granddaughter of Bernabó Visconti, Lord of Milan from 1354 to 1385.

71·PROSPERO DA CAMOGLI *to the*

DUKE OF MILAN

Francia, cart. 525. Orig.

El hé qui a pié del Delfin doi principali: l'uno hé Monsignor de Montoban,[1] *quale hé tuto del Duca de Bertagna et per la Dona, chi hé descesa dal condam Illustre Domino Bernabò et cetera, tuto contrario ala liga nostra; l'altro hé* il Magnifico Cavaler Domino Iohanne Batardo de Armignaco, Marescalco del Dalphinato, il qual, *per dispecto et rispecto et cetera,* se diporta optimamenti cum mi. Per tanto m'hé parso de darne adviso a V. Ex., adcioché s'el gli parerà, lo possi rengratiar per littere speciale a lui, semper tamen remettendomi a quello parerà a V. Ex.; et cossì il Spectabile Gofredo Alamano, Signor de Castelnovo, cusin de Gulielmo de Mugnon, el quale me dicono commendarsi supra meriti de V. Ex., ala qual humiliter me racomando.

March 3, in the morning:

The news here is that the King of France has been gravely ill for six days. Also, my lord of Charolais has letters from Bruges reporting that the King of England has joined with the English Queen, that the Earl of Warwick and his army, dazed, were shouting "Peace! Peace!" and that the Earl has fled to Calais. However, my lord of Charolais sends word to the Dauphin that, on the Dauphin's behalf, he will see to it that the Duke of Somerset is not made privy to the Dauphin's designs —in the way that Warwick has been and is kept informed[1] [by the Dauphin]. *If more certain news arrives, I will inform Your Lordship.*

Same day, in the evening:

In a letter that the Dauphin received today from my lord of Croy, further news from England is reported, namely, that the King of England had joined with the Queen; but it is added that the Earl of Warwick had united with [Edward,] *Earl of March, son of the Duke of York, and many other English princes and they had laid siege to the King and Queen very near London. Nevertheless, the Dauphin himself does not believe the letter, though it is written by my lord of Croy, and fears that the report is an invention aimed at creating such consternation as events like these would indeed cause. I am sending a copy of my*

72·PROSPERO DA CAMOGLI *to the*

DUKE OF MILAN

Francia, cart. 525. Orig.

Die 3 martii, in mane

El hè novelle qui come el Re de Franza hè stato sei dì malato grave-menti; similiter come Monsignor de Iharloes ha littere da Brugges come lo Re de Anglia se era coniuncto cum la Regina de Anglia et lo Conte de Varvich et la sua banda stopiditi cridavano "pace" "pace," et ch'el ditto Conte de Varvich se ne hè fugito a Cales; tamen manda a dir epso Monsignor de Iharloes al Delfin ch'el farà per la S.ria Soa ch'el Duca de Sambrecet non serà lanco[a] *a suoi designi come sii stato et sia lo Conte de Varvich;*[1] *se altro ne harò più certo, advisarò Vostra Excellentia.*

Die ea, in sero

Per littere che scrive Monsignor de Crovi al Delfin hoggi recepiute, sonno refrescate le novelle de Anglia; videlicet ch'el Re de Anglia se era coniuncto cum la Regina, ma se subiunge ch'el Conte de Varvich se era adunato cum D. Marichie, figliolo del Duca de Iorch, et multi altri principi de Anglia; et che se eran posti al assedio contra el Re et Regina de Anglia assai presso de Londres; tamen el Delfin proprio non crede ben ditta littera, quantumque sii scritta da Monsignor de Crovi, et teme

---

a. Probably: largo.

lord of Croy's letter together with other reports, which, for good reason, bear no heading or signature.

In addition, between the Duke of Burgundy and his son there exists greater discord, as I understand it, than I believed; let me say that the Dauphin in the meantime does not know what to do. Considering everything, I greatly fear—with this division in the House of Burgundy and the ruin of their hopes concerning England, on the one hand, and given, on the other, the great advantages being offered the Dauphin to come to terms with the King of France—that necessity may move the Dauphin to espouse the King's cause, which, as I formerly wrote to Your Lordship, he has all along indicated to me he is not only much inclined but eager to do.

Thus, *Your Lordship* is now informed of everything and can decide as you think best. I await guidance and instructions from you. I am humbly and faithfully ready to carry out all your orders.

[March] 4:

At this hour I have learned that the Dauphin is sending to the Duke of Burgundy his emissary who had been to the King of France, in order to take the necessary steps for sending the emissary back to the King of France, and he is leaving today. I am also told that the Duke of Burgundy and his son will shortly come here, one from one region and one from another. It is impossible to express the Duke's veneration for the Dauphin.

I recommend myself to Your Excellency.

HISTORICAL NOTE.

1. i.e. though the Dauphin intrigues with the Yorkists, whom the Count of Charolais detests, the Count will not disclose these secret dealings to the Lancastrian Henry Beaufort, Duke of Somerset. Charolais, descended through his mother from John of Gaunt, Duke of Lancaster (1340–99), es-

non sii cosa retrovatta ad repalpar tanta consternation de animi come merita de far tanta cosa come era questa. De la qual litera de Monsignor de Crovi mando la copia cum le altre littere de le novele sensa titulo per bon respecto. Preterea el me par intender che dal Duca de Bergogna al figliolo sii discordia maior che io non credeva; dico intanto che el Delfin non sa ben che fare et io, considerando tutto, dubito forte che occurrendo da l'uno canto questa discordia et la ruina de le speranse se havevan de Anglia et cetera, da l'altro canto invitando lo partito grasso de la composition dal Re de Franza al Delfin, la necessità non strenga epso Delfin a prender lo partito del Re de Franza in el quale, come per altre scrivo a la Vostra S.ria, el me monstra a la bella destesa de inclinar non solamenti assai sed volunteri. Siché Vostra S.ria hè mò advisata del tutto et potrà deliberarsi come gli parerà, del che aspecto norma et advisamento. In omnia mandata humiliter fideliterque paratus sum.

Die 4 [martii]

In questa hora ho inteso come el Delfin manda al Duca de Bergogna lo suo chi fu al Re de Franza per prender la expedition necessaria de remandarli al Re de Franza, et va via hoggi; similiter me [se] dice ch'el Duca de Bergogna et lo figliolo veniran qui de brevi, l'un da uno paese et l'altro da l'altro, et non se potria dir la veneration chi se ha al Delfin. Me racomando a la Excelentia Vostra.

poused the Lancastrian cause; and in 1459–60, when the Duke of Somerset was vainly attempting to drive Warwick from Calais, Charolais and Somerset had become close friends.

On the fourth of this month I dispatched to Your Excellency by the courier *a full report of treaty negotiations and of my views on them* and also an account of the news here. In this letter I will briefly summarize what I then wrote so that, should the courier meet with any hindrance —as I trust he does not—Your Excellency will not be deprived of information which you should have.

Regarding the treaty, the Dauphin shows the best disposition toward Your Lordship; but, whether it be that out of honor he feels himself obligated to recompense Giacomo, or that it seems to him he has given up his own special interests—which entailed no small obligation in the future on Your Lordship's part etc.—having never requested anything but the preservation of Giacomo, and finally was even willing to relieve Your Lordship of the burden of warring on the Duke of Savoy—whether it be one or the other, he insists that there be disbursed more than 12,000 florins and, besides, that an honorable lodging be provided, namely, a castle for Giacomo, with a monthly income of 100 gold ducats for his wife and his family. No argument nor complaint that I have made has been able to move him from this stand, and he has refused to listen to any justification of Your Lordship's position and to any blame directed against Giacomo, declaring that it is a prince's obligation to relieve, not destroy, the afflicted. I also wrote that before mak-

73·PROSPERO DA CAMOGLI *to the*

DUKE OF MILAN

Francia, cart. 525. Orig.

A li 4 del presente scripsi a la Ex.tia V. per lo cavalaro de quella abundanter quanto era occurso fin a lì, cossì in la *materia,* come de le *consideratione mie;* similiter de le novelle del paese; et per questa, sutto brevità, in substantia replico adciochè se per caso, quod absit, lo cavalaro recepessi impedimento alcuno, non manche a la Ex.tia V. li debiti advisamenti. *Quanto a la materia de la liga la substantia hè questa: che il Delfino monstra optima disposition verso la S. V., ma sia per la honestate che gli par exiger da lui che D. Iacomo sii recomperato* [sic], *sii per parergli essersi remisso de ogni sua specialità et non haver mai requesto salvo la conservation de D. Iacomo, et in le quale sua specialità gli era pur de non picole reciproce de la S. V. in futurum et cetera; et ultimatamenti remissossi de non voler che la S. V. habia carico alcuno de guerra con el Duca de Savoya et sta pur in scacco de recheder che si sbursano più de li duodecimillia florini, et ultra sii dato uno logiamento honesto, videlicet uno castello a D. Iacomo cum provision mensuale de ducati cento d'oro per la dona sua et sua famigla; nè a moverlo de questo proposito hè valuto argumento, nè condoglensa che io habbi fatto, cum sit che per cosa chi pertegna a excusar V. S. cum inculpation de D. Iacomo non gli ha paruto de accapparla, dicendo che hè cosa da principe relexar li afflicti et non confunderli; et scripsi come avanti questa sua determination el me haveva legeramenti licentiato, dicendo che da l'un canto*

ing this conclusive reply, he had on the spur of the moment given me leave to depart, saying that, on the one hand, he considered himself *obligated to recompense Giacomo and that, on the other, he did not think Your Lordship should pay the Dauphin's debts and that thus, it seemed to him, the only conclusion was that no treaty should be made.*

This is the sum of what I wrote concerning our negotiations.

The news which I sent and which I herewith repeat and confirm is *that the Dauphin has been in close negotiations about reconciling himself with the King of France and he is sending back ambassadors to the King; and I fear that an agreement will be reached—on the part of the King of France, because he is a sick old man and to an aged father the recovery of a son is a great consolation, especially in circumstances of such high political importance; on the part of the Dauphin, because the agreement is necessary to him, for his patience is almost exhausted, what with day-after-day of remaining in such a bad situation and what with despairing of the hopes he had concerning English affairs, which remain obscure. I hold to my opinion that there is no hope of an English invasion of France, and the Dauphin himself, who up to now had indicated to me a different opinion, is changing his mind.*

The conditions of the projected accord between the Dauphin and his father, which I have from the Dauphin himself on the word of a prince, are these: The King of France is content to give him Genoa, and governorship of Asti, and the control of the state of the Duke of Savoy; to yield him Dauphiné; and to grant him lands lying between Dauphiné and the Burgundian territory, for if otherwise the Dauphin is unwilling to go through with such a scheme, the offer of Genoa, Asti, and of other inducements in Italy is made, as the King of France openly indicates, so that the Dauphin will restrain the Duke of Milan from aiding King Ferrante and will favor Duke John. The only difficulty up to now concerns certain jurisdictional matters pertaining to the Duke of Burgundy, which, from what I understand, are being ironed out.

On this subject, I reported to Your Lordship the question the Dau-

gli pareva debitore compensare D. Iacomo, da l'altro non gli pareva de-
bito V. S. pagasse li debiti del Delfino, et che per termine de medio a li
[gli] pareva che non se facesse nulla de liga. Questo hè lo effecto circa
questa parte.

De le novelle scripsi et cossì replico et confermo *ch'el Delfino hè in*
streta partita de reconciliarsi cum el Re de Franza et gli remanda am-
bassatori, et la cosa me dubito non venga fatta per parte del Re de
Franza per rispecto de la invalida antiquità, che pur a uno padre vechio
hè specie de grande consolatione la recuperation de uno figlolo, maxime
in tanto peso de stato, et per parte da [sic] Delfino iera la necessità che
pur la patientia hè quasi straca de tanta diuturnità de star male et la
desperation de le cose de Anglia, quale sian come si vogli, io ne sto in
mia opinione che de passar in Franza io non ne spero, et lui medesmo,
che fin a qui me monstrava altra opinione, se va rendendo. Le condi-
tione de l'acordio sonno queste, secundo che ho da lui, Delfin, in fide
vera principis: el Re de Franza hè contento de darli Zenoa et lo guverno
de Ast et lo governamento del Stato del Duca de Savoya, rendergli el
Delfinato et darli terre contigue dal Delfinato al paese del Duca de Ber-
gogna, nam alioquin el Delfino non si vol desferrar de tal retratta. Le
offerte de Zenoa, Ast, et quelle cose de là sonno, secundo apertamenti
monstra el Re de Franza, perchè epso Delfino restrenga el Duca de Mi-
lano da favori del Re Ferrando et favorisca el Duca Iohanne; la diffi-
coltà fin a qui [é-] de certe cose de iurisdictione pertinente al Duca de
Bergogna, le quale per quello [che] ho, se adaptano; et in questo scripsi
a V. S. de la domanda me fece de come me pareva che la [el] se potessi
conservar, facendo liga cum V. S., et prendendo partito cum el Re de
Franza chi monstrava apertamenti esser contrario a V. S., et la resposta
che io gli feci che era in summa che se pur el haveva facende in Italia,
lo temon e la tremontana de suoi pensieri doveva esser la S. V., et s'el
Re de Franza lo mandava a mal proposito in quelle labrusche come lui
le adulcisse meglo el pareria più saggio, et s'el Re de Franza li mandava
a bon fin, come epso Delfino facesse meglo ch'el Re de Franza potria

phin asked me about resolving his dilemma if he leagued himself with
Your Lordship and then took part with the King of France, who
openly shows himself to be against Your Lordship; and I reported my
reply: if he undertook an enterprise in Italy, the rudder and pole star of
his thoughts should be Your Lordship; if the King of France sent him
to no good purpose into tangled thickets the more he was able to soften
the King's intentions, the wiser would he show himself to be; and if the
King sent him to good purpose, the better the Dauphin did, the more
content could the King be with him. I then reminded Your Lordship
that it would be well to look to Genoese affairs etc.

The news received here from England grows wilder day by day
and hour by hour. A letter written to the *Dauphin* by one who was at
the great battle[1] on Shrove Tuesday recounts in detail the princes and
number of troops engaged on both sides, the assaults and blows exchanged, the tumults on each side. The essence of the matter is this: on
that day the King's troops were encamped ten miles [from London]
near a town called St. Albans, some 120,000 men, no few of whom took
their departure because of lack of victuals. In the afternoon the Duke of
Somerset came with 30,000 horse to smell out the position of the Earl of
Warwick and the King's forces. Somerset and his men launched a very
feeble assault; Warwick then decided to issue from his fortified position
and cut his way through the enemy; and so with 4,000 men he thrust
right through to St. Albans, where the Queen was stationed with 30,000
men. The Earl, finding himself alone and twilight coming on, returned
to his entrenched position, constantly harried and pursued by Somerset's men. On reaching his lines and hearing some of his men yelling to
the enemy, he feared that treason was afoot and so fled the field as best
he could.

The King had been placed under a tree a mile from the battlefield,
where he laughed and sang, and when word came of Warwick's defeat,
he kept with him, by guaranteeing their safety, the two princes [Lord
Bonvile and Sir Thomas Kyriell] who had been left to guard him. Very
soon the Duke of Somerset and the victors arrived to greet him. He gave

esserne più contento; et feci ricordo a V. S. che ben seria prevenir le cose de Zenoa, etc.

De le novelle de Angliterra se ha qui straniesse assai dì per dì et hora per hora; et per littera che scrive al *Delfino* uno chi fu a la grande batagla[1] lo martedì de Carlevaro[a] et rende raxon distinctamenti de li Principi, de li numeri de le gente, de li assalti et de li colpi ferite et voce che furon quello dì da l'uni a li altri etc. Lo effecto hè che in quello dì eran acampate le gente del Rei presso a X migla ad una terra chi se noma Albano, ben CXX^m, de li quali se ne partitte per diffecto de victualia non puochi. Lo Duca de Sambreset post meridiem venne cum cavalli XXX^m ad anasare lo Conte de Varrvich et la gente del Rei et li fecero assai lasso assalto, et lo Conte de Varrvich se deliberò de usir del campo et erumper contra loro et cossì cum 4^m homini lo cassò fin dentro Albano, unde era la Regina cum homini XXX^m, et lo Conte, vedendosi solo et lo dì basso, se ne ritornò al campo, sempre hortato et cassato da li Sambreceti; et quando fu al campo intese de quello se vociferava dal campo suo a l' inimici, et dubitò ymo vedette acti de tradimenti et se partì meglo ch'el possette. Lo Rei era posto longi de lì uno miglo, sutto uno arboro, unde se rideva et cantava, et essendo voce de la rupta del Conte de Varrvich, ritenne supra sua fede li doi Principi chi gli eran stati lassiati a la guardia. Assai tosto vennero lo Duca de Sambrecet et li vencitori a salutarlo, a quali el fece bon volto et se ne andò cum loro ad Albano a la Regina, et l'un doman [sic] uno de li doi ritenuti in fede sua fu decapitato, l'altro incarcerato.[2] Morte gli fu de qualche IIII^m di quello dì tra una scaramucia et un'altra, dal medio dì fin a media nocte. Lo Conte se retaxe [sic] cum Monsignor de la Marcha et subito recolsero ben homini CC^m, et restava la cosa in tal contrapesi, che pareva unde Londres inclinasse lì esser la victoria. Doppoi, per littere venute heri pur al *Delfino,* se ha da persona dignissima come Monsignor de la Marcha et lo Conte de Varrvich havian ben CL^m homini, la più bella gente che mai fussi veduta in Angliterra, et per alcuni acti non ben legi-

---

a. Read: Carnevale.

them a good welcome and went with them to St. Albans to the Queen, and on the morrow one of the two lords whom the King had promised to protect was decapitated, the other imprisoned.[2] In one engagement or another, some 4,000 men were killed that day, the battle lasting from midday to midnight.

The Earl joined with my lord of March and they immediately assembled a good 200,000 men. The issue then hung so in the balance that it appeared that the side to which the city of London inclined would have the victory.

Subsequently, in letters which reached the *Dauphin* yesterday, we learn from a most reputable source that my lord of March and the Earl of Warwick have indeed 150,000 men, the finest troops that were ever seen in England, and that because of some illegitimate acts committed by the King and his army, London inclined to my lord of March and the Earl of Warwick. So, in desperation, the Queen and the Duke of Somerset persuaded the King to resign the crown to his son [Edward, Prince of Wales], and this, out of his goodness, he did. This act accomplished, they abandoned him and withdrew—the Queen and her son and the Duke—into Yorkshire, which lies in the northern part of England and is one of the most rugged regions in the island. The rest of the princes and people, moved to indignation [against the Lancastrians] proclaimed my lord of March as King [Edward IV]. This is confirmed by several letters worthy of credit. Nevertheless since the news is so amazing it is not entirely believed, but within three days fresh tidings are expected. My lord, I am ashamed to mention such thousands and thousands, which seem to me more suitable for counting loaves from ovens. However, everyone affirms that on that day there were some 300,000 men in arms, and that indeed all England was stirred, so that it is said there were even more than 300,000 combatants.

If thus things stand, *my crossing the Channel, after I have settled matters here, to visit the new King* [Edward IV] *and congratulate him etc. would perhaps be even more useful than my projected visit to his father, the late Duke of York. However, I will do as Your Lordship*

timi del Rei et de la banda sua, inclinava Londres verso Monsignor de
la Marcha et lo dicto Conte de Varrvich, et cossì desperata la Regina et
lo Ducha de Sambrecet havian persuaso lo Rei a deponer la corona in
lo figlolo et cossì fece per sua bontà. Quo facto, lo han lassiato et se son
retratti, la Reina, lo figlolo et lo Ducha in Horch, chi hè una parte paese
forte de la isula verso tremontana. Lo resto de li Principi et populi, indignati, havian creato Rei lo dicto Monsignor de la Marcha. Questo se
ha per più littere degne de credito; tamen, come cosa grandissima, non
se gli dà piena fede, pur fra tri dì se ne aspecta novelle vive. Signor, io
ho qualche vergogna de tanti numeri de miliara, chi me pareno numeri
da fornaciari; pur ognun afirma che quello dì fosseron in arme homini
da CCC^m et demum tutta l'Angliterra esser commossa, perchè el se ne
dice anchora più. Se cossì fusse, *el seria forse più cunveniente che io
transferisse, composte le cose, a visitar lo Rei et congratular et cetera,
che la visitation del quondam Duca de Iorch suo patre; pur ne starò a
quello me ne cometterà la S. V. a la quale se cossì parerà, ricordo che
serà necessario haver nove litere* [sic] *de credensa etc. Fra 4 dì serò dal
Duca de Bergogna, si Deo placebit, per visitarlo et retenerlo in amicicia
cum la S. V., ma de la difficultà de la liga cum el Delfino* non me
par dirgli altro, essendo la cosa reducta [.....]^b *a dinari.* Me racomando a la Ex. V., che Dio feliciti.

---

b. Two words crossed out and illegible.

thinks best to command. I make note that there must be new letters of credence etc.

Within four days I will be at the Burgundian court, if God pleases, to pay respects to the Duke and to maintain the friendly relations between him and Your Lordship, but I see no reason to say anything to him *about the difficulty over the league with the Dauphin* since the business has now been reduced [. . . . .] *to a question of money.* I recommend myself to Your Excellency, whom God prosper.

HISTORICAL NOTES

1. Feb. 17, the second battle of Saint Albans.

2. Both were decapitated; it was Warwick's brother John, Lord Montagu, captured by the Lancastrians, who was spared.

This most illustrious prince [the Dauphin] has today requested me to write to Your Excellency about favoring one Benoit de Montferrand, on whom the Pope has conferred the abbacy of Saint Anthony, in Dauphiné, at the request of his lordship; and it appears that, for certain reasons, it is important that "Fra" Benoit be recommended to Your Excellency. Hence the Dauphin has earnestly charged me to recommend him to Your Excellency. Therefore I now write to Your Excellency to beg you to show him favor, which act not only will be most pleasing to the Dauphin but will put under obligation to Your Excellency certain gentlemen and Benoit's worthy relatives at the court of the Duke of Burgundy, who have often made this request of me. I will not take the time to explain his situation here, since through a letter from the Dauphin, Your Excellency will learn everything. As always I humbly recommend myself to you.

Magnificent Lord Cicco: You will learn from the enclosed letter to his lordship what has happened since the courier Martino departed, and I therefore will not repeat it here. Further, I hope that from Martino you have received all the letters I wrote to his lordship and to you, and hence I will not write at length now. Always, nevertheless, I beg for Your Magnificence's favor for me and my affairs, I mean my family;

74·PROSPERO DA CAMOGLI *to the*

DUKE OF MILAN *and to*

CICCO SIMONETTA

Francia, cart. 525. Orig.

Questo Ill.mo Principe m'ha hoggi ditto como el scrive a V. Ex.tia per racomandation de uno Messer Fra Benedetto de Monferrant, al qual la S.tà del Summo Pontifice ha conferto una Abbatia de S.to Antonio, che hé in lo Dalphinato, a richesta de Sua S.ria; et per alcuni bisogni accadeno, pare che pertegna ditto Fra Benedetto essere racomandato a V. Ex.tia, et cossì m'ha multo incarricato che per mie littere io lo vogla etiam render ben racomandato a V. Ex.tia. Pertanto cossì scrivo questa, supplicando ala prefata Ex.tia V. vogli farlo haver per recommisso, la qual cosa, ultra che serà acceptissima a questo Ill.mo Principe, etiam obligherà a V. Ex.tia alcuni gentilhomini et da bene, suoi parenti, che stan in la Curia del Ill.mo Monsignor lo Duca de Bergogna, li quali multo me ne han pregato. Non me extendo in narrar qui il caso suo, cum sit che per littere del prefato Ill.mo Principe Monsignor lo Dalphino V. Ex.tia intenderà il tutto, ala quale humiliter semper me racomando.

M.ce Domine Ciche. La V. M. intenderà per la littera inclusa che io scrivo al S.re quello che hé in substantia de la materia et le novelle supravenute doppoi la partenza de Martino, perché io non replico qui. Insuper per Martino spero haverà essa M. V. recepiute tucte littere et quelle similiter che ho scritto a V. M.cia, perché non me extendo qui.

for there is no point in asking favor for affairs since they are governed by the grace of God and the operation of fortune. And so I continually recommend myself to his lordship.

The present messenger serves Benoit de Montferrand, Abbot of St. Anthony's in Dauphiné, who is at present in Milan and on whose behalf the Dauphin is writing to our lord. The Dauphin has charged me, among other things, that I recommend Benoit warmly to Your Magnificence, in whom his lordship seems, up to now, to place great trust. I report no further details concerning Benoit, for Baude Meurin has written what is necessary.

Semper tamen prego V. M. vogli havere per racomandato me et le mie cose, videlicet la famiglia mia. Nam le cose per gratia de Dio et exercicio de fortuna non bisogna racomandar, non essendo in rerum natura. Et cossì continue racomandarmi al S.re. Preterea lo presente messo hé de Fra Benedetto de Monferrant, Abbate de S.to Antonio in lo Dalphinato, il quale hé al presente a Milano et per lo qual questo Ill.mo S.re scrive al S.re nostro, et m'ha incarricato inter cetera che io lo racomande strettamenti a V. M.cia dela qual el monstra Sua S.ria fin a qui haver bona fiducia. Nam, ultra quello gli ho referto etc., Baudison ha scritto quello che bisogna. Data ut in litteris.

+[1]Not having had further information recently nor a way of dispatching a letter to Your Excellency, I had kept here the present courier in order to be able to report to Your Excellency what was pertinent and I wrote you four letters:

One, about our journey through Germany and the hindrances that delayed us; a second, about events in this region; a third, about the negotiations, etc.; a fourth, giving my opinions, as Your Excellency instructed me.

Since I received today by way of Bruges Your Excellency's letters written on February 15,[2] I have thought it better to send the important dispatches by that route and to allow the courier to return by the way he came. Hence by him I am sending only one letter to Your Excellency, an account of our journey, and I have also given him letters for the Duchess and others, all of which are to be referred to those that, I hope, will arrive before the courier. Sending letters by way of Bruges will be quicker and more secure.

I recommend myself humbly to Your Excellency, whom God keep in happy state. Also by way of Bruges I have made reply to what Your Excellency writes me in the letters I received today. In great haste.

75 · PROSPERO DA CAMOGLI *to the*

DUKE OF MILAN

Francia, cart. 525. Orig.

+[1] Non havendo a questi dì altro adviso né via da scriver a V. Ex.tia, io havia retenuto qui il presente cavalaro per scriver a V. Ex.tia le cose pertinente; et scriveva a V. Ex.tia quatro littere. La una del camin nostro fatto per la Alamania et deli impacii n'han retardato, l'altra de le novelle del paese, l'altra de la substantia de la materia etc., l'altra del apparer mio cossì come m'ha imposto V. Ex.tia; siché hoggi recepiuto per la via de Brugs le littere de V. Ex.tia, date ali 15 del meise,[2] m'é paruto meglo mandar le importante per quella via et lassiar lo ditto cavalaro retornarsene a suo camino. Et cossì per lui solum scrivo a V. Ex.tia une littere [sic] del camino nostro fatto, et hogli etiam dato altre littere ala Ill.ma Madona et altri, che tutte se referen a quelle che, spero, antiveniran lo ditto cavalaro, et per la dicta via de Brugs seran più presto et più sicure. Siché me racomando humiliter ala Ex.tia V., che Dio conservi in stato felici. Similiter per la ditta via ho fatto res-posta a quanto me scrive V. Ex.tia per ditte littere hoggi recepiute. Raptissime.

HISTORICAL NOTES

1. The significance of this sign, placed before the salutation, is explained by Prospero in the next doc. 76, p. 165.
2. This letter of Feb. 15 has not been found.

Today I received a letter of yours by way of Bruges together with one from our lord, to which I am replying by the enclosed communication. Both letters brought consolation to me at a moment when I was almost in despair. I appreciate the kindness of Your Magnificence in sending me those particulars, whereby I see that, with such a mass of matters, no trouble has been taken to answer my little private queries; and I beg you to attend to my business, not neglecting to bring it to the attention of our lord, and give it the dispatch it deserves, which I will indeed attribute to Your Magnificence.

Of other matters here I will say nothing more, save to make this observation: if one leaves aside those familiar ways of the *Dauphin,* which *in Italy would be regarded as frivolities* but which are the natural manners of *the French*, there is none superior to him in perspicuity, intelligence, efficiency and in true magnanimity, in my opinion, which I indeed remit as always to any better judgment.

I assure you that in rebuffing the blows aimed at *Giacomo di Valperga*, the Dauphin gives me blows on all sides. Nevertheless he seems, personally, to be very well disposed but by the replies I reported in the letter devoted to my crude opinions, you may see that there is danger in delay; and I can tell you that our cause is being deliberately injured, especially through the agency of the *Duke of Brittany*. The *Dauphin*

76·PROSPERO DA CAMOGLI *to*

CICCO SIMONETTA

Francia, cart. 525. Orig.

Hoggi ho recepiuto una vostra per la via de Brugs cum una del S.re nostro, a quale respondo per cedulam et utreque fuerunt mihi iam prope afflicto solatium. Rengratio la humanità de V. M.cia in quelle particularitate, unde vedo non si grava in tanta mole rerum responder a mie particulare minutarie; et prego la vogli proseguir et non negliger de prender il tempo a piè del S.re et che se dii spachio ala causa et execution al mio debito, el quale in vero reputerò da V. M.cia. De le altre cose de qui io non replicherò altro, salvo questa conclusion che se si potesse torvia dal *Delfin* qualche familiaritate che *in Italia serian reputate legerese* et qui sonno il natural de *Franza,* in reliquo acumine, ingenii et velocitate ac vera magnanimitate nihil melius, a mio iudicio, quale remetto ben semper a chi meglo gli vede; et vi prometto che in rebatter li colpi, che erano adriciati contra *D. Iacomo Valperga,* el me ne dà de sutto et de supra, etc. Tuttavia lui, come lui, monstra lo animo optimo, sed per li risposti scrivo in la littera del rude apparer mio, periculum in mora; advisando V. M., che qui hè chi noce assai a la cosa a posta, maxime del *Duca de Britannia,* et epso *Delfin* hè inversato del animo verso *Re Ferrando* et tutto inclinato in lo *Duca Iohanne,* sed hac in litteris.

Ceterum, M.co Messer Cicho, Vostra M.cia sa et vede ben che io sum de quella che me sia qualità saltem netto et puro servitore, et se io

has changed his mind in regard to *King Ferrante,* and now entirely favors *Duke John*—but this I have reported in my letters.

For the rest, Messer Cicco, you know well that I am, whatever else, a frank and loyal servant and if, perhaps, I do not put my dispatches in the proper form, I beg you to rephrase them as they ought to be; and if you think I should write in a different way, do please let me know so that my dispatches are not faulty, except from lack of knowledge on my part or perhaps from excessive zeal that causes me to take the shortest route, that is, the plain, direct way.

Further, if the occasion arises, I beg Your Magnificence to show favor to my little mother and my family, so that they at least be given some support, and let it be sufficient justification that I am here at the ends of the earth, whence, as always, I recommend myself to Your Magnificence, whom God prosper.

For the rest, I am writing *to our lord* a letter *marked at the top thus* + *, which is unimportant, being written only for the sake of the safety of the other letters, and in which I give the appearance of writing an authentic dispatch.* I am writing to our lord and to Your Magnificence by way of Bruges, which seems to me safer.

[On the back] *Baude Meurin* has written to the *Dauphin* from *Florence* and has spoken very highly of the *Duke of Milan* and of *Lord Cicco,* the which indeed aids our cause, and I am doing all that I can and I hope for the best.

non sporgo le cose cum quelli modi si conveniria, forse, io prego V. M.cia, transformi le cose ala stampa debita; et s'el vi pare che habbi a tener altri modi in el mio scriver, perdio, datime lo adviso che non mancha, salvo per non saper o forse per nimia affection che me fa andar per la corta, hoc est per la dritta via.

Preterea, si accidat, prego V. M.cia habbi racomandato la matreciola et li mei, che saltem gli sii resposto de qualche chiappe et basti che io sum qui in finibus terre, unde et semper me racomando a V. M.cia, che Dio feliciti.

Ceterum, io scrivo *al S.re* una littera *signata in capite sic* +, quale per adviso, *hè vaca e facta solum per salve de l'altre, quale monstro de dir.* Scrivo al S.re et ala M. V. per la via de Brugs, che me par più sicura.

[A tergo]: *Baldizon* ha scritto qui de verso *Firenza* al *Delfin* et multo se hè laudato del *S.re* et de *D. Cico,* le quale cose iuvan pur et io me aito et spero pur bene.

On the sixth of this month[1] I sent a dispatch to Your Excellency by a member of the *Dauphin's* household in which I reported a number of things; I will now recapitulate the news of what had up to then happened here and add what has since happened. I wrote in those letters of the battle [of Wakefield, Dec. 30, 1460] between the Queen of England and the late Duke of York, in which perished the Duke, one of his sons [Edmund], the father and two brothers [one, Sir Thomas Neville] of the Earl of Warwick, and some 15,000 men, and many others have been killed in various battles fought about the same time throughout the island.

I also wrote that *the son of the Duke of Burgundy* [Charles, Count of Charolais], a bitter enemy of *my lord of Croy* [Antoine, Count of Porcien], had laid complaints against Croy before *the Duke* and then formulated certain specific accusations, some of which he claims to be capital charges, against *Croy;* and the matter has been submitted to the ducal council. On this account the *Dauphin,* who was then with the *Duke of Burgundy,* returned to Genappe in order to avoid being imbroiled in such a dangerous quarrel and counseled me not to think of going to the *Duke* until the matter was decided; the *Dauphin* also advised me not to go *to England* because matters there are completely topsy-turvy at present.

77·PROSPERO DA CAMOGLI *to the*

DUKE OF MILAN

Francia, cart. 525. Orig.

Ali 6[1] del presente scripsi a V. Ex.tia per uno famiglo del *Delfin* diverse cose, et replicherò per quello specta ale novelle del paese de quello era alhora et hé accaduto doppoi. Scripsi in quelle littere del conflicto havia dato la Regina de Angliterra al condam Duca de Iorch et, morto epso Duca et uno figlolo, morto lo padre del Conte de Varrvich et doi figloli, morti insuper a quella batagla da homini XV^m et multi altri in diverse altre batagle, exinde seguite in quello medesmo tempo per la insula. Scripsi insuper come *lo figlo del Duca de Bergogna,* indignato contra *Mon.re de Crovi,* se era condoluto gravementi cum el *Duca de Bergogna* et tandem ha formato certi capituli contra de *Mon.re de Crovi,* inter li quali pretende essergene de capitali; et la cosa hé a Consiglio, per il che *el Delfin,* chi tunc era cum el *Duca de Bergogna,* se ne era venuto per non impaciarsi de tali impacii et pertanto me consigliava che io non pensassi de andar dal *Duca de Bergogna,* finché la cosa non prenda termine, et cossì finaliter del andata mia *in Anglia,* perché le cose sonno tutte indisposte al presente. Doppoi sonno venute de Angliterra più littere et messi, et de le littere pertinente mando qui le copie ala Ill.ma S.ria V. Deli messi principaliter hé venuto uno gentilhomo deli più privati del *Duca de Bergogna,* quale el havia mandato più dì fa dal *Conte de Varvich,* et ha portato littere de epso *Conte* al *Delfin,* quale ho vedute multo reverente et amorose etc.[2]. Lo effecto

Since, there have come more letters and messengers from England. I enclose herein copies of the pertinent letters for Your Lordship. Of the messengers the principal one is a gentleman, one of the *Duke of Burgundy's* intimates whom the Duke had sent many days ago to the *Earl of Warwick.* He has brought letters from *Warwick* to the *Dauphin,* which I have seen and which are most respectful and affectionate etc.[2]

The essence of the letters is that the King [Edward IV] is going northward with all the forces of [southern] England, an army of 120,000 men which is commanded by the Earl of Warwick. They are marching to give battle to the Queen, who has withdrawn to that part of the island which faces French Brittany.[3] The Yorkists have therefore assembled a fleet so that she cannot escape by sea. The Yorkist host is marching in three divisions: the first of 20,000 men; the second, of 40,-000; and the third of 60,000.

The Queen nevertheless has taken her stand in a strong place and it is said she has some 30,000 troops. The result is expected within fifteen days; great, cruel, and profoundly significant, no matter who wins.

On the third of the present month the Earl of March won a victory over two of the princes of the island who favor the Queen, and there were killed in that battle some 8,000 men, of whom it is computed that 200 or more were nobles, knights, and squires.[4] By that victory the Earl of March recovered his province of Wales, in the extreme western part of the island facing Ireland, which is a lordship belonging to the Duke of York and now, consequently, to his son.[5] In sum, anyone who computes the violent changes and overthrows of that island must affirm that, from the time of the Caesars who first conquered it, up to now, there have not occurred so many calamities as have befallen the island since the murder of the Duke of Gloucester.[6] It appears, further, that many more calamities are to come.

I also wrote to Your Excellency that at the request of *Charles, Count of Maine, the Dauphin* had sent an emissary to the *King of France,* who was much caressed by the *King* and honored by the whole court. This emissary returned on the seventh of this month, and that

hé ch'el Rei va cum tutte le forse [sic] de Angliterra contra ala Regina et ha homini CXX^m, deli quali lo capo et guida hé lo Conte de Varvich; et se va incontra ala Regina, la quale hé in la parte dela insula chi guarda la Bertagna Gallica,[3] et perciò se hé proveduto de armata per mare, adcioché ella non possi scapar per mare. Tanta multitudine hé ordinata in tre squadre: la prima de XX^m, l'altra de XL^m, l'altra de LX^m. La Regina tamen hé in loco forte et se dice ha combatenti da XXX^m. Lo exito se aspecta fra XV dì: grande, crudele et sententioso de multe cose, vencia chi si vogli. Et ali tre del presente[4] lo Conte dela Marcha havia guadagnato una iornata contra doi deli Principi dela insula, chi favoriscono la Regina; et era morto in quella batagla homini VIII^m, tra li quali se computan CC in più cavaleri et nobili scuderi, et per quella victoria havia recuperato il paese suo de Gales, chi hé in le parte extreme dela insula verso Irlanda, quale hé Signoria del Duca de Iorch et per consequens de lui figlolo.[5] In summa chi computa li squaderni de quella insula afferma che dali Cesari chi la sottoposero in qua, non ha havuto quello Regno tante calamitate come dala occision del condam Duca de Gloseste[6] in qua, et par che sia per haverne assai più. Scripsi item a V. Ex.tia come a petition de *D. Huicine Karlandagar, el Delfin* havia mandato dal *Re de Franza* uno suo messo, quale era multo carezato dal *Re de Franza* et honorato dali altri. El ditto messo se ne retornò ali 7 del presente, et statim la sera *el Delfin* mandò per me et mi disse in longa serie tutti quelli accidenti de quella cavalcata, quali in conclusion sono questi. *El Delfin* domandava primum el *Delfinato* et altre cose pertinente a uno *figlo del Re de Franza,* sed inter cetera paese contiguo *dal Duca de Bergogna al Delfinato,* et che el *Re de Franza* promettesse de lassiar *in pace el Duca de Bergogna.* Al che, dice et *Delfin,* el *Re* haver "due" [sic] fatto resposte: la una in scritti generale et dele più belle parole et offerte che fu mai possibile devisar, sed al proposito del *Duca de Bergogna* verbum nullum; tamen non monstra *el Re* de farne caso, et volendo *el Delfin andar* una volta *dal Re,* el dice el *Re* haver cose da dirgli da solo a solo et ch'el serà il più contento ch'el fussi mai et similia. Io non ho veduto lo scritto, ma m'hé stato promisso la copia.

very evening *the Dauphin* sent for me and told me at length all the circumstances of that mission, which, in sum, are these:

The Dauphin asked first for *Dauphiné* and for other things appropriate for a *son of the King of France*; among them, for the lands lying *between Dauphiné and Burgundian territory;* he also asked that the *King of France* promise to leave the *Duke of Burgundy in peace.*

According to the *Dauphin, the King* made two replies. The first, a general answer in writing, contained the most flattering words and the handsomest offers that could ever be devised, but on the subject of guaranteeing peace to the *Duke of Burgundy,* not a word; though the *King* does not seem to make an issue of this. Further, if *the Dauphin* is willing *to see the King himself* just once, the *King* has things to tell him, for his ear alone, that will content him more than ever he has been contented, etc. I have not seen the writing but I have been promised a copy. The other reply, by word of mouth, the *Dauphin* says, was as follows: if the *Dauphin* was, however, unwilling to go to the *King,* the *King* is content to grant him his request for certain lands bordering *Dauphiné and the territory of the* Duke of Burgundy and is willing to give him *Genoa and Asti* and, together with *Dauphiné,* the control of the *Duke of Savoy,* to which *the Dauphin* much aspires. The *King* makes this offer so that the *Dauphin* will favor *Duke John in Italy* and prevent the *Duke of Milan* from *aiding King Ferrante,* and the *King* proposed many other such schemes and designs, in the *French* manner. *The Dauphin* then made certain observations to me which I send in the enclosed note[7] to Your Excellency.

Now, the *Dauphin* tells me that his emissary's mission was handled at the French court by [Gaston IV,] *Count of Foix,* since *Charles, Count of Maine,* to whom the *Dauphin* had addressed his emissary, was absent. *Maine* has sent letters to excuse his absence and his consequent inability to forward the mission, and so he urges the *Dauphin* at all costs to send his emissary back to the *French court* since *Maine* will be there in a few days and the *Dauphin* need have no doubts that he will obtain everything he asks for. *Maine* adds that he will be the master of

L'altra resposta a bucha, dice *el Delfin,* esser questa: che se pur el non vol *el Delfin andar dal Re, el Re* hé contento de dargli certe terre, chi continuan el *Delfinato con el Duca de Bergogna;* et vole dargli *Zenoa et Asti* et insieme cum *el Delfinato* lo governo del *Duca de Savoya,* al quale *el Delfin* aspira multo; et questo adciò ch'el favorisca *in Italia* el *Duca Iohanne* et reprima *el Duca de Milano* dali *favori* de *Re Ferrando,* et multe altre cose circa ciò opportune cum multi designi facti in questo proposito al modo de *Franza.* Et qui me fece doppoi *el Delfin* lo ragionamento, che mando per cedula[7] incluso a V. Ex.tia. Or el me dice el *Delfin* che la expedition de questo suo hé stata fatta per man *del Conte de Fois,* absente *D. Huicine Karlandagar,* al qual epso *Delfin* havia adriciato lo messo suo et lo qual *D. Huicine Karlandagar,* essendo absente, ha priso excusa per littere del non posser esser intervenuto ale cose; et per questo conforta multo che omnino el lo remande poso puochi dì ch'el serà dal *Re de Franza,* et non dubite el *Delfin* che obtenirà tutto; et gli manda a dir che epso *D. Huicine* serà lo maistro del *Re* et che el *Conte Don Martin* serà anullato. Et me par intende [sic] ch'el fa questo per due cause: la una per guadagnar el *Delfin* ali *favori* de *Duca Iohanne;* l'altra per haver dal *Delfin* la *confirmation* de alcuni privilegii. Et computando io lo parlar dele cose del *Re Ferrando* ch'el me fece l'altra volta, cum quelo ch'el me fa al presente de tutta quella *stirpe,* come vederà *la V. S.* per cedula, a me pare intender ala bella destesa ch'el gli adherisse multo et maxime ch'el gli dole assai star cossì longo tempo a *dinari* del *Duca de Bergogna;* et se una volta el mette in securo lo quieto del *Duca,* quanto il resto da *Re* a *Delfin* me pare, secundo intendo, aquietato et pacato honorabiliter per l'una parte et per l'altra. Et cossì de brevi remanderà suo *oratore al Re,* adriciato a *D. Huicine Karlandagar.* Io gli ho confortato ch'el indusii a remander fin ché si veda lo fin *de Anglia,* et questo ho fatto per haver spacio de advisar *V. S.,* et me n'ha dato speransa. Credo ben sii etiam qualche differentia in questo fatto, perché el *Re de Franza* vorria ch'el *Delfin andassi da* lui et lui omnino non lo vol fare; et m'ha ditto chiaramenti che cossì come *Papa* non può esser *excommunicato, el Re* non può esser *traditor;*

the *King* and that [Antoine de Chabannes,] *Count of Dammartin* will be reduced to a cipher. I think that Maine acts thus for two reasons: one, to win the *Dauphin* to *Duke John's cause;* two, to secure from the *Dauphin* the *confirmation* of some privileges.

When I compare the way the *Dauphin* formerly spoke to me about *King Ferrante* with the way that at present he speaks of that whole *family* [the House of Aragon], as *Your lordship* will see from the enclosed note, it seems amply clear that he is now attached to the Angevins, especially since he greatly complains of having lived so long on the *bounty* of the *Duke of Burgundy;* and if once he can secure a guarantee of peace for the *Duke,* the remaining issues between the *King* and the *Dauphin* will, I think, be honorably resolved on both sides. Thus it is that the *Dauphin* will shortly send back his *ambassador to the King,* with instructions to work through *Charles, Count of Maine.*

I have urged the Dauphin to delay sending back his emissary until we see what finally happens *in England,* and he gives me hope that he will do so. I have acted thus in order to have time to inform *Your Lordship.*

I believe that there is some impediment blocking an accord between the *Dauphin* and his *father,* for the *King* would like the *Dauphin* to come to him but the *Dauphin* is under no circumstances willing to do it; and he has flatly said to me that just as the *Pope* cannot be *excommunicated, the King* cannot be *a traitor,* and he also adduces the example of the one I write about in the separate note.[8] In sum, I do not know what will happen.

The *Dauphin* also says that his *emissary* has reported that a *Genoese ambassador* was at the *French* court to request of the *King* an *experienced governor.*[9] The emissary reports that there was also at the *French* court an *ambassador,* named [Bertrand de Beauvau, Lord of Précigny] from the *King of Sicily* [King René] who was requesting *aid for Duke John* and who, up to the time the *Dauphin's* emissary left, had not been favorably received and was discontented, saying openly that *Duke John* is in *bad shape.*

et poi allega lo exemplo de quello che scrivo in parte per cedula[8] etc.;
siché non so quello serà. Dice insuper el *Delfin* che ditto suo *oratore*
gli ha ditto che a pié del *Re* era uno *oratore* de *Zenoa* per recheder al
Re uno *savio rector*[9]; et ultra che era lì similiter a pié del *Re* uno *oratore*
del *Re de Sicilia,* chi se chiama *Be.,* chi rechede *auxilia per el Duca
Iohanne* et era fin alì non ben veduto et mal contento, dicendo apertamenti che el *Duca Iohanne* sta in *mal punto.*

Insuper heri sera el *Delfin* m'ha ditto che per non tenerme secretto
alcuno suo, hé alcuni dì che *il Conte de San Paulo* gli ha mandato a dir
ch'el gli vogli mandar lo più fidato ch'el habia, perché gli vole dar
adviso pertinentissimo ala composition dal *Re* al *Delfin;* et cossì gli ha
mandato uno che hé a pié del *Delfin,* come *D. Cico* a pié de *V. S.*[10], et
hé quello dela cui absentia io scrivo a V. S.ria per altre littere; siché non
hé ancora ritornato, ma sii che si vogli, la cosa se tratta quasi come ch'el
celo et le stelle tutte inclinan a *pace* de *Re* et *Delfin.*

Deli movimenti de Catalogna et quella presa del Principe et la novitate deli populi de Catalogna, io non scrivo a V. Ex.tia altro, perché non
dubito V. Ex.tia ne sii per altri modi meglo advisata. Pur lo Rei de
Castella par se approximi cum gente d'arme al Regno de Catalogna
sutto pretension de aspectative ch'el gli allega etc.

Lo Legato hé partito de Angliterra, secundo m'ha dicto uno gentilhomo del *Delfin,* et se hé tolto da rumori de *barbari; lo secretario*[a] del
Delfin hé ritornato *dal Conte de San Polo,* cognato de *Karlandagar,* et
dice faran per *el Delfin* a pié del *Re* mirabilia: Dio vogli pur sian fatti
de *Franza.* Preterea el *Delfin* me dice che li *oratori*[11] de *Franza,* chi
furon in Italia a Venetia et [al] *Duca de Modena* per frescamenti, sonno
andati *dal Re de Franza* et tutto quello faran et ragioneran m'el saperà
dire et m'el dirà; et non ne dubito, perché van per lo camin de *Karlandagar,* chi hé pur quello me despiace. Signor mio, io do li advisi a
V. Ex.tia che me sonno dati a me; et se in questo paese se parlassi ad
arte io non me ne affermeria forsi in tutto, sed vedendo *che qui se*

---

a. Here Prospero used the cipher symbol for Cicco Simonetta instead of writing out
the word "secretario."

Yesterday evening the *Dauphin* told me, explaining that he keeps secret from me none of his affairs, that some days ago the *Count of St. Pol* [Louis of Luxembourg] had requested him to dispatch to the Count the most trustworthy man he has because the Count wished to give him very important information regarding his projected accord with the *King*. So he sent him a man who has the same relationship to the *Dauphin* that *Lord Cicco* has to *Your Lordship*,[10] and he is the one about whose absence I wrote to Your Lordship in a previous letter. He has not yet returned, but, be as it may, matters are developing almost as if the heavens and the stars all incline to an *accord* between *King* and *Dauphin*.

Concerning developments in Catalonia and that arrest of the Prince [Don Carlos, by his father] and the uprising of the Catalan people, I write nothing more to Your Lordship because I do not doubt that Your Excellency has been through other channels better informed. However, the King of Castile [Henry IV] is apparently approaching the kingdom [i.e. Aragonese province] of Catalonia with an army, under the pretext of the claims to it that he advances.

The papal legate has left England, according to what a gentleman of the *Dauphin's* has told me, and has removed himself from the uproars of the *barbarians. The Dauphin's secretary* has returned *from the Count of St. Pol,* brother-in-law of *Charles, Count of Maine,* and reports that the Count says he will accomplish wonders for the *Dauphin* at the *French* court. May it be God's will that they are *"French* deeds" [i.e. empty boasts].

In addition the *Dauphin* tells me that the *French ambassadors*[11] who *went to Venice and to the Duke of Modena* have recently returned *to the King of France* and that he will be able to, and will, tell me everything that they do and say. I do not doubt that he will do so, for their affairs will be handled by *Charles, Count of Maine,* which is indeed a fact that displeases me.

My Lord, I pass on to Your Excellency the information that is given to me. As to whether the people here speak with *guile and dis-*

inculpa lo parlar dele *circuicion* de *Italia* et che el *Delfin* in tutte le altre cose va netto, io me ne credo bona parte; tuttavia remettendomene al meglor sentimento de V. Ex.tia, ala quale m'hé paruto de sporgerle, come quale et de unde si sian; et de quello accaderà ala iornata, darò li advisi me seran possibili, a V. Ex.tia, ala quale humiliter me racomando.

simulate, I would *not* swear that they do so in everything. Indeed, seeing that here they criticize *"Italian deviousness"* and that the *Dauphin* in everything else proceeds straightforwardly, I believe a good part of what is told me. Nevertheless I remit my opinions to the better judgment of Your Excellency, to whom I have thought it good to report under what circumstances and from what sources I have secured my information. Of what subsequently happens from day to day I will send the best account that I can to Your Excellency, to whom I humbly recommend myself.

HISTORICAL NOTES

1. This dispatch has not been found.

2. One of the Dauphin's followers, the Lord of la Barde, was at this time at Warwick's side and would take part, fighting under the Dauphin's banner, in the battle of Towton, March 29, 1461.

3. Prospero had but a hazy idea of English geography; the Queen was in Yorkshire, which faces Denmark across the North Sea.

4. On Feb. 3 (not March 3) he crushed the forces of James Butler, Earl of Wiltshire, and Jasper Tudor, Earl of Pembroke, at the battle of Mortimer's Cross in Herefordshire.

5. The Duke of York possessed extensive estates in the Marches of Wales, but the Principality of Wales, attached to the crown, was nominally under the lordship of the royal heir, the Prince of Wales.

6. Humphrey, who died in somewhat suspicious circumstances on Feb. 23, 1447, after being put under arrest by his Lancastrian enemies headed by William de la Pole, Duke of Suffolk.

7. See next doc. 78, p. 179.

8. Evidently the example of Don Carlos, heir of John II of Aragon, whom his father had imprisoned [see next doc. 78, p. 179 and doc. 60, n. 9, p. 63].

9. Louis de Laval, Lord of Châtillon, formerly Governor of Dauphiné for the Dauphin, was appointed Governor of Genoa by Duke John when the latter sailed to attempt the conquest of the Kingdom of Naples; Châtillon failed to maintain a firm grip upon the city [Beaucourt, VI, 332].

10. i.e. Jean Bourré, the Dauphin's first secretary.

11. See doc. 55, n. 6, pp. 19.

The Dauphin bitterly detests what the King of Aragon has done in taking prisoner his son;[1] and in commenting on the inherent treacherousness of that House, he entered upon the following discourse:

It is true that he is related both to the Duke of Orléans and to Duke John of Lorraine; but he loves Duke John the more and not because the Duke is a relative. Therefore for the sake of the genuine honor and true well being of Your Lordship, he thinks it better for you to enter into a marriage relationship with Duke John than with King Ferrante[2] because he comes of a nobler and more ancient House; and, in the Dauphin's opinion, such a marriage would do more to ensure the safety of your state both now and in the future, and would give you greater prestige in the eyes of the Venetians and throughout Italy for you would thus be able easily to reconcile yourself with the King of France, who is much irritated by the projected marriage contract with King Ferrante as by other action that Your Lordship has taken against Duke John. Furthermore such a marriage would reconfirm the old tie between France and the Sforzas.

Many other things he said to me on this subject, which I will not write to Your Excellency, for, I am certain, you perceive and see, looking at all sides of the question, where your veritable well being and

78·PROSPERO DA CAMOGLI *to the*

DUKE OF MILAN

Francia, cart. 525. Orig.

Per cedula. *Detestando extremamenti el Delfino lo acto che ha fatto lo Re d'Aragon in prender suo figlolo,*[1] *et qui facendo commenti dela natural infidelità de quella casa, el me intrò in questo ragionamento: ch'el hé vero ch'el ha parentato cum lo Duca de Orliens et cum lo Duca Iohanne de Lotaringia, ma ch'el ama più el Duca Iohanne et non per parentato ch'el habia; sed per puro honor et vero ben de V. S., gli pareria meglo che V. S. se strengesse de parentato con lo Duca Iohanne che con el Re Ferdinando,*[2] *perchè hé più antiqua et nobel casa et se ne veneria a suo parere a metter meglo in saldo il Stato de V. S. in futurum et de presenti cum maior reputatione apiè de Venetia et tutta Italia, perchè se reconcilieria per questo modo facilmenti con el Re de Franza, il qual se hé così sdegnato de questo, come de altra cosa che habbi fatto V. S. contra el Duca Iohanne, et se repeteria la antiqua Francia sforsesca.* Et multe cose me disse in questo proposito che io me supersedo de scriver a V. Ex.tia, la qual sum certo chi intenda et veda ex omni parte il vero suo ben et honore. Pur come *oratore* de *V. S.* et fidele servo m'hé paruto debito mio dargli lo adviso.

Insuper havendo sigillate le altre littere, ho receputo la littera de *V. S.* de XX Ianuarii[3] et veduto la continentia. Il che, ultra che m'hé stato de grande consolatione, credo etiam serà stato utile ala materia et

honor lie. However, as *Your Lordship's ambassador* and faithful servant, I have thought it my duty to inform you of this.

In addition, after I had sealed the other letters I received *Your Lordship's* letter of January 20, the contents of which, besides giving me great consolation, will also, I believe, be useful for our cause; and Your Excellency may be certain that I will do my best and will not allow to fall to earth fruit that can be put to use, especially since if that result follows, the *Genoese business* will be similarly successful.[3]

I would like to urge (may any who deem me *presumptuous* in so doing pardon me), and indeed for what I think good reason I will not forbear to beg, Your Excellency *to ignore the rash and grandiose pronouncements of the Dauphin, which, uttered merely for what use he can make of them and not out of any regard for Your Excellency's welfare, hint at wonders so illusory that he would not dare express such thoughts in plain speech; and I beg Your Excellency, having put such statements aside, to do everything, by means of sweetly reasonable inducements, which are the way of princes, to bring the Dauphin to terms as quickly as possible so that the offers of the King of France may come to naught; and I in the meanwhile will, to the best of my ability, urge him to hold off.*

HISTORICAL NOTES

1. See doc. 60, n. 9.

2. Here the Dauphin is reviving an earlier proposal to have Duke John marry Ippolita, Sforza's daughter, who in 1455 had been betrothed to Ferrante's eldest son, Alfonso.

3. Though this letter of Jan. 20 is no longer extant, another from the Duke to Prospero on Jan. 17 [see doc. 60, p. 61], which may contain the substance of the missing communication, suggests, in its reporting on the successes of King Ferrante, that the "result" to which the ambassador here refers is the final triumph of Ferrante over Duke John.

habbi per certo, V. Ex.tia, che me ne tenirò io bon et non lasserò cader in terra fructo chi se ne possa metter a uso; et perchè me par che seguendo quello effecto, seguirà similiter quello de *Zenoa*. Io saperia laudar et per quello, che perdonemi chi m'ha reputato *passionato,* me par intenderne per vera ragione non ometterò de supplicar a V. Ex.tia *che, posto da canto li precipiti et dispendiosi ricordi de che per sua utilità più che per ben de Vostra Excellentia dano speranse de far quello de che non ardirian parlar, Vostra Excellentia per la via deli boni, quale hé la via deli Principi, facia tutto a mettergli modo, come più presto adciochè si rumpa l'argumento del Re de Franza in quelle cose, et io interim conforterò le dilatione quanto* me serà possibile. Datam ut in litteris.

GENAPPE [GENEPIE], MARCH 13, 1461
BRUXELLES [BROCELLIS], MARCH 15, 1461

On March 4 I dispatched Martino, Your Excellency's courier, with a detailed report of how things stood up to then. After that, by a servant of "Fra" Benoit, Abbot of St. Anthony's in Dauphiné, who was being sent to Milan with letters for Your Excellency, I forwarded a summary of the report Martino was bearing so that if anything happened (and I hope nothing did happen) to one of the messengers—for the journey is long and arduous—Your Excellency, by one way or the other, would have the necessary information. Then yesterday by Guglielmo Cyname,[1] a merchant of Lucca, I sent a report to *Lord Cicco* of what had since happened, a copy of which is enclosed. [omitted]

What has since occurred I am reporting below to Your Excellency, in whose presence I would like to be for one day because in letters it is impossible to explain everything. Indeed, if it were not that leaving here would seem almost a desertion and would put our business to silence— not to mention that I must await a reply from Your Excellency—I would without fail take my departure and return to you.

The matter is this: *since March 6 the Dauphin has played the savage with me and used veiled and ambiguous language. I therefore sought to learn the cause of this strange behavior. Since there are factions at this court, as there are at most courts, I probed this person and that one at opportune moments; and from one I learn that the sister of*

79 · PROSPERO DA CAMOGLI *to the*

DUKE OF MILAN

Francia, cart. 525. Orig.

Ali 4 dì del presente spachiai Martino, cavalaro de V. Ex., per lo quale scripsi plenamenti a quella quanto me pareva esser fin a lì. Doppoi per uno famiglo de uno Domino Fra Benedicto, Abbate de Sancto Antonio in lo Dalphinato, chi era adriciato cum altre littere ala Ex. V., scripsi il compendio de quanto havia scritto per lo dicto Martino adcioché se caso alcuno, quod absit, essendo il camin longo et dispendioso, intervenisse ali messi, V. Ex. havesse o per uno modo o uno altro li advisi necessarii. Doppoi per Gulielmo Cynami,[1] mercatante Luchese, heri subiunxi quello me occurreva per littere directe a *D. Cico,* lo exemplo de la quale littera hé ut infra final data. [omitted][a]

Et poso questo m'hé innovato quanto scrivo qui de subto a V. Ex., a pié dela quale me desydero per uno dì, cum sit che per littere non si può ben exprimer il tutto; et perdio se non fusse che partirme de qui quasi pareria uno resecar et metter in silentio la cosa et ultra hé debito aspectar la resposta de V. Ex., io me parteria omnino per ritornar da quella. La cosa hé questa: *da 6 dì in qua el Delfin monstra multo il salvatico et usa parole ancipite et de doi sentimenti meco et, parendomi stranio, ho studiato de intender quello si può, et percioché questa Curia hé divisa, come acade la maior parte per tutto, io ho temptato uni et*

---

a. There follows, virtually word for word, a repetition, except for the first paragraph, of Prospero's dispatch of March 9 to Sforza, doc. 73, pp. 147.

the Duke of Brittany, aware of the Dauphin's poverty, sent to offer him money and that he was inclined to accept the offer, perhaps up to 4,000 ducats. There is no doubt that if such an offer has been made, it has been made indirectly by the Duke of Brittany and to no good end—not, from what I understand (see below), to persuade the Dauphin to act against Your Lordship, but only to separate him from you, for what cannot be accomplished at present they do not want to give up hope of accomplishing in the future; and the Duke of Brittany thinks there has never been so good a time as the present to drive a bargain with the Dauphin. I was told on oath that this is true, and at times the Dauphin himself has told me that, since he has relatives and friends in the French royal household to whom his leaguing with Your Lordship would be a mortal blow, he thinks it practical to secure some reciprocal advantage from Your Lordship by which he can justify the alliance to everybody.

By others I am told that the Dauphin has been informed—as Your Lordship will have learned from my previous letters—that Your Lordship is merely dallying with him and that, because of the faith he puts in this report and of the suspicions he has nursed from the beginning, he is therefore perplexed and undecided and so suspends judgment until he receives a reply from Your Lordship.

Having learned this, I yesterday entered into conversation with the Dauphin, congratulating him on the success Baude Meurin has had with the Pope—for Baude writes that the Pope, out of respect for Your Lordship, has done everything that could be wished. The Dauphin replied that this was true, but he did not, I may say, speak with the enthusiasm that I thought the situation merited. He added that he was informed that Your Lordship was sending Count Galeazzo and another of your sons to visit the Venetians. He then observed that many cities, with dangers close at hand to be warded off, have often times found a better remedy in securing support from a distance than from nearby.

In order to keep his promise to me about giving me information concerning the [Italian] negotiations of the ambassadors of the King of

altri cum li ragionamenti opportuni; et da uni intendo che essendo notitia dela necessità, la sorella del Duca de Bretagna gli have mandato a proferir dinari et inclinava ad aceptarne parte forse fin in 4.000 ducati; et nulli dubium che se tal offerta hé fatta, hé fatta per indirectum per el Duca de Bretagna et a non bon fine, non perché per quello intendo ut infra per enodepar [sic] contra V. S., ma solo per disiunger el Delfin da V. S., perché de quello non si facia al presente, non se voleno precider la speransa in futurum et gli pare non fu mai tempo haver bon mercato del Delfin, salvo al presente; et questo ho da persone cum sacramento, che cossì hé vero et qualche volta m'ha ditto el Duca de Bergogna[b] *che havendo deli parenti et amici in casa del Re de Franza, ali quali seria culpo mortale la liga del Delfin cum V. S., el par utile haver qualche reciproca da V. S. cum la quale el si possi honestar cum tutti. Da altri ho ch'el Delfin hé stato advisato, come per altra via intenderà V. S. per altre mie littere, che V. S. gli dà bone parole et dando fede al adviso cum le coniecture ch'el se n'ha concepto dal principio fin a qui, el ne sta indingabunato et suspeso et solo se conten fin ala resposta de V. S.. Io, veduto questo, me sum introducto heri in ragionamenti cum el Delfin congratulandomi dela bona expedition ha havuto Baldizon dal Papa, il qual Baldizon scrive che el Papa per rispecto de V. S. lo havia expedito ad votum et el Delfin me disse ch'el era vero, sed non iam cum quelli sapori me pareva a dover meritar la cosa. Subiunxe doppoi ch'el era advisato che V. S. mandava lo Conte Galeacio [sic] et un altro deli figloli a visitar Venetiani et che multe terre vicine a periculi de vivere spesse volte han data megliori rimedii a palificar dala larga de supra che apresso; et che per satisfarmi di quello m'havia promisso in darme l'advisi deli trattamenti de li ambassatori del Re de Franza et Duca de Bretagna, el me advisava che uno Messer Henrico de Blancavila, homo del Duca de Bretagna, interrogato dela facenda, havia ditto che s'el Re de Franza attendeva le promisse al Duca de Bretagna, el Duca proseguiria la cosa, ma ch'el ditto Re non gli attende; tamen subiunxe el*

---

b. Ciphering error for: Delfin.

France and the Duke of Brittany, he informed me that a Messer Henri de Blancheville, a man of the Duke of Brittany's, interrogated concerning those negotiations, has said that if the King of France kept his promises to the Duke of Brittany, the Duke would undertake the enterprise but that the King of France gives him no encouragement. Indeed the Dauphin added these words, in essence: that from the report made by the ambassadors on their return from Italy it is considered evident at the French court that Your Lordship can have no reason to fear at present.

I then remarked that, with King Ferrante prospering, I did not think it sound counsel on the part of some of the French to put forth such thoughts etc.

He replied, "King Ferrante will never be able to aid the Duke of Milan, Prosper; and I, and others too, are of the opinion that, if the royal House of France does not take care in the future perhaps our successors will not have reason to rejoice at such a demonstration of friendship [as the Duke of Milan is now making] *toward the Venetians, who, however, will not accept it—and I so say for no other reason than the natural one that everybody can understand."*

Since these matters are beyond my limited understanding and since my failing to report them properly might make a difference to the decisions Your Lordship has come to, I have wanted in this letter to tell you precisely what the Dauphin said, and I also want to report on another matter that belongs to this business, concerning which, as I have noted above, Your Excellency will be informed in another way.

It might perhaps be that my suspiciousness gives me doubts that I have no reason to entertain, but I have wanted Your Lordship to perceive all the pangs of my heart. In the meantime, I am doing, and will do, the very best that I can by whatever replies and other diplomatic activity seem effective.

For the rest, at this time that I mentioned above, there came to the *Dauphin* one of the *Duke of Brittany's* knights, *My lord of Pessi,* who has been having long conversations with the *Dauphin.* This morning

Delfin queste parole in effecto che ale relatione de ditti ambassatori
quando ritornoron de Italia se ha per chiaro in la Corte del Re de
Franza che V. S. non può dubitare pro presenti, al che io allegai etiam
che prosperando el Re Ferrando non me pareva che fussi sano consiglo
de alcum de Franza far tali pensieri etc.; et lui disse che potrà iuvare el
Re Ferrando mai al Duca de Milano, Prosper, et altri che io, et io sum
de tal sententia che se la Casa del Re de Franza non se ne prende cura
in futurum forse che nostri successori non se relegrerano de tale demon-
stratione verso Venetiani, chi non le acceptano perciò *et ch'el non m'el*
dice sensa cagione altra che la naturale che ognun può intender. Et
perché queste cose sonno supra la tenuità del sentimento mio et, negli-
gendole per non intender tutto, potria far interesse ala deliberation che
ha a prender V. Ex. in questi fatti, ho voluto dar lo adviso formaliter
per questa et cossì de un'altra cosa che mira a questo signo, dela quale
ut supra dico, V. Ex. serà per altro modo advisata. Potria forse esser
che la zelosia che ho me fa dubitar de quello che altramenti non bisogneria, tamen ho voluto che V. Ex. intenda tutti li mei pongimenti de
core; interim tamen io me aito et aiterò cum le resposte et li modi me
pareran opportuni de quello che io so et posso.

Ceterum, infra questo tempo che dico de supra, hé venuto dal *Del-*
fin uno Cavaler del *Duca de Bretagna,* chi se domanda *Monsignor de*
Plessi, il qual ha longhi ragionamenti cum el *Delfin;* et questa matina
se n'é ito dal *Duca de Bergogna,* per la qual cosa me par de prender la
occasion de andar a visitar epso *Duca de Bergogna* et sforsarmi de
intender se qualcosa gli hé. Ben saperia laudar che V. Ex. si deliberi più
presto si può in questa materia *si non fussi mai per altro, salvo per non*
star in pratiche, maxime chi dovessero esser *sensa effecto chi potessero*
generar più suspitione de quelle sonno in Italia dela Ill.ma S.ria Vostra,
ala quale humiliter me racomando. *Genepie,* die XIII martii [1461].

Post scripta. *Io sum venuto qui al Duca de Bergogna, dal quale*
quantumque adhuc non sum stato; tamen Monsignor de Crovi se lauda
extremamenti de V. S., et me fano grande acoglense et m'ha dato in
compagnia lo figlolo[2] delo illustre condam Marchese Leonello da Este.

he has gone to the *Duke of Burgundy,* on which account I think it good to take this occasion to visit *that Duke* and try to discover if something is going on.

I would like to urge Your Excellency that a decision be reached as quickly as possible concerning this matter, *if for no other reason than for not remaining in negotiations,* especially negotiations that are likely to be *without result, a situation that could generate, among those in Italy, more suspicion* of Your Most Illustrious Lordship, to whom I humbly recommend myself. *Genappe,* March 13 [1461]

Postscript. *I have come here to the Duke of Burgundy, on whom, however, I have not so far called. However, my lord of Croy* [Antoine, Count of Porcien] *speaks very highly of Your Lordship and makes me a great welcome and has given me for a companion the son of the late Marquess Leonello of Este.*[2]

My lord, I find here hardly less war between the Duke of Burgundy and his son than that between the Dauphin and the King of France, and it only requires that the Duke banish his son for the parallel to be complete. From what I am learning, the Dauphin is trying to avoid taking sides, but he has incurred a certain amount of jealousy,[3] *and it is this that necessitates his making peace with the King of France. Perceiving how highly the Duke's son is esteemed and how much he is hated by my lord of Croy, I think that my lord of Croy cultivates me to enhance his status by securing the greater favor from Your Lordship. I will therefore take the requisite steps to dispatch my business here quickly, and I shall then go to Bruges, where I shall await the reply from the courier sent back to Your Lordship, to whom I humbly recommend myself. Brussels,* 15 March [1461]

Lord Cicco:

I beg Your Magnificence to read this *privately to our lord.* A man whom up to now I have found to be a good and true friend assures me that ten days ago the *Dauphin was informed by a Milanese person of importance*—and so the report comes from other sources *than the Mar-*

*Signor mio, io trovo qui puocho menor guerra dal Duca de Bergogna al figlolo come se sia dal Delfin al Re de Franza, né gli mancha salvo bandirlo in tanto che per quello vado intendendo el Delfin sta ancipite tra l'uno et l'altro, et ne hé accaduto qualche zelosiette³ chi sonno pur de quelle chi necessitan la pace dal Re de Franza al Delfin; et intendendo quanto hé apreciato lo ditto figlolo et quanto el hé artomacato*ᶜ *de Monsignor de Crovi, io penso che epso Monsignore me vogli far più honor per favorirse più de V. S.; et per questo userò lo debito temperamento inde speciarme presto de qui et menandarò a Brugs unde attenderò la resposta del cavalaro remandato a V. S., ala quale sedullo humiliter me racomando. Brocellis,* die 15 martii 1460. [1461]

Magnifice Domine Ciche etc.. Io prego V. M. chi vogli leger *separatamenti* questa *al Signore.* Uno che fin a qui trovo bon amico et veritader me acerta ch'el *Delfin* da X dì in qua *hé advisato da persona degna de* nostro paese *delà,* altri, et ultra *ch'el Marchese de Monferrato* et suo fratello, che io sum *qui per darli bona verba.* Idem sub *iuramento teribili* dicendomi ch'el hé cossì, *m'ha ditto che in* Consiglo *del Re de Franza,* poso lo ritorno deli *ambassatori* del *Re et del Duca de Bretagna* etc., se hé ditto che *Venetiani* apertamenti monstran de desiderar *Cremona* et tunc *farian et dirian* etc.; siché vi prego, per Dio faciati intender al Signore che io me doglo a morte che fin a qui non gli haby potuto scriver littera se non *agarica,* et ne faciati la excusa mia perché io non so unde meglo ricorrer come ala pura verità. Tamen mediante la summa sapientia de *V. S.* et li boni et iustificati deportamenti suoy per li advisi ne aspetto, spero che reduremo *lo agarico in zucaro,* perché pur el *Delfin* cum tutti quelli supraventi fin a chi, quanto al effetto de la cosa che ho scritto per Martino sta in fermo, et usque huc in concusso proposito de *la liga con el Signore,* et prego V. M. adrici et temperi cum li modi convenienti tutto quello che io scrivo, ala qual semper me offero et racomando.

---

c. Read: estomacato.

quess of Montferrat and his brother—that I am *here only to make empty offers.*

Swearing to me by *a fearsome oath* that this is true, my friend also *told me that in* the council *of the King of France,* after the return of the *French and Breton ambassadors,* it was said that the *Venetians* openly indicate that they want *Cremona* and therefore *would do and say* etc. Hence I beg you, for heaven's sake, to make our lord understand how mortified I am that up to now I have been able to write him *nothing but unpleasant* letters. And do make my excuses, for I know no other recourse except to report the exact truth. Nevertheless, through the high wisdom of *Your Magnificence* and by means of the effective steps you will take to procure the advices I am awaiting, I hope that *the bitter* will turn *sweet*; for indeed the *Dauphin,* despite all the difficulties that have come up—those that I reported by Martino—still firmly desires *a league with our lord.*

I beg Your Magnificence, to whom always I offer and recommend myself, to modulate and appropriately emend everything that I report.

HISTORICAL NOTES

1. Guglielmo Cinami, member of an ancient family of Lucca, which in the middle of the fourteenth century had established itself in France and Flanders as cloth merchants and bankers [L. Mirot, "Études lucquoises," *Bibliothèque de l'École des Chartes,* XCI (1930), 100 ff.; cf. two letters of recommendation for Cinami, corrupted into "Sentina," by the Dauphin to Sforza and Cicco Simonetta, Genappe, March 12 and 13, [1461], *Francia,* cart. 525; *Lettres,* I, 156–58].

2. Francesco, seventeen year old natural son of Leonello d'Este, Marquess of Ferrara, 1441–50.

3. i.e. the Duke suspected that the Dauphin favored his son.

Enclosure in a letter to Prospero.

Prospero, we are writing you this letter[1] so that you can show it to my lord the Dauphin and read it to his excellency. If it will help sufficiently so that you are able to conclude the treaty, make every effort possible to conclude it in accordance with your commission, for we hold this of great importance. In case you cannot conclude, return here with the good grace of my lord, telling his serenity that although no written treaty has resulted from the negotiations for an alliance, nevertheless we consider that alliance as completely concluded and established as if there had been drawn up a thousand treaties, and such, we believe most certain, will be the attitude and intention of the Dauphin, and we will always remain in this most firm opinion.

Concerning the Marquess of Montferrat and [his brother] lord Guglielmo, try your best to discover the means they use in sending there information about our affairs etc.—how and in what way they procure the information and by what method they forward it to the Dauphin, and if anyone from here gives information, and in what way etc. Look into and explore this matter as thoroughly as possible so that you come back well informed.

[About other matters, too, you are to keep us informed:] item, the business of the Dauphin's accord with his father; item, my lord of Bur-

80 · *The* DUKE OF MILAN *to*

PROSPERO DA CAMOGLI

Francia, cart. 525. Minute

Poliza in litteris Prosperi.

Prospero, te scrivemo questo littera[1] perché tu possi mostrarla ad Mons.re Delphin et legerla ala Ex.tia Soa, et s'ella giovarà che tu possi concludere, sforzate de farlo iuxta la comissione che tu hay et in questo te sforza quanto te sia possibile, perché l'averimo multo caro; caso non sia possibile, cum bona gratia d'esso Monsignore te ne ritorna, dicendo ad Soa Serenità che quantunche non sia seguita né facta scriptura de questa intelligentia et liga praticata etc., tamen Nuy la tenerimo per ferma, facta et stabilita, quanto se ne fussero facte mille scripture, et cossì ne rendiamo certissimi che sarà la mente et intentione de quello I. S., et Nuy con questa firmissima opinione viveremo continuamente.

Sforzati sentire deli Marchese de Monferà et S. Guillelmo, li modi servano là in advisare deli facti nostri etc., et como et par quam viam lo sentono et per quale mezo lo sporgono al Delphin, et si altri de qua advisa etc., et per quale via etc., et vogli in ciò speculare et explorare quanto te sia possibile che tu vegni bene informato. Item deli facti delo accordio del Delphin con lo patre; item de Mons.re de Borgogna; item del fiolo d'esso Monsignore; item deli facti de Ingliterra et Scotia etc.; item deli facti del Duca de Savoya; item del Duca d'Orliens et Bertagna etc.; item confortaray et salutaray mille volte Mons.re de Crovi etc.

gundy; item, my lord's son [Charles, Count of Charolais]; item, the affairs of England and Scotland etc.; item, the affairs of the Duke of Savoy; item, the Duke [Charles] of Orléans and the Duke [Francis II] of Brittany. Item: you will greet and compliment my lord of Croy [Antoine of Croy, Count of Porcien, or his brother John, lord of Croy] etc.

HISTORICAL NOTE

1. This letter, which was to accompany the present note, has not been found. In fact there are no letters extant written in March, 1461 by Sforza to Prospero [Cf. doc. 102, p. 331]. The contents of this note, however, are closely connected with those in Sforza's letter to his envoy of April 1 [15?], 1461 [doc. 92, p. 263], and in note *g* to this letter there is a quotation of a passage which is identical to the second sentence in the note. It may be that an earlier draft of the April letter was prepared on March 15, but was never sent.

For reasons that I wrote to you and sent word by Martino, I left
Genappe yesterday to go to Bruges and remain there until the return of
Martino. I left there at Genappe with the honorable François Royer,
brother-in-law of the honorable Pietro da Gallarate, a rough-haired
bitch, cousin german of the dog Nobile. She is very clever: she will
fetch sticks that are thrown in the water or anywhere else; she will
faithfully retrieve anything; and, in addition, if something is lost or
falls along the road, she will, when sent for it from the distance of a
mile beyond, find it and faithfully bring it back. She is the handsomest
and best dog that I have found in all these regions; and I wanted to try
her out in all these things before I sent her to Your Magnificence, to
whom I would like to send something worthier. Nevertheless, such as
the gift is, I beg Your Magnificence for the present to accept it kindly.
Among other things, beware that she is not beaten, but always praised
for doing well; for otherwise this breed becomes recalcitrant and you
will not have good service from her. A member of François Royer's
household, who is traveling on foot, will take her as far as Peverino and
from there she will be forwarded to you; for a man on horseback could
not bring her unless he had a cart, because she is wider than she is
long.

81·PROSPERO DA CAMOGLI *to*

CICCO SIMONETTA

Francia, cart. 525. Orig.

Perciochê per li rispetti vi scripsi et mandai a dir per Martin cavalaro, io me partitti heri da Genapio per andar a Brugs et lì demorar fin al ritorno de epso Martino. Io ho lassiato lì a Genapio al Spectabile Francisco Royer, cognato del Spectabile Petro da Galerate, una cagna pilosa, cosina germana de Nobile, la qual hé industriosa, ariverà a prender li verotoni chi si lansano in le aque et per tutto, a portar deretro fideliter ogni cosa; et ultra se si domenticassi o cadessi per camino qualcosa, per uno miglo remandata indietro, troverà et reporterà fideliter; et hé la più bella et la meglor che io habbi trovato in tutti questi paesi; et prima la ho voluta provar a tutte queste cose, anci che io la mandassi ala M. V., ala qual io vorria mandar cosa più digna. Tamen tal qual el hé per lo presente, prego la M. V. la accepti gratiosamente; et inter cetera caveat che ella non sii batuta, sed semper bene faciendo sia festiata [sic], aliter enim sonno stirpe disdegnosa et non haresti bon servitio. Uno famiglo del ditto Francesco, chi va a pede, la condurà fin a Peverino et de lì vi serà mandata, nam homo a cavallo non la porria condur sensa carretta, perché hé più larga che longa.

Ceterum qui se dice che la Regina de Angliterra, doppoi ch'el Rei ha renunciato la corona al figlolo, ha dato veneno al Rei, il qual almanco ha saputo in questa vita morire, s'el non havesse miga saputo far

For the rest, it is said here that the Queen [Margaret] of England, after the King [Henry VI] renounced the crown in favor of his son [Edward, Prince of Wales], gave poison to the King—who at least has known in this life how to die, if in the past he has not known how to do anything else. It is said that she will marry [Henry Beaufort,] the Duke of Somerset. Nevertheless this is uncertain rumor, and I consider it the more doubtful since the English Channel has been stormy and unnavigable for the past ten days. I recommend myself to Your Magnificence.

altro per lo passato; et dicessi che ella se coniungerà al Duca de Sambrecet. Tamen questo hé rumor incertus et io lo reputo tanto più incerto, quanto ch'el mare da Angliterra qui hé fortunale et innavigabile da X dì in qua. Me racomando a V. M.tia.

Enclosure.[1] Master Zanetto has run into great trouble with Master Roger, a most notable painter,[2] and it has required the intercession of the Dauphin. Nevertheless he is promised fifty ducats for a year for his living and is not to drink wine during the year, and so Master Zanetto has promised. He is in truth a young man of good discretion and talent and honesty, and if you think it good to intercede with our lord for twenty-five ducats, it will be a charitable deed, notwithstanding that he has, on this account, dedicated the first of his works to our lord and to Your Magnificence. So that there be no delay, he has already gone to his master and has begged me to recommend him to Your Magnificence and to request that you condescend to give him some reply and if possible make this provision for him in some way.

Dated as in the letters.

HISTORICAL NOTES

1. This note was enclosed, it would seem, in Prospero's letter to Cicco Simonetta of March 11 or in that of March 15.

2. Zanetto Bugatto or Bugatti, a portrait painter at Sforza's court, worked in Brussels (1460–63) in the studio of Roger van der Weyden [F. Bologna, "Un San Gerolamo lombardo del Quattrocento," *Paragone,* N. 49

82·PROSPERO DA CAMOGLI *to*

CICCO SIMONETTA

Francia, cart. 525. Orig.

Per cedulam.[1] Magistro Johannetto hé corso a grande fatica cum Magistro Rogero, pictore nobilissimo,[2] et hé stato necessaria la intercession de Monsignor lo Dalphino. Tamen per uno anno se gli hé promisso ducati L.^ta per lo viver suo et non debe bever vino questo anno, et cossì ha promisso Magistro Iohannetto. Et in vero hé iuvene de bona discretion et virtù et honestà, et se pare ala M.V. intercedere a pié del S.re per ducati 25, el hé una elymosina, non obstante ch'el ha per ciò dedicato le primicie del suo operagio al S.re et ala M.V.; siché non se daran de badda [sic], el se n'é ito al suo mastro et m'ha pregato che io lo recomande a V. M.tia, che si digne de fargene qualche resposta et si fieri potest provedimento per qualche via.

Data ut in litteris.

(1954), 48]. In 1467 he was sent to France by Galeazzo Maria Sforza to execute a portrait, now lost, of his future bride, Bona of Savoy. Around 1472 Louis XI commissioned him to paint portraits, no longer extant, of the late Duke of Milan and of Galeazzo Maria [G. D'Adda, *Indagini storiche, artistiche e bibliografiche sulla Libreria viscontea-sforzesca del Castello di Pavia. Appendice alla prima parte* (Milan, 1879), 82–83].

Some days ago I sent Your Illustrious Lordship a hasty account of the civil strife in England. Now I am sending you, enclosed, copies of letters from there, by which Your Lordship will learn what has since happened in England up to the fifth of the present month; and you will also learn, from an addition in my hand written on the back of one of the copies, what is most recently reported and believed. Although there is yet no positive confirmation, it is believed nonetheless that the new King whom the English have elected [Edward IV] will, together with the Earl of Warwick, accomplish wonders.

If Your Lordship will consider past happenings and what I have written and what the lords of this [Yorkist] party have written, [you can see that,] should a sign be provided by the Church [i.e. a Cardinal's hat for Coppini], which is called for because of the importance of such a realm and of such high matters initiated by me and brought almost to completion, it would be an easy thing to achieve greater and more worthy deeds than have been heard of in these parts for 500 years. If it please God that this come about, He will provide for it, for never has the time been so propitious as now.

I left [England] for a little while because necessity required, and Warwick counselled, me to do so; but from day to day I am expecting

83 · FRANCESCO COPPINI *to the*

DUKE OF MILAN

Autografi, cart. 51, fasc. 6. Orig.

A dì passati scripsi ad Vostra I. S. in pressa[a] la substantia delle cose d'Inghilterra. Hora vi mando incluse le copie delle lettere ricevute de là, per la quale [sic] vederà prefata V.I.S. quanto era seguito per fine a dì 5 de questo; et per una aggiunta di mia mane a tergo d'una de dicte copie, quanto novamente si dice et si crede. Et benché non se n'abbi anche vera sotitia, si crede nondemanco che questo novo electo insieme cum VVarvico [sic] faranno cose maravigliose. Et se V.I.S. considera le cose passate, et quanto ho scripto, et quanto hanno scripto questi Signori de questa parte, se qui si trovassi un segno della Chiesa, quale richiede la reputatione de tanto Reame et de così gran cose cominciate per me et deducte quasi ad perfectone [sic], sarebbe leggier cosa ad fare li maggiori et più degni facti che siano uditi da 500 anni in qua in queste parti, se a Deo piacerà che si facci, li provederà che ancor é tempo più che mai. Io mi partì perché così richiedeva la necessità, et anche per consiglio de Vvarvico, per un pezo, et de dì in dì aspetto ritornar, secundo il caldo che haremo de costà; et de qua non dubitamo far ben se de costì semo aiutati, altrimenti meglio é pigliar altra provincia et altre faccende, dove forsi poterò far utile. Attendo che ha facto

---

a. Read: in fretta.

to return, according as how the situation there heats up; and we have no doubts about doing well here if, from your side, we are given aid. Otherwise it would be better to take another province and another mission, in which I could perhaps be of use. I await word of what Messer Antonio [della Torre] has done and what it may seem good to Your Lordship to do, to whom I recommend myself, for either there or here I am and will be yours.

I am often with the Duke of Burgundy, by whom I am most warmly received, for he has proof that I am zealously devoted to his state. I have written enough.

Messer Antonio et che parer sia quello de V.I.S., ad la quale mi raccomando, perché ho là o qua suo sono et sarò.

Sono spesso con questo I.S. Duca et da quello optimamente visto, che ha provato sono zelante del suo Stato et basta.

We wrote to his illustrious lordship about developments in England and we believe they will please him. Because of press of business we wrote in our own hand and in furious haste. This present messenger also bears letters on the same subject that I am writing to the Pope. You will see all, so I say no more, recommending myself always to our illustrious lord and to you. If, on your side, fire were applied to the bombard, I will see to it that the explosion resounds even more loudly in your ears than it does in England, and it will be all that you could wish. However, I will be believed only after the fact and then it will be too late. Farewell in the Lord, and, as I said, recommend my affairs to his lordship, to whom you know how much I am devoted, and whether here or there I intend to be and remain his.

Your faithful Legate from Terni, in his own hand and hastily.

So that his lordship and you may know something of what we accomplished for the Church, we are sending you, enclosed, a copy of an account of our sea-passage [i.e. expedition to England] which we wrote in England when we were in those parts [. . .].

84 · FRANCESCO COPPINI *to*

CICCO SIMONETTA

Autografi, cart. 51, fasc. 6. Orig.

Scrivemo ad quello I.S. delli processi de qua d'Inghilterra et credemo li piaceranno; et per le grande occupationi scrivemo de nostra mano et in furia, et anche queste medesime cose per lo presente messo scrivo ad N.S. Vederete tutto, siché non dico altro; raccomandomi sempre ad lo nostro I.S. et ad voi. Et se de costì fussi dato foco ad la bombarda, io vi farò sentir lo romore de più là che Anglia et bastivi. Dopo il facto sarò creduto e sarà tardi. Valete in Domino et, ut dixi, raccomandatene ad quello S., del quale sapete quanto sono devoto, et qua o là intendo essere et vivere suo.

Vester fidelis Interamnensis Legatus manu propria et veloci.

Perch'el S. et voi vedate qualcosa de nostri bon tempi che havemo per la Chiesa, rimandamo inclusa la copia del nostro passo di mare che scrivemo in Anglia quando fum in pa[. . .].

If indeed I have, up to now, written a great deal to Your Excellency, and perhaps to the point of tediousness, I think it pertinent to your deliberations concerning the treaty with the Dauphin that you be informed of what I am reporting below; for on coming here in order to try to learn more about matters, I made such discoveries that I feel almost as if I had emerged from a cloud and had now reached open sky.

As I wrote in previous letters sent by way of Bruges, I came here on March 14 and then on the 16th I had an audience with the Duke of Burgundy, who received me honorably, as I explain in the enclosed missive. After that, on the 18th, I had a long private conversation with my lord of Croy [Antoine, Count of Porcien], in which he spoke freely about everything, thus showing the trust he reposes in Your Lordship and Your Lordship's emissary. He produced a great many wise and far-reaching and elevated observations and also important explanations concerning the state of affairs here.

Among other things, he made clear to me that the projected accord of the Dauphin and the King of France had neither the approval nor the assent of the Duke of Burgundy, but rather the contrary. He complained that as result of the Duke's harboring the Dauphin and swearing homage to him as Dauphin and future King, the King of France

DOCUMENT 85. CIPHERED DISPATCH OF PROSPERO DA CAMOGLI TO THE DUKE OF MILAN.
BRUSSELS, 23, 26 MARCH, 1461.

85·PROSPERO DA CAMOGLI *to the*

DUKE OF MILAN

Francia, cart. 525. Orig.

Seben fin a qui io ho scripto ala Excelentia Vostra assai et forse fin a tediosamente, per esser io venuto qui et parutomi intender più ultra de quello che avanti io non intendeva, reconoscendomi quasi esser stato inusito [sic] de nubilo et al presente pervenuto al sereno, m'hé paruto pertinere al deliberarsi dela Excelentia Vostra in la materia cum el Delfin che ella sia advisata de quanto scrivo infra. Come per altre per la via de Brugs scripsi ala S. V., io venni qui ali 14 del presente et poi quelle ali 16 fui dal Duca de Bergogna, il qual me recevete honorabiliter, come scrivo per l'alligata ala S. V.; postea ali 18 fui cum Monsignor de Crovi in longo et privato sermone et hebbe meco una conferentia libera de tutte cose, monstrando che tal fede gli pareva prender dela S. V. et de ogni suo, et dissemi de multi saggi et grandi et relevati argumenti et alte conclusione del stato dele cose de qua. Inter cetera me feci intender chiaramenti che l'acordo del Delfin con el Re de Franza non hè nè grato nè de consentimento del Duca de Bergogna, imo lo contrario, dolendosi che havendolo receputo el Duca fin dal principio et iuratolo come Delfin et futuro Re de Franza, el Re se ne ha preiso uno implacabile sdegno contra el Duca adiuncto ali altri antiqui despecti et che essendo le cose de Anglia in suspeso, le quale importan la sententia del pacifico del Duca, aut dela turbation sua, non gli par honesto etc.. Et qui disse talmenti che epso Delfin non par essersi

had conceived an implacable hatred against the Duke, to add to the long-standing causes of enmity between them; and given the fact that the strife in England hangs in the balance, the outcome of which will mean peace or trouble for him, the Duke does not think it honorable [of the Dauphin to make overtures to his father at such a time]. *Croy then implied that the Dauphin had not given this matter the weighty deliberation and consideration that such a prince should employ.*

Item: concerning the business of Genoa and the other Italian offers the King of France was making to the Dauphin, about which I have written to Your Lordship, my lord of Croy told me that the Duke of Burgundy has had no advices from the Dauphin about them, nor does my lord of Croy believe in these offers. If they are a fact, Croy does not think that the Dauphin is acting honorably. He added that since the Duke of Burgundy had received the Dauphin, the Duke would see to it that he never lacked anything; but the Duke would never try to persuade him or dissuade him in any way and if the Dauphin is set on going, he will let him go. Nevertheless Croy thinks that an accord between the Dauphin and the King of France will not take place, and he told me how his brother [Jean, Count of Chimay] *had served as a ducal ambassador to the King—in an effort, I believe, to obtain information and undermine these negotiations and for many other reasons. All circumstances, it seems to me, fit this conjecture. On the other hand, I now see more clearly what Lord Alberico* [Maletta] *reported on his return* [from a mission to Savoy]—*that the Dauphin was annoyed with the lukewarmness of the Duke of Burgundy as evinced in the representations the Duke's ambassadors made to the Duke of Savoy.*[1] *Furthermore, since the Dauphin, made uneasy by the Duke's advanced years and bad health, is now drawing closer to my lord of Charolais, it appears that the great love which the Dauphin and the Duke once showed for each other has cooled.*

Item: since the Dauphin has spent a great deal of money, especially on religious charities, without being willing to watch his accounts or stay within his means, he has found himself in still another sort of

aducto a questo cum tutta quella ponderata premeditation et consideration che debe uno tale Principe.

Item, m'ha ditto che del fatto de Zenoa, nè dele offerte dele cose de Italia, che io scripsi ala S. V. che el Re de Franza offeriva al Delfin, el Duca de Bergogna non ha dal Delfin advisatione alcuna, nè epso Monsignor de Crovi crede cossì sia; et se cossì hè, non gli pare che dal canto del Delfin si serva honestà, subiungendo che poichè el Duca de Bergogna lo avia ricolto, mai non gli mancherà nè mai li suaderà nè dissuaderà cosa alcuna et s'el se ne anderà, lo lasserà andare. Tamen ch'el ha opinione che la cosa dela pace del Delfin al Re de Franza non harà loco et me disse come suo fradel era ito ambassatore del Duca de Bergogna al Re de Franza, credo io per intender et lavorar de cava subterranea et multe altre ragione, et m'hè paruto comprender che tutte cadeno in questo proposito. Dal altro canto hora me paio chiaro di quello che fin del ritorno del Magnifico Domino Albrico el me parse comprehender ch'el Delfin ha havuto sdegno dela tepidità del Duca de Bergogna usata per suoi ambassatori a piè del Duca de Savoia,[1] et ultra iam tacitamenti restrengendosi cum Monsignor de Iharloes, figlolo del Duca de Bergogna, per diffidentia dela vechiessa et mala sanità del Duca de Bergogna, par la cosa esser distratta da quello grande amore chi se mostrava dal principio.

Item, etiam per haver el Delfin expeso largamenti, maxime in elimosine sensa voler reveder li computi et la possibilità, se ritrova in altre necessità et non ha dal Duca de Bergogna excepto ducati dua milia in mense et se pare necessitati per questo ala pace con el Re de Franza. Ceterum monstrò epso Monsignor de Crovi ch'el Duca de Bergogna habia havuto grande consolatione de tal visitation per parte dela V. S. dicendomi, cossì che cum sit, che vivendo questo Re de Franza, el Duca de Bergogna non può sperare de ben nè de pacifico et similiter vivendo el Duca de Bretagna et Orliens, la V. S. non si può far alcuno bon concepto del Re de Franza, imo semper esser, serrà de ogni nocumento che al Re fusse possibile, gli par che la natura conduca ben V. S. et el Duca de Bergogna a strengersi insieme. Et questo me

difficulty; and since he receives only 2,000 ducats a month from the Duke of Burgundy, he thinks it necessary, for this additional reason, to make peace with the King of France.

For the rest, my lord of Croy declared that the Duke of Burgundy took great pleasure from the fact that Your Lordship had sent an emissary to him. He went on to say that, since as long as the King of France lives the Duke of Burgundy cannot hope for anything good or for peace and since, similarly, as long as the Dukes of Brittany and Orléans live Your Lordship cannot expect anything good from the King of France, but rather can be assured of being done every injury by him that he can inflict, it seems to my lord of Croy that nature herself urges Your Lordship and the Duke of Burgundy to draw together. Croy then pressed me to stay here until there is news from England. Such news is expected within a few days, and it is thought that it will be very good or very bad, for the issue is bound to be decided soon, as I explain in the enclosed missive to Your Lordship.

Here is the essence of what I gathered from his commentary on English affairs: if the Earl of March, son of the Duke of York, and the Earl of Warwick lose, the Duke of Burgundy thinks that some injury from the King of France is to be feared, and he believes therefore that in every way possible the Dauphin should be humored. I do not know whether in speaking thus Croy might have had in mind requesting something of Your Lordship. In any case, in order to hold the pass I confined myself as much as I could to generalities, and I stated, among other things, that under commission from the Pope, master of the league of Italy, Your Lordship has had to assume a great many burdens, and has others besides. In sum, I made him a very cautious reply, and if anything else is said to me on the subject, I will do the best I can with such general answers as are prescribed in Your Lordship's instructions until I hear otherwise from you. As a matter of fact, according to my feeble judgment I don't know whether it would be so terribly bad for your state if there were indeed a war between the Duke of Burgundy and the King of France.

To give Your Lordship the latest news I have—it is said here that

confortò assai che io volessi attender finchè se habi novelle de Anglia,
quale se aspecteno grandementi bone o grandementi triste in puochi dì,
perchè hè reducta la cosa a ioco de puoche tavole, come scrivo per
l'aligata ala S. V.. Et m'hè paruto che suoto [sic] el suo parlar inteso è
questa substantia, che s'el Duca dela Marcha, figlolo del Duca de Iorch,
et Conte de Varruich perdeno, el Duca de Bergogna reputa dubitar de
qualche nocumento del Re de Franza (contra de lui) [a]*; et gli pareva*
tunc omnibus modis retener in bona el Delfin, et in questo non so s'el
gli passassi mai per mente de richeder in aliquo la S. V.. Al che io per
preocupar lo passo, quamvis dala larga et in altri propositi, gli recordai
come de commission del Papa, maistro della Liga de Italia, la S. V.
havia havuto deli carichi assai et havia per Anglia. [b] *Et in reliquis, gli*
resposi assai cauto, et se altro circa ciò me ne serà ditto, me aiterò de tale
resposte generale, come se conten in la instruction dela S. V., finchè
habia altro da quella maxime che per lo mio povero iudicio non so se
dovessi esser tutto el mal del mondo al Stato vostro questa guerra, se
cossì fussi dal Duca de Bergogna [c] *al Re de Franza. Et perchè la S. V.*
intenda più avanti, qui se ha come el Re fa quantità de gente d'arme et
navili in Guasconia et non se sa a che fine et unde miri indubitatum
videtur aut a Cales aut a favori dela Regina de Anglia. Quanto specta
a Cales, el Duca de Bergogna va a una terra chi si domanda Sant Omer[2]
sutto color dela Tuexon, come scrivo per l'altra, et ha comandato a
ognun de quelli van seco che habiano le arme loro cum loro. Quanto
specta al stato de Anglia, etiam el serà vicino lì et dicemi Monsignor
de Crovi che sia del Delfin quello si vola, se al Duca de Bergogna serà
mossa guerra, el Duca harà presti tra cavalli et fanti centomilia; et per
quello intendo tacitamenti, el Duca se provede et sta cum lo ochio
aperto ala guardia et ha mandato in Bergogna Monsignor lo Marescalco
de Bergogna suoto specie de andar a solatio a casa sua, et dellà mante-
gna in ordine quello bisogna là.

---

a. Brackets in the original.
b. The cipher reads "Anglia" while C. C. has "Anglia" crossed out and replaced with "altro" which is probably what Prospero intended to write.
c. C. C. reads: Dalfin.

the King of France is assembling a large quantity of troops and a fleet in Gascony; it is not known for what purpose but it is thought that they will be used to attack Calais or to aid the Queen of England.

As regards Calais, the Duke of Burgundy is going to a town called St. Omer[2] under pretext of holding an assembly of the Order of the Golden Fleece, as I write in the enclosed letter, and he has ordered all those who are going with him to have their armor with them. As regards the English situation, he will, at St. Omer, be closely in touch with events. My lord of Croy tells me that, whatever attitude the Dauphin takes, the Duke of Burgundy, if the French make war on him, will have ready, what with horse and foot, 100,000 men; and from what I am tacitly given to understand, the Duke is prepared to defend himself and stands on guard with his eyes open and has sent the Marshal of Burgundy into the Duchy of Burgundy, under pretext of his enjoying a holiday at home, so that he may take whatever steps are necessary there.

For the rest, according to my information my lord of Clèves, my lord d'Estampes, my lord the Bastard[3] and all those of the Duke of Burgundy's line hold with the Duke's son against my lord of Croy, and the Duke of Burgundy alone sustains Croy, as being the honorable thing to do. However, it is said that the government of this state will change, for the Duke of Burgundy is old and not in good health and thus thoughts of the future make everyone incline to the Count of Charolais.

My lord, I am the first hound that Your Lordship has sent into these fields and if I am not on the right scent and the right track, i.e. if I am not reporting truths and the essential matters, as Your Lordship would desire and as my mission requires, I beg Your Lordship to excuse me. The point is, I send you these advices as I receive them from moment to moment so that Your Lordship, who is most perceptive, may discern what conduces to your welfare. I beg you kindly to give me directions as to what are the pertinent matters.

Since these issues here seem to me well worth Your Lordship's giv-

Ceterum, per quello che io sento, li illustri Monsignor de Cleve, Monsignor d'Etamps, Monsignor lo Batardo,[3] *et tutti quelli dela linea del Duca de Bergogna, tengono con lo figlo del Duca de Bergogna et contra Monsignor de Crovi, et solo el Duca sustene per bono exemplo Monsignor de Crovi. Pur se ha opinion che lo governo de questo Stato se muterà, nam el Duca de Bergogna è pur antiquo et non ben sano et questa diffidentia fa inclinar ognuno al Iharloes.*

Signor mio, io sum lo primo braco che V. S. habi mandato in queste stobie, et se non fusse cossì sul dritto nasto et orme dele cose vere et necessarie, come V. S. desideraria et seria officio de servo, io prego V. S. chi me habi per excuso; tamen do li advisi, quali e da chi li ho de momento in momento, adciochè la S. V., chi hè prudentissima, discerna quello conduce al suo bene et ala quale io suplico che di quanto hè pertinente me vogla dar resposta et legge. Nam parendomi queste cose degne da far pensero ala S. V. sule cose de qua, io me proforserò de suspendermi del parlar nè del far coseta alcuna, excepto generaliter, finchè habia resposta de questa. Dico etiam se Vostra Excelentia, per resposta de quanto ho scripto per Martino cavalaro, me comettessi che io facesse conclusion alcuna, come fundata su l'advisi dati per Martino, et dico me suprastarò tanto quanto possibile me serà a salvamento, et interim per tutte le vie possibile tenderò ad haver undique advisi, nam da multi puochi se può far ricolta de qualche certeza.

Circa le cose del Delfin, io me tengo verso la Signoria Soa cum tutte le dulcesse possibile et de queste cose non gle n'ho voluto dar adviso alcuno, adciochè qualche legeressa galica non me metessi in scandali. Vedo ben ch'el Duca de Bergogna et Monsignor de Crovi lo tengono in grandissime parole bone in tanto che de omnibus et singulis io non so ben che creder. Prego Dio chi me conceda gratia de poter satisfar ala vogla dela S. V., ala qual humiliter me racomando. Brocellis, die vigesima tertia martii.

Die 26, post scripta. Heri, essendo io in man de medico per dogle de coste che quasi tutto me cingono, credo per fredi preisi questo

ing thought to, I will try to confine myself to generalities and refrain from doing the smallest thing until I have a reply from you. I say also that even if Your Lordship, as a result of what I dispatched to you by Martino the courier, should commission me to make any settlement— that is, give me instructions based on the information brought by Martino—I say that I will still try to hold off as long as I safely can, and in the meanwhile by all ways possible and from all quarters I will try to gather information, for from many bits and pieces some reliable advices can be harvested.

Concerning the Dauphin, I conduct myself in my relations with him with all possible delicacy, and I have refrained from saying anything to him about what I have been told here, lest Gallic impulsiveness and imprudence put me in an impossible situation. I note, however, that the Duke of Burgundy and my lord of Croy treat the Dauphin with the greatest deference, and so what with one thing and another I really do not know what to believe. I pray that God will grant me the grace of being able to satisfy the will of Your Lordship, to whom I humbly recommend myself.

March 26, *Postscript. Yesterday as I was in the hands of a doctor because of pains in my ribs that encircle almost my entire body—the result, I believe, of a cold I caught this winter—Giacomo di Valperga came here to see me and told me that the Dauphin was with the Duke of Burgundy at Our Lady of Hals, three leagues from here, and wished to speak with me. Today therefore I went to him and was given a grand reception.*

In the course of a long conversation he told me about the capture of Bertrand, a servant of his, and one Laurentio, a servant of Your Lordship—I think it is Lorenzo de' Bernardini[4]*—who were arrested in territories that Duke John holds. However, he has written a letter about the matter and would like to believe that they will be released.*

The Dauphin then said to me, "Prospero, I once promised you to tell you everything that I learn about the Duke of Brittany. I can inform you that the Breton ambassador, who, I told you the other day,

inverno, venne qui D. Iacomo de Valperga a vedermi et dissemi ch'el Delfin era cum el Duca de Bergogna a Nostadona de Aus [sic] *qui vicino a 3 leghe et me voleva parlare. Sichè hoggi gli sum ito et m'ha fatto grande ricolta; et in longis sermonibus me disse dela presa de Bertran, suo famiglo, et de uno Laurentio de V. S., che estimo Laurentio de Berardino,*[4] *preisi sule terre del Duca Iohanne et come tamen gli havia scripto oportune et voleva creder seriano relaxati. Et doppoi me disse: Prospero, io te ho una volta promisso de dirte tutto quello sentirò del Duca de Bertagna. Io te adviso come lo suo ambassatore, che te dissi l'altro dì esser dal Re de Franza, se ne ritorna al presente dal Duca de Bertagna spaciato in questa forma ch'el Re de Franza gli ha resposto che cum sit che Italia bisogna de esser più tosto inganata che sforsata; parendogli in lo anno presente le cose de Franza non ben propicie in Italia, par al Re de Franza ch'el Duca de Bertagna se suprastia per questo anno, ma che in lo anno futuro gli serà de bone cose assai et che tunc meglo se potrà fare. Io rengratiai el Delfin et lo interrogai se in queste speranse, che dava el Re, fussi mai la opinione de pace dala Signoria Soa al Re. Il che feci per descalcar più a fundo deli ragionamenti de questi dì, repetendo a Sua Signoria quelle raxone che gli dissi a questi dì, per le quale per suo honor et bene se ha da far concepto dela inteligentia et liga con V. S. più tosto che de attender a vani tituli et designi, che se devisano de qua* etc.. *La Signoria Soa me feci questa resposta che, provedendosi per la S. V. al fatto de D. Iacomo de Valperga, la qual cosa seria una honestation soa, a piè de tanti parenti et amici che dano contra V. S., omnino et deliberatamenti disponeva de servarmi la promessa et fermar la liga, ut scripsi; et che quando ben* [fusse] *d'acordio con el Re de Franza et el Re volessi che lui fussi averso, tamen havia pensato lo modo de esser in secreto et effecto de bona liga con V. S., dela quale el se ne farà concepto che di padre, et che di questo io non dubiti.*

Quantum vero pertinet ala pace dal Re de Franza ala Signoria Soa, el me afferma in primis che s'el Re acerterà el Duca de Bergogna[d] *de*

---

d. C. C. reads: Delfin.

was at the French court, has now returned to the Duke of Brittany with this report of his mission: The King of France told him that, since in Italy guile works better than force and since he does not think that French affairs in Italy are going to prosper this year, he believes that the Duke of Brittany should do nothing this year, but in the year following the situation will be much more favorable for the Duke and then more can be accomplished." I thanked the Dauphin and asked him if, in this hope that the King of France held out to the Duke, there might have been the thought of peace between his lordship and the King.

I said this in order to probe more deeply into what the Dauphin had recently said to me. I also repeated what I had recently told him, namely that for his honor and his own interest he would do better to consider an understanding and league with Your Lordship than to pay attention to the empty schemes and designs that are hatched in these parts, etc.

His lordship made me this reply: if Your Lordship would make due provision for Giacomo di Valperga, which act would serve to preserve the Dauphin's honor in the eyes of those relatives and friends who are opposed to Your Lordship, then he was entirely and firmly prepared to keep his promise to me and conclude the league, as I previously wrote; and if indeed he made an accord with the King his father and the King wished him to oppose the Duke of Milan, he has thought of a way of still remaining in secret but effective alliance with Your Lordship which alliance, I may be sure, will mean more to him than his father will.

Concerning the peace between himself and his father, the Dauphin affirmed, in the first place, that if the King of France would assure the Duke of Burgundy of a good peace, and would give him, the Dauphin, control of Savoy and the lordship of Dauphiné and regions beyond, he would make the accord. Otherwise, never. Concerning Genoa he said nothing this time, and I am almost inclined to think that he would just as soon you had it as he had it.

I have, in this connection, some information, which could very

*bona pace et gli dà lo governo del Stato del Duca de Savoya et regnum
ultra Delphinatum, el se contenterà. Aliter nunquam. Et de Zenoa non
me disse altro et quasi me par comprhender ch'el non seria manco contento ch'el la fussi in V. S., come in Sua Signoria. Io ho perciò qualche
adviso et non sum fuori de opinione, tamen non lo acerto che tutta la
differentia dal Delfin al Re de Franza resti in che el Delfin vada una
volta dal Re, la qual cosa el Delfin fin a qui non monstra voler far,
etiam s'el celo ruinasse; et tra questo et forse qualche desturbetto che
dà el Duca de Bergogna, forse non venirà a seguir l'acordio, lo qual non
seguendo et restassi identidem doppoi el Delfin in qualche scandalo chi
scopiassi dal Duca de Bergogna a lui, io dubitaria in tale caso che el
Delfin non s'areattacasse ad acceptar aiuti, che in la prima forma de
liga se sporgevano per parte de V. S.. Sichè io non so voltar questo
malato in lato che non dogla; nam s'el se acorda cum el Re de Franza*
ut supra, *el ven più vicin che non par al mio pocho intellecto faci per
nui, benchè el dice el Delfin ni bene verso la V. S.; s'el resta desfavorevel
dal canto del Re et del Duca de Bergogna, el vorà forse più cose in liga
ch'el non havia acceptato prima; et sia che si vogli altramenti non
aquistandolo V. S., el me par che hariamo perduto qualche cosa et tanto
più quanto se altri se lo attrahesse. Questi sonno li dubii in che io con-
verso et vedo ben che mi può esser obiectato tropo timidità et de scon-
forti che io do; ma Signor mio, tra quello che io sento et quello che io
vedo et la zelosia che ho del ben de V. S., benchè io non so quanto V. S.
reputi al suo Stato pertener le pratiche de qua, doppoi che V. S. m'ha
posto in questa cura, a me par mio officio scriver il tutto et bona costuma al ben consiglar proponer il peio chi possi advenir cum ciò sia che,
consiglato lo maior periculo, lo resto resta in guadagno.*

*Insuper me disse el Delfin ch'el Duca de Bertagna hé malato de una
fistula in la gamba et de una altra se ne dubita in la testa;*[5] *et che
quanto ale speranse che gli dà el Re de Franza per lo anno futuro, ch'el
crede sia la opinione de meglori fatti del Duca Iohanne et dela Regina
de Anglia.*

Ceterum Gascon non me aiuta in aliquo, excusandosi ch'el Delfin

well be true but I do not guarantee it—namely, that the entire difference between the Dauphin and the King of France lies in the fact that the King wants the Dauphin to come to him at least for one visit and the Dauphin up to now appears unwilling to do so though the heavens fall. Between this and some objection that the Duke of Burgundy may be making to the accord, it will perhaps come to nothing. Should that accord not be concluded and if I continued to remain here until some scandalous explosion occurred in the relations of the Dauphin and the Duke of Burgundy, I would fear, in that case, that the Dauphin might want to accept the kinds of aid that in the first form of the treaty were offered by Your Lordship.

In sum I don't know how to turn this patient to the side that does not ache; for if the Dauphin accords with the King of France, as above, it does not seem, to my poor intellect, that he will maintain his alliance with us, although he says he will do so. If, on the other hand, he remains at odds with the King of France and has trouble with the Duke of Burgundy he will perhaps demand greater guarantees in the treaty than he required before; yet, no matter what happens, if Your Lordship does not secure an alliance with him, it seems to me that we have lost something, and so much the more if he is won over by others.

These are the doubts and fears that preoccupy me, though it can be objected that I am too timid and that I look on the bad side of things. However, my lord, what with what I learn and what I see and my jealous concern for Your Lordship's welfare—though I do not know how important Your Lordship considers negotiations here—since Your Lordship had given me this mission, I think it my duty to write everything and I think it a good usage in offering counsel to put forward the worst that can happen because when one has pointed out the most dangerous possibility, whatever occurs that it is not so bad as that represents so much profit.

In addition, the Dauphin told me that the Duke of Brittany is suffering from a fistula in the leg—and he has no doubt that the Duke has another in the head.[5] As to the hope that the King holds out to the

*gli ha commesso ch'el non se impaci de questa cosa; et per quello m'hé
ditto, volendosi excusar cum el Delfin de quello de che l'era inculpato
per vostro* [respecto], *el ha messo a campo la copia de quella benedeta
scritta ch'el fece dar a V. S.,*[6] *la qual cosa se l'ha aitato lui, non iuva già
a quello perché io sum qui. Tamen, Signor mio, per quello che io so et
posso non mi manco de bono animo, et non obstantibus suprascriptis,
sum de bona vogla quanto vedo esser pertinente al fatto dela S. V., ala
quale humiliter me racomando. Brocellis,* ut supra.

Magnifico Meser Cicco,[e] *io prego la Magnificencia Vostra qui vogli
leger questa al Signore, da solo a solo, sensa che nè el Conte Gasparo nè
Piero de Pusterla n'habian notitia; l'un perch'el non mi scandalisasse,
perchè me ama como sapiti; l'altro perchè non me intendubene* [sic] *et
el Signore debe voler che la pura fede sia secura in casa dela Sua Signoria. Dico questo per quanto toca li desfavori dal Delfin. Prosper,
manu propria.*

*In questa festa dela Tueson sarà da bona banda che se sia per far
due vel tre grande deliberatione secrete, et fin a chi non so quid; ma
non* [sic] *el Duca de Bergogna hé un fiume profundo et qui curre
surdo. Penso ch'el pensi d'acautelarsi in qualche modo più ch'el potrà
deli supraventi del Re de Franza. Io starò sul aviso et de tuto adviserò el
Signore. Idem Prosper.*

---

e. This note to Cicco Simonetta is missing in the C. C.

Duke for the coming year, the Dauphin believes it is based on the King's expectation that the affairs of Duke John and of the Queen of England will go better.

For the rest, Gaston [du Lyon] *gives me no help at all, offering as his excuse that the Dauphin has ordered him not to meddle with the Valperga negotiations; and from what he has said to me, in an attempt to exculpate himself in the Dauphin's eyes from the charges of being too favorable to you, he has put in the field a copy of that blessed memorandum that he drew up for Your Lordship,⁸ which document, if it has helped him in the past, no longer aids him because I am here.*

Nevertheless, my lord, to the best of my ability I will keep up my spirits, and, despite what I wrote above, I will do with good will whatever I see to be useful for forwarding the affairs of Your Lordship, to whom I humbly recommend myself. Brussels, as above.

Magnificent Messer Cicco, I beg Your Magnificence to read this to the Duke when you are alone with him and to see that neither Count Gaspare [da Vimercate] *nor Piero da Pusterla have any knowledge of it—the one, so that he cannot make trouble for me, for you know how much he loves me; the other, because he does not wish me well; and the Duke should want loyalty such as mine to be protected in his household. I say this on account of the Dauphin's disfavor* [which I have incurred because of "leaks" from Milan]. *Prospero in his own hand.*

For this feast of the Toison d'Or there will be a goodly assemblage; whether it is being held in order to make, in secret, two or three great decisions, I do not know. However, the Duke of Burgundy is a deep river that now holds hidden undercurrents. I think that he is seeking the best possible way of insuring himself against some attack by the King of France. I will remain on the alert and report to the Duke of Milan everything I learn. Prospero.

HISTORICAL NOTES

1. These representations concerned the plight of Valperga and the arrears in dowry payments owed by the Duke to the Dauphin [see doc. 55, n. 4, p. 18 and doc. 59, n. 5, p. 58.

2. St. Omer is twenty-four miles southeast of Calais.

3. Jean, Duke of Clèves; Jean of Burgundy, Count d'Estampes; Antoine, called the Grand Bastard of Burgundy, most famous of the Duke's numerous illegitimate children.

4. Bertrand: unable to identify him; Laurentio: probably Lorenzo de' Bernardini de Orvieto, appointed (1457) *Podestà* and Castellan of San Colombano [Santoro, 404, 633].

5. The Dauphin's irony was apparently lost on Prospero.

6. See the Memorandum of Gaston, Nov. 30, 1460, doc. 57, pp. 27–37.

On the 14th of this month I wrote to Your Excellency about my coming here to pay a visit on your behalf to this most illustrious prince, the Duke of Burgundy. I think it appropriate, and indeed called for, for me to inform you by a special letter about the reception I was given.

On the 16th I was conducted immediately after the Duke had dined—which was at the first hour of night—into the presence of his lordship. In my greeting to the Duke I performed those parts of my mission which, I thought, were fitting for the occasion, in accordance with Your Lordship's instructions.

The Duke in his reply spoke as benignly and admiringly about Your Excellency as could be expressed, always calling you his "good cousin of Milan" etc.,[1] thanking you for the daily courtesies his men receive in Milan, and in return offering his services to Your Excellency and his good offices to me for anything I might want. Then the collation was brought and I was told that I should partake of it since it is regarded here as a courtesy custom.[2]

The following day I was with my lord Antoine [of Croy, Count of Porcien], who made me great offers of service and much lamented that his brother Jean [of Croy, lord of Chimay] was not present to hear news of Your Lordship, Jean a few days before having gone as ducal ambassador to the King of France. He made an appointment with me

86·PROSPERO DA CAMOGLI *to the*

DUKE OF MILAN

Francia, cart. 525. Orig.

Ali 14 del presente scripsi a V. Ex.tia del mio esser venuto qui a visitar per parte de quella questo Ill.mo Principe. Doppoi de quello hé seguito m'hé paruto conveniente et debito mio advisarla per particolare littera dela coglensa m'hé stato fatto. Ali 16 io fui conducto statim, poso il desnar de la S.ria Sua, hoc est ad una hora de nocte, al conspecto de Sua S.ria, ala quale feci quelle parte dela ambassiata che me parsero convenir a quanto m'havia imposto V. Ex.tia; ala quale Sua S.ria rispose tanto benignamente et honorevolmente verso la Ex.tia V. quanto dir se potessi, sempre in la denomination de V. Ex.tia dicendovi et appellandovi suo bon cusin de Milan[1] etc., rengratiando V. Ex.tia de le quottidiane cortesie che se fan in le terre de V. Ex.tia ali suoi, et per contra offerendosi a V. Ex.tia et a me facendo ogni oblatione etc.. Et cossì fu portato la collatione et mi fu ditto che io faresse collatione, perché cossì hé costuma de questo Ill.mo Principe in le honoratione tale.[2] L'undeman doppoi io fui cum Monsignor de Crovi, il quale me fece grande offerte et dolsesi assai ch'el Magnifico D. Iohanne, suo fratello, non fussi qui per intender de novelle de V. S.ria, il qual Messer Iohanne puochi dì avanti era andato ambassator de questo Ill.mo S.re al Rei. Doppoi conclude di esser l'indeman in li ragionamenti necessari meco per sua satisfactione, come quello chi volunteri ragiona de V. Ex.tia, et cossì me fece dir che io dovessi andar a disnar cum Sua S.ria et cossì feci. In lo

to have a conversation next day concerning matters he wanted to hear about, explaining that he was always happy to talk about Your Excellency, and he sent me an invitation to dinner, which I accepted.

At the dinner there were eight of the principal knights and lords who are at this moment at the Duke's court, four of whom wear the livery of the Order of the Golden Fleece. Membership in this Order, as I explain below, is counted in this country the highest honor. In the course of the dinner some ten or twelve gentlemen approached the board, men who, in passing through Milanese territory at various times, had been received, as they express it, "ala ducale sforsescha" [i.e. in the magnificent style for which the Sforza Duke is renowned]. They gave thanks and the highest praise to Your Excellency, and offered me anything I could ask for, mentioning money and horses, if ever I, running into difficulties so far from home, should be in need.

I gave them appropriate thanks and begged them to take the treatment Your Excellency had given them as an expression of his esteem even though—whether for our not being familiar with Burgundian etiquette or not having had sufficient notice of their arrival—they had not been received as worthily, in the household and the territories of Your Excellency, as the Duke of Burgundy's men deserve to be.

There then followed a long and excellent discussion of the magnanimity, liberality, and incomparable genius of Your Excellency, in the course of which numerous gentlemen had much to say. The Marshal of Burgundy questioned me at length about your modes of government and personal demeanor both in peace and war, and he listened with pleasure to my replies, which, if they were not what they should have been, were at least to the height of the capacity that God has granted me. This conversation gave me great comfort and aid, both because of the talk about Your Excellency and also for providing me with a little relaxation in the whirlwind of courses throughout this lengthy dinner, which is the custom here.

After dinner my lord of Croy took me aside and spoke to me at length, inquiring after the good health and well being of Your Excel-

qual disnar eran 8 li principali Cavaleri et S.ri, chi sian al presente in questa Curia, et inter cetera 4 de quelli che portan la leverea dela Tueson, chi hé, come scrivo qui de sutto, in questo paese grande sublimità; et lì supra tavola vennero diversi gentilhomini circa X vel XII, quali in diversi tempi, passando per le terre de V. Ex.tia sonno stati recepiuti, secondo che dicono, ala ducale sforsescha; pertanto rengratiando et laudandosi summamente de V. Ex.tia, me fecero offerta de ogni cosa, specificando argento et cavalli, se forsi per esser venuto a tempi incommodi et in paese lontano, mi bisognava cosa alcuna. Li quali io rengratiai convenienter, pregandoli che volessero prender in grado li trattamenti de V. Ex.tia se o per non saper noi cossì de là come se sa di qua, o per non esser tutta la piena noticia de loro esser, non fussero stati recepiuti cossì degnamenti come meritan quelli de questo Ill.mo Principe in casa et paese de V. Ex.tia. Et cossì se intratté in longhi et excellenti ragionamenti dela magnanimità et liberalità, incomparabile virtute de V. Ex.tia, dicendosi circa ciò da uni et un altri multe predicatione; et fui assai interrogato da Monsignor lo Marescalco de Bergogna, qui era inter dicti, del stato et contegni de V. Ex.tia, si in guerra come in pace; et li piaque audir de quello che io gli resposi se non secundo il merito, almanco secundo Dio me amaistra; lo qual predicamento a me fu de grande consolatione et sucurso, sì per parlar de V. Ex.tia, sì etiam per haver qualche passatempo in tante furie de piatti et diuturnità de prandio, il qual fu al modo de qua etc.

Post prandium el ditto Monsignor de Crovi me ridusse da parte et me ragionò assai, demandandomi de la bona sanità et prosperità de V. Ex.tia et dela Ill.ma Madona, lo Ill. S. Conte Galeaz et tutti li illustri figloli de V. Ex.tia, subinde del stato de Italia et dele cose de qua et de Angliterra, confortandomi ymo strengendomi che io volessi dimorar de qua, havendo a star in lo paese, et che lo Ill.mo S. Duca me faria monstrar le artiglerie che ha Sua Ex.tia a Lilla, quale sonno per carri mille ducento in più, adcioché io ne possessi [sic] far relatione a V. Ex.tia, chi ha il nome dela guerra et dela pace; et cossì se altra cosa degna serà de qua, de che possa esser grato a V. Ex.tia haver noticia, fa-

lency, my lady the Duchess, Count Galeazzo and all the other illustrious sons of Your Excellency, then asking about the situation in Italy and speaking of affairs here and in England. He constantly urged me to stay here, since I had to remain in the country; and he promised that the Duke would arrange for me to inspect his artillery park at Lille, where he has 1,200 and more ordinance wagons, so that I could send an account of it to Your Excellency, who bears the palm in war and peace. My lord of Croy likewise said that there might be other things here about which Your Lordship would be pleased to have notice. He concluded that if, on behalf of Your Excellency or to aid me, there will be anything he can do, I should by all means let him know, because of the deservings of Your Excellency both in respect to the supreme honors paid to the Duke of Clèves and the gift of his brother's life, not so much preserved as actually restored.[3] To these statements I made what reply seemed to be fitting.

There is little news here except that the Duke of Burgundy is leaving Brussels for a town of his called St. Omer, which is near the coast of Flanders and six leagues from Calais, where he has decided to hold the splendid festival of the Golden Fleece. The people of Brussels sought to persuade him to hold the festival here and guaranteed to give him 20,-000 Rhenish florins and to furnish him with a great hall, which they are erecting in time for the meeting. However, I believe that because of the advantages of the situation of St. Omer, which is more convenient for the Princes of the Golden Fleece, who have to be at the ceremony, the Duke decided to leave Brussels and so left here on March 23 to keep Easter at Ghent, then go to Bruges, and thence to St. Omer.

The Order of the Golden Fleece, as I believe Your Excellency is informed, has a device of a golden fleece, which about thirty princes and dignitaries wear, some of them French and some Burgundian. Among the French are the Duke of Orléans and certain others. The members of the Order, leagued in a sort of brotherhood, assemble from time to time to commemorate the deceased members, to elect new ones, and to take note of what is needed for the conservation of the Order.

cendomi questa desinentia che se per V. Ex.tia o per alcun mio bisogno accadeva cosa alcuna a farsi per Sua S.ria, io non me ne ritenesse per nulla celato a Sua S.ria, per merito dela Ex.tia V. et per li honori supremi fatti alo Ill.mo S. Duca de Cleve, et per lo beneficio dela vita non tanto conservata, quanto restituita a suo fratello.[3] Ali quali ragionamenti io feci quelle resposte me parsero digne et conveniente.

De le novelle de questo paese gli hé puocho, excepto che quello Ill.mo S.re va de qui ad una sua terra, chi si domanda San Thomer verso le Marine de Flandria, presso a Cales a 6 lenche [sic], unde se hé deliberato de tener la festa solenne dela Tueson. Questo populo lo ha cercato de retener a far ditta festa qui, et se obligarano a dargli fiorini Rheni XX milia et fornirgli una sala grande che gli fa questa comunità dentro dala festa; tamen credo per la opportunità del sito dela terra chi é più consa ali Principi dela Tueson, che han ad esser a ditte cerimonie, Sua S.ria se hé deliberata de partir et cossì partitte de qua ali 23 del presente et farà le feste de Pasca a Gant, deinde irà a Brugs, deinde a San Thomer. La Tueson, come credo V. Ex.tia esser informata, hé una liverea del aureum vellus, che portano circa XXX^{ta} Principi et principali de questo paese tra Francia et qui, inter li quali de Francia gli hé lo Ill. S. Duca de Orliens et certi altri, li quali de ditta liverea han come liga ad idem velle et nolle, et de tempo in tempo convengono insieme a far memoria deli defuncti et suplir de altri, et rememorar quello bisogna ala conservation de tal Ordine. Lo prefato Ill. S. Duca de Orliens, per quello sento, non gli venirà per lo presente personaliter et ha havuto una sententia in lo Consiglo de Paris contra de Sua S.ria de uno Contato, chi hé de le bone cose havessi Sua S.ria; vero hé che chi debe recuperar lo Contato ha da pagargli certa non picola quantità de argento.[4] Credo questo Ill.mo Principe demorerà ala ditta terra de Sant Homer uno pecio per cambiar aere.

De Angliterra credo haver scritto a V. Ex.tia continuamenti li processi de quelle straniesse; et ali 6 del presente et doppoi ali 14 advisai V. Ex.tia per la via de Brugs come se diceva ch'el Rei de Angliterra havia renunciato la corona in lo figlolo, quamvis se dice che Sua M.tà

The Duke of Orléans, from what I hear, will not be present at this coming meeting. He has obtained a judgment in the Parlement of Paris against the Duke of Burgundy concerning a county, one of the Duke's prized possessions. True it is that anyone who expects to regain the county will have to pay the Duke no small amount of money.[4] I believe the Duke will remain a little while at St. Omer for the change of air.

Concerning England, I believe I have written to Your Excellency about the shifts in fortune and the strange happenings there. On March 6 and then on the 14th I sent word to Your Excellency by way of Bruges that it was being said that the King of England had abdicated in favor of his son—although it is reported that at a previous time the King had remarked that the boy must be a son of the Holy Ghost, etc., but these are perhaps the words of violent partisans, such as are now to be found in England.[5] I also sent the news that the Londoners, the most important people in the island, and others, along with certain lords, moved by indignation [against the Lancastrians], had created a new King, Edward [IV], son of the Duke of York, formerly the Earl of March. Afterwards, it was widely reported that he had indeed been chosen new King by princes and people in London. According to the most recent letters received, this King has accepted the scepter, the staff of royalty, and all the other regal appurtenances except the holy oil and the crowning, which he has postponed until he has got rid of the other king, brought peace again to the realm, and, among other things, exacted revenge for the murder of his father and of so many knights and lords who were recently killed. To accomplish this, the Earl of Warwick left London, according to the latest word, with some 12,000 armed men to join with King Edward, who had gone into the country to raise thousands of troops more for the battle with the King and Queen, which battle some say he is seeking of his own will; others say, out of necessity.

As is usual with great matters that affect many, conflicting things are being said. According to those who report the claims of Edward and Warwick, Edward's advantages are great: partly because of the exten-

alias habia ditto che conven ch'el sii figlolo del Spirito Santo etc.; le quali, forse, sonno parole de vulgi furiati, come al presente sonno in quella insula.[5] Et scripsi come se haveva che altri populi et Londres, capo de li populi dela insula, insieme con alcuni altri S.ri, indignati, haviano creato novo Rei Edoardo, figlolo de quel Ill. S. Duca de Yorch, quale si appellava Monsignor de la Marchia, il quale per quello si ha doppoi undique hé pur cossì, come si dice, electo novo Rei da Principi et populi in Londres; et per le ultime littere se han, Sua S.ria havia acceptato lo sceptro, bachetta regale et tutte le altre cerimonie, excepto la unctione et la corona, dale quale se hé suspeso fin a tanto che haby anullato l'altro Rei, et spianato in bon pacifico la insula et lo Regno, et inter cetera fatto le debite unce dela occision del padre et tanti Cavaleri et S.ri che furon trucidati questi dì; et per questo se dice che ultimamenti lo Ill. Conte de Varruych era usito de Londres cum homini armati da X^m in XII^m per retrovarsi cum lo ditto Edoardo novo Rei, il quale era per lo paese adunando miglara de gente per andar ala iornata, hoc est ala bataglia contra la Regina et lo Rei, chi dice per disposition propria, chi dice per necessità. Li parlari sonno, come accade in le cose commune et grande, diversi et secundo la passione. Chi fa bona la ragion de Edoardo et Varruich dice cossì che li favori de Edoardo sonno grandi sì per la Signoria grande ch'el ha in la insula et in Yrlanda, sì per le iniurie che gli ha fatto crudelmenti la parte dela Regina, sì etiam per Varruich et Londres che hé tutta inclinata in la parte de ditto Rei novo Edoardo et Varruich, la qual per esser richissima et la più opulenta cità de Cristiani rende le parte, unde ella inclina, molto favorabile [sic]; al che etiam se adiunge la bona opinion che hé del temperamento et moderation de dicti S.ri Edoardo et Varruich. Chi volta carta dice che la Regina hé prudentissima et stando su la diffesa cum gente assai, come se dice che ha, redurà le cose al iugero et straquerà questi impeti de populi, quali quando vederan non esser sul camin del pacifico, facilmenti veneran a prender altro partito cum ciò sia che la propria natura deli populi, maxime liberi, hé de non lassiarsi mai tanto amalar che non possino dar una volta; ma sia la cosa come si vogli, come per altre ut supra scripsi a

sive lordship he exercises in England and in Ireland; partly because of the wrongs cruelly inflicted on him by the Queen's party; and also partly because of Warwick and because of London, which is entirely devoted to the cause of King Edward and Warwick, and the fact that it is the richest and most opulent city in Christendom gives the party whom it favors a tremendous advantage. There must be added the good opinion that prevails of King Edward's and Warwick's moderation. On the other hand, those who favor the Queen say that she is acting most prudently and that by remaining on the defensive with a very large army, as it is said she has, she will contain and then exhaust the attacks of the [Yorkist] people's army, who, when they see that they are not on the road to peace, will quickly come to take the other part, since it is the nature of the common people, especially when they are free, never to let things get so bad that they cannot shift their loyalties. In any case, as I have previously written to Your Excellency, the game is now reduced, since it has been played so long and hotly, to but a few moves and must shortly be won by one side or the other.

Most clement lord, what we have heard here of the inhumanity and cruelty used in this civil war passes belief. Setting aside the thousands who have killed each other with such mad fury that neither age nor rank nor princely station can save a man from the swords of the victors, within London itself there was a citizen who, going to the Mayor, chief magistrate of the city, succeeded in securing the condemnation of a man who had been arrested on mere suspicion, and this prisoner, without trial or judicial sentence, was beheaded and his head borne by the hair to his door and set above it, as is done with game. I was told this by a trustworthy knight who himself saw that deed and many other incredible acts of violence. Whoever wins then, if God does not intervene it is believed that terrible barbarities will be committed. May God choose the better side.

The legate [Francesco Coppini], as I wrote to Your Excellency, has left England after being in extreme danger from both sides. The reason, it is said, is that he promised Warwick to go to the field of battle

V. Ex.tia, lo iocho per essere stato longo et fervente hé reducto a puochi scacchi, et bisogna si metti in brevi a l'una parte o a l'altra.

El seria, clementissimo S.re, una cosa supra fede chi recitasse de quello havemo de veduta qua de la inumanità et crudelità se usa in quelle controversie. Lassiamo andar le miglara chi se estingueno cum tanta rabia, che non hé chi per età o dignità o principato si possi salvar da la victoria de quelli ferri, ma etiam dentro da Londres proprio hé stato Burgese, chi hé andato dal Mere, hoc est magistrato dela cità, unde se formava processo contra de uno preiso per suspicione et piglato dicto pregione sensa aspectar processo né sententia iudiciale, et lì taglatogli il collo et portato la testa per li capelli a plantarla su la porta sua, come se fa de le salvadisine. Questo m'ha referto Cavaler degno de fede, chi se trovatte là al acto et multe altre feritate incredibile; siché sia vencitor chi si vogli, se Dio non gli metti la mano, credessi che gli seran de le barbaresche assai: Dio elega il meglo.

Lo Legato, come scripsi a V. Ex.tia, hé partito de là et stato in extremo periculo da l'una parte et da l'altra. La cagion, se dice, hé perché havia promisso a Varruich de andar in campo et excomunicar li inimici, et dar la benedictione a li seguaci de Varruich; et vedendo el mal tempo dela possansa de la Regina, non sentendosi bene, non andò. Del che Varruich remase mal contento et lui trette partito; et essendo ià in nave, in terra era venuto gente a cherirlo, et se ne venne de qua, unde de haver sapiuto ben fugir in tempore opportuno, el se ne relegra assai. Io non lo ho adhuc veduto; s'el serà a Brugs, spero de vederlo queste feste de Pasca et di quanto intenderò più ultra adviserò V. Ex.tia.

Ceterum el m'hé dato qui in compagnia il M.co Francisco, Marchese da Este, figlolo del quondam Ill. S. Leonello, il qual in vero me par de bon proposito et de vigile sentimento; et per quello me dice, hé intentionato in brevi de dar una volta fin in lo paese verso Ferrara, et dice venirà a visitar la Ex.tia V., dela quale el se lauda quottidie summamenti, et ad essa io humiliter me racomando.

and excommunicate the enemies of the Yorkists and give his blessing to Warwick's adherents, but sensing that the Queen's power made the climate unfavorable for this enterprise, and not feeling well, he did not go. Warwick being angered by his refusal, the legate decided to leave the country. Even as his ship was putting to sea, men sent to seize him reached the harbor. Having arrived in these parts, he rejoices indeed at having had the sense to flee at the right moment. I have not yet seen him; if he will be at Bruges I hope to see him at Eastertime, and I will further inform Your Excellency of what I learn.

For the rest, I have here been given for company the Magnificent Francisco, Marquess of Este, son of the late Marquess Leonello, who in truth seems to me to have good judgment and an alert mind; and, from what he tells me, he intends shortly to make some changes in regard to Ferrara, and he says he will come to visit Your Excellency, whose praises he sings daily, and to whom I humbly recommend myself.

HISTORICAL NOTES

1. "Cousin" only in the sense that Sforza's wife, Bianca Maria, illegitimate daughter of Filippo Maria Visconti, the previous Duke of Milan, was the niece of Valentina Visconti, wife of Louis, Duke of Orléans, second cousin of the Duke of Burgundy.

2. A collation of wine, spices, and wafers was customarily served to signify the conclusion of the first ceremonious audience granted an ambassador [see, for example, Philippe de Commynes, *Mémoires,* ed. by B. de Mandrot, 2 vols., (Paris, 1901), I, 9].

236

3. See Vol. I, doc. 48, n. 2, p. 342.

4. The county was one that Orléans had pledged to the Duke of Burgundy in return for the Duke's contributions to the ransom Orléans paid the English in 1440, in order to secure his liberty.

5. Yorkist propaganda, as Prospero suspected, had insinuated that Margaret of Anjou's son Edward, Prince of Wales (1453–71) was not sired by Henry VI—the King's frail, monklike nature providing some color for the rumor.

By Bertram, a servant of the Dauphin, I today received a letter of Your Lordship of the last of February. Bertram did not arrive sooner because he and his companions, on account of their connection with Your Lordship, were detained and maltreated by officials in *Duke John's* territories. I herewith make reply to that letter.

[Prospero summarizes what he has written in previous missives: the Dauphin's demands for Valperga and his ordering G. du Lyon not to meddle with the matter; bad relations between the Duke of Burgundy and the King of France; the Dauphin's negotiations with his father and their effect upon the Duke of Burgundy; Prospero's reception by the Duke of Burgundy and the Duke's decision to hold the assembly of the Golden Fleece at St. Omer; the expectation of a final, bloody resolution of Yorkist-Lancastrian strife; the vain hopes of the Duke of Brittany and the Dauphin's attitude toward that Duke; concerning the Empire, the unpopularity of Frederick III and the belief that the Duke of Burgundy, if he wished, could secure the imperial diadem; news that the Dauphin's secretary, Baude Meurin, has been well received at Florence and Rome; letters from the Montferrats and other sources in Italy discounting Sforza's sincerity in negotiating with the Dauphin; Prospero's estimate of Valperga's character.]

For the rest, I eagerly await news from hour to hour that Genoa will follow the way of the Cremonese[1] for it seems to me that such an

87·PROSPERO DA CAMOGLI *to the*

DUKE OF MILAN

Francia, cart. 525. Orig.

Per Betram, famiglo del *Delfin,* a questo dì ho recepiuto una littera dela S. V. de ultimo februarii et non più tosto per esser stato epso et li compagni, come cose de V. S., destenuti et mal tractati dali officiali del *Duca Iohanne* in le terre sue. Respondo per questa ala parte de quella. [omitted][a]

Ceterum io attendo cum desiderio tutto el dì che del Stato de Zenoa se adimpisca lo iudicio del Cremonese,[1] perché el me par che facia per V. S. mettersi in securo da quello canto; nam posto in bon termino lo Stato del Re Ferrando, unde doppoi V. S. ha questo Delfin et se reconcilia in Franza, el me par che per merito et virtù et per bona opera la S. V. deba esser commendata per tutto'l [sic] mondo per veramenti prudentissima. Siché prego Dio me ne conceda la consolatione che aspecto. Nam quantumque el Delfin sia sticioso cum ognuno per la condicione che hé al presente, pur facendo la S. V. cosa perché io gli possi far intender ch'el ha da contentarsi etc., io spero che l'harimo al designo de V. S..

Del ocello mandato et del desiderio ha V. Ex.tia in far cosa grata etc., scuserò in tempore opportuno. Lunedì, se a Dio piacerà, irò ad Brugs et lì attenderò la resposta de V. Ex.tia, ala quale humiliter me racomando.

---

a. For the contents of the omitted passages, see the translation.

event will make for Your Lordship's security in that quarter. For if King Ferrante's position becomes stabilized and then Your Lordship secures the Dauphin and is reconciled with the French, I think that for merit and genius and high accomplishment Your Lordship should be commended by the whole world as being truly the most politic of men. I therefore pray God to concede me the joyful news that I am looking for. For although the Dauphin is tetchy with everyone on account of his present situation, if Your Lordship will make him an offer which I can show him to be one he should settle for, I hope that we will have him as Your Lordship plans.

Concerning the falcon that was sent and Your Excellency's desire to do something better than that to please the Dauphin etc., I will make the due excuses at an opportune moment. Monday, God willing, I will go to Bruges and will there await the reply of Your Excellency, to whom I humbly recommend myself.

Given as above.

I beg Your Excellency that, as regards what I write *in disfavor of the Dauphin and in blame of the Marquess of Montferrat and Lord Guglielmo, you not allow others to know it;* and indeed Your Excellency should desire this secrecy so that *your faithful servant does not suffer for reporting the truth*—and I am not moved to ask this without legitimate cause. And so I recommend myself to Your Excellency. Given as in the letter.

HISTORICAL NOTE

1. Prospero is here expressing the hope that, following the revolt of Genoa on March 9, 1461 [see doc. 89, n. 1, p. 250], Sforza would be able to wrestle control of the city from the French, just as he had recaptured Cremona and its territory from the Venetians in the autumn of 1453.

Data ut supra.

Io supplico a V. Ex.tia che de quanto perten a quello che scrivo *in desfavor del Delfin et in carico del Marchese de Monferrato et lo Signor Gulielmo, Ella non vogli che altri lo sapia;* et debe voler il simile V. Ex.tia adcioché *la pura fidelità del servitor si conservi;* et non me ne movo sensa legitima causa, et cossì me racomando a V. Ex.tia. Data ut in litteris.

I believe that Your Excellency has, despite the claims of the Pallavicino,[1] understood the justice and honesty of my position; and there
still remains to be received from them about seven hundred pounds,
most of it spent on food and lodging and paid for some of them.

When Your Excellency sent me here the first time, I begged you
kindly to provide for my payment and so the Magnificent Cicco told
me to go to Messer Lorenzo,[2] who would make the necessary provision
etc. I returned to Milan and found nothing done. Similarly, for this
mission I made the same request, and again I was told that Messer
Lorenzo handles matters by attending to his own business and leaving
mine aside, which treatment, beyond the fact that it is not, I may say,
honest, I do not believe I merit at his hands since I was the main promoter of his appointment. Therefore remembering the inherent benignity of Your Excellency, who never fails to protect his servants, and
seeing myself here at the ends of the earth on a mission Your
Excellency has been good enough to intrust to me, I do not think myself in a lower station than if I were present there. Hence I beg Your
Excellency kindly to see to it that I am not given such unmerited
blow. The way of preventing it is simple: let orders be given to Messer
Lorenzo, and if necessary to Messer Girrardo, my substitute, and confirmed by Your Excellency, that no proceedings be taken in the actions

88 · PROSPERO DA CAMOGLI *to the*

DUKE OF MILAN

Francia, cart. 525. Orig.

Io credo che la Ex.tia V. habbi in tante disputatione Palavicine[1] inteso a chiaro la mia iusticia et honestà, et restando a recever da loro circa lire VII cento, la maior parte spese su le hostarie et pagate per alcuni de loro. Quando V. Ex.tia me mandò de qua la prima volta, io supplicai a quella che ella si dignasse de far proveder al mio pagamento; et cossì me disse il M.co D. Cicho che io andassi a Messer Laurentio,[2] chi provederia necessariamenti etc. Ritornai a Milano et trovai nihil factum. Similementi in questa ultima partensa supplicai, et similement me fu ditto ch'el dicto Messer Laurentio provederia. Hora intendo che epso Messer Laurentio procede in le cose et attende al fatto suo et lassia il mio da canto. La qual cosa, ultra che cum supportation non hé honesta, io non credo meritarlo da lui per esser stato principal promotor de la denomination de lui. Per il che, ricordandomi dela bona et naturale benignità de V. Ex.tia, quale ala protection de suoi servitori non mancha in aliquo, et vedendomi qui in queste ultime parte del mondo a servicii de li quali epsa Ex.tia V. se hé dignata darme cura, non reputo esserne in peior grado come se io fussi presente là. Pertanto supplico a V. Ex.tia che ella si digne che io non receva tal botta non meritandola. Et lo modo hé apto, silicet [sic] che sii imposto ad epso Messer Laurentio et cossì, se bisogna, a messer Guirardo, mio substituto et confirmato da la Ex.tia V., che non si proceda in le cause che non sia fatto il mio pagamento de

until I be paid what I have proved I am owed! and if, concerning the remaining sums that I claim to have spent—as my notary knows and the others that have handled the accounts—anybody wishes to raise doubts, at least let the matter be put aside until my return there, and I can clarify it, for I would be terribly ashamed to make instances to Your Excellency about anything unjustifiable. Otherwise, I would indubitably stand to lose, beyond that amount, such a great sum as would be a ruinous blow to me, and one I do not believe I merit from Your Excellency, to whom I humbly recommend myself.

HISTORICAL NOTES

1. See Introduction, p. xvii.

2. Lorenzo de Terentiis de Pesaro, Doctor of Law and since 1456 *Vicario Generale e Sindicatore* [Santoro, 104]. Ducal Commissary at Parma, and member of the *Consiglio Segreto* (July 14, 1461), he was twice (Nov. 1461 and Dec. 1467) sent on missions to Louis XI [Lazzeroni, "Il Consiglio Segreto," 120, n. 86].

quello consta. Et se del resto che io pretendo haver speiso, come sa lo notaro mio et li altri chi han menata la spesa, altri volesse inculcar et instipular dubio alcuno, sian almanco dipositi, finché al mio esser de là, io possa chiarirli. Perciò che io me vergogneria del mondo ad far instantia a V. Ex.tia de cosa indebita. Altramenti io veniria a perder ultra che indebitamenti, etiam tal et tanto grande summa chi seria botta dannosa più che non credo meritar dala Ex.tia V., ala qual humiliter me racomando.

On Easter Sunday [April 5] the *Duke of Burgundy* sent for me to join his observances of the day, as is his custom on such an occasion, and in the course of a conversation he told me that four days ago he had had news *of the uprising in Genoa*[1] [March 9]; and because of his great *hate* of *Duke John* and all *Duke John's* line, whom he reputes to be the ones responsible for *his troubles with the King of France,*[2] he could not conceal from me his pleasure at the news, though he said he had not told me sooner because it was not fitting to discuss worldly matters during this holy season. He questioned me closely about whether *Your Lordship* had *numerous trusty adherents in Genoa.* I gave as honorable and appropriate an answer as I could, but *about the uprising* I did not know what to say since I had no information whatsoever, although *the Duke* told me that the news was confirmed in letters from *Milan* written on March 22.

I then came here, where I have found out not only about the events of the uprising but about differing *attitudes* toward it within the city, for the *Genoese* here belong to some of the principal families and they have inside information. Their feelings about the matter vary, some being pleased and some sorry, but all those who are well-wishers of *Your Lordship* agree entirely in fearing that control of the city seems to be in dispute between the *Fregoso and the Adorno and in believing that*

89·PROSPERO DA CAMOGLI *to the*

DUKE OF MILAN

Francia, cart. 525. Orig.

El dì sancto de Pascha el *Duca de Bergogna*[a] mandò per mi ad festigiare, come se sole in tal dì, et inter ragionar me disse che l'era 4 dì havia novelle *dele novitate de Zenoa;*[1] et per *l'odio* grande ch'el ha al *Duca Iohanne* et tutta sua linea, quale reputa esser quella chi gli ten *lo squaderno cum el Re de Franza,*[2] *V. S.*[b] non mi posseva celar lo piacer ne havia, dicendomi che non più tosto me l'havia ditto per rispecto deli dì alieni da cose mondane. Et domandomi assai se *la V. S.* havia *fideli assai in Zenoa.* Al che resposi per lo honor et debito quello mi parsi el meglo, ma *de la novitate* non sappi che dire, non havendone adviso, quantunche *la S. Sua* me disse che per littere de 22 del passato date a *Milano* se era confirmato la novella. Venni doppoi qui unde ho inteso non solamenti lo processo, ma etiam li *sentimenti* che ne hanno uni et un'altri a *Zenoa,* perché quelli de *Zenoa* chi sonno qui, sonno deli principali et hanno li advisi intrinsechi. Li sentimenti loro sonno varii et a chi ne piace et a chi ne dole, ma la paura universaliter de chi ama lo ben de *V. S.* hé ch'el si vede la cosa esser in altercatione da *Fregosi a Adorni, cum sit che come ella fussi più prestamenti et sensa controversia exequita et puoi aquatata, meglo seria per la S. V. per rispecto dele zelosie de Venetiani.* Advisando V. Ex.tia che ho da uno domestico de *An-*

---

a. C. C. incorrectly reads Delfin.
b. Read: Sua S.ria.

the more quickly that dispute were pacified and a settlement reached,
the better it would be for Your Lordship because of the suspicions of
the Venetians. I have learned from a man who dwells in the same
house as does *Andrea Bragadino*[3] who is on intimate terms with him,
that [the Venetians?] *here keep talking in such a way that it would be*
no marvel if they embraced Duke John's cause, for they say that Your
Lordship puts Genoa in an uproar in order to take it for yourself by
that means, and many other things, more out of malice than for any
truth or reason.

By a fortunate coincidence there came to me this evening *Ambro-*
gio Ruffino, a Milanese. He told me that last evening there passed by his
place of business two Venetians, who were talking about Your Lord-
ship, and he sent a boy to follow them and learn what they were saying.
The boy followed them closely but *he could not understand clearly*
what they were saying, for they spoke in low voices, except that finally
one said to the other, "If thus it will be, it will be in the beard [i.e. at the
expense] *of the Duke of Milan." Ruffino also says that the Venetians*
here openly show a most malicious and barbarous attitude—I cannot
think why they should, unless on account of the Genoese uprising or on
account of Duke John, whom I do not see to have any other escape
open to him but that of withdrawing by way of the gulf.

I do not venture to make a statement to Your Lordship nor to press
my opinion, for it is not my place to do so; but, although it is said that
Prospero Adorno has been chosen Doge, I should desire that, concern-
ing Genoa, Your Lordship consider that it is a matter of great impor-
tance and at this moment many are waiting to see how prudent Your
Lordship is. Although the whole Genoese ruling class[4] are an inferior
and untrustworthy lot, nevertheless since they are split into factions,
Your Lordship may choose the least unsatisfactory one—that is, the one
supported by the majority of the nobles and of the other good houses of
Genoa—and settle on that one and not abandon as a prey for evil people
nor as a plaything for children one of the most noble members of
Christendom, which is of such great importance to the state of Your

drea Braghedino,[a] et chi ha stretta compagnia qui cum lui, chi dice che[******] [c] *chi sonno qui, van in ragionando per modo che s'el si vedesse che imbraciassero la cosa del Duca Iohanne non seria meravigla, dicendo che V. S. mette Zenoa in rixa per torsela de medio et multe altre cose più per malignità che per né verità né ragione.* Et per bona iuncta el hé venuto da me questa sera *Ambrosio Rufin, milanese, dicendomi che heri de nocte passavano per la contrata sua dui Venetiani, quali ragionavano de V. S. et gli mandò de retro uno garsone ad intender;* et il qual referse haver atteso assai, *sed non haver possuto mai ben intender, perché parlavan basso, salvo che infine uno disse al altro: Se cossì serà, serà ala barba del Duca de Milano. Et dice che qui aperte monstrano lo animo malignissimo et ferito. Io non so coniecturar che possi essere se non o de Zenoa overo del Duca Iohanne, el qual non vedo possi haver a suo scampo altro exito, salvo quello de retrarsi per la via del gulfo.*

Io non ardisco de recordar né laudar ala S. V., perché non specta a me; ma quantumque si dice Prosper Adorno esser electo, io desideraria che in li fatti de Zenoa la S. V. facessi uno computo che l'hé uno grande peiso et a questo trato multi starano a mirar la prudentia dela V. S.; quamvis tutti li capelacii[a] *me pareno de mal pilo et puocha fede, tamen doppoi che han facto la factione la S. V. ne elegesse il manco tristo, hoc est quello in chi più riposassi la mente deli nobili et altre bone casate de Zenoa, et riposassi in quello et non lassiar andar in preda de mala gente né in ludibrio de puti lo più nobile membro dela cristianità chi ven tanto ben in concio al Stato de V. S.; determinandone sic eum volo manere donec veniam*[d] *et s'el tempo al presente non par servire ala S. V., forsi servirà altra volta, perché quanto muttili boni che io anaso, non vedeno altra forma de quieto, salvo lo Stato dela S. V.. Nam aliter aut che regerà a loro despecto serà cum spesa de chi vorrà sustener, aut se ne anderano tutti et quella cosa chi può et potrà aliquando de esser utile ala S. V. veniria ad esser damnosa. Signor, questo loco hé il fundego de*

---

c. The intended word for this blank is probably Venetiani.
d. John 22.

Lordship. You may support the government of your choice as long as it suits you, and if the present moment does not serve the ends of Your Lordship, perhaps a later time will serve; for, however many changes for the better I can conceive, I see no other means of bringing peace and order to Genoa except through Your Lordship's government.

For otherwise, either a governor who is hated by them will cost dear whoever supports him or they will all go smash together, and thus a thing of value to Your Lordship would be ruined. My Lord, Genoa is the object of the hopes and fears of Italy. However, Your Lordship, being most prudent, will substitute for my views those that seem best to him, and I will say once for all "Thy will be done, thy kingdom come."

I beg Your Excellency kindly to be willing to see to it that there be restored what was formerly promised to me, as is known to *Lord Cicco,* and this is a good opportunity to do a benefit to a faithful servant without any expense to Your Excellency. I have written more fully to *Lord Cicco* about it, so that "into your hands, Lord, I commend my spirit," *which will always be Your Excellency's to whom God give happiness.*

HISTORICAL NOTES

1. On March 9, 1461, the Genoese populace, exasperated by oppressive taxes to finance the Angevin war at Naples, revolted against the ineffectual Governor, Louis de Laval, who had supported the nobles and rich merchants in their efforts to escape much of this taxation. Laval quickly took refuge in the *Castelletto* while the old rival leaders, Paolo Campofregoso, Archbishop of Genoa, and Prospero Adorno entered the city at the head of two columns of their clients in an effort to control the city with the aid of the populace. Subseqently Campofregoso agreed to back Adorno for the Dogeship, thereby achieving a united front against the French garrison besieged in the *Castelletto.* On March 12, Adorno was elected Doge [Simonetta, B. XXVIII, 441–42].

2. A generation before, the Duke of Burgundy had backed René of Anjou's rival in a struggle for the Duchy of Lorraine. Capturing René at the bat-

tutti li sentimenti dele nobile terre de Italia. Pur la V. S., chi hé prudentissima, metterà a loco de questi advisi quello gli parerà, et io dirò semper fiat voluntas tua dummodo adveniat regnum tuum. Ben supplico ala Ex.tia V. chi vogla degnarsi per me far proveder che io sia restaurato de quello che alias mi fu promisso, come sa *D. Cico;* et questa hé bona opportunità a far beneficio al servo fidele sensa constero [sic] de V. Ex.tia. Io ne ho scritto a pleno al dicto *D. Cico,* siché in manus tuas Domine commendo spiritum meum, quale semper serà de V. Ex.tia, che Dio feliciti.

tle of Bulgnéville, 1431, and holding him prisoner for several years, the Duke had finally released him in return for pledges of ransom, which, René being unable to pay, exacerbated the ill feeling between the two Houses.

3. A Venetian merchant and later (1471) *Savio ai ordini* or member of the Board of Admiralty. Venice had always opposed Milanese domination of Genoa [Perret, I, 358–59, 579].

4. According to Pius II [*Commentaries,* B. V, 371], the *Capellazzi* formed a distinct Genoese class of rich merchants with many clients, monopolizing the Dogeship and distinguished from the other two classes—the *popolari* (plebeians) and the feudal nobility. Actually the citizenry were roughly divided into *popolari* and "nobles," but the distinction was more apparent than real for each class included rich merchants with extensive land holdings, and both groups exercized political power through their *alberghi* or clans [J. Heers, *Gênes au XVe siècle. Activité économique et problèmes sociaux* (Paris, 1961), 564 ff.].

Through Angelo Tani[1] I wrote nine days ago to Your Excellency *about many affairs here.* I also reported, concerning the news from England, that bonfires of rejoicing were lighted at Calais, and then soon after doubt was cast upon the accuracy of the news.[2] Now I inform Your Excellency that today letters arrived from London with the authentic information that the battle was fought fifteen days ago at a place near York, 170 miles from London.[3] King Edward [IV] and Warwick came off the victors. There were 28,000 killed and more, all counted by heralds, among whom on Warwick's side more than 8,000 were slain and four lords, while on King Henry [VI]'s side 20,000 perished and fourteen lords.[4] King Henry, the Queen [Margaret], their prince [Edward] and [Henry Beaufort,] the Duke of Somerset, with two other lords withdrew to Newcastle, a fortress of the island which is on the sea and near Scotland, whither the victors sent 20,000 men to besiege them. After the letters were sealed, it was added that there was news at London that the fortress was taken and all within it.

I am snatching a moment to write this brief missive to Your Excellency. Within four days, please God, I will write more at length and in orderly fashion about the battle and the names of the lords [who were killed] and what *seems to me to be the significance of this event. I add now that henceforth England is considered to be under the control of*

90·PROSPERO DA CAMOGLI *to the*

DUKE OF MILAN

Francia, cart. 525. Orig.

Per Angelo Tani[1] scripsi hoggi sonno 9 dì a V. Ex.tia quanto era *in multe cose de qua,* et dela novella de Angliterra come se faciano li falodi in Cales et come puocho doppoi se venne in dubitation dela cosa.[2] Hora adviso V. Ex.tia che in questo dì sonno littere de Londres certe, come la batagla fu hoggi XV dì, longi da Londres migla 170 presso a Iorch.[3] Lo Rei Edoardo et Varruich restoron vencitori: de morti gli fu in summa XXVIII[m] et più, tutti computati per certi araldi, inter li quali dal canto de Varruich se ne trova 8 milia in più et Principi 4; dal canto del Rei Henricho vintimilia et Principi 14.[4] Lo Re Henrico, la Regina, lo Principe et lo Ducha de Semesetreht [sic] cum doi altri Principi se erano retratti ad Neumburg, che hé uno castello dela insula sul mare et vicino ala Scocia, unde li vencitori haviano mandato homini vintimilia per assediarlo. Doppoi sigillate le littere se adiunge che a Londre era novelle ch'el dicto castello era preiso et cossi li inclusi.

Questa scrivo ala Ex.tia V. sutto brevità, ala ventura; fra 4 dì, se piacerà a Dio, scriverò più ala destesa et per ordine lo loco et li nomi deli Principi, et quello *me par esetir* [sic] *de retro questo fatto; cum ciò sia che hoggimai se reputa la Angliterra aspianata per Domino dela Marcha et Varruich cum grande loro reputatione.* Me racomando humiliter ala Ex.tia V., che Dio feliciti.

the Earl of March [Edward IV] *and Warwick, a fact which has exalted their reputations.* I humbly recommend myself to Your Excellency, whom God prosper.

HISTORICAL NOTES

1. Angelo di Iacopo Tani, manager of the Medici Bank at Bruges from 1450 to 1465 [R. de Roover, *The Rise and Decline of the Medici Bank, 1397–1494* (New York, Norton paperback ed., 1966), 338–39], had lent money to the Dauphin during this period, and was a financial agent of the Duke of Burgundy.

2. In another dispatch of Apr. 9, which survives only as a summary made by the Chancery [*Sommari,* cart. 1560, fasc. 2], Prospero reported events in England immediately before the battle [see next note], the substance of which is repeated in this dispatch and in that of Apr. 18, doc. 95, pp. 285–297.

3. The battle was fought near the village of Towton, twelve miles southeast of York, on Palm Sunday, March 29.

4. These undoubtedly exaggerated figures represent the "official" Yorkist tally of the dead [see CSPM, I, 60–67].

The other day by Angelo Tani, who left here April 10, I sent a dispatch [1] to Your Excellency recounting in full events here up to then and reporting sentiments concerning Genoa and the opinion held about the Venetians among these Italian merchants here, who, for being men of importance, know a great deal and who, for being in a place where they do not have to watch their step, say everything.

Now, revolving in my mind the revolt at Genoa and having now heard of the transformation of the Genoese state and the election of Prospero Adorno as Doge, and recalling that I am a follower of Your Excellency and therefore without other patron or protector, save Lord Cicco, whom I know to be temperate and moderate, I think it necessary, occupied though I am in greater affairs, to make a statement about myself to Your Excellency on such an occasion. Whether from the beginning I passed a just judgment on the House of Adorno or not, at least it served to put the subject on the table, although from the result it is evident that I am not passionately biased as some about Your Lordship have declared—may God pardon them for saying so—and on that account I am not about to take service again with anyone of the Adorno family nor with any other, except such a connection as Your Excellency would consider useful. Therefore I beg Your Excellency not to disdain to arrange for me in the state of Genoa some form of compensation, to

91·PROSPERO DA CAMOGLI *to the*

DUKE OF MILAN

Francia, cart. 525. Orig.

L'altro dì per Angelo Tani, partito de qui ali deci del presente, scripsi [1] ala Excellentia Vostra ad plenum quanto era fin a lì et deli sentimenti erano qui dele cose de Zenoa et dela opinione hé de Venetiani a pié de questi italici mercatanti de qui, li quali per esser homini de pecio senteno assai et per esser in loco fuori de rispecto, dicono tutto. Hora revolvendomi in lo animo lo fatto de Zenoa et havendo mò inteso dela transformatione nova del Stato et dela election de Prospero, ricordandomi per esser io de directo dela linea de Vostra Excelentia, et pertanto sensa altri né procuratori né patrone, salvo D. Cico, quale io cognosco temperato et modesto, item occupato in maioribus, me paio necessitato ad ricordarmi ala Excelentia Vostra in tale occasione; et quantumque se io iudicai fin dal principio iustamenti dela casa Adorna o non, scilicet quanto perteneva a rumper la glacia, benché per lo exito consta che non hebbi mai le passione che me obiectavano a pié dela S. V. de quelli a chi Dio perdona, et per questo io non sum per readomesticarme cum alcuno de dicta casa né altro, salvo tanto quanto parerà et piacerà per suo utile ala Excelentia Vostra.

Pertanto, Illustrissimo Signor, io supplico a Vostra Excelentia che in tale occasione non si sdegne farme ordinar del Stato de Zenoa a qualcun deli comodi et restauri, che io haria potuto sperar vivendo cum loro; et sia Adorno vel Fregoso, vogli Vostra Excelentia che mi sia dato

which I could have looked forward if I had continued to live with them. Be the Doge Adorno or Fregoso, may it be the will of Your Excellency that I am given whatever amount of money seems suitable to you, by means of which I can make my nest under your wings, as I have already begun to do and am disposed to do. Beyond the sum of money, the late Messire Perrino[2] promised me the consulate of Tunis or that of Alexandria in Egypt, as Lord Cicco knows, which consulates can be of great worth because of the variety of Genoese commerce throughout the world; and therefore I think I can and should have more from the Adorno family than from others. Considering that I have a brother in Lombardy and a son, four years in the service of King Ferrante, I beg you kindly to consider my request as coming, not so much from unreasonable greed, for I have lost much more than I ask for, nor from ambition, for with the predecessors of these Adorno I held a higher place than my present hopes represent, nor from sheer presuming, for I believe I merit this much from Your Excellency, but rather from the necessity I have of restoring my financial position in this world; and if I am to be useful and hatch eggs, I need a nest and something to line it with. I desire to bring this matter about without any cost to Your Excellency, who, I know well, is financially burdened by a great many others, and in whose service, whether it be that I am provided with less or more, I would like to play the role of Petro Brunori,[3] that is, such and so much as will be in everything pleasing to Your Excellency; nor will it ever be otherwise for I hope that, if only for your honor, you would like to think that I have made a good change in moving from Spinola[4] and the Adorno to you, and so humbly I recommend myself to you.

Magnificent Lord Cicco, I write the above to the Duke not so much to make demands on him as to record my need and infirmity so that if the time were ripe I could not be accused of negligence. Since Your Magnificence is the overseer of opportunity and you know what the Duke is and is not willing to do and what is easy and what is

quella quantità de dinari che piacerà et parerà ad essa, deli quali io me possi far lo nido mio sutto le ale de quella, come ho ià principiato et sum disposto; et perciò che ultra la summa deli dinari, condam messer Perino[2] me promesse lo consulato de Tunexe, aut quello de Alexandria de Egipto, come sa lo dicto D. Cico, li quali consulati possono esser de altra [alta?] condicione per le varietate deli commercii de Zenoa per lo mundo, parendomi posser et dover haver più dal Adorno che da altri; attento che pur ho fratello in Lombardia et figlolo ali servicii del Re Ferrando quatro anni fa, et qui pur sonno et viveno servitori a Vostra Excelentia, supplico a quella se digne de prender lo designo mio non tanto per apetito irrationabile perché ho perduto multo più, né per ambitione, perché cum li padri de questi Adorni io era più alto che per tale cose, né etiam per presumptione che io habbi de richeder questo, perché io me creda tanto meritarlo dala Excelentia Vostra, quanto che ho pur necessità de restaurarmi in questo mundo; et si debo covar, bisogna nido et substancia de qualcosa. Et desidero de sortir questo sensa carrico dela Excelentia Vostra, quale cognosco ben haverne deli altri assai et a pié dela quale perciò sia quello più et quello manco che si vogli, io sum disposto de esser per la rata mia, Petro Brunoro,[3] hoc est tale et tanto, quale et quanto in tutto piacerà ala Excelentia Vostra, né mai serò altramenti, ché pur spero, se non fussi mai, salvo per suo honor, vorrà che io habbi fatto bon cambio da Spinole[4] [sic] et Adorni ad essa et cossì humiliter me gli racomando.

Magnifico Messer Cico [Simonetta], *io scrivo la suprascripta al Signore non tanto per fargli instantia de me, quanto per uno ricordo de lo mio bisogno et infirmità, ad ció che se lo tempo fussi, non mi possessi esser imputato negligentia. Et la Magnificentia Vostra, chi hé suprastante de opportunitate et chi sa quello hé in voluntà del Signore et non, et quello hé facile o grave, facia quello manco et quello più gli pare, et cossì come a padre adricio la fortuna mia; pregando Vostra Magnificentia chi ne vogli haver ricordo et proponerlo come et quando gli parerà, et non tenere puti temerario, perché pur la età me ne admonisse;*

difficult, please do for me what little or more seems good to you, and thus to you as to a father, I commit my fortunes. I beg you to put my matter forward how and when will seem best to you and not to consider me a rash boy, for my situation has forced me to take this step. If you think that my request would be displeasing to the Duke or might be difficult because it runs counter to other affairs of his, I am content [that you do not bring it up]—*indeed, I beg you not to make any mention of it since I can easily console myself by citing the proverb, "He asks a great deal who, giving good service, is silent."*

HISTORICAL NOTES

1. These dispatches were received by Sforza on the evening of Apr. 29 [Vincenzo della Scalona to the Marchioness of Mantua, Milan, Apr. 29, 1461, A. S. Mantova, *Carteggio-Milano*, B. 1621].

2. Pietro Campofregoso, former Doge of Genoa who had given the city to Charles VII (1458), and in September of the following year had been killed in an unsuccessful attempt to expel Duke John from Genoa.

3. Pietro Brunori, an old friend and comrade in arms of Francesco Sforza, who in 1443 betrayed him and joined his enemy, King Alfonso of Naples [Simonetta, B. VI, 125–27]. Prospero evidently wishes to emphasize the close friendship between Brunori and Sforza, not the subsequent betrayal.

4. The Spinola, like the Adorno, were a powerful Genoese clan rivaling the Campofregoso for the Dogeship. Prospero owed allegiance to both [see Introduction, p. xvi].

et quando pur paresse a Vostra Magnificentia che la cosa fussi molesta al Signore, aut aliqualiter difficile per non desconciar altri suoi fatti, io sum contento; imo prego Vostra Magnificentia non ne faci mentione alcuna, cum sit che facilmenti io me diporterò sul commentar il proverbio che: assai domanda chi ben servendo tace. Data ut supra.

Third version

We recently received all your letters of the 17th, 18th, and 28th of February and of the 3rd, 4th, 9th, and 15th of March; and from these we have learned how benignly and graciously the Dauphin received you and the great honor he paid, and pays, you. We wish you to render infinite thanks to his most illustrious lordship because we consider such honors as given to our own person. Concerning his excellency's thanks for the honor we paid Gaston, there is no cause for them because we were not able to do what our debt and obligation to his excellency call for and what the virtues of Gaston merit.

By your letters we also remain fully informed about everything you have accomplished with his lordship: the representations you have made to him on our behalf, the answers his lordship gave you, and your replies to him. In everything we commend you; and in response we say that we can never render sufficient thanks to his lordship for such good will, such love and high affection, such magnanimity and generosity as he has demonstrated and demonstrates to us; but we must pray God, the rewarder of all acts of goodness, that He be the one to render to his lordship reward and recompense on our behalf and to place his lordship in that prosperous and happy state that he desires, and we desire

92 · *The* DUKE OF MILAN *to*

PROSPERO DA CAMOGLI

Francia, cart. 525. Minute[a]

Tercia et huiusmodi reformata.

Havemo havute questi dì tutte le toe littere de dì XVII, XVIII et XXVIII de febraro et III, IIII, VIIII [b] et XV de marzo proximo passati, et per quelle inteso quanto benignamente et graciosamente quello Ill.mo S. Delfin te ha recevuto et lo grande honore te ha facto et fa. Vogliamo tu renda infinite gracie ad Soa Ill.ma Sig.ria perché tutto tenemo essere facto alla persona nostra propria. Del regraciare che Soa Ex.tia ne fa del honore havimo facto ad Guaston, questo non bisogna, perché Nuy non havimo possuto fare quello che rechiedeva el debito et obligacione nostra verso la Soa Ex.tia, et anche quello meritano le virtù del dicto Gaston. Et per dicte littere ancora restamo difusamente et copiosamente avisati da ti de tutto quello hay exequito con el prefato Ser.mo Mon.re,

---

a. There are two other minutes in cart. 525. One, marked "prima," is dated April 12, 1461; the other, marked "secunda," is dated April 13. The third and final draft, which follows, was first dated "XV aprilis 1461," but "XV" is crossed out and above it appears the word "primo." Below this date there is written: "dupplicata die XVII aprilis." We are unable to offer an explanation for this change to "primo" other than it may be an error by the scribe for the third minute follows logically the preceding two, and Prospero wrote to Cicco Simonetta on May 9, 1461, that he had received the duplicated letter of April 17 [doc. 93, p. 275]. Consequently it appears that the third minute was written on April 15.
b. Prima and *secunda* add: XIII

for him; and we pray that God grant us the power to be able to fulfill our obligations and carry out our desire in regard to his lordship.

As to the replies his lordship has made to you regarding the matter of Messer Giacomo di Valperga, we say that we have always loved him, and continue to love him, for his virtues, him and his House also. We learn from your letters that the Dauphin would like us to recompense lord Giacomo for the damages he has suffered: namely to give him more than 12,000 ducats; item, to give him 100 gold ducats a month for subsistence; item, to give him a castle, near his brother's possessions etc., that would provide a good income for his family. We answer that for him as a friend and servant of the Dauphin and a gentleman, we would always do everything possible, but not in this way. We are greatly amazed at such a demand, because it is not we who are obligated to make good his losses nor is the Dauphin so obligated, because neither his lordship nor we are the one who took his property from him. On the contrary, his excellency has always done everything to preserve Valperga's estate and so, on our side, have we done. As to his lamenting that he has lost his property because he was not aided by us, we reply that such is not the case; for Gaston is fully informed, and you are also, that we made every attempt and provision possible, compatible with honor, to preserve his property in many times sending him soldiers. Of those we sent from our own Milanese subjects and others, many were hanged, greatly to our charge because of our being willing to give him aid. There were also many we sent who could not enter the fortress of Masino; and many others in addition turned back, from fear that they might be given the treatment that some within had received, who had been hanged, and also because of the outrageous deeds committed by lord Giacomo's men within Masino, about which the brother of Gaston who was there is well informed—which reprehensible acts were the reason that many of the men we last sent, preferred to disobey our commands and return to face being at our discretion and mercy rather than to go there where such treatment was meted out. Indeed, in the end, if Valperga's wife and his adherents within Masino had not yielded the

et dele exposicione et ambassate gli hay facte per nostra parte, et dele resposte te ha facte Soa S. et dele replicacione gli hay facte. De tutto te commendamo; et respondendo dicemo che a Nuy non ne pare essere sufficienti de potere rendere gracie ad quello Ser.mo Sig.re de tanta bona disposicione, tanto cordiale amore et dilecione, et tanta magnanimità et liberalità ch'el ha monstrato et demonstra verso Nuy; ma pregamo Dio, quale é retribuitore de tuti li beneficy, che sia quello gli renda retribucione et merito per Nuy, et che lo reponga in quello prospero et felice stato che la S. Soa desydera, et ancora Nuy, et che ne presti gratia che possamo fare el nostro debito et adimpire el nostro desyderio verso Soa S.

Quantum autem alla parte che la S. Soa te ha dicto et resposto circa li facti del Mag.co Misser Iacomo de Valperga, dicimo che Nuy l'havimo sempre amato et amamo per le soe virtù luy et casa soa; et perché per le toe littere intendiamo che Mon.re voria che facessemo contento D. Iacomo et lo restaurassemo deli danni suoy, cioé dargli più de XII^m ducati, item donarli ducati cento d'oro el mese de provisione, item donarli uno castello che fosse de bona intrata per la soa fameglia, presso le cose de suo fratello etc., dicimo che a luy como amico et servitore de Mon.re et como gentilhomo faressemo sempre ogni cosa ne fosse possibile, ma non per questa via;^c maravigliandosse assay de tale domanda, perché non siamo quelli che habiamo ad restaurare li suoy danni né ancora Mon.re el Delphino, perché la S. Soa non é quella gli l'habia tolte, né ancora Nuy. Immo la Ex.tia Soa ha facto ogni cosa per conservarglile, et cossì Nuy dal canto nostro; et perché intendemo luy s'é pur lamentato che le ha perdute per non essere stato aiutato da Nuy, dicimo che la cosa non é cossì, de che Gaston é informatissimo et ancora tu che Nuy facessemo ogni prova et ogni experiencia et provisione

---

c. Prima: Nuy sarimo ben contenti donare ad Mon.re quello tu hai in commissione et farlo moito volunteri et poy la Sig.ria Soa lo daghi a luy o ad chi gli pare. [Crossed out]: Et se questo gli pare poco, dicemo che Nuy sapemo che non poressemo far tanto che potessemo satisfare pur ad una parte del debito nostro verso el prefato Mon.re, ma le de' havere discretione et compassione alle spese et necessità nele quale se trovamo al presente. [The first part is crossed out and the second is missing in the *secunda*.]

place as they did—not out of necessity but of their own free will—his property would have been saved and he would still have it. In sum, as is said, his losses are not due to the culpability or negligence of the Dauphin or of us, but to the aforesaid conduct and handling of affairs that were used etc.

In regard to the Dauphin's statement that everything we would do for lord Giacomo he would consider as done for himself, we say that for his lordship, as is said, we will always be prepared to do anything; but this in this way we will not do because it would mean, and give notice, to everyone that we are the one, and not lord Giacomo di Valperga, who made war on the Duke of Savoy; and such an occurrence would be greatly to our disgrace, which we are most certain that his lordship, loving us as we are sure that he does because of his benignity, would not wish, because it would be his own. Therefore, for the said considerations and reasons we could not do what lord Giacomo requests in the way that he asks.

[In addition to this difficulty about lord Giacomo, the Dauphin raises another, which seems more significant: namely that, should he come to an accord with the King his father—as he says he is doing because it stands with his lordship to accept the accord etc.—he does not know how he can observe our treaty since the will of his father runs counter to ours etc. We say we do not consider that such an accord has to make difficulties for, or break, our treaty with his lordship; because as a result of his reducing himself to the grace and love of the King his father, His Majesty, we are most certain, will want to honor him and treat him worthily, as every father should treat his good son; and his lordship, we are certain, will govern himself with such prudence that he will enjoy the credit with his father that every good son should by right enjoy. Therefore we conclude that the more status, authority, and power he will have with his father, so much the better means will he have of aiding and favoring us and keeping us in the love and grace of His Majesty; because we have never gone contrary to the will of His Majesty but rather have always been his loving and most devoted serv-

ad Nuy possibile con honestà per conservargli le cose soe in mandargli gente in più volte; et de quilli mandassemo molti ne forono impicati de nostri subditi Milanesi et de altri, con assay nostro incarico, per volere Nuy aiutare le soe cose; et molti gli ne mandassemo qualli non possetero intrare in la Rocha de Masino et ancora molti altri se ne tornarono in dreto per dubio non gli fossero facti deli portamenti, che erano stati facti ad l'altri inanti, qualli eranno [sic] stati impicati, et ancora per li stranii portamenti erano stati facti per quelli de D. Iacomo, qualli erano in Maxino, como é bene informato lo fratello de Guaston che era dentro là; quali sinistri portamenti forono casone che molti de quilli nostri mandassemo ultimamente, più tosto volsero rompere li comandamenti nostri et retornare indreto et stare ad discrecione et misericordia che andare là dove se gli facevano tali tractamenti. Et pur in ultimo se la dona soa et li suoy che eranno [sic] dentro de Masino non havessero dato el loco, non per necessità, ma motu proprio et de soa spontanea voluntà, como fecero, le cose se sariano conservate et le haveriano ancora. Siché como é dicto non sonno perdute per colpa né pe defecto del prefato Mon.re né nostra, ma per li tractamenti, governy et modi predicti servati etc..[d] Et perché el prefato Mon.re dice che tutto tene facto ad se stesso quello che Nuy facessemo ad D. Iacomo, dicimo che per la S. Soa, como é dicto, Nuy saremo sempre apparechiati fare ogni cosa; ma questa per questa via non faressemo, perché saria ad dire et fare noto ad ciaschuno che Nuy fossemo stati quilli[e] che havessemo facto guerra al Duca de Savoya et non D. Iacomo de Valperga; el che ad Nuy saria grande vergogna, la quale siamo certissimi che amandone el prefato Mon.re cordialmente, como siamo certi che fa per soa benignità, siamo certi non la voria, perché saria soa propria. Siché per le dicte casone et rasone non poressemo fare quelle cose che rechiede el prefato D. Iacomo per quella via ch'el dice. [Et perché oltra questa difficultà de

d. *Prima* and crossed out in the *secunda:* Siché chi non ha colpa, non debe portare pena.
e. *Prima:* che havessemo facto fare ad D. Iacomo quello che fece, [crossed out]: et che Nuy havessemo havuto pensamento de fare altro che fosse contra la forma et della Pace et dela Liga in Italia etc.

ant and are determined to remain so as long as we live. His Majesty has always, out of his great goodness, borne for us the greatest affection and love, although many have continually pretended that the reverse was true; and since he has, out of his graciousness and benignity, persevered in his true affection and love toward us, he will do so all the more when the Dauphin will be reconciled with him.]

Therefore we wish you to supplicate and move his excellency—with the tact, persuasiveness and charm that we are certain you know how to use—to condescend, in the same spirit of love, charity, benignity, and greatness of mind that he has up to now demonstrated to us, to come to a conclusion, regarding our treaty, in accordance with the commission that you have brought in writing and by word of mouth. We are most certain that his excellency will want to demonstrate in deed what up to now he has demonstrated in words, because such a conclusion will give great comfort, great hope, and great consolation and pleasure to us and to our sons. Therefore in this matter employ all your abilities and diligence and use every care and vigilance with the Dauphin so that he be willing, in the happy frame of mind and good disposition that we are certain he bears toward us, to come to the said conclusion—indeed, we cannot in any way believe that his excellency is not going to come to such a conclusion. Therefore see to expediting the matter as quickly as possible, using always that moderation, that honor and reverence which you know represents our attitude and our obligation toward that most serene prince. If, after you have done everything possible, the Dauphin should seem, for some legitimate and important reason, unwilling to conclude the treaty, we wish you to take leave of his excellency and, with his good will, return to us.

Concerning the Kingdom of Naples, according to letters from Antonio da Trezzo in Naples, of the 24th of March, King Ferrante's cause continues to prosper.

Item: we wish you to convey our compliments to my lord of Burgundy, offering to his excellency us, our state, and our resources as fit-

D. Iacomo, Mon.re ne adduce un'altra, quale pare mazore, cioé che accordandosse con el S. Re suo padre, como dice fare, perché sta ad la Sig.ria Soa ad acceptare l'acordio etc., che non sa como potesse observare la nostra intelligencia per essere la voluntà de suo padre contraria alla nostra etc., dicimo che Nuy non tenemo che tale accordio habia ad difficultare né interumpere la intelligentia nostra con Soa Sig.ria, perché reducendosse alla gratia et amore del Ser.mo S. Re suo patre ne rendiamo certissimi che la Soa M.tà el vorà honorare et tractare dignamente, como debbe fare caduno patre el suo bon figliolo; et la S. Soa siamo certi se governarà con tale prudencia che potrà presso Soa M.tà quello debbe rasonevolmente potere caduno bon figliolo presso el patre. Il perché concludimo quanto più l'haverà Stato, auctorità et possanza presso el S. Re suo patre, tanto più haverà meglio el modo de aiutarce et favorirce et conservarce in l'amore et gratia della M.tà Soa, perché Nuy non fossemo may contrarii della voluntà della M.tà Soa; immo gli siamo stati sempre amorevele et devotissimo servitore, et cossì deliberamo essere finché viveremo; et la M.tà Soa per soa summa bontà ne ha sempre portato summa dillectione et amore, quantunche molti l'habiano continuamente simulata al contrario, et tamen la Soa M.tà per soa gratia et benignità ha perseverato in la bona affecione et amore verso Nuy et maioremente farà quando el prefato Mon.re Delfin sarà presso la M.tà Soa.] [f] Unde vogliamo che preghi et supplichi la Soa Ex.tia con quella humanità, suavità et dolceza che siamo certi tu saperay fare, et operare che la se digni con quello dolce amore, carità et benignità et con quella grandeza de animo, che s'é demonstrata fino al presente verso Nuy, inclinarse et descendere alla conclusione, secondo le commissione che tu hay portate in scritto et ad boca, perché ne rendiamo più che certissimi che la Soa Ex.tia ne vorà monstrare con vero effecto quello che fino al presente ne ha monstrato in parole, perché de tale conclusione Nuy ne prenderimo grande conforto, grande speranza et grande consolacione et piacere per Nuy et figlioli nostri. Siché in questo

---

f. Bracketed section missing in *prima.*

tingly as you can; and do the same with lord Charles, his son, and with the Duke of Clèves.

Concerning the business of Genoa we will say no more because we are certain that you will have learned what has happened there: namely that on March 9 the whole population rose and drove out the governor [Louis de Laval, lord of Châtillon,] who had been appointed by the King of France, and also his officials and soldiers, who withdrew to the citadel and are still there.

The Genoese created a popular republic, fired by wrath and indignation against any gentlemen who adhered to the said governor, and those gentlemen have been in great danger of feeling the displeasure of the populace. Then the people unanimously chose Prospero Adorno as their doge. He now governs the state peacefully and the people busy themselves with pressing the siege of the citadel, which they have so tightly blockaded that it is believed the besieged will soon be reduced to terms and take their departure. In this Genoese business we have played no part, either in the beginning, the middle or the end, but we have left it up to them; and if some say otherwise, you will reply emphatically that the accusation is false, for, in all truth, it will not be found that we ever meddled with the affair in any way.

Milan, April 17, 1461

Post datum: having today received letters from Bruges dated April 10 informing us that the new King of England, namely King Edward, with the Earl of Warwick and his other adherents defeated the army of the Queen and besieged her and now dominates affairs in such a way that without doubt the new King will secure the Kingdom, we wish that, matters being thus, with the permission and good will of the Dauphin you make the journey to visit King Edward and deliver to him our compliments and offers of service, as you think appropriate, being guided by the legate. Inform yourself fully about all affairs there; then you will send word immediately about everything and you will return to us as soon as possible.

vogli usare ogni tuo inzegno et industria et ogni solicitudine et vigillancia con lo prefato Ser.mo Mon.re, ch'el se digni con alegro animo et quella bona disposicione, che siamo certi ch'el ha verso de Nuy, venire ad dicta conclusione che non possamo credere per niente che Soa Ex.tia non debia venire ad tale effecto. Siché cura expedirte quanto più presto te sia possibile, usando sempre quella moderacione, quella honestà et reverencia che tu say é nostra intencione et nostro debito verso quello Ser.mo Principe; et quando tu haveray facto ogni opera et studio ad te possibile, et che al prefato Ill.mo S. paresse per qualche legitima et importante casone et respecto de non venire al effecto de dicte conclusione, vogliamo che prendi licencia da Soa Ex.tia et con soa bona gratia te ne venghi da Nuy.[g]

Delle cose de Reame, per quanto havimo per littere de Antonio da Trezo in Napoli de XXIIII del passato, passano tutte prospere per lo Re Ferrando.[h]

Item volimo ne recomandi ad Mon.re de Bergogna, offerendo alla Soa Ex.tia Nuy, lo Stato et facultate nostre tanto dignamente, quanto te parerà opportuno; et con lo Ill. S. Chiarles, suo figliolo, faray el simile et con Mon.re Duca de Clevi.

Circa li facti de Zenoa Nuy non ne extenderemo altramente, perché siamo certi che tu haray inteso como le cose son passate;[i] cioé che ad dì VIIII de marzo proximo passato se levò universalmente tutto el populo et tolsero via el Governatore, quale gli era per lo Ser.mo S. Re de Franza, et cossì l'altre gente et soldati che erano con luy al governo, quali se redussero in Castelleto et lì sonno; et se hanno facto Stato de

---

g. *Prima* and crossed out in the *secuda:* dicendo ad quello Ill.mo S.re che quantunque non sia sequita et facto scriptura de questa intelligentia et liga practicata etc., tamen Nuy la tenerimo per ferma et facta et stabilita tanto quanto se ne fossero facte mille scripture, et così ne rendiamo certissimi che sarà la mente et intencione de quello Ill.mo S.re, et Nuy cum questa firmissima oppinione viverimo viveremo [sic] continuamente.

h. *Prima* and crossed out in the *secuda:* in toto Regno et spera il dicto Re presto obtenire el facto suo. De novo non gli é altro.

i. *Prima:* lo populo, motu proprio, hanno mutato lo Stato gl'era et electo Duxe Prospero Adorno, et così stato in Ducato attende ad stringere Castelletto. [This is the extent of the reference to Genoa.]

libertà con grande ira et indignacione contra deli gentilhomini quali adherivano ad dicto Governatore, et sonno stati dicti gentilhomini in grande periculo ch'el populo non gli habia facto dispiacere, donde unanimiter hanno ellecto Prospero Adorno Duse [sic]; et cossì governa el Ducato pacifice, et attende el populo ad stringere Castelleto, quale hanno strecto in modo che se crede che presto debia ad redurse ad pacti et pigliare partito. Et Nuy in questa cosa de Zenoa non ne siamo impazati né in principio né mezo né in fine, ma lassamo pur fare ad loro; et se altri dicesse altramente, respondi gagliardamente che non é el vero, perché con el vero non se troverà may che Nuy se ne siamo impazati in cosa alcuna.[j]

Milan, April 17, 1461

Post datum: perché se sono hozi havuto qua littere da Bruge de dì X del presente, como lo novo Re de Ingliterra, videlicet lo Re Adouardo con lo Conte de Veroich et l'altri suoi hano rotto l'exercito dela Regina et assediatola et reducto le cose in modo che senza dubio esso Re novo obtenirà lo Stato, volimo che, essendo così, con licentia et bona voluntà de quello Ill.mo S. Dalphino tu te transferissi alla M.tà del prefato S. Re ad visitarla et offerirnegli et reccomandarnegli como te parerà convenire, facendo capo ad Mon.re el Legato, et informandote compitamente de tutte le cose dellà et deinde ne avisaray subito particularmente del tutto et te ne retorneray da Nuy quanto più presto te sii possibile.

---

j. *Secunda,* crossed out: salvo che Nuy gli havimo mandato. [The sentence is thus interrupted.]

Having returned from England, I some days ago wrote to Your Excellency from Bruges about English affairs, about the reason for our coming here, and about what afterward happened and what the English hope will come about if they are aided as Your Lordship has written and given firm expectation that they will be. I await what will happen as a result of the coming [to Milan] of Messer Antonio della Torre, who will arrive fully furnished with what Your Lordship requested. Now, although the situation in England has undergone great change, nonetheless in the end my lord of Warwick has remained in control and created a new King [Edward IV], the Earl of March, son of the Duke of York, who was with Warwick when we crossed to England [from Calais, in June of 1460]; so that affairs are in such shape that if the Yorkists are given aid, as we have many times written and solicited, there will be accomplished a significant deed, more glorious than any that has occurred in these parts in 500 years; because this new King is young, shrewd, and of aspiring mind and if he is encouraged by the Pope with my assistance—provided I am given the requisite authority and prestige—everything he does will be of high significance. Otherwise all our plans will fall in ruins together with my labors. Since I know well that this matter is in Your Lordship's hand, I remain optimistic; otherwise, I would already have taken the road of return.

93 · FRANCESCO COPPINI *to the*

DUKE OF MILAN

Borgogna, cart. 514. Orig.

A dì passati da Bruggs, essendo tornato d'Ingheterra, scripsi ad la
V. Ex. delle cose de là et della cason de nostra venuta; et appresso
quanto sucedeva et quanto speravo poter seguir, essendo aiutato come
V. I. S. havea scripto et datone ferma speranza. Aspecto che sia seguito
per la venuta di Messer Antonio de la Torre, el quale venne fornito
pienamente de quanto V. I. S. richiedeva. Hora benché le cose d'Anglia
habbino havuto più mutatione, non dimeno ad fine Mons. de Varvich é
rimaso al di sopra et fatto uno novo Re, quello figlio del Duca Ebora-
cense, Conte de Clemantia, el quale fu insieme cum Varvich ad tornar
cum nostri in Anglia; siché le cose passano in forma che se sono aiutate,
come havemo più volte dicto et solicitato, si farà cosa degna et de maggior gloria che fussi da 500 anni in queste parti, perché costui é iovane,
prudente e magnanimo et se vede il caldo del S. P. colla assistentia mia,
con reputatione debita, ogni cosa farrà degna et grande; alias van in
ruina tutti li nostri pensieri et le mie fatiche. Et perché cognosco bene
che questo fatto é in mano de V. I. S., ne sto de bona voglia; altrimenti
io sarei già in camino al venirne. Siché degnisse la S. V. hora lavorar
che é il tempo et aiutar la materia, de la quale per lo passato V. Ex. ha
sollicitato, ma che questo é uno tratto maraviglioso d'aconciar lo stato
de Italia et lo vostro spetialmente per sempremai. Pensate, S. mio,
quanto verisimilmente ve apparecchierà la fortuna: 1. comodità sifatta;

Therefore I beg Your Lordship to labor, because the time is ripe, and give aid to a cause which, in the past, Your Excellency has worked for but which now represents a marvellous opportunity for you to settle the affairs of Italy, and especially your own, forever more. Consider, my lord, what fortune in all likelihood is preparing for you—one, an opportunity such as this; and two, a man so fervently disposed by his nature to be devoted to you. Let us leave aside whether that man's mind can rise to the occasion, for Your Lordship fully knows the answer from experience. I know that you have been begged to intercede by such men who perhaps do not suit you. My lord, these are events of high importance and such events do not come often; if Your Lordship believes that I am the man that I think I am, please show it, now that you have the opportunity, and I am, in your hands.

I know the secret and I know the truth about the Curia; I need say no more. If Your Lordship does his part, everything will begin to develop—and it will cost you no more than words. Pardon me, Your Lordship, if I speak so boldly—for it appears that thus the Creeds of the Church a long time ago bade men speak—especially now that, just as I have been from infancy your servant, partisan, and son so should you be a father to me, and this is the time to show it, to the honor of God and to the Church's glory and yours.

On the third of May next coming the Duke of Burgundy is holding his council near Bruges in a castle called St. Omer [sic], where will assemble those of his Order of the Golden Fleece, and I am to be there and I will inform Your Excellency of what happens. I have learned that an emissary of yours is there [i.e. Prospero da Camogli]. It will be convenient if, through a letter from Your Lordship, he and I can have an understanding, and therefore, if the idea seems good to you, Your Excellency can so notify him, instructing him that in matters pertaining to Your Lordship he should readily hear all I have to say. I say this for a good purpose, and I stand prepared to help, especially because, thank God, the Duke of Burgundy cherishes me more than he does most, for so have experience and trust decreed.

et 2. homo, che ci sia così fervente et naturalmente disposto ad vostra devocione. Lassiamo stare se li basta l'animo o no, che di questo sa la V. I. S. assai per la experientia. Io so che sete pregato interceder per tali che forsi non vi vanno per l'animo. S. mio, questi sono casi de grande importanza et che non vengono spesso; se V. S. crede che sia, quello che io sono, degnisi mostrarlo hora che può et sto in vostre mani. Io so il secreto et so il vero della corte et basta; se Vostra I. S. fa la sua parte, ogni cosa cresce et non ci mettete se non parole. Perdonimi, V. S., se così securamente parlo, perché ne par che così vogliono li credi gran tempo fa et maxime hora che così come io vi sono, ab infantia, stato servitore et partisano et figlio, così mi debbiate essere padre, et questo é il punto da monstrarlo con honore de Deo et gloria della Chiesa et vostra.

A dì 3 del mese di maio proximo che viene, lo I. S. Duca de Borgogna tiene suo consiglio appresso Bruggia in uno castello dicto Sancto Odomaro, dove saranno quelli della sua livrea del Vellum d'Oro, et io mi vi debbo ritrovare et adviserò V. Ex. de quanto seguirà. Ho inteso che lì é uno de vostri. Sarà conveniente cosa che per lettera de V. I. S. ci possiamo intendere insieme et così, se vi pare, può Vostra Ex. notificare al prefato; dica che nelle cose appartenenti ad V. S. ne oda volentieri tutto. Dico ad bon fine, et sto per iovare, et maxime perché da Sua I. S., gratia de Deo, sono amato et fuor del generale, perché così vole la experientia et la fede.

Di poi volendo serrar questa, ho lettere del Spectabile Messer Antonio dala Torre et inteso le provisioni fatta [sic] per V. I. S.. Assai ne piaceno et sommamente ringratio V. Ex. et supplico che così seguiti, che dapoi ch'é in mano sua ne voglia havere honore.

Io ho novamente nuove d'Anglia per uno de miei, che mandavo adposta, et ad Bruggia ha trovate le nuove, come nelle incluse copie si contiene; et per questo vedrà V. Ex. la bella occasione che Dio ne manda, s'el S. P. et V. Ex. l'aiuterà, come certamente credo et aspetto. Et per questa speranza io mi movo domani per andare ad Bruggia ad trovar lo I. Duca de Borgogna, et havuti colloqui cum Sua Ex., per passare in Anglia, aspettando de certo che dietro à mandato nuovelle

Subsequently, as I was about to close this, I had a letter from Messer Antonio della Torre from which I learned of the steps taken by Your Lordship. We are highly pleased and most heartily thank Your Excellency and pray that you follow the matter through since it is in your hand, so that you will have the honor of it.

I have just had tidings from England by one of my household whom I dispatched for that purpose and who at Bruges found the packet of news, copies of which are contained in the enclosed. By these Your Excellency will see the wonderful opportunity that God sends us, if the Pope and Your Excellency will give aid, as certainly I believe and expect. In this hope I will tomorrow set out, first to go to Bruges to find the Duke of Burgundy and then, having conferred with him, to cross to England. I am confident that you will send good news after me, such as reveals that it is your will to aid the enterprise; and if you do so, I hope in one year without fail, even within this coming summer, to report matters that you will be singularly pleased to hear. May it please Your Excellency to send the enclosed copies to the Curia, directed to Messer Falcone, where are kept the Pope's letters concerning these advices.

My lord, please be patient with this miserable handwriting of mine because I wrote in the most furious hurry and I cannot, in all propriety, communicate these matters to others, and I have so much to do that, being almost alone, I marvel that I am alive; for I have to keep my eye on affairs in England, France, and Italy at the same time, without taking into account the operation of my legation in these parts of Burgundy and Flanders; and I therefore pray you to trust the writer when the writing is incoherent.

Postscript. I have learned that the Duke of Anjou, alias King René, has occupied Avignon, to the disparagement of the Church.[1] Concerning the news, I say to Your Lordship that if I will be given the authority, I will make the Angevins wish to attend to their home affairs, by means of England. Enough said.

This matter has greater import than our folk at the Curia seem to understand. They have only to say the word and yet they do not under-

bone et tali che s'intenda che l'ampresa [sic] si vole aiutare; et così faccendo, spero sanza fallo in uno anno, et ancor questa state, farvi sentire cose che singularmente saranno grate.

Piaccia V. Ex. mandare queste incluse in Corte, che si drizano ad Messer Falcone, dove sono littere de N. S. de questi advisi.

Degnisi V. I. S. haver patientia con questa trista scriptu[ra] de mia mano, perché la fo in grandissima furia, et non posso acconciamente comunicarle ad altri; et ho tanto da fare che ritrovandomi quasi solo, é maraviglia che sono vivo, bisognando haver l'occhio al stato d'Anglia, de Francia et Italia ad uno tempo medesimo, sanza le faccende della legatione che ho in queste parti de Borgogna et Fiandra; et supplisca la fede dove la scriptura é incomposta.

Post scripta. Ho inteso ch'el Duca d'Angiò, alias Rex Renato, ha occupato Vignone in dispregio della Chiesa.[1] Ad che dico ad la I. S. V. che se mi sarà data reputatione, io li farò venire voglia dal canto de qua attendere ad casa per mezo dell'Inghiltera et basta. Questa materia importa più che li nostri di corte non par che intendano, et possono provedere con parole, et non lo sanno. Verrà tempo che se ne pentiranno et pertanto la V. S., che conosce, li porta la mano.

Como[a] per la inclusa se monstra, la parte adversa é disfatta in tutto se questo nostro Re é favorito dala Chiesa; e non c'é altro modo honesto se non che se ne ritorni là sotto colore de reformare lo stato della Chiesa, como havea cominciato; et amo che habbi più reputatione si torni [sic] con exaltatione, secondo che per lo Re vecchio et per questo medesimo novo et per tutti é stato demandato; et lì é Messer Antonio con le commissioni tutte, siché qui non manca se non il sollicitare di cosa, et da poi che Deo ha proveduto che questa cosa sia in vostra mano, piacerà ad voi condurla ad fine, perché questi casi non vengono spesso et io so ben assai che ho da fare et so dove tengo li pié. Per lo messo del Papa, che

---

a. What follows was written in sympathetic ink between the first eighteen lines of this dispatch. At the chancery the paper was treated with a chemical reagent which made the writing visible. Thus the writing between the lines is of a darker color than the rest, and the paper itself shows traces of being treated with some sort of solution.

stand it. *The time will come when they will repent of their attitude; meanwhile Your Lordship, who understands the matter, may please put his hand to it.*

As the enclosed shows, the adverse party is completely overthrown, if this King [Edward IV] *is favored by the Church, and there is no other honorable mode of accomplishing this except for me to return there, with the pretext of reforming the government of the Church, as I had begun—and, for greater prestige, to return there elevated* [to the Cardinalate], *according as has been requested by the old King* [Henry VI] *and this new King and by everybody.*

Now there [in Italy] *is Messer Antonio* [della Torre] *with all the requisite documents, so that it remains only to solicit my elevation and then, since God has seen to it that this affair be in your hands, may it please you to conduct it to its conclusion; for these chances do not come often and I know very well indeed what I have to do and I know where my allegiance lies.*

By the Pope's messenger who bore the brief to Your Lordship and by other secret ways I am informed that you are being urged to bring about the promotion of a new bishop created in your territory, the which would interfere with our affair. I hope then that Your Lordship will not abandon the old way for the new, especially not knowing how the new is fashioned. I have such faith in Your Excellency as you, because of my merit, should have in me and as, by your letters and by Messer Antonio, you have given me to think you have; and I hope in God that you will aid me as God has given you the power to do, for you will be as happy with the outcome as ever you have been in anything you have done for a servant. Think, my lord, where I have put myself out of love and loyalty for you, and, accordingly may it please you to employ me.

portò il Breve ad V. S., et per altre secrete vie, sono advisato che sete stimulato per la promotione d'uno novo vescovo facto nel vostro ter-reno, il che sarebbe impaciare il facto nostro; et non de manco io spero che Vostra I. S. non lascerà la via vecchia per la nova, et maxime non sa-pendo come la nova sia facta; et ho tanta fid[ucia in] Vostra Ex., quanto merita la mia in verso de quella, et quanto per vostre lettere et per Messer Antonio m'havete dato. Et spero in Deo se n'aiutarete, così come Deo v'à dato il potere, che V. S. se ne loderà quanto de cosa che facisse mai per uno servitore. Pensate, S. mio, dove mi sono messo per amore et fede et secondo quello ne degnate adoperare.

HISTORICAL NOTE

1. Avignon and its evirons at this time belonged to the Church; as Count of Provence, René had long desired to incorporate this district into the rest of Provence. Coppini's tidings were false.

We wrote the enclosed letter to our illustrious lord, as you will see; please read it, as usual, and having understood everything in it, please take such steps as you think our business requires, according as our hopes are in you, and remember that these chances and opportunities do not occur often—except that there is no need to string out words with you when fidelity combined with deeds speaks for itself. Nonetheless, since these are great affairs and when such affairs are conducted by rumor they usually meet with great obstacles, I thus write, remind, and solicit you to be very watchful in order to be able to guard yourself against envy, because there is no greater devil in courts, and you know it. Recommend my affairs to his lordship, to whom I hope that I will be a useful servant, if God gives him the honor of the enterprise. With this will be some letters addressed to Messer Ia. Delingrati in Holland. Please dispatch them faithfully by your messenger to the hands of Messer Santo de Vergilio for the messenger who will carry the other letters to Rome.

94 · FRANCESCO COPPINI *to*

CICCO SIMONETTA

Inghilterra e Scozia, cart. 566. Orig.

Scrivemo al nostro I. S. per la alligata littera, come vederete, la quale vi piaccia leggere al modo usato, et, inteso il tutto, provedere come vi pare che rechieda il nostro fatto secondo come havemo speranza in voi; et ricordatevi che questi casi et queste opportunità non occorrono spesso, ma che [non] bisogna extendersi in parole appresso di voi, dove la fede con le opere sollicita per sé medesimo. Nondimanco perché queste son gran cose et quando sono conducte sula voce sogliono haver de grandi impacci, però vi scrivo, ricordo et sollicito che siate oculati per potervi guardar da la invidia che in corte non é il maggior diavolo, et voi il sapete. Raccomandatene al prefato Illu. S., al quale spero che sarò utile servitore, se Deo li dà honore dell'ampresa. [sic]

Con questa saranno alcune littere ad Hollandam [?] ad Messer Ia. Delingrati. Piacciavi per lo messo vostro mandarle fidelmente in mano di Messer Santo de Vergilio per quello messo che porterà l'altre ad Roma.

On April 12 I took the opportunity of dispatching word to you, by a messenger my lord of Arras [Jean Jouffroy, Bishop of Arras] *sent into these parts,* concerning what reliable news we had here about English affairs; and in this letter I will repeat what I then wrote, namely:

On March 29 the forces of King Edward and Warwick joined battle with those of King Henry, the Queen and that party at a place near York which is 170 miles from London. The struggle was intense and cruel, as happens when men fight for a realm and for their lives. In the beginning fortune seemed to be on the side of King Henry: those banners of the Queen that are inscribed, "Judge me, O Lord, and distinguish my cause from that of unholy people," appeared to have won the field, and 8,000 men and more of King Edward's and Warwick's army were killed, among whom were lords Scrope and Fitzwalter.

Then the wind changed and Edward and Warwick came off victorious, and of the army of Henry and the Queen more than 20,000 men were killed and the princes named below. In sum, thirteen princes and more than 28,000 men lost their lives, all counted by heralds after the battle, among the dead being many knights and gentlemen.

King Henry, the Queen, and the Prince withdrew to a fortress named Newcastle, which is on the sea near Scotland, and with them, the Duke of Somerset, the Duke of Exeter, Lord Roos, Lord Rivers. It

95·PROSPERO DA CAMOGLI *to the*

DUKE OF MILAN

Francia, cart. 525. Orig.

Ali dodeci del presente, per uno messo mandato in queste parte per Monsignor de Aras, scripsi a ventura quelle certificatione havevamo qui de le cose de Angliterra et per questa replico pur quello medesmo; ciohé che ali 29 de martio le gente del Re Edoardo et Varruich se appicioron cum le gente de Re Henrico, la Reina et quella banda, vicino a Iorch, longe da Londre milia cento 70 [sic]. Et la suffa fu grande et cruda, come accade unde si contende de Regno et vita; dal principio monstrava la fortuna esser dal canto del Re Henrico et quelle bandere dela Reina, chi sonno inscripte:—Iudica me Deus et discerne causam meam de gente non sancta—etc., fecero vista de vincere et fuoron occisi dele gente del Re Edoardo et Varruich homini octomilia in più, tra quali eran de Principi lo Signor de Scruppo et il Signor de Finaitter. Doppoi, mutato il vento, restoron vencitori Edoardo et Varruich et furon occisi dela banda de Henrico et la Regina homini XX^m in più et li infrascripti Principi. In summa morti Principi XIII et homini 28 milia et più, tutti computati per araldi poso la batagla, inter li quali vi eran multi cavaleri et gentilhomini. Lo Re Henrico, la Regina et lo Principe se erano retrati ad uno castello, che si domanda Neumburg, hoc est novo castello sul mare, vicino ala Scotia et cum loro lo Ducha de Sambresetrh, lo Ducha de Cetrh, il S.re de Ros, il Signor de Rivera; al qual castello, se diceva, li vencitori haver mandato obsidione de XX^m

was said that the victors sent 20,000 men to besiege this fortress and then news reached London that all the Lancastrians were captured, the which I do not believe for good news always gives birth to false flowers. Because Edward and Warwick have behaved themselves well their prestige is high, and because they have conquered their popularity is enormous.

Tomorrow, it is said, two younger brothers of the Earl of March, son of the Duke of York [i.e. Elward IV] [1] *are coming here, to whom the Duke of Burgundy has ordered great honor to be paid.*

In my letter of the 12th I wrote that I would later set forth what I think will follow from these events, and I will do so in this letter, not so much because I presume to assert myself, as to carry out the instructions Your Excellency gave me, namely to express my opinions, which, as always, I remit to the judgment of Your Lordship. I deem it necessary to impart the following information.

First, if King Henry, his Queen and the aforementioned fugitives are not captured, it seems certain that in time they will stir up fresh disturbances and strife, to which the common people are not averse since the tempest falls as much on the heads of the princes as on their own; and the fewer lords that are left, the happier the people will be, for they will thus think themselves closer to securing political freedom, to which, I am told, the citizens of London much aspire.

If, however, these Lancastrian fugitives are captured, then it can be thought that the kingdom will remain settled and quiet under King Edward and the Earl of Warwick; and since they are on very good terms with the Dauphin and the Duke of Burgundy, it is to be believed that, partly because of the hostile moves the King of France has made against the Duke of Burgundy and partly because of the Dauphin, who does not think things can remain as they are, perhaps the scheme of an English invasion of France will be carried out, especially if the Dauphin does not come to terms with the King of France, concerning which I have no further reliable news and I continue to hold the views that I expressed in the note in the letter given to Angelo [Tani]. *I have*

homini, et più era novella in Londres che erano tutti prisi, la qual cosa io non credo, cum ciò sia che semper in le bone novelle nascono de vani fiori.

La reputation de Edoardo et Varruich per loro ben viver hé grande et la gratia per haver venciuto hé grandissima; *et domane, se dice, vengono qui doi fratelli minori de D. dela Marchia, figlolo del Duca de Iorch,*[1] *ali quali el Duca de Bergogna ha deputato fare grandi honori. Io scripsi per la dicta de dodeci a V. S. che scriveria doppoi quello che mi par venga apresso queste cose et cossì facio per questa, non tanto perché io presumisca de allegarme, quanto per observar quanto me comette V. S. in la instruction, scilicet de render raxon del mio apparer del che ideo semper me remetto ala V. S.; et parmi da advertir* ut infra.

Primum, se la Regina de Anglia et el Re de Anglia cum li altri supradicti fugiti non sonno presi, el pare cosa certa che a tempo debano resuscitar remor et nove rixe, ale quali li populi non sono disformi, doppoi che la tempesta cade cossì ben sul tecto deli Principi come sul loro, et quando manco Signori gli serà, più seran contenti; et gli parerà esser più vicini al'occasion dela libertà, unde secundo m'hé dicto aspiran multo quelli de Londres. Si vero fussero preisi, el si può reputar quello Regno saldo et quieto in Re Edoardo et Conte de Varruich, et tunc essendo affecti al Delfin et al Duca de Bergogna, hé da creder che sì per li supraventi che ha fatto el Re de Franza al Duca de Bergogna, come per rispecto del Delfin, a chi par non posser star, cossì forsi se proseguirà lo designo de passar in Franza, maxime s'el Delfin non fussi in pace con el Re de Franza, del che fin a qui non ho altro de certo, et sum del parer [che] *scripsi per cedula in le littere date ad Angelo. Et ho notato lo grande fundamento che se fa el Duca de Bergogna de Anglia, che lui ha tenuto cum el Conte de Varruich, et lo figlolo con la Regina de Anglia, adciochè cadesse la cosa come si volesse, Anglia havessi vinculo de amicicia in casa del Duca de Bergogna. Et se cossì serà ch'el Stato de Anglia sii quieto in D. dela Marchia, figlolo del Duca de Iorch, et Conte de Varruich, el se reputa le cose del Duca de Bergogna esser in grande favore; et seguitando che per le novitate de Zenoa el Duca*

noted the great importance the Duke of Burgundy attaches to England,
he holding with Warwick and his son with Queen Margaret so that,
whatever happens, England has a tie of friendship with the House of
Burgundy.

If, then, England remains quiet under King Edward and War-
wick, it is thought that the affairs of the Duke of Burgundy will
thereby prosper, whereas because the rebellion at Genoa has weakened
Duke John and strengthened King Ferrante, the affairs of the King of
France do not look too good, the Dauphin not being in accord with
him and demanding a guarantee of peace for the Duke of Burgundy. I
am therefore willing to believe that the King of France, a man of great
intelligence, will, if he has not already done so, be more inclined to an
accord with the Dauphin. Hence, since in the House of France Your
Excellency is regarded hostilely because of your attitude toward the
King of Sicily [René] *and Duke John, whose party governs the King of*
France at present and is mortally hated by the Duke of Burgundy—on
which account Your Excellency may think that the situation here is of
importance to your state—it would seem to me useful for you to be
linked with the Duke of Burgundy and with his son, seeing that such a
link is a counterpoise to France; and if there would be no impediment
because of the regulations of the Order of the Golden Fleece, which
require that members support each other and the Duke of Orléans is a
member, I am persuaded that the Duke of Burgundy would be happy
to do anything that would strengthen his relations with Your Lordship.

I can tell you that the Duke speaks highly of you and I also under-
stand from a reliable source that the Duke of Burgundy's son has the
greatest esteem for you and speaks most warmly about Count Gale-
azzo; and I am told that he is thinking of dispatching a messenger to
the Pope and writing to Your Lordship and sending a little present to
Count Galeazzo. It therefore crossed my mind that if it could be
effected that Count Galeazzo were made a member of the Order of the
Golden Fleece, that membership would confer great honor and favor
on Your Lordship's House and would represent a great acquisition of

Iohanne si debiliti et el Re Ferrando si fermi, si reputa le cose del Re de Franza de non troppo bona facia, non essendo el Delfin in pace cum el Re de Franza et perché se vol far la ragion del compagno. Io voglio creder ch'el Re de Franza, chi pur hé de grande mente, forsi s'el non lo harà facto fin a qui, inclinerà più ala pace con el Delfin. Et doppoi che in casa del Re de Franza hé dato qualche carrico ala S. V. per rispecto del Re de Sicilia et Duca Iohanne, la cui parte hé quella che governa al presente el Re de Franza et hé in capital odio a pié del Duca de Bergogna,[a] unde la Excelentia Vostra reputi pertener al Stato suo le cose de qua, a me pareria utile conglutinarsi con el Duca de Bergogna et lo figlolo, attento che questo hé contrapeso de Franza; et s'el non obstassi lo Ordine dela Tueson, chi rechede che l'un sii favorevele al altro, et inter quelli gli hé lo Ducha d'Orliens, io me persuado ch'el Duca de Bergogna faria assai et volunteri ogni cosa chi pertenesse a strengersi cum la S. V.. Et qua molte parole sue de V. S. sonno humanissime, et cossì intendo per bona via lo figlolo far grande concepto de V. S., et parlar humanissimamenti del Conte Galeazio et m'hé ditto ch'el pensa de voler adriciar uno messo al Papa et scriver a V. S., et mandar uno presentetto ad epso Conte Galeazo. Et me passava per animo se mai si potessi fare che se gli donassi lo dicto Ordine dela Tueson, la qual cosa seria de grande honore et favore ala casa de V. S. et de grande aquisto de coniunction de Signori; et sento che epso Monsignor de Iharloes qualche volta n'ha ragionato cum una persona sua stretta. Siché se paresse a Vostra Excelentia ch'el Conte Galeazo cominciasse de visitarlo de qualche littere conveniente et mandargli qualche presente de barde da cavalli, non dico armature, perché non ne ha troppo, vogliate [mandarle] *qui;[b] et la Vostra Excellentia gli scrivesse qualche littere de credensa in me, io visiteria la Sua Signoria, che non ho facto fin a qui, et anderia intorno dextramenti a tastando il fundo. Et non dubiti la*

---

a. C. C. incorrectly reads: Delfin.

b. The cipher actually reads: "perché non noia troppo vulgate qui," which is obviously garbled. C. C. has interpreted thus: "perché non ne ha troppo, vogliate mandarle qui," which seems to be what Prospero intended to write.

princely alliances; and I understand that my lord of Charolais at one time mentioned this possibility to an intimate of his.

I suggest, therefore, that, if Your Excellency approves, Count Gale-azzo might begin an acquaintance with Charolais by writing an appropriate letter and by sending him some gift of horse-armor—not armor for himself—because he does not have much; and if Your Excellency would write some letter of credence for me, I would pay a visit to the Count of Charolais, which up to now I have not done, and would set about adroitly probing the situation. Your Lordship need have no fear about the quarrels and broils within the Burgundian court, about which I have sent you word, for I have dextrous means of learning what requires to de done. My lord d'Estampes, nephew, and the Bastard [Antoine], son, of the Duke of Burgundy are here; they are devoted to the Count of Charolais, as I have formerly written to Your Lordship, and they are also, let me point out, members of the Order [of the Golden Fleece]; and, from what I understand, the Dauphin has secret intelligence with Charolais, who has a reputation for prudence and valor. Nevertheless I mention all this only in case Your Lordship should find anything advantageous in affairs here, and as always I remit my observations to the judgment of Your Excellency.

Concerning Genoa, I learn that one Percivale Grillo,[2] *a Genoese who is resident at the French court* but is somewhat volatile and shallow, *has written here that the King of France blames himself for the mismanagement of the Genoese situation and does not blame the nobles; that the king is making provision to succor the citadel [into which the French garrison had withdrawn]; that the King of Sicily [René] is to send to Genoa a fleet of nine galleys; and that the Genoese nobles, saying they unanimously support the King and Duke John, give the King hope that he will recover the city. I learn also however that Girolamo Spinola*[3] *has always had a secret understanding with Your Lordship, but that Battista, his father-in-law, is entirely opposed and that consequently they are not on good terms.*

For the rest, *since the Dauphin's ambassador has returned from the*

S. V. che, perché sia qui deli garbugli et diferentie, de che ho dato adviso a Vostra Excelentia, io ho per ciò li modi dextri ad intender quello
bisogna. Qui hé Monsignor d'Etamps, nepote, et Monsignor lo Batardo,
figlolo de questo Duca de Bergogna, chi sonno affectionati a Iharloes,
come per altre ho scritto a V. S., et perciò che sonno eiusdem ordinis, io
lo ricordo voluntieri ala Excellentia Vostra, advisando quella che, per
quello sento, etiam el Delfin ha intelligentia secreta cum epso Iharloes,
il quale ha reputation de prudente et de valente Principe. Questo sia
tamen ricordato da me in caso che V. S. faci interesse dele cose de
qua, et di tutto me remetto perciò semper ala Excelentia Vostra.

In le cose de Zenoa io sento che uno Princival Grillo[2] de Zenoa, chi
sta a pié del *Re de Franza*, il qual hé perciò alquanto passionato et
legero, *ha scritto qui ch'el Re de Franza inculpa lui stesso dela improvi-
dentia ch'el ha havuto in quello Stato de Zenoa et non dà culpa alcuna
ali nobili; et fa providimenti da sucurre Castelleto, et che el Re de Sicilia
gli debbe mandar l'armata de nove galeas; et li nobili dan speransa al
Re de Franza ch'el si recupererà et sonno universaliter inclinati in el Re
de Franza et Duca Iohanne. Ma intendo etiam che Ieronimo Spinola*[3]
in secreto [sic] *ha semper sentito cum V. S., ma Baptista, suo socero,
contrariissimo et stano non bene insieme.*

Ceterum, *perciò che l'ambassatore del Delfin hé ritornato dal Re de
Franza et se dice variamenti de quello che ha fatto, come accade in le
cose alte, unde ognun ioca de sua opinione overo passione. Io sum stato
questa matina cum Mon.re de Crovi, il qual m'ha ditto che el suo ambassatore del Delfin*[c] *non ha fatto nulla, né crede deba fare, maxime per
lo rispecto che per altre ho scripto a* Vostra Excellentia, videlicet *dela
differentia etiam deli suspecti dal Re de Franza al Duca de Bergogna.
Affirmo et replico che ogni dì cresce il vento, maxime per la armata et
exercito* [del] *Re de Franza, che hé grande et multiplicata de novo; et
monstra el Duca de Bergogna star in dubio che sutto color de Cales non
schiopii qualcosa in suo paese, et cossì m'ha ditto Mon.re de Crovi. Io*

---

c. C. C. reads: Duca de Bergogna.

King of France and various things are being said about what he has done—as happens in important matters, where everyone joins in the game with his opinion or bias—I went this morning to my lord of Croy [Antoine], *who told me that the Dauphin's ambassador* [Houaste de Montespédon] *to the King, has accomplished nothing nor does he believe that anything will be accomplished especially for the reason I previously reported to* Your Excellency, namely, *the state of antagonism and suspicion that exists between the King of France and the Duke of Burgundy. I affirm and repeat that every day the wind grows stronger, especially because of the King's large fleet and army, which have recently been increased in size; and the Duke of Burgundy, as my lord of Croy has told me, seems to fear that under pretext of* [attacking] *Calais, the French may make a thrust into his territories.*

I would be happy to remain here in order to see the splendid ceremony of the Golden Fleece and to learn what decisions these lords might take—for all kinds of things are predicted—and also in order to await Your Excellency's reply somewhere else than in the Dauphin's presence; but if I hear anything else about the report of the Dauphin's ambassador, I will perhaps go to the Dauphin within three days.

In addition, I am advised by many that I should be very careful about my return journey, and since my regular route would be through Germany, I do not know if I should return that way, especially because of the documents I will have with me. I know of no route safer than that of Bavaria, but since we do not know the language nor was I ever there, I am informing Your Excellency; *and if you know things about that road, or another likely one, that I do not know, your advice in the matter will be my law.*

Concerning English affairs news arrives here from hour to hour: today is the third consecutive day that letters have come here from trustworthy English merchants at Calais. Item: it is said for certain that King Henry, the Queen, the Prince of Wales, the Duke of Somerset and his brother, Lord Roos, and the Duke of Exeter were captured, of whom the Duke of Somerset and his brother were immediately be-

stava voluntieri qui per veder questa solemnità dela Tueson et intender qualche deliberation facian questi Signori, perché pur se dice non so che, et ultra per attender resposta de Vostra Excelentia in altrove che a pié del Delfin; tamen se sonerà altro del suo ambassatore ritornato, forse che anderò fra tri dì dal Delfin.

Preterea io per me sonno advisato de multe parte che mi deba haver bona advertentia in el mio ritorno, per modo che quasi per haver frequentato Alamagna, non so se deba ritornargli, dico maxime per rispecto dele scriture; et non so camin più sicuro come quello de Bavera, et perciochè non savemo le lingue né mai gli fui, io ne adviso volunteri la Ex.tia Vostra, adciochè se per là, aut per altro camin opportuno gli fusse deli rispecti che io non so, lo adviso di quella mi sia legge.

Dele cose de Angliterra, perciochè de hora in hora se ha novelle, hoggi hé il tertio dì che sonno qui littere de anglesi mercatanti de fede; item de verso Cales come di certo lo Re Henrico, la Regina, lo Principe de Gales, figlolo, lo Ducha de Semesetrh, lo Signor de Ros, suo fratello, lo Ducha de Setrh erano preisi, deli quali subito fu taglata la testa alo Ducha de Semesetrh et suo fratello; et cossì seguitandosi sul Ducha de Setrh, quasi in lo puncto dela decolatione, venne voce ch'el scampassi; et per esser cognato de Re Edoardo, de chi ha la sorella, se dice esser stato salvato, tamen perché hé fero et [i..gu..r..ale], se extima lo faran morir a morte più honesta. Io me era suprastato a scriver questo per veder se si affermava altramenti; se cossì hé per certo tra Re Edoardo et Varruich puocho avanti rupti, afflicti et expulsi,[4] et Re Henrico et la Regina vencitori, et chi gli pareva haver spianato il mondo serà uno singular exemplo de quella che li prudenti homini, in excusa deli errori humani, han nominato fortuna; et chi ben consydera le infelicitate de quella Regina et le ruine deli occisi, et attenta la ferocità del paese, cum che animo resti li vencitori! Veramenti me par habbi a pregar Dio per morti et non manco per vivi.

De quello che habbi a seguitare, multi sonno li examini chi se ne fan, attento quello Regno orbato de tanti Principi naturali et reduto [sic] solamenti in dui chi habiano nome et reputatione de Principi, et

headed. Then, just as the Duke of Exeter was likewise to be beheaded, there came word that he should be spared. It is said that he was saved because he is married to King Edward's sister [Anne], but since he is fierce and [. . .], it is thought that they will nonetheless have him put to death, but in a more honorable fashion.

I had stopped writing this letter in order to see if the news might be confirmed from another source. If what I have reported is indeed correct, then what with King Edward and Warwick only a little before this broken, pursued, and driven from England [4] and King Henry and the Queen completely victorious, it can certainly be said, first, that anyone who thinks he has subdued the world will prove to be a vivid example of the operations of what prudent men, in excusing human error, have called fortune; and, second, that everyone who considers the wretchedness of that Queen, the destruction, the number killed and who, knowing the ferocity of the country, understands in what state of mind the victors remain, truly it seems to me must pray to God for the living no less than for the dead.

Concerning what will now happen in England many analyses are put forward, seeing that that kingdom has been deprived of so many princes, its natural leaders, and that there remain only two who have the name and reputation of princes [namely, King Edward and the Earl of Warwick], who by their prudence and their exemplary behavior in the face of virulent enmity have recovered from such persecution and overcome all. However, since it would not be appropriate for my slender intelligence to try to take the measure of, nor to grasp in its entirety, a matter of such high significance, I am waiting to hear more; and as long as I have to be here, I will continually keep Your Excellency informed of all events. As always I humbly recommend myself to Your Excellency.

Postscript. At this point there arrived here letters and Genoese merchants come from London, and also a Genoese squire of the Earl of Warwick. These men do not confirm the capture of King Henry and the Queen and the rest of their company, as recounted above; though they

chi per prudentia et ben viver loro cum la animosità se sian recuperati da tante persecutione et habian superato tutto. Tamen, percioché ala mia tenuità non conven né squadrar né metter al tondo cose de tanta grandessa, io ne starò ad audir et tanto quanto harò ad esser de qua, adviserò continuamenti la Ex.tia V. de tutti li accidenti, ala qual semper humiliter me racomando.

Post scripta. In questo puncto sonno iuncte qui littere et mercatanti zenoesi venuti da Londre, inter cetera uno zenoese scudero de Varruich, per li quali non se afferma la preisa del Re Henrico et la Regina et compagni ut supra. Ben dicono che essendo a Cales se faceva fochi et falodi correspondenti a quelli si facevano a Sanduchio et Dobla in Angliterra, perché si comprehende et crede esser doppoi seguito cum sit che dela obsidione ognun lo afferma. Per il che io me remetto ala verità; semper in mandata paratissimus.

Nota de Signori morti [in] Angliterra dela parte dela Reina ala batagla che fu a 29 de marcio.

Il Conte di Nortamburlant
Il Conte de Vuestemburlant
Il Conte de Devenscire
Il Sig.re de Cliffort
Il Sig.re de Nivelle
Il Sig.re de Bramont
Il Sig.re de Duelles
Il Sig.re de Vuelby filius
Il Sig.re Arigho de Bochinchamb
Antonio de Rivera, Sig.re di Scales
Il Signor Daties
Andrea Trolop, cavaler
et più morti multi cavaleri et gentilhomini con XX^m persone.

Dela [parte] del Re Edoardo:

say that when they passed through Calais, there were bonfires and fireworks corresponding to those that were being made at Sandwich and Dover in England. Hence it is believed that the Lancastrians were indeed afterward captured since everyone affirms that they had been besieged.

On this subject I remit myself to the truth, always most ready to obey your orders.

List of the Lancastrian lords killed at the battle [of Towton] on March 29:

The Earl of Northumberland
The Earl of Westmoreland [false]
The Earl of Devon [captured after the battle and beheaded]
Lord Clifford
Lord Neville
Lord [Viscount] Beaumont [false]
Lord Welles
Lord Willoughby's son
Lord Harry of Buckingham [Sir Henry Stafford] [false]
Anthony of Rivers, [i.e. Anthony Woodville, son of Lord Rivers]
[false]
Lord Scales [captured after the battle]
Lord Dacres
Andrew Trollope, knight
and many knights and gentlemen along with 20,000 others.

Lords killed on King Edward's side:

Lord Scrope [of Bolton] [false]
Lord Fitzwalter [died shortly after of his wounds]
and more than 8,000 others.

Those said to be captured: [false, except for Lord Rivers]
King Henry
the Queen

Il Sig.or de Scrupp
Il Sig.or de Finaiter   } morti
et più VIII^m persone

Et se dice esser preisi:
Il Re Henrico
La Reina
Il Principe
Il Ducha de Somersetrh
Il Ducha de Sestre
Il Sig.re de Rosa
Il Sig.re de Rivera

the Prince
the Duke of Somerset
the Duke of Exeter
Lord Roos
Lord Rivers

HISTORICAL NOTES

1. George (1449–78), later Duke of Clarence, and Richard (1452–85), later Duke of Gloucester and King Richard III, had been sent from London to the Low Countries when the Lancastrian army, after the second battle of St. Albans (17 Feb.), was threatening the capital.

2. Percivale Grillo, member of one of Genoa's leading clans with considerable banking interests both in France and England [Heers, *Gênes au XVᵉ siècle*, 85, 569].

3. Except for Girolamo, the Spinola had supported the French at Genoa [Simonetta, B. XXVIII, 442].

4. In October, 1460, after their defeat at Ludford near Ludlow by the Lancastrians.

After what I wrote today, there arrived here the two brothers of King Edward of England, youths, the one, eleven years old [George, born Oct. 21, 1449] and the other about ten, [Richard, actually eight years old, born Oct. 2, 1452] whom the Duke of Burgundy, as he is in all things most benign, has been to visit at their lodgings and has treated with great respect. I had gone to thank his excellency for the kindness he has done me out of regard for Your Lordship and to request permission to return *to the Dauphin in order to find out if anything has happened. His lordship urged me to remain here until there is really certain news from England and I thought it good to comply.*

I recommend myself to Your Excellency, whom God preserve.

96·PROSPERO DA CAMOGLI *to the*

DUKE OF MILAN

Francia, cart. 525. Orig.

Post hodie scripta, hoggi sonno iuncti qui li doi fratelli del Re Edoardo de Angliterra, iuvenetti l'uno de XI, l'altro de X anni vel circa, li
quali questo Ill.mo S.re, cossi come hé in tutte le cose benignissimo, hé
stato a visitar al logiamento et gli ha fatto grande reverentie. Io era andato per rengratiar Sua Ex.tia dele caresse m'ha fatto per rispecto de
Vostra Ill.ma S.ria et domandar licentia per ritornarmene *dal Delfin
per intender si quid est* etc.. *Sua Signoria mà confortato che io resti qui
fin che de Anglia se habia certessa ferma et cossì non m'hé paruto de
non obedir.* Me racomando ala Ex.tia V., che Dio conservi.

I have informed Your Illustrious Lordship of English events, by several letters, and especially a few days ago, by a servant of mine who should be there in twelve or fourteen days. Now I am sending Your Lordship copies of letters received from England, notably from the Chancellor [George Neville, Bishop of Exeter], a brother of the Earl of Warwick, and from two other bishops, from which you will be informed of the final most wonderful victory gained by the Earl of March, the newly made King [Edward IV], and by Warwick, and will learn what a cruel battle it was, since on both sides a total of 28,000 men have been killed.[1] Of these, ten of the greatest lords of the other party perished, whereas our King lost only one baron and 800 other men. Things are changing for the better, and never was there a more propitious time for the Pope and for Your Lordship, if the matter is rightly understood. Since you see from the contents of the letters that my returning to England is welcome, I am on my way back there and, for my part, will do all that I should, and more. It remains for those in your quarter to do what is needful, concerning which all hope of success lies in your authority and in your hand. I am in despair, my lord, because I see so many glorious opportunities at hand and yet I am neither aided nor understood; however, I am consoled by the trust I have

97·FRANCESCO COPPINI *to the*

DUKE OF MILAN

Inghilterra e Scozia, cart. 566. Orig.

Per più littere ho advisato V.I.S. delli successi d'Inghilterra et maxime a dì proxmi [sic] passati per fante proprio che dovea essere costì in
12 o 14 dì. Hora mando ad V.I.S. la copia delle littere havute d'Inghilterra et maxime dal cancelliere, fratello del Conte di Warwic, et da dui
altri Vescovi, per le quali intenderà la prefata V.I.S. la final et mara-
vigliosa victoria che ha havuta lo Conte della Marcia, che é facto nuovo
Re, et decto Warwich et quanto crudel battaglia é stata, che da una et
dall'altra parte sono morti XXVIII milia homini[1] infra quali sono X
maggior signor dell'altra parte e di questa summa non sono morti
della parte del nostro Re se non I° barone et VIIIe altri. Sono le cose
disposte ad reformarsi et mai fu il più bel tempo per N.S. et per V.I.S.
se ben s'intende la cosa; et perché come vedete per tenor delle littere la
mia tornata é grata, sono in camino per andar là et proseguir dal canto
mio il debito et più che debito. Resta che di costà si facci il bisogno, del
quale tutta la speranza é in vostra auctorità et in vostra mano. Io mi dis-
pero, I.S. mio, che veggo apparechiate troppo gloriose cose et non sono
aiutato né inteso, ma pur mi conforta la fede che ho in Vostra I. S. che mi
fa mettere ad ogni sbaraglio. Con questa saranno littere in corte ad Messer Falcone, et scrivo ad N.S. tutto. Piaccia ad V.I.S. mandarle per
fidato et far di là provisione che par necessaria. Fui advisato per littera

in Your Lordship, which prompts me to take any risk. With this missive will be letters addressed to Messer Falcone at the Curia, and I am writing everything to the Pope. Will Your Lordship please forward those letters by a trusty messenger and make such provision as appears necessary.

I am informed, by a letter of March 4 from Messer Antonio della Torre, of what on that side was arranged and I replied by the above-mentioned messenger. My lord, it is not who begins but who perseveres that will be saved. I am, today, to be with the Dauphin, who awaits me in Brussels in order to confer about matters of great import pertaining to this affair; and within three days I will be at the council of the Duke of Burgundy [i.e. assembly of the Order of the Golden Fleece], from which place I will send information to Your Lordship. In God's name, aid this enterprise, and quickly, if you wish to see great things such as have not been seen for many ages. I recommend myself to Your Lordship; may God preserve you long.

Held back until May 1: I found here letters from Your Illustrious Lordship concerning the going of Messer Antonio della Torre to Rome. I have nothing else to add, for already Your Lordship can see from the foregoing the propitious occurrences here, which can result in many good things, provided that support is forthcoming. Your Lordship can see that here no one is sleeping. I go tomorrow to the Duke's council, where I hope to find your Messer Prospero, and I will write again. Then I will cross to England in order to deal with the matters that need attention. May Your Lordship do what is necessary there so that here it is not necessary to solicit.

HISTORICAL NOTE

1. These three letters are published in translation in CSPM, I, 60–67.

di Messer Antonio da la Turre a dì 4 di marzo di quanto costì era ordinato et risposi per lo messo soprascripto.

I.S. mio, non qui inceperit, sed qui perseveraverit salvus erit. Io debbo essere oggi con lo Illu.mo Delphino che m'aspetta in Borsella per conferire di grandi et degne cose appartenenti ad questa materia et infra tre dì sarò al Consiglio dello Illu. Duca, dal quale luogo advisarò V.S. Per Dio aiutate questa impresa, et presto, se volete vedere cose degne et gran tempo non viste. Raccomandomi ad V.S. che Dio ne conservi lungo tempo.

Tenuta a dì p° di maggio: et ho trovato qui littere di Vostra I.S. sopra l'andata de Messer Antonio dalla Torre ad Roma; et altra cosa non accade, perché già di sopra vede la I.S.V. li felici successi di qua, che potranno essere acconcio di molte cose bone, se saranno aiutate. I.S., vede la S.V. che di qua non si dorme et io vado domani al Consiglio di questo I. Duca, dove spero trovare il vostro Messer Prospero et scriverò iterum. Di poi ne andrò in Anglia per tener le mani su queste cose che ne hanno bisogno. Faccia la S.V. quanto bisogna de là, che de qua non bisogna sollicitare.

Since we are about to take horse, we will not write to you at length; you will see what I write to our illustrious lord and the glorious victory won by our friends in England, the like of which was never heard of. We are going there in order to arrive while matters are fresh and to pursue our enterprise; and if we are given aid, we will do wonders. It has been the will of God that we left England so as to be saved and to return when things were secure in order to accomplish deeds honorable to God and to the Church and to the whole state of Italy. You will see from the letters that 28,000 men have perished in one battle, in which have fallen eleven great lords of the other party. God pardon them and give us the grace to do well. I recommend to your care the enclosed letters that we wrote to the Pope and others in the Curia, directing them to Messer Falcone. It seems to me that our illustrious lord the Duke might do well to write some letter to England, and perhaps we will send you a memorandum of what we think would be appropriate. We have perceived from the letters of Messer Antonio della Torre your diligence and zeal in our affairs. Continue to act thus with sincerity, as we have hopes of gratifying you.

Held back until May 1, at Bruges. We have had letters from our lord and from you concerning the coming of Messer Antonio della Torre.

98 · FRANCESCO COPPINI *to*

CICCO SIMONETTA

Inghilterra e Scozia, cart. 566. Orig.

Perché semo per montar ad cavallo non vi scrivemo lungo, ma vederete quanto scrivo al nostro I.S. et la gloriosa victoria havuta per li nostri amici in Anglia che mai fu udita simile. Et noi andemo là per arrivare ad cose fresche et seguitare le nostre imprese, et se saremo aiutati, faremo cose mirabili. É stata la voluntà di Dio che ad tempo ne partissimo per esser salvi et ritrovarci al tempo sicuro da far cose honorevoli a Dio et ad la chiesa et tutto lo stato di Italia; voi lo vedete et intendete che sono morti in una battaglia XXVIII^m homini, dove sono caduti XI li maior Signori dell'altra parte. Dio li perdoni, et ad noi dia gratia di far bene. Raccomandovi le littere alligate che scrivemo in corte ad N.S. et altri, drizandole ad Messer Falcone; parne che lo N.I.S. Duca debbe scrivere qualche littera in Anglia et forsi vi manderemo la nota secondo il nostro disegno. Havemo visto per littere di Messer Antonio dalla Torre la vostra diligentia et fervore in le nostre cose. Seguite con l'animo franco che speramo farvi consolati.

Tenuta a dì primo di maggio in Bruggia: et havemo littere dello I.S. et vostre della venuta di Messer Antonio dala Turri; et altra cosa non bisogna, perché già di sopra havete il bisogno, et per questa volta non credo che aspettassino meglio. Fate hora voi de costì che qui non si dorme.

No need to write further, because already from the foregoing you have what is necessary. I do not believe that for the present a better opportunity could be expected. You there now be doing, for here nobody is sleeping.

It happens that I have many things to write to Your Excellency *and it is an essential part of the loyalty I owe to you to write strictly what I hear, for it is not my place, but* Your Excellency's, *to evaluate information, especially since I know no more than I do about what is of importance and what is not of importance to Your Lordship's state. I make this statement purposely so that certain others will not think my diligent reports to be merely mental vaporings.*

One who up to now I find to be a good servant of Your Excellency *writes me from Nivelles, where the Dauphin has a residence, that, by a relative of his come from the French court, he is informed that the son of the Bailli of Asti* [Regnault de Dresnay] *recently went to the King of France and, his business immediately dispatched, returned to Asti; that the King of France had decided on 400 lances for Lombardy, of which half were already in Dauphiné; that everyone at the French court was saying that Your Lordship was the author of the revolution at Genoa, that the Dukes of Brittany and Orléans were very speedily to be at court and many other nonsensical braggings in the French manner and in blame of Your Lordship.*[1]

I have likewise been assured of all this by the Dauphin's ambassador [Houaste de Montespédon], *now returned from the King of France, who came here to the Duke of Burgundy, and very restrained and*

99·PROSPERO DA CAMOGLI *to the*

DUKE OF MILAN

Francia, cart. 525. Orig.

El accade scriver de multe cose a V. Ex.tia, *et hé necessario ufficio dela fede debo a quella scriver secundo che io sento, cum ciò sia che a me non specta, sed ala* Ex.tia V., *discerner li uti* [li] *advisi dali vacui, maxime non sapendo più de quella o che io so esser pertinente o inpertinente al Stato dela* S. V.; *questo scrivo volunteri acioché la mia diligentia non paresse a qualcun altri fumosità de cervello.*

Uno che io trovo fin a qui bon servitor dela Ex.tia V., *me scrive da Nivella, che hé stantia del Delfin, che per uno suo parente venuto dela curte del Re de Franza, hé advisato come lo figlolo del Baglo de Ast era venuto dal Re de Franza frescamenti et subito spaciato se ne era ritornato; et che el Re de Franza havia deliberato quatrocento lance per Lumbardia, dele quale era ià la mettà in Dalfinato; et che lì per tutto se diceva la* S. V. *esser stato la autore dela novità de Zenoa; et che el Duca de Bertagna et Orliens dovevano esser multo presto ala curte, et multe altre iactantie farsi al modo de Franza et in carrico dela* V. S..[1] *Et così me ha affermato l'ambassatore del Delfin, revenuto dal Re de Franza, il quale ambassatore hé stato qui dal Duca de Bergogna multo continente et basso, perché cumprendo nulla habbi fatto; tamen lo vero sii in suo loco et procurerò de saperlo.*

Item, qui hé iuncto uno currero de Zenoa mandato a mercatanti qui, il qual, dicendo de multi pauori del Stato de Zenoa novo, dice che

humble he was, which leads me to think that he has done nothing. However, let the truth be in its place, and I will seek to ferret it out.

Item: *there has arrived a Genoese courier sent to the merchants here, who, speaking of the many fears of the new government of Genoa, says that the Venetians have sent ambassadors to Your Lordship because of their suspicions regarding Genoa and are assembling a fleet, it being uncertain whether it is to be sent against the Turk or to Apulia. I do not believe the Venetians have any such evil intentions, but such murmurings as are being made, prompt me to send this word to Your Lordship.*

For the rest, I decided today that there would never be much for me to do here and that, because of the return of the Dauphin's ambassador, I should go back to the Dauphin to learn what I could. I therefore had recourse to my lord of Croy, who, however, urged me to remain here and then persuaded me that I should go to see the Duke of Burgundy. On doing so, I was told by the Duke that he would like me to remain here until there was reliable word about what had happened in England. The situation there remains as follows: Neither the Queen of England nor her son was captured, as it was reported. Messengers and letters, however, give assurance that they are besieged, as I wrote. Hence, I remained here, my lord of Croy telling me that if I wanted information about French affairs, I would secure better and more truthful information through his brother [Jean, Count of Chimay], *who has returned and is to be at the assembly of the Golden Fleece, than through the Dauphin. His brother and Messer Simon de Lalain,[2] who had gone on embassy to the King of France, have come back without having had audience; and from what I learn there is not much love lost, in private, between the Duke of Burgundy and the Dauphin, as I have written and now affirm; and I fear that the Dauphin may incur a great deal of blame for taking too much on himself, which he does either because he is over ambitious or because he feels that necessity compels him to—and it may be for both reasons. Nevertheless, I do not presume to set this forth as fact, and I refer myself to the truth.*

Venetiani havian mandato ambassatori a V. S. per zelosia de Zenoa et
che fan armata, del che hé incerto o per lo Turco aut per Apulia. Io
non credo miga mal de Venetiani, tamen tante susuracione se ne fan,
me strengono ad advisarne la S. V..

Ceterum, parendomi hoggi mai non far troppo de qua, et per la
ritornata del ambassatore del Delfin esser meglo a ritornarmene dal Del-
fin per intender qualcosa, etc., ho havuto ricorso da Mon.re de Crovi, il
qual me *confortò pur a restar qui et demum laudoe* [sic] *che io stesso*
fussi cum el Duca de Bergogna. Et cossì fui dala Signoria Sua. Me re-
spuse[a] *piacerli che io restassi qui fin a qualche certessa dele cose de*
Angliterra, quale sonno pur ancor cossì: nam né la Regina de Anglia né
el figlolo furen preisi, come se disse; li messi et le littere acertan ben che
sonno assidiati, come scripsi. Cossì me restai, dicendomi Mon.re de
Crovi che se pur era mio desiderio de intender dele cose de Franza et
del Re de Franza, io le intenderia meglo et più veracementi per la via de
suo fratello, chi hé ritornato et debe esser ala Tueson, che per via del
Delfin; il qual suo fratello et messer Simon de Lalain[2] *erano ambassa-*
tori al Re de Franza, et se ne sonno ritornati sensa haver havuto audi-
entia et, [per] *quanto comprendo, dal Duca de Bergogna al Delfin non*
gli hé gratia troppo in intimo, et affermo quanto ne scripsi; et dubito
che [al] *Delfin non se gli dia troppo culpa per far troppo o per neces-*
sità, et forsi che hé per l'una causa et per l'altra. Tamen non presumisco
de affirmarlo et me reporto ala verità.

Io vedandomi [sic] *retener qui per cose generale, primamenti hebbi*
suspicion ch'el Delfin, chi non volse a questi dì patir che io me retra-
hesse da canto, come scripsi a Vostra Excelentia, per attender risposta
de quanto scripsi per Martino cavallaro, et a chi forsi gravava il cor-
responder ali honori fatti per la S. V. a Gaston, non fusse quello chi me
havesse piantato qui per uno termine de medio; et per questo io era al-
quanto perplexo de quello che me havessi a fare, maxime che havendo
la S. V. honorato assai quelli del Duca de Bergogna,[b] *non paresse che*

---

a. The cipher reads "me scluse" but C .C. has "me respuse" which is more appropriate.
b. C. C. incorrectly reads: Delfin.

Seeing myself being detained here for no specific purpose, I first suspected the Dauphin. As I wrote to Your Excellency, he had not wanted me to withdraw from his court while I awaited your reply to the dispatch I had sent by Martino the courier—his reluctance perhaps caused by embarassment in comparing such treatment with the honors Your Lordship had paid Gaston—and I suspected that he might have planted me here in the meanwhile. I was therefore perplexed about what I should do, especially because I did not want it to be thought that I was here to redeem the courtesies that Your Lordship had so splendidly accorded to visitors from the court of Burgundy. But after I had, on that account, made an attempt to obtain license to depart from the Duke of Burgundy, his lordship sent to me a Messire Claude Molongion,[3] who had formerly been at Milan with the Duke of Clèves. This gentleman, after urging me to remain and see the ceremonies of the Golden Fleece, then went on at weary length to tell me that the Duke of Burgundy was awaiting certain answers and advices, in consequence of which the Duke perhaps would have more to say to me than he had so far said. I gave no sign that I understood what he meant, though it is true that for the many offers the Duke of Burgundy had made me I thanked him, and since I did not think it befitted Your Lordship's honor for me to overlook, nor indeed could I avoid, the attentions he paid me, i.e. the offers he made and his telling me that the Duke of Burgundy wished to present to me etc., I thus signified my appreciation. However, my purpose remained to withdraw myself from this situation so that, as I note above, it would not look as if Your Excellency sent me here to redeem the courtesies that Your Lordship extends out of sheer benevolence; and I therefore showed some reluctance to go to St. Omer to the festival of the Golden Fleece, indicating that I did not think myself of sufficient rank to attend such a high ceremony. The Duke of Burgundy, however, signified to me that it was his wish that I be there; and so I will go, and of what I learn there I will inform Your Excellency, to whom I humbly recommend myself.

Among these Genoese merchants here, there are indeed some who

io fussi qui per rescoter le cortesie, etc.. Ma dopoi perché [per] *tal rispecto ho fatto instantia de prender licentia dal Duca de Bergona, la Signoria Sua me mandò uno Messer Clacaudo Molongion*[3] [sic], *chi alias fu là cum lo Duca de Cleve, il qual, confortandomi a restar et a veder la festa dela Tueson, stracurse in dirme ch'el Duca de Bergogna aspectava certe resposte et advisi per li quali forse la Signoria Sua me ragioneria più avanti che non ha fatto. La qual cosa io non monstrai intender; ben hé vero che a multe proferte me ha fatto el Duca de Bergogna io lo ho rengratiato, et non parendomi conveniente al honor de V. S., né posser obviar ale caresse me fa, quanto specta ale offerte et a quello me era dicto ch'el Duca de Bergogna voleva presentarmi, etc., io ho fatto signification et sum per farne lo effecto in tuto de abstrarmi de tal cosa, adcioché come dico de supra, non paresse che Vostra Excellentia m'havesse mandato qui per riscoter quelle cortesie che Vostra Signoria fa gratis, etc.; feci qualche repugnantia per non voler andar a San Thomer ala festa dela Tueson, per non parendomi in grado degno de tali spectaculi. Tamen el Duca de Bergogna m'ha significato esser suo desiderio che io gli sii; et cossì gli anderò, et de quanto intenderò là, adviserò Vostra Excellentia, ala quale humiliter me racomando.*

Inter questi mercatanti de Zenoa qui gli hé pur de quelli chi rugiscono de quella transformation del Stato de Zenoa, et hé chi dice che tra'l Duce et li Fregosi comincia nascer rugine, ma che tutto sta coperto per esser ancora Castelleto in mano de Galli.

are raging about this alteration in the government of Genoa, and it is said that trouble is beginning to develop between the Doge and the Fregoso but that it remains entirely concealed because the citadel is still in the hands of the French.

HISTORICAL NOTES

1. Sforza's secret agents had in fact aggravated popular discontent against the French, and his troops were soon involved on the side of the rebels. Moreover, the Duke had been instrumental through his envoy, Tommaso Moroni da Rieti, in keeping Archbishop Paolo Campofregoso and Prospero Adorno united in their efforts to expel the French garrison from the *Castelletto* [Simonetta, B. XXVIII, 443; cf. Sforza to Ottone del Carretto, Milan, March 14 and 20, 1461, *Roma,* cart. 50]. Charles VII sent to Milan his Councilor and Master of Requests, Henry de Merle, bearing a letter [Mehun, Apr. 19, 1461, *Francia,* cart. 525; published by Beaucourt, VI, 494-95] reproaching Sforza for his anti-French activity, contrary to his previous protestations of devotion to the French monarchy, and requesting the withdrawal of Milanese troops from Genoa and aid for the besieged garrison. The King invited the Duke to state his intentions on this matter so that he could take appropriate action. The envoy did not arrive in Milan until the evening of May 28, having been delayed by his efforts to recruit troops in Piedmont for raising the siege of the *Castelletto,* and left the city on May 31 [Vincenzo della Sca-

lona to the Marchioness of Mantua, Milan, May 18, 20, 28, and 31, 1461, A. S. Mantova, *Carteggio–Milano,* B. 1621; cf. Bartolomeo Birago to Sforza, Asti, May 21, 1461, *Asti,* cart. 476]. In compliance with the royal request, the Duke dispatched Iob de Palazzo to Genoa with a written order [June 6 and July 2, 1461, *Reg. Ducale* 160, pp. 453, 483] recalling his forces and requesting his "adherents" to give transit and supplies to French troops marching towards the city. Iob was also instructed to go to Asti and advise its Governor, Dresnay, and Henry de Merle of this action [Iob to Sforza, Asti, June 12, 1461, *Asti,* cart. 476]. These "official" orders did not deceive the French Ambassador, however [Bartolomeo Birago to G. Simonetta, Asti, Aug. 13, 1461, *ibid.,* cart. 476], for it was known that Sforza continued to aid the rebels with money and troops [see doc. 120, n. 8, p. 451].

2. Simon de Lalain, lord of Montegny, councilor and chamberlain and experienced diplomat, was "one of the most notable lords of the Duke of Burgundy's household" [Beaucourt, *Charles VII,* VI, 24].

3. Unidentified; evidently a gentleman of the Duke of Burgundy's household.

We have written often about English events to his illustrious lordship and to you, and have shown the situation there to be such that, if vigorous support is provided from your quarter, the outcome will be glorious, for never was there a more propitious time. We await, following upon the arrival [in Italy] of Messer Antonio [della Torre], an answer from there to some effect.

In addition, we found here the honorable Messer Prospero da Camogli, from whom we have received letters of his lordship and have learned of the commission Messer Prospero has to cross to England. Having left that country and now, because of the happy turn of events there, being requested to return, we desire Messer Prospero to go there also, which will be very advantageous to our designs for he seems to me a man of brains and experience. However, although he has said that he is willing to do what we think best, nonetheless he makes some difficulty about it. Upon our inquiring what the trouble was, he said that he was not properly prepared to go and, next, that the main reason for his coming here was not to cross to England—and indeed when he had concluded his main mission, concerning which he awaits reply from your lordship, he desired to return to Italy, especially because of some changes that have occurred in those parts [i. e. the Genoese rising against the French], in which he has no small interest, as he says Your

100 · FRANCESCO COPPINI *to*

CICCO SIMONETTA

Inghilterra e Scozia, cart. 566. Orig.

Noi havemo scripto spesso delli progressi d'Inghilterra ad quello Illu. S. et ad voi et demonstrato le cose essere in termini che, se virilmente se li dà favor di costà, haranno glorioso fine né mai fu più bel tempo. Aspettemo, dopo la venuta di Messer Antonio, risposta di là con qualche effecto. Havemo insuper ritrovato qui lo Spec.le Messer Prospero Camulio, dal quale havemo ricevute littere del prefato Illu. S. et intesa la commissione che havea passar in Anglia per ritrovarci. Hora essendo noi passati di qua et dipoi per li felici successi, essendo in Anglia richiamati, desideramo la venuta di decto Messer Prospero di là, che al proposito dell cose disegnate sarà molto opportuna, perché ne pare homo di cervello et prattico; pur, benché ne habbi risposto voler far nostro parere, niente di manco ne fa alchuna difficultà et, volendole noi intendere, ne dice non haver ben il modo, et appresso che la principal casone di sua venuta di qua non era il passar in Anglia; et pertanto, quando havesse absoluta la principal commissione sopra la quale aspecta risposta dal S., desiderava ritornarsi in là et maxime per alcune novità di quelle parti, dove ha non pocho interesse, come dice essere noto ad V. M.tia; et così da lui non havemo explicita risposta. Pertanto cognoscendo noi che la sua compagnia ne può essere gran favore ad li nostri disegni, et maxime per lo Stato della Chiesa et di tucta Italia, et havendo noi desiderato da quel S. uno suo huomo, come da Messer Antonio po-

Magnificence knows, and so we have not had an explicit reply from him. Consequently, since we know that his accompanying us can be very helpful to our designs, particularly for the state of the Church and for all Italy, and since we had already requested of his lordship a man of his, as you can learn from Messer Antonio, Messer Prospero's cooperation seems to us both profitable and necessary; and I therefore beg you to exert yourself with his lordship so that he forthwith instructs Messer Prospero to obey his commission and come to England when the time seems right, and that in the meantime his lordship provided him with appropriate letters of credence, as also we mentioned briefly in letters we wrote to his lordship, which you will see.

Afterward, we wrote a letter to the Holy Father concerning these plans, of which we are sending you the original and a copy so that his lordship can see it and, if he thinks good to do so, send it on. We did all this for a good purpose, namely, that His Holiness may understand in every detail how useful and effective for him and for the Church are the operations of his illustrious lordship. For the rest, we recommend ourselves cordially to Your Magnificence, and so may it please you to recommend me to his lordship.

As a result of the change in government in England, the French are issuing orders on a great scale for the mustering of a fleet and an army. Some are afraid that the object is to give trouble to the Duke of Burgundy, and he fears so. Others think the movement is aimed at England, but the French will come too late, according to what people think. If in your quarter speedy provision is made for our business, all will go well. God grant that you do the right thing.

teste intendere, ne par utile et necessario; et così vi prego che odoperiate col prefato Illu. S. che quam primum commetta a dicto Messer Prospero che seguiti la commissione et che passi di là quando ne parerà il tempo, et interim provedali di lectere opportune, come anche tocchamo succintamente nelle littere che scrivemo al S., le quali vederete.

Appresso scrivemo una littera al Sancto Padre sopra questa parte, della quale vi mandamo la copia et la originale, acciò che la veda il prefato Illu. S. et parendoli di mandarla, la mandi. Tutto facemo ad fin di bene, acciò che Sua S.tà intenda per ogni verso le opere del prefato Illu. S. officiose et grate per lo Stato di Sua S. et della Chiesa. Ceterum ne raccomandemo ad V. M.tia cordialmente, così ve piaccia raccomandarne al prefato Illu. S.

Dopo queste novità d'Inghilterra li Franzesi fanno grandi cenni d'armata per mare et per terra. Alchuni dubitano che siano per dare noia ad questo S. et lui ne dubita. Altri stimano per Inghilterra, ma arriveranno tarde secondo che si crede. Se di costà si provede presto al bisogno, ogni cosa anderà bene. Dio vi dia ad prender bon partito.

By my last, written a few days ago from Bruges, I informed Your Illustrious Lordship about English affairs and sent copies of the letters concerning all that happened up to that day. I wrote also to Your Lordship that, having learned of the presence in these parts of the Honorable Messer Prospero, your emissary, I would attempt to get in touch and cooperate with him, and I requested Your Lordship to send him word to the same effect. After I arrived at the court of the Duke of Burgundy, who is holding his council [i.e. the assembly of the Golden Fleece] here in St. Omer, a day's journey from Calais, I found Messer Prospero, from whom I received letters of Your Lordship to the desired effect, although because of the changes that have occurred in English affairs and my departure from that country and also because of his own preoccupations, up to now he has not crossed *to England*. I have similarly taken pleasure in discovering that in his *negotiations* with *the Dauphin* he began well and has continued up to now with good prospect of success, and I thus see that we are all firing at the same target; for, before I saw Messer Prospero or knew of his proceedings, I had a long conversation with *the Dauphin* in which I introduced the question *of English* affairs and dropped a few significant hints—although *Your Lordship* was not especially *named,* nevertheless the Dauphin was able to understand that if he took a lead in these affairs, *he would find Your*

101 · FRANCESCO COPPINI *to the*

DUKE OF MILAN

Francia, cart. 525. Orig.[a]

Per le mie ultime, pochi giorni avanti da Bruggia, advisai V. I. S. delle cose d'Inghilterra et mandai le copie delle lettere di tucto il seguito fin quel dì. Scripsi etiam ad V. I. S. che havendo inteso essere in questi parti lo Spectabile Messer Prospero, vostro messo, me forzerei retrovarlo et intenderemi [sic] seco, confortando V. I. S. che per sua lettera li scrivessi in simile effecto. Di poi sono arrivato in corte di questo I. S. Duca, qual tiene suo Consiglio qui in Sancto Odomaro presso ad Cales ad una zornata, et ho ritrovato decto Messer Prospero dal quale ho ricevuto lettere di V. S. in quel effecto che desideravo, benché per le novità seguite et per la mia partita et anchora per le occupationi sue fin mò, non sia passato *in Anglia;* et trovando *la pratica* dello *Illustre Delfino,* per lui cominciata et continuata fin mò in assai bon termini, similiter ne ho havuto piacere, vedendo che tutti tiramo ad uno segno, perché avanti che vedessi decto Messer Prospero o sapessi de suoi progressi, essendo io stato ad lungo parlamento con decto *Monsignor Delfino,* havevo introducta pratica delle cose *de Anglia* cum qualche movi-

---

a. The original dispatch was filed in *Borgogna,* cart. 514, while the deciphered Chancery copy was found in *Francia,* cart. 525. The two have now been filed together in cart. 525. Since no key for Coppini's cipher has been found, it was necessary to derive it with the aid of the Chancery copy. The dispatch was then transcribed from the original, as always.

Lordship disposed to support him in every way, though I had no wish to push matters further until I had talked with Messer Prospero. Hence it has worked out well indeed that this *negotiation* has continued up to now, for my talk with the Dauphin has served to confirm the sincerity of your position.

From what my capacity for perception and my knowledge tell me about the condition of *western* affairs, I believe it useful to continue the *said negotiation,* and even to pursue it more closely than has been done, because of events *in England,* as a result of which *the Dauphin* might be invited *to make engagements* that afterward could render his relationship with *Your Lordship* more difficult; for this *victory of King Edward is a great blow,* as everyone knows, *to the King of France,* who perchance might prefer to turn to his son than to await [an attack by] *his enemies.*

Because the situation of the *Dauphin* depends, for reasons in great part known, on the *Duke of Burgundy,* I again urge and counsel *Your Lordship* to continue and indeed increase the good will *and understanding* you have with the Duke, which will be easy because he is naturally inclined *to the party of King Edward.* I previously put my hand to the matter, and now have done so **again, and** I intend to follow up by confirming the Duke in this *attitude* and in his warm relationship with you. For all these respects and for the reasons *Messer Antonio* [della Torre] will have reported to *Your Lordship,* I, being about to *return to England,* as by previous letters I have informed you, think it well done and useful that Messer Prospero should also go there in order to see and learn; and, in addition, his presence will go well with the proposals I have made to these English princes concerning an *alliance* between them and *Your Lordship,* as by *Messer Antonio* and by letters *Your Lordship* was informed, and Prospero's presence will also confirm the impression of *Your Lordship* that we have created in the minds of these lords. In this case, it will be advisable to provide letters of credence *to the new King, Edward* [IV], and to those who wrote to Your Lordship, but these two [i.e. Edward and Warwick?] are the

mento che, benché *la S. V.* non fussi spetialiter *nominata* assai, tamen poteva intendere che mettendo il capo a decte cose retroveria *la S. V. disposta a tucti i suoi piaceri, favori.* Ma non m'ero voluto extender più avanti finché con decto Messer Prospero m'aboccavo, unde cade bene a puncto che questa *pratica* sia tenuta et continuata fin mò et lo mio parlare si viene ad verificare. Et per quanto l'ongegno [sic] et la notitia et la dispositione delle cose *occidentali* mi porge, credo che sia utile continuare *decta pratica* e ancora stringerla più che l'usato per le cose occorse *in Anglia,* per le quali decto *Delfino* potrebbe essere invitato *ad partiti,* che di poi farebbeno la cosa sua con *la S. V.* più difficile, perché questa *victoria del Re Edoardo é uno grande scacco,* come tutti intendeno, *al Re de Franza,* el quale per aventura porria voltarsi più tosto *al figliuolo,*[b] che aspectare *l'inimici sui.* Et perché i facti del *prefato Delfino,* per le casoni note in gran parte, dependono da questo *Duca de Bergogna,* ancora lodo et conforto *V. S.* ad continuare et crescere la benivolentia *od intelligentia* con ipso, la quale sarà facile cosa, perché natuaralmente é inclinato *ad questa parte del Re Edoardo.* Et io già prima, et hora di nuovo, li ho messo le mani et intendo seguire per confirmarlo in questo proposito et in questa *intelligentia.* Et per questi tucti respecti et per le casoni che per *Messer Antonio* ad *V. S.* saranno riferite, dovendo io *ripassare in Anglia,* come per le altre mie scripsi, ne par ben facto et utile che decto Messer Prospero ancora vi si transferisca per intendere et vedere, et etiam perché viene bene ad proposito delli principii per me per me [sic] dati della *intelligentia* di quelli Signori con *V. S.,* come per decto *Messer Antonio* et per lettera fu *V. S.* advisata, et confirmerassi quella impressione che di *V. S.* havemo facta nelle menti di quelli Signori. Et in questo caso sarà opportuno provedere di nuove lettere *al novo Rei Edoardo*[c] et ad quelli che scripsono ad *V. S.,* ma questi 2 sono il fondamento; et interim se pur occorresse *il nostro passar di là,* scuseremo con quelle lettere che decto Messer Prospero ha il meglio che si potrà, benché lui m'abbi facto alcune exceptioni del modo

b. C. C. reads: alla Anglia volo.
c. C. C. reads: Varuich.

main ones. *If we should cross to England* in the meantime, we will make our excuses, as best we can, in using Prospero's old letters of credence. He has, however, made some reservations concerning the mode and time of his crossing, in order to await reply from *Your Lordship.* By your next letters, then, will you please confirm his instructions to cross, because for a long time I have desired a man of yours of this standing, as by Messer Antonio I informed you. At present I know nothing else worth writing to Your Lordship except to remind you that you should *direct your efforts toward English* affairs. As I have often written, never was a time more *propitious for our plans,* if they are well managed, and with celerity, particularly since I now have the aid of Messer Prospero—had I had that aid in the past in these parts, I certainly believe that *great results would have been seen*—and especially if in your quarter *there is no sleeping,* for it much helps the cause to have a coadjutor who has a brain and experience, above all in matters of this nature, concerning which I would to God that others whom this affair concerns might have the skilful judgment the business demands.

My illustrious lord, *Your Lordship knows that grand affairs* are not managed without danger and great diligence; and it is impossible for anyone, even the wisest lord, to bring them to consummation *unless he bestows aid* and *trust upon his faithful ministers,* who often, by the most rigorous diligence, seeing themselves trusted and supported by their lords, produce greater results than were expected or hoped for. And Your Excellency has some proof of this *in England.* Therefore, Most Illustrious Lord, please lay hand to the work in whatever way is required, so that our accomplishments do not, after such toils and perils, come to ruin before our eyes, *with shame and loss of reputation by the states of Italy.*

With respect to what Messer Prospero has, and will have, to accomplish with the *most serene Dauphin,* and with respect to keeping on good terms *with this prince,* I will not fail to do what Messer Prospero requests and will request, and I will hit upon effective measures to that end. Hence, with one on one side and the other on the other, we will all

et del tempo del passar suo per aspectar resposta da *V. S.,* la quale si degni per le prime confirmare la comissione del passare, perché già gran tempo ho desiderato uno vostro homo di questa qualità, come per Messer Antonio advisai. Altro non so che, al presente, sia degno di scrivere ad V. S., se non recordarle che ad le cose *de Anglia tenga le mani.* Come più volte ho scripto, mai fu tempo più *dextro al proposito nostro,* quia se son ben guidate et con presteza et maxime ritrovandomi havere l'aiuto del prefato Messer Prospero, el quale se havessi havuto per lo passato in queste parti, credo certamente se ne saria *visti grandi fructi,* maxime se di costà *non se dormisse,* perché fa molto al proposito havere coadiutore che habbi cervello et pratica et maxime nelle cose di questa natura, delle quali, volessi Dio, che altri ad cui toccano havessi tanta peritia quanta richiede il bisogno.

Illustrissimo Signor mio, *le gran cose sa V. S. sensa periculo* et gran diligentia non si conducono; et é impossibile per qualunque, etiam sapientissimo Signore, poterle mandare ad perfectione *se non si dà favore* et *credito ali ministri fideli,* i quali spesse volte per la exactissima diligentia, vedendosi da suoi Signori creduti et favoriti, producono maggior fructi che li sperati o aspectati. Et V. Ex. ne ha visto qualche prova *in Anglia.* Siché, Illustrissimo Signore, piacciavi metterci le mani in quel modo che richiede il bisogno, accioché le nostre opere non si vedano essere perdute con tanti affanni et periculi et finalmente *con vergogna et damno in reprobrio deli Stati d'Italia.* Et per quanto specta ad quel che ha et harà da fare el prefato Messer Prospero con lo prefato *Monsignore Serenessimo Delfin,* et del intertenere *questo Principe,* io non mancherò di quel che m'à richiesto et richiederà decto Messer Prospero et me accaderanno delli propositi apti acciò. Siché, l'uno da l'un canto et l'altro dall'altro, tireremo tutti ad uno segno et con speranza di qualche *degno fructo se saremo aiutati.*

Raccomandome ad V. Ex.. Raccomandone ad la V. S. dalla quale attendo con desiderio aviso delli progressi di Messer Antonio.

Di poi ho parlato *con alcuni astrologi* et maxime con uno valente, che é religioso et prelato, et dice et così ha dato in scripti [sic] già più

fire at the same target, in hope of some *profitable result if we are aided*. I recommend myself to Your Lordship, from whom I eagerly await word of the progress of Messer Antonio.

[Postscript.] I have since spoken *with some astrologers,* in particular with a skilled one, a prelate of an order, who says, and has put in writing many times *for the Duke of Burgundy, that the King of France will this summer stand in the* greatest *danger of death, and if he escapes* it will be a miracle rather than the course of nature. Around August the result will be seen. I inform you of this because it greatly concerns your business, and I would think it good to accelerate Messer Prospero's negotiations.

tempo *al Duca de Bergogna, che el Re de Franza in questa state* porta grandissimo *periculo di morte, et se ne campa,* sarà più tosto miraculo che corso di natura et circa agosto si vedrà l'effecto. Advisovene perché tocca grandemente al facto vostro, et parmi d'accellerare la praticha di Messer Prospero. Laus Deo.

I believe that up to now Your Magnificence has recognized me to be a man frank and without deceit; and always, I am confident, I will be found so, for such is my nature. However, putting aside circumlocutions, it seems strange to me that since my leaving there I have had from our lord only two letters: one, informing me that the armies had gone to winter quarters; the other, full of the magnificence of Gaston [du Lyon], *which magnificence would fit into a grape seed.*[1] *As for good will, I have hope of it, but, because of the hidden motivations of men, I do not dare to affirm its existence; and I am not one to believe in anything except deeds. In sum, of changes in affairs there, of some hoped for good word about a new alignment at court, and of the proper answers to questions that are asked me here, I have no knowledge, and dare to say nothing beyond what I already know; and therefore find myself little better than a clothed beast. On account of this anxiety and feeling of shame, I am leaving here, although I thought it useful to remain some days longer; and this grieves me so much the more because this lord* [the Duke of Burgundy], *in reciprocity, is happy to honor servants of the Duke of Milan.*

If it was not thought worthwhile to write me news, at least I might have been given notice of the receipt of my letters and been sent a courier with blank paper so that it would look as if some account were

102 · PROSPERO DA CAMOGLI *to*

CICCO SIMONETTA

Francia, cart. 525. Orig.

Io credo che fin a qui Vostra Magnificentia me habi cognosciuto homo netto et sensa busche et semper me confido serò trovato tale, perché cossì hé mia natura; et pertanto, posto da canto le circuitione, el me par stranio che doppoi che sum partito de là non habbi mai havuto dal Signore excepto due littere: l'una dela gentedarme ite ale stantie, l'altra tutta plena dela magnificentia de Gaston, quale magnificentia staria in uno pignolo.[1] Nam del bono animo, quantumque io ne spero bene, pur non ausi [sic] m'affirmare propter occultas hominum voluntates et non sum per creder excepto ale opere. Insuma in tanta innovatione de cose per de là, in tanta expectatione de sentir nova bona banda qualcosa, et in tante interrogatione che me ne sonno state fatte qui, non havendone io altro né ardiando de dir cosa che io non sapessi, io me sum trovato qui asiatamenti [sic] una bestia vestita et per questo metus verecundia me ne vo via, quantumque me pareva utile demorargli qualche dì più; del che tanto più me dole quanto che questo Signore, per reciproca, honora volunteri quelli del Signore. Et se non me se dignava de scriver novelle, almanco me fussi stato dato adviso dele littere recepiute et mandato uno correro cum paper bianco, adcioché parà che si fa computo dele cose de qua.

Io non credo né per demeriti de mei deportamenti né per negligentia mia, che la fede et la devotione porto al Signore et lo desiderio

being taken of affairs here. I do not believe that, either of faults of conduct or negligence, the loyalty and devotion I bear to the Duke of Milan and the desire I have to please him merit this treatment. Nevertheless, for my part, so that Your Magnificence does not call me irascible, I say no more. However, considering that often when intelligence is insufficient, reputation lends a helping hand, I can but lament and excuse myself if my failure to understand matters here as well as I should, has not been redeemed by reputation and thus my accomplishments do not correspond to the desire of our lord. Nevertheless I am eager to do everything that I possibly can. However I remind you that, just as in agriculture there is no use carefully planting a tree unless subsequently it frequently rains, so there is no use to have carefully planted me here on the extreme shore of the lands of the earth and then not give me the breath of life which letters represent, or information or that good encouragement that all servants should receive. I reached this conclusion out of grief, for I should be not only [. . . .] but I am content with everything, in regard to myself, that is pleasing to the Duke of Milan and to Your Magnificence. However, for the true welfare of our lord, I say that, given the exalted rank of the Dauphin and the Duke of Burgundy, and the great prestige and fame that the Duke of Milan enjoys here, it would be more honorable and useful if a man of higher authority and greater name were here and one better acquainted with the policies of our lord's government than I am. Under those circumstances there would be no need for so many messengers and letters. Besides, the exalted station of those here will thus be more fittingly complied with, a consideration that is especially important seeing what the Legate [Francesco Coppini] requests concerning English affairs.

Therefore, to put things in one bundle, these affairs are of greater weight than my back can rightly bear, and if they are so considered among you, you will understand why I am moved to request that I be replaced. Otherwise, if not, better it would certainly be not to have sent me.

porto de fargli cosa grata meriti questo; tamen quanto per me, adcioché
Vostra Magnificentia non mi appelli colerico, io taceo. Ma considerato
che spesso unde la raxon non vale, iuva la reputatione, se per non in-
tendersi de qua tutto quello che vole la ragion, lo mancamento de repu-
tatione causasse in me che non correspondessero le opere mie al desid-
erio del Signore, io me ne doglo et scuso; non tamen obstante questo,
sollicitaturus omni studio quello et quanto me serà possibile. Ben vi
ricordo che cossì come in agricultura non basta plantar uno arboro bene
se doppoi non gli piove spesso, idem non so se sia ben havermi plantato
qui in littore orbis terrarum extremo et non darme né spirito de littere
né adviso; né questo per certo hé de quella bona saliva se debbe far
tussavia[a] *ali servitori. Fo questa conclusion et d'acorrosato, perché io*
debo esser non solum [****] sed contento de tutto quello piace de me
ala Signoria Sua et a Vostra Magnificentia; sed lo dico per lo vero ben
de Sua Signoria che attenta la grande sublimitate del Delfin et Duca de
Bergogna, attento la gran reputatione et fama che ha el Signore de qua,
seria suo honor et utile che fussi in queste cose homo da più et de maior
nome, et qui sapia meglo li propositi del Stato del Signore che non so
io, et a questi modi non bisogneria tanti messi et tante littere. Preterea
etiam la sublimità de questoro ne serà meglo satisfacta, maxime etiam
attento quello che richede lo Legato per le cose de Anglia, che a fare
tutto uno fascio, queste facende sonno de maior peso che non voleria la
schina mia; et se sono reputate apud vos per tale, intenditi che io me
movuo ben a desiderargli altri che io. Sin autem non, meglo era per
certo a non mandar.

HISTORICAL NOTE

1. i.e. Sforza's letters of Jan. 17, doc. 60, p. 61, and Feb. 27, doc. 68, p. 113.

---

a. Read: tuttavia.

*What, according to Your Lordship's instructions, remained for me
to do, I was not up to this moment able to accomplish under the circumstances, i.e. my being involved in the situation here. Now the case is
altered for I have finally met with the Legate* [Francesco Coppini], *to
whom I have thought it good to give some information about the
league with the Dauphin, indicating that I was instructed by Your
Lordship to share all that I knew with him. This I have done for two
principal reasons: one, so that he will be the freer in sharing what he
knows with me; two, because he is indeed in negotiation with the Duke
of Burgundy and the Dauphin; and since he is entirely devoted to Your
Lordship, he can give me many useful tips about forwarding Your
Lordship's cause as the need arises. And he has indeed promised to aid
me in all ways possible. Since he has great experience in affairs here and
since I am alone, I have thought it most useful to confer with his lordship in order to be the better informed and guided.*

Concerning the battle fought in England, I affirm what I have
written to Your Excellency: true it is that the news of King Henry's
and the Queen's capture is certainly false, but I recall that I reported it to
be doubtful. It is said that 160,000 men took part in the battle. For my
opinion regarding these English affairs, I remit my judgment to what, I
believe, the Legate has written concerning them to Your Excellency;

103·PROSPERO DA CAMOGLI *to the*

DUKE OF MILAN

Francia, cart. 525. Orig.

Quello che per la comissione de Vostra Excelentia me restava a far et che fin a qui per esser involupato qui, come ho scripto ala Vostra Excelentia, non me era possibile, havemo sortito qui a caso che iam tandem me sum retrovato cum lo Reverendissimo Monsignor lo Legato cum lo quale m'hé paruto de comunicar qualcosa dela liga cum el Delfin, monstrando de haver in commission da V. S. de participar cum la Signoria Sua tutto. Et questo ho fatto per dui principali rispecti: l'uno adcioché me vegna a me in rebus suis più libero; l'altro perché pur ha pratica cum el Duca Bergogna et el Delfin, et essendo lui tutto dela S. V., me può far mille bone scorte a favorir la S. V. de passo in passo a bisogni; et cossì m'ha promesso m'adeiuncta[a] in melius gli hé [possibile], ché per esser la Signoria Sua praticissima dele cose de qua, trovandome io solo, m'hé paruto utilissimo conferir cum la Signoria Sua per più adviso mio et adricio.

Dele cose de Angliterra quanto specta ali conflicti, affermo quello ho scritto a V. Ex.tia. Vero hé che acerto la preisa delo Rei Henrico et dela Regina non esser vera, benché mi ricordo perciò haverla scritta per dubia; dicesi che havevan al dì dela batagla homini centosexanta milia. Del apparer mio in dicte cose anglie me ne remetto a quello credo epso

---

a. Read: m'aiterà or m'adiuterà.

for indeed I have seen a regular flow of letters written by him to Your Excellency and by Your Excellency to his lordship, who, beyond the fact that in all matters he seems to me very shrewd and experienced, in this particular matter seems an English Aristotle; and in truth, my lord, I am most happy to find his lordship to be such, and to be so devoted to Your Excellency.

The Legate has strongly urged me to cross to England, for the honor and greater prestige of Your Excellency and for the forwarding of his affairs, etc. I replied that I am ready to do whatever he urges and persuades me to undertake; but concerning the "when" and the "how" I made some reservations, namely: concerning the "when," that I was awaiting a reply from Your Excellency, having informed you, in the dispatch carried by Martino the courier, of the changes in England and of the choice of the new king and having reminded you that if you wanted me to carry out my mission to England, it would be well for me to have letters of credence addressed to that new king; concerning the "how," that for the sake of Your Excellency's position, it should not appear openly that Your Lordship is taking pleasure in working, on all sides, against the King of France, but I added that I had devised a means by which our purposes will be concealed. If I learn that Your Excellency wishes me to go to England, I will regret not being able to see Your Excellency first so that I might clearly understand just what you want me to do.

In addition, the Legate has talked at length with me concerning the change of government in England, about which I have been informed and am daily informed by the English themselves, who confess, or rather preach, that the Legate has been the author of King Edward's and Warwick's elevation and the guiding rule by which they have directed themselves, and at present he is being urgently requested to return there.

In advising with me freely concerning the welfare of Your Excellency's state, the Legate said, on the subject of an English invasion of France, that, since even with eyes closed anyone can see and hear the

Monsignor haverne scritto a V. Ex.tia, perché pur ho veduto censuetu-
dine de littere da epsa a V. Ex.tia a Sua Signoria, la qual ultra che in
tutte le cose mi pare prudentissima et pratica, in queste me pare uno
Aristotile anglico. Et in vero, Signor mio, io me sum relegrato assai de
trovar Sua S.ria tale et de tale affectione verso V. Ex.tia. *La Signoria
Sua multo m'ha confortato de passar in Anglia per honor et più reputatione de Vostra Excelentia, et al proposito dele cose sue etc. Al che ho
risposto che sum apto a farne quanto et quello me conforterà et suaderà,
verum del quando et del come ci ho fatto qualche reservationetta;
videlicet del quando in aspectar risposta de Vostra Excelentia, ala quale
per Martin cavalaro, havendo scripto dele mutatione de Ingliterra et
dela election del novo Re, ricordai se gli pareva che io havessi a proseguir lo viagio seria ben haver littere in lo novo Re de Ingliterra; del
come etiam feci mentione per lo reguardo da Vostra Excelentia, che non
si intenda ala scoperta che ella si delecti de temptar per tutto contra el
Re de Franza, ma a questo gli ho devisato il modo chi serà coperto; se
intenderò Vostra Excelentia contentarsi dela andata mia, ben seria stato
contento de veder de Vostra Excelentia, perché io intendesse in questo
de far cosa de che epsa sii contenta.*

  *Insuper epso Monsignor lo Legato ha conferto largissimamenti
meco del Stato de Ingliterra, in el quale quanto specta ale sublimatione
del Re, figlolo de D. dela Marchia, et Conte de Varuich, io ho inteso et
intendo tutto el dì per Anglesi proprii ch'el confessano, imo lo predican, la Sua Signoria esser stata lo autor et la regula cum che se sonno
adriciati et al presente multo hé richesto là. Et avisando la Signoria Sua
meco liberamenti per quanto riguarda il ben del Stato dela Vostra Excelentia che Anglesi si tranfundessi [sic] in Franza, perché etiam ad
ochii chiusi se vede et intende el Re de Franza dolersi dela S. V., per
uno remedio dala larga chi spesso iuvano non manco che d'apresso,
incumbe la Signoria Sua assai in adaptar questa cosa; et gli pare che
cum ogni puocho de che se aitassi el figlo de D. dela Marchia et el
Conte de Varuich, se buterian al opera fornito che havessero contra el
Re de Ingliterra, la Regina [et] figlolo, adunche salvo semper lo apparer*

King of France complaining about Your Excellency, it is incumbent upon his lordship to return to England in order to promote that antidote to the French King's hostility, for a distant remedy may be no less helpful than one close by. He thinks that with only a little aid the new King and Warwick would undertake the enterprise once they have finished with King Henry, the Queen, and their son—saving always the judgment of Your Excellency. We together canvassed the possibility that if some portion of the funds to be collected in England by the skill of the Legate might, with the Pope's approval, be made available—no great sum, only enough to hire six large Genoese ships for four months —this would constitute a grand present and a most substantial aid to the new King and Warwick since they would then hold the mastery of the sea, the which security would stimulate all the people of England to take arms against the French; and the present government of Genoa should take a favorable view of the idea, for in thus bringing low the French, the Genoese would be the more firmly of a mind never to think any more about, nor put hopes in, the King of France.

As far as I am concerned, however, such ideas are worth nothing unless they are approved by the principals. Whether this or another method of pushing the English into war with France will seem useful to Your Excellency, I would suggest we take advantage of the fact that we have a Pope who is well disposed to you, especially considering the fragility of human life. In truth, one good provision in regard to English affairs that might be made at present would be to effect an increase in the authority of the Legate, because often things can be accomplished by prestige that cannot be accomplished by reason; and I also think it would be a good idea to provide ships, as mentioned above, which would serve to reinforce the Earl of Warwick's fleet. This is what we conferred about, the Legate and I.

This is the thirty-first letter that I have written to Your Excellency, and I have had no reply to any of them nor even advices of their being received. This I mention for the information of Your Excellency, to whom I humbly recommend myself. From Saint Omer of the "Morini"

et iudicio de Vostra Excelentia. Nui examinavamo insieme cossì, che se de quello che per industria dela Signoria Sua se traesse de Ingliterra cum bon contentamento del Papa se daesse il modo al spender, etiam non grande quantità, basteria haver sei grosse nave de Zenoa per quatro mesi, et seria grande presente et substantialissimo aito al Re novo et [al] *Conte de Varuich, cum ciò sia che serian siguri del mare, la qual securessa faria butar tutti* [li] *populi de Ingliterra ala guerra in Franza; et hé cosa che al presente Stato de Zenoa debe esser grata, perché destruendone el Re de Franza se incaparerian meglo a non pensar mai più né sperar supra el Re de Franza.*

Questi tali pensieri quanto per me sonno designi chi non valeno se non se approbano per li principali; et unde questo o altro modo a inforsar ben Ingliterra cum Franza paia utile a Vostra Excelentia, io saperia laudar che doppoi se ha uno Papa ben disposto ch'el si gaudesse, attenta maxime vite humane fragilitate; et invero uno deli boni provedimenti si possessi far al presente in le cose de Ingliterra, seria questo dar et crescer autorità al prefato Monsignor lo Legato, perché spesso se fa per la opera dela reputatione quello non si può far per ragione; et ultra se provedesse dele nave ut supra, *il che seria scorta al altra armata del Conte de Varuich. Questo hé de quanto havemo conferto lo prefato Monsignor lo Legato et io. Et questa hé la trigesimaprima littera che ho scritto a Vostra Excelentia et de che fin a qui non ho né resposta né adviso dele recepiute, il che sii in notitia dela prefata Excelentia Vostra, ala qual humiliter me racomando.*

Post data. *Lo Reverendissimo Monsignor lo Legato ha pur voluto intender da me come scrivo a Vostra Excelentia del spender de quello che per soa industria se cavarà de Ingliterra, et ge li ho ditto; al che el fa questa postila: che tal movimento procedeva in animo suo per de Vostra Excelentia; non ch'el volessi* [che] *de questo el Papa possessi mai intender che epso desiderassi de metter man in la farina del iubileo,[1] ma che monstrandosi per parte de Vostra Excelentia a pié del Papa confortar che etiam se si dovessi spender qualcosa in Ingliterra per irritarli et spengerli in Franza, ch'el pareria ben fatto a Vostra Excelentia, al*

[a tribe of Belgic Gauls] *in Artois, on the ninth of May, fourteen hundred sixty-one.*

Postscript. *The Legate wanted to know how I was writing to Your Excellency about the expenditure of the funds which his lordship's skill will extract from the English. On my telling him, he made this statement: that, in his mind, such action should proceed through Your Excellency; that he did not want the Pope ever to be able to think that he had any desire to "metter man in la farina del iubileo";*[1] *but that it should be signified to the Pope, through Your Excellency, that anything contributed to stir up the English and send them into France would be regarded by you as a favor and that you would supply whatever additional funds were needed—and then the Legate would see to it that no such addition was necessary. Nevertheless, my lord, I do not well understand these schemes and I remit myself to Your Excellency.*

The Legate awaits only a reply from the Earl of Warwick and secure passage to England, the sea here being full of Norman and French pirates so that safeguards are required, etc.

In sum, considering these things in earnest, my lord, I see a great many matters that, in my judgment, *should not be neglected; but to put my hand to them I do not dare because I do not consider myself up to it, and I prefer to confess my sin rather than by rashness to falsify ruinously the opinion that Your Excellency might have of me. Therefore if you consider these matters to be important* etc., *I would suggest that you replace me with someone else. Otherwise, I beg Your Excellency not to take my advices in any other way than as representing the diligence of the servant who always humbly recommends himself to you.* Given as above.

HISTORICAL NOTE

1. Evidently a colloquial phrase of the time meaning "dip into Church funds."

che etiam se mancassi qualcosa Vostra Excelentia supliria, et tunc epso Legato provederia che non gli mancheria nulla. Tuttavia, Signor mio, io non intendo ben questi tratti et me ne remetto a Vostra Excelentia. Epso Legato non aspecta altro che resposta dal Conte de Varuich et passagio sicuro per Anglia, perché tutto'l mare qui hé pleno de Normandi et gente de Franza, corsari, et bisogna andar cum securtà etc.. Siché ricoglendo io trette queste cose vedo, Ill.mo S.re mio, essergli al mio iudicio de le cose assai che non mi paiano *da negliger; et pur abraciarle io non ardisco, perché non mi vedo sufficiente ad ciò et più tosto voglo confessar il pecato mio, che per temerità de fraudar cum damno la opinion che Vostra Excelentia avessi di me; per il che se a quella pare* queste cose esser toccante etc., *lauderia altro che me; sin autem prego Vostra Excelentia non prenda tanti mei advisi excepto in parte de diligentia del servitor, il qual semper humiliter a quella se racomanda.* Data ut supra.

*That Your Excellency may be informed of the news here: there
arrived yesterday letters and messengers from England that swear to
and confirm the capture of King Henry, the Queen, and all those previously mentioned. Nevertheless I do not know what to certify as true,
and if Your Lordship should be amazed at such uncertainty, let me tell
you that there is not here that organization to be found in your government, and no news arrives here except what comes by chance, a situation that is owing to the nature of those in power. For the Duke of
Burgundy attends to his "devotions"* [1] *and leaves the policies and cares
of state to his officials, who, since they lack that supernatural aptitude of
princes, cannot exercise that vigilance and foresight that God has con-
ceded to lords. Nevertheless, whatever the precise situation in England
is or will be, things are going supremely well for the new King and the
Earl of Warwick, concerning which I remit myself to the knowledge of
the Legate, for, in the opinion of the English themselves, he is an oracle
in these matters.*

*Concerning affairs here, a fortnight ago the Duke of Burgundy
arrived here and then just about the same time 1500 horse of the King of
France, entering ducal territory, approached to within little more than
half a day's journey of St. Omer, but remained harmlessly in their en-
campment. The Duke dispatched a herald, who, according to what was*

104 · PROSPERO DA CAMOGLI *to the*

DUKE OF MILAN

Francia, cart. 525. Orig.

Ad ciò che Vostra Excelentia sia advisata dele novelle sonno de qua, heri vennero littere et messi de Ingliterra chi iurano et acertano la preisa delo Re Henrico et [dela] *Regina et de tuti quelli de che se diceva. Tamen io non so che acertare, et se la V. S. prendessi admiratione de tanta incertitudine, io dico che non sonno qui li ordini de quella et non se scrutta* [sic] *qui novelle, salvo se vengono o volano, et questo accade per la natura de questi governi. Nam el Duca de Bergogna attende a sue devotione[1] et lassia il pensiero et la cura del Stato a servitori, in li quali non essendo quello supranatural instructo de Principi, non possono esser de quella vigilantia et antiveder che Dio ha concesso in li Signori. Tuttavia, quicquid sit aut futurum sit, le cose del novo Re et* [del] *Conte de Varuich sonno in supremi favori, del che,* ut supra, *me refero al prefato Monsignor lo Legato, perché hé uno oraculo de quelle cose a iudicio de epsi proprii de Ingliterra.*

Dele cose de qua, hoggi sonno 15 dì che iunxe qui questo Illustrissimo [Signore] *Duca de Bergogna et tunc assai in quelli dì iunxeno cavalli del Re de Franza, millecinquecento, presso de qui a puocho più de media iornata sul paese de questo prefato Duca de Bergogna, quali tamen stavano sul hostarie innoxii; et gli mandò uno suo araldo, qual, secundo se diceva, haveva inteso da loro che erano venuti per levar lo obsedio che havevano quelli de Cales ad uno castello qui vicino che si*

said, learned from them that they had come to raise the siege that the [Yorkist] *Calais garrison had laid to a castle nearby that is held for King Henry and the Duke of Somerset.*[2] *On discovering that the siege had been raised, the French departed, but three days ago some 12,000 of them returned.*

Relations between the Duke of Burgundy and the King of France are much embittered, as formerly I wrote to Your Excellency.

Your Lordship can understand how things are managed in these parts: the Duke of Burgundy, as I said, allows himself to be entirely governed by others, a situation about which, I believe, there will be made in the assembly of the princes of the Golden Fleece some far from gentle mention; the King of France is continually under the domination of women, a situation about which there are many complaints. Those in power here, then, conduct themselves very differently from their counterparts in Italy, especially Your Lordship's administration, and they are scheming people who consume a great deal of time and mental energy in devising empty plans. Nevertheless, in their house it sometimes thunders so much that it does rain. For a long time the French thundered about taking Genoa and they thundered about invading the Kingdom of Naples, of which noise little account was taken; but finally the rains came to both places, and in quantity. Therefore, as a servant who should fear and take into consideration everything, I write to Your Excellency all aspects that strike me.

True it is that I have been with the brother [Jean, Count of Chimay] *of my lord of Croy* [Antoine], *the lord who made me great offers and gave me great thanks here. On my asking Croy's brother what he thought the King of France's attitude was toward Your Lordship, he answered that he understood it to be menacing indeed. When remarks in that vein were made in his presence, he so effectively pointed out the integrity, statesmanship, power, etc. of Your Lordship that those who had been making such remarks then fell silent. He says that not too much account is made of the Duke of Orléans; more, of the Duke of Brittany. He believes that because of all the King of France has on his*

ten per lo Re Henrico et Semesetrh² et, *inteso che lo dicto obsedio se era levato, se ne eran ritornati; hora hoggi sonno tre dì, sonno ritornati pur lì in quelli medesmi contorni ben dodecimilla. Et quanto da Duca de Bergogna al Re de Franza le cose sonno multo sgonfie, come iam diu scripsi a Vostra Excelentia.*

Può intender la S. V. come et quali sono li governi de qua. El Duca de Bergogna, ut dico, se lassia tutto reger da altri, del che credo qui in questo convento de Principi se farà qualche non dulce mentione. El Re de Franza protinus hé in governo de femine et rugiscono; et quantumque habiano diportamenti diformi de quelli de Italia, et maxime de V. S., et chi siano gente devisatoria et chi consumano assai de suoi ragionamenti et tempi in designi vacui, tamen pur qualche volta tona tanto a casa loro che piove. De Zenoa se disse longo tempo non secreto, et pur fu andata in regnum Neapolis se faceva puocho computo, et pur han dato tempesta assai; siché a modo de servitore chi semper debe temere et rispectar, io scrivo voluntieri a Vostra Excelentia tutti li riguardi chi me pongeno. Vero hé che sum stato cum lo fradello de Mon.re de Crovi, il qual m'ha fatto qui de grande offerte et rengratiamenti, et lo ho domandato de quello ch'el pensa del Re de Franza verso Vostra Signoria. Risponde haver inteso de minacie assai et, quando se hé parlato in presentia sua de tale cose, ha resposto dela probità et providentia de Vostra Excelentia et dela possansa etc., *pre modo chi rugiva avanti, taceva doppoi. Et dice che de Orliens non se fa troppo computo, ma del Duca de Bertagna pur;*[a] *crede che per li bisogni se haran a far de qua, le cose del Re de Franza verso la S. V. seran più modeste; ben dice esser grande despecto al Re de Franza la mutation de Zenoa, et di questo esserne multo culpato la S. V., et me fa questa conclusion: che s'el Duca de Bertagna farà cosa non grata a V. S., per contra a lui la S. V. troverà continuamenti de qua multo più favori che contra Orliens, quale hé del Ordine dela Tueson, per vigor del quale bisogna esser propicii et favorevoli l'uno al altro. Il simile et più a pleno et più chiaro*

---

a. Read: più.

hands here, the pressure he brings to bear on Your Lordship will be modest indeed. However, he says that the overthrow at Genoa has greatly angered the King and that Your Lordship is much blamed for having had a hand in it. In conclusion he told me that if the Duke of Brittany makes any hostile move against Your Lordship, you will always find here at the court of Burgundy many more opposed to the Duke of Brittany than would be opposed to the Duke of Orléans. This comes about because of Orléans' belonging to the Order of the Golden Fleece, whose regulations require members to be helpful and favorable to each other. The Duke of Clèves told me the same thing, but more fully and explicitly, saying that if it were not for this respect, the Duke of Burgundy, for his part, would like to make all the demonstrations toward Your Lordship that one brother could make to another.

To return to the subect of the Duke of Burgundy's position: as far as my slender intellect can see, the Duke of Burgundy is deliberately staying under cover, not giving the appearance of favoring one side more than the other because the situation in England is by no means stabilized; and since it is the nature of these people to back and fill and since because of their volubility it is impossible to be certain of what they mean, one can do no more than refrain from complaining about the things they do that militate against our objectives etc.

It is because of this state of affairs that the King of France suffers all the ear-boxings and nose-tweakings that are administered to him. Nevertheless I assure Your Excellency that almost every day here councils are held until dawn, during which all the threatening moves of the King of France are mocked. It is thought that the French are to besiege Calais with both an army and a fleet, which enterprise the King undertakes in order to provoke the Duke of Burgundy and see what he will do. Here, there seems to me to be no other thought at present than to see to it, secretly, that Calais is strong, and so the English say that for a year they have no fear in the world. This is the present state of affairs here.

For the rest, the ceremonies of the Golden Fleece have been cele-

m'ha dicto lo Duca de Cleve, dicendomi che, se per tal rispecto non fussi, el Duca de Bergogna vorria far dal canto suo tutte le demonstratione verso la S. V. che fussi possibile da uno fratel cum fratelo [sic].

Per ritornar al proposito del presente esser del Duca de Bergogna, per il picolo intellecto mio, me par veder che el Duca volunteri sta coperto; et non si manifesta pender più da uno canto che de un altro, essendo le cose de Ingliterra non de tutto in sicuro et per natura naturata [sic] *de quelle gente, essendo cossì incerte et unde non si può per loro volubilitate far fermamento alcuno, salvo non dolersi de male che habiano et piacersi de ogni bene che sia a propositi nostri* etc.. *Et per questo el Re de Franza conporta tutte le orechiate et toccate de naso che se gli fano; et tamen prometto a Vostra Excelentia che si sta in consigli fin a dì chiaro, quasi ogni dì, et si buffa de tanti supraventi del Re de Franza. Se extima che debiano metter lo campo a Cales, et per exercito et per armata, la qual cosa el Re de Franza faci per stimular el Re de Franza*[b] *et veder quello farà; et qui non me par se faci altro pensiero al presente, che proveder secretamenti che Cales sii forte, et cossì dicono quelli de Anglia che per uno anno non dubitan al mondo. Questo hé il stato presente dele cose de qua.*

Ceterum la solemnità de questa Tueson hé fornita et celebrata, in le quale cerimonie questo Ill.mo Principe fece demonstratione de tre cose: Religione, Sublimità et Apparati. Religione: ch'el stette in genuchie devotissimamenti quanto durò lo officio fin a due hore post meridiem, semper contemplando le arme et insegne dela Sacra Maiestà de Re Alphonso, quale haveva ante oculos, come spechio de la humana condition. Sublimità: per haver tanti Principi reverenti et ch'il reconoscono per suo Ducha, padre et superiore, quantumque el li ten in honor de fradelli. Apparati: in el culto divino et humano supremi

Era lo ordine dela celebratione in questo modo. In li suggesti del choro sedeva in testa, da man dritta, il Signor Duca, et da l'una parte et l'altra del choro erano le insegne, nomi et tituli de tutti Principi,

---

b. Ciphering error for "Duca de Bergogna" not corrected in C. C.

brated. In these the Duke of Burgundy exemplified three themes: worship, lofty solemnity, ritual. Worship: the Duke remained most devoutly on his knees throughout the divine service, which lasted until two o'clock in the afternoon, constantly contemplating the arms and insignia of King Alfonso, [of Aragon, died 1458] which he had before his eyes as a mirror of the human condition. Lofty solemnity: in that he has such revered princes who acknowledge him their Duke, Father, Lord, although he honors them in sharing the bond of brotherhood. Ritual: in the cult, divine and human, of the Highest.

The ordering of the celebration was as follows. In the stalls of the choir sat at the head and on the right the lord Duke, and along both sides of the choir were ranged the insignia, names, and titles of all the princes, barons, and knights of the Order. All wore the vestments of the Golden Fleece, scarlet hoods and scarlet mantels that reached to the feet and were fringed with gold, and had about their necks the collar of the Golden Fleece. In the stalls of those absent sat their proxies; in the stalls of the deceased were hung black cloths displaying their insignia, names, and titles. I was given the first place on the left side, beneath the head of the barons on that side. At the offertory, *Golden Fleece,* chief of the Duke's heralds, ceremoniously called the roll of the Order by name and title, except that there was announced the suspension of the Duke of Alençon on acount of his being a prisoner, until his case, if indeed there were a case, is considered by the Order.[3] Subsequently *Orléans'* name was called, *as Duke of Orléans and Count of Blois, but he was not given the accustomed title of Duke of Milan, at which point the Duke of Burgundy gave me a significant glance.*

The church, which is very large, was splendidly hung with arras depicting with magnificent artistry the Apocalypse. The choir was similarly embellished, with hangings of cloth of gold depicting various stories from the Old and New Testament. The altar, as a thing divine, was adorned with religious objects: namely, first a very large cross containing a piece of the True Cross; then eighteen images, of gold not silver, of the length of an arm; and in the middle the holy Fleur-de-Lys, more

Baroni et Cavaleri del Ordine; et loro tutti vestiti de capucii et manteli de scarlata, longhi fin a pedi, cum le fimbrie d'oro et al collo lo colaro delo Aureum Vellus. Ali lochi deli absenti erano li procuratori; ali lochi deli defuncti erano le insegne, nomi et tituli in panno nigro. A me fu dato lo primo loco a man mancha, a pié del capo deli baroni da quella man. Al offertorio furon, per la Tueson D'oro, chi hé superiore deli araldi, domandati solemniter per nome et titulo, salvo che fu fatto publica suspension del Duca de Lanson per esser pregionero, finché sii inteso la causa sua per lo Ordine, se cossì fusse.[3] Subsequenter fu rechesto *Orliens, come Duca de Orliens et Conte de Bloes, et non gli fu dato il solito titulo de Milan, al che me riguardò cum bono ochio el Duca de Bergogna.*

La chiesia, ch'é assai grande, tutta distincta de panni de Arass, in li quali se representava la Appochalypsi ordinatissimamenti. Lo choro similiter destincto de tali panni intexuti d'oro, in li quali se representava diverse hystorie del Testamento Novo et Vechio. Lo altare, come cosa divina, era distincto de cose supranaturale; videlicet, in primis gli era una cruce del vero ligno assai grande; et auree et non argentee ymagine 18 de grandessa de uno bracio; et in medio la sacrosancta flor de lys, piena de reliquie divine et coperta de zoie preciosie in quantità et qualità, quale hé grande per longo uno bracio et più et per traverso puocho mancho. De cantori, araldi et tale cose era numero infinito et aptitudine grande a tutte le cerimonie. La sala del convivio, quale hé dela grandessa dela sala dela Ill.ma Madona, licet hé più alta, era tutta coperta de panni de Arass ut supra, intertexti [sic] d'oro, mirabili opere, in li quali se representava tutta la hystoria del Aureum Vellus, demisso da celo a Gedeon per insegna, in virtù dela quale el dovesse interprender la salute del populo de Ysdrael. Al loco del suggesto deli Principi erano panni serici et d'oro altre opere. La argentera per contra multo richa et tutta de vasi o d'oro o inaurati, et quatro aricorni ad organo l'uno maior che l'altro, vaselli cristalini et de altre petre pretiose in copia; et quale argentera fu intacta quello dì, tanta era la copia deli argenti destinati al servicio. Lo convivio fu, sedente medio lo Duca et li altri da l'una parte

than an arm's length tall and almost as wide, which contained holy relics and was crusted with jewels, precious both in their quantity and quality. Of singers, heralds, and such appurtenances, there was an infinite number, all superbly contributing to the ceremonies.

The banquet hall, which is of the size of that of the most illustrious lady, the Duchess, but with a higher ceiling, was completely hung with tapestries of cloth of gold, as above, marvellous works depicting the whole story of how the golden fleece was sent down from heaven to Gideon as a sign that he was to undertake the salvation of the people of Israel. Behind the dais where sat the princes were silken hangings and other adornments of gold. Opposite was a display of plate, very rich and all of vessels of gold and silver gilt, four unicorn horns arranged in order of size like organ pipes, and many vessels of crystal and of other precious stones. This plate remained untouched that day because so much of it does the Duke have that there was plenty of additional plate for the dinner service.

At the banquet the Duke sat at the middle of the board with the others ranged on either side in accordance with their seniority in the Order. On the extreme right was my lord [Charles] of Charolais; at the other end [Antoine], the Bastard of Burgundy, both sons of the Duke. Each of the princes of the Golden Fleece had his own service, and the banquet consisted of fifty courses, each served by fifty servitors and the courses borne through the hall in a grand procession of trumpeters and other musicians, with the other nobles then being served. These ceremonies were held on May 2.

The number of the princes of the Order is established by the constitution at thirty-one. There are two main bases of the Order: a vow to defend Holy Church, and a vow to maintain all honor, morality, and good custom without stain, these vows being part of the articles of the Order, of which articles I hope to be able to obtain a copy because I think they are worthy and useful. Stemming from these vows is the requirement *that all members of the Order be in league, confraternity, and identity of wills with each other. The Duke of Burgundy finds this*

et da l'altra, secondo che erano avanti intrati in lo Ordine. Dal extremo dela man dritta era Monsignor de Iharloes; da l'altra, Monsignor lo Batardo de Bergogna, ambi figloli del prefato Principe. In lo convivio fu fatto ad ciascuno deli Principi lo suo plato et L.ta imbandisone, quali heran copiose, per cinquanta corpi humani per ciascuna, tutte portate in grande procession de trombe et altri ministerii subsequentibus aliis nobilibus. Questo fu lo dì de II maii.

Lo numero deli Principi de dicto Ordine hé per institution XXXI. Li fundamenti de questo Ordine, Ill.mo S.re mio, sonno doi: voto de defensione dela Sancta Chiesia; et voto de tutta honestà, moralità et bon costume sensa reprochio, come si conten in li capituli de dicta institution, quali spero de posser haver per copia, perché me pare cosa degna et utile. Lo hedificio di questi fudamenti [sic] hé *che questi sono in liga et confraterna intelligentia ad idem velle et nolle, et el Duca de Bergogna se ne vale assai, perché gli ha aiti et consigli. In suplimento deli morti, quali erano sei, se hé stato in multi consigli secreti iuxta morem; et per quello che m'han ditto de loro proprii, credo resupliran al presente de 5, se non cambian proposito. Nam in loco de condam Re D'Aragona, credo per honor de Sua Maiestà, se suprastaran per suplir de un altro Rei et penso reserven lo loco al Re Ferrando, se le cose lo permeteran. Questo hé mio extimo.*

Siché, considerando io la natura de questo Ordine dela Tueson, et parendomegli a questo de honor et favor, io confesso haverla intra me stesso assai desiderata al Illustre Conte Galeazo. Nondimanco, non intendendo ben che contentamento ne dovesse haver Vostra Excelentia, cum ciò sia che io non so se ali proposti de quella tale demonstratione servan o deservan, me sum contentato de farne alcuna vel minima demonstratione. Pur quello ho potuto far, traversando dala larga, io ho fatto, come visitar de questi Principi, ragionar cum loro Signorie de Vostra Excelentia, deli modi et governi di quella, dela iusticia, dela liberalità, dela gratia et autorità che ha universaliter per tutto et similia; et come in questi costumi, cum grande et mirabile sublimatà de animo et ingenio, se aleva et hé Cavalero il prefatto Signor Conte Galeaz. Credo haver-

brotherhood of great value to him because he has their aid and counsel.

To supply the places of the deceased members, six of them, many secret councils were held, as is customary, and according to what they themselves have told me, I believe that at present they will elect five *new members, unless they change their minds. I believe that, in honor of the late King of Aragon, they will not fill his place until they elect another King, and I think they are reserving the place for King Ferrante, if matters permit. This is my judgment of the situation.*

Considering then the nature of this Order of the Golden Fleece and the honor and prestige that it confers, I confess to have within me a strong desire for Count Galeazzo to be elected to it. Nonetheless since I do not know how Your Excellency feels about the matter and since I also do not know whether, in this procedure, indication of a desire to be elected does a service or disservice, I have contented myself with offering a certain indication, or rather a very small one. However, what I have been able to do, acting with discretion, I have done, such as calling upon these princes in order to speak with them about Your Excellency and to describe your manners and modes of government, your justice, liberality, the grace and authority that all universally find in you, and similar things, and to explain how in these customs, with great and marvelous loftiness of spirit and intelligence, has been reared, and made knight, Count Galeazzo.

I believe that by these means I aroused the right feeling among these princes, and if the obstacle of the Duke of Orléans did not stand in the way, which I do not like to believe, I am not without some thought that they may have elected Count Galeazzo, although neither I nor others know for certain because it is a custom of the Order never to announce the names of outsiders who are chosen until they consent to become members, and this is for the honor of the Order. This is my view of the matter, reserving always the judgment of Your Excellency. Would that thus it was, because it would seem to me that in this honorable way, and without incurring the dislike of any lord in the world, you would acquire a league with the Duke of Burgundy and with the

gline suscitato quelli sentimenti bisognano, et s'el obstaculo del Duca de Orliens non lo prohibisse, il che non mi piace creder, non sum sensa qualche opinione lo habian electo, quantumque io non ne so' certo né altri lo sapia per rispecto del costume del Ordine, che hé de non publicar mai li electi extranei finché non consenteno; et questo hé per honor del Ordine. Et quanto per me, reservato semper lo apparer de Vostra Excelentia, utinam così fussi, perché me pareria Vostra Excelentia per modo honorevole, et non de alcun carrico a pié de Signoria del mondo, haver aquistato liga con el Duca de Bergogna et tanti altri sensa spesa etc.; *quale liga può qualche volta venir ben inconcio, cada la cosa come se vogla. Ben acerto Vostra Excelentia che ha reputation qui in queste parte maior che havessi mai altro chi se sia stato Duca de Milano, parlando semper cum suportation. Se così serà, gli serà mandato messo degno a V. S., ala* [sic] *qual, piacendo a Vostra Excelentia, serà da far grande et bon honore* etc.. *Pur io non acerto nulla, perché non vorria proponer a Vostra Excelentia cibi non cotti; pur, come dico, ne ho qualche opinione, et per questo lauderia ch'el prefato Illustre Conte se adomesticasi* [sic] *cum littere et altro aliquando cum lo figlolo del Duca de Bergogna.* Me racomando ala Ex.tia V. humiliter. Data ut supra.

other lords of the Order without expense etc., *which league could some time come in very handy, however things turn out. I can well assure Your Excellency that you have a greater reputation in these parts than —speaking always with permission—has had any other who has been Duke of Milan. Should Count Galeazzo be elected, the news will be brought to Your Excellency by a worthy emissary, to whom, if Your Excellency agrees, it will be well to pay high honors, etc. However, I offer no assurance about all this, for I would not want to send Your Excellency unbaked dough* [i.e. opinion masquerading as fact]. *However, as I say, I have some hopes about the matter, and therefore I would strongly suggest that Count Galeazzo become acquainted, through letters and a little something more, with the son of the Duke of Burgundy.* I humbly recommend myself to Your Excellency. Given as above.

HISTORICAL NOTES

1. Since the Duke was not over religious and was notoriously fond of his pleasures, Prospero is probably being ironic or else means by *devotione* "things one is devoted to," i.e. private interests.

2. Hammes Castle, one of the fortresses defending the English "Pale" of Calais, finally yielded to Warwick's troops in October, after Angelo Tani [see doc. 90, n. 1, p. 254] paid 250 pounds, on behalf of the Treasurer of Calais, to the Lancastrian defenders.

3. Jean, Duke of Alençon, detected in treasonable practices with the English, was arrested in 1456; in 1458 at a solemn "Bed of Justice," presided over by Charles VII, Alençon was condemned to death but consigned to prison. Attempts by the French to link the Duke of Burgundy with Alençon's treasonable dealings with the English had exacerbated the bad feeling between the King and the Duke.

We have received all the letters you have written since the departure from here of Martino, our courier, the last of which is of the 28th
of April. We have noted all that you wrote in those letters concerning
developments in England and in other matters etc. We reply briefly
that you have done well; we commend you on all counts; and we bid
you to continue acting thus as long as you are there. We wish you to
maintain most cordial relations with the Duke of Burgundy and with
my lord Charles [Count of Charolais,] his son, to whom you will pay a
visit on our behalf and offer the complimentary greetings that seem to
you fitting. We address to them the enclosed letter of credence for your
person.[1] Similarly you will convey compliments on our behalf to my
lord [Antoine] de Croy, lord John his brother, the Duke of Clèves, and
to such other lords as will seem best to you. Concerning the ceremonies
of the Order of the Golden Fleece, you will inform us in detail of the
proceedings, of the lords who took part, of the ceremonial usages, and
of everything else, as fully as possible.

Otherwise, because, as you know, the Bishop of Terni, the apostolic
legate, is there, we want you to be with his lordship and, since he is
extremely well informed about English affairs, you will consult with
his lordship on the subject and do what he thinks best.

Concerning the principal business with the Dauphin, we believe

105 · *The* DUKE OF MILAN *to*

PROSPERO DA CAMOGLI

Francia, cart. 525. Minute

Havemo recevuto tutte le toe littere ne hay scritto dapoy la partita de qua de Martino, nostro cavallaro, l'ultime dele quale sonno de dì XXVIII del passato, per le quale toe littere havimo inteso tutto quello ne scrivi sì deli progresi de Inglitera [sic], como dele altre cose etc. Breviter respondemo che hay facto bene et de tutto te comendamo et cossì te sforza fare per l'avenire finché tu saray lì; et volimo ne tenghi continue recomandato ad quello Ill.mo S. Duca de Bergogna et ad Mon.re Chiarles, suo figliolo, quale andaray ad visitare per nostra parte et gli faray quella visitacion et offerte te parerano conveniente; gli scrivamo l'aligate littere de credenza[1] in tua persona. Similiter confortaray per nostra parte Mon.re de Crovi, D. Io. suo fratello, Duca de Clevi et quilli altri Sig.ri che te parerà; et dela Tueson, avisane particularmente como serà passata, deli Signori gli serano stati et cossì deli modi servati in quelle et de ogni altra cosa tanto distinctamente quanto te serà possibile.

Ceterum perché como tu say el se trova de là el R. Mon.re lo Vescovo de Terani, Legato apostolico, volimo sii con la S. Soa et circa li facti de Ingliterra, perché luy ne é informatissimo, te intenderay con la S. Soa et faray quello gli parerà.

Circa la cosa principale con Mon.re el Delfin, Nuy credemo che tu haveray hormay recevute le littere te havimo, per Martin cavallaro,

that you have already received our letters that we dispatched by courier Martino. Therefore we make no further reply because, by Martino, we have written to you what is necessary. If you have concluded the business with the Dauphin, you can return, unless his lordship commands you to do otherwise. If you have not concluded and the Duke of Burgundy wishes you to postpone your departure for some days, we wish you to do what the Duke desires, and send word to us immediately.

HISTORICAL NOTE

1. Dated May 16, 1461 [*Francia,* cart. 525].

scripte, perciò non te replicamo altro, perché per esso Martin te havimo scrito [sic] quanto bisogna. Se haveray expedito con Monsignore Delphin, poray retornare, salvo se esso Monsignore te comandasse altramente; caso non havessi expedito et che Monsignore de Borgogna volesse che tu tardassi qualche dì, volimo fazi quello vorà la S. Soa et advisarci subito del tucto.

We have received your letters, by which we were informed about the propitious developments in affairs there. We answer that the news has given us great pleasure and we thank Your Lordship for those tidings, urging and praying you to do the same in the future concerning all you learn about developments there, and also we urge Your Lordship to bend all your efforts to giving effective direction to affairs, as you are accustomed to do and as we are certain you will do because of your prudence and great abilities. We for our part will not fail you here in any way. Prospero da Camogli, our secretary, is there and will be with Your Lordship in order to come to an understanding with you and will in all do what seems best to Your Lordship; and so have we written to him that he is to do as long as he remains there. Concerning your business, we have written many times to Rome, and in persuasive terms; and in addition to writing letters we have given strict instructions to the Honorable Messer Agostino Rossi,[1] whom we sent a few days ago to His Holiness, so that Your Lordship may be of easy mind— we shall no more neglect anything that we can do in your behalf than we would if we were soliciting in our own behalf, for not otherwise do we consider the welfare and desire the promotion of Your Lordship than as our own.

106 · *The* DUKE OF MILAN *to*

FRANCESCO COPPINI

Inghilterra e Scozia, cart. 566. Minute

Havemo recevuto le vostre et per quelle inteso quanto ne scriviti deli prosperi successi delle cosse dellà. Rispondemo che ne havemo ricevuto piacere assay et regraciamo la S. deli avisi ne ha dati, confortandola et pregandola ad fare el simile per lo avenire de tutto quello intendereti de li progressi de quelle cose dellà et cossì confortamo la S. Vostra ad sforzarse de drizare le cose bene, secondo é solita, et siamo certi che farà per la prudencia et virtute soa. Nuy dal canto nostro non gli mancaremo de qua in cosa alcuna. Prospero Camulio, nostro secretario, se trova dellà et sarà con la S. Vostra per intenderse con quella et farà in ogni cosa quanto alla S.V. parerà et cossì gli scrivemo ch'el faci fin ch'el starà dellà. Del facto vostro havimo scripto più volte ad Roma et in bona forma et oltra le littere ne havimo data strecta commissione al Spectabile Messer Augustino Rosso,[1] quale pochi dì sonno havimo mandato dalla S.tà de nostro S., siché la S. Vostra stia de bono animo che Nuy non gli mancaremo de cosa che sapiamo et possiamo, pur come s'el fosse facto nostro proprio, perché non altramente stimamo el bene et desyderamo la exaltacione de V.S. ch'el nostro proprio.

HISTORICAL NOTE

1. Member of a powerful family of Parma, experienced lawyer and diplomat, Rossi had entered Sforza's service in 1450. Eight years later he was ambassador to John II of Aragon, who granted him the privilege of adding Aragon to his name. From 1463 to 1468 he served as ambassador at the papal court, and at his return he was made a member of the *Consiglio Segreto*. In 1476 he was knighted by the Pope [Lazzeroni, "Il Consiglio Segreto," 133, n. 109].

I do not know whether to sing the "Gloria in excelcis" or recite the "Laudato dio" etc. in rendering thanks for "Sir Courier," Martino having arrived here yesterday and he himself having brought the news of how he had fared since leaving me on March 9. I do not say that it should come to sending me special couriers, for the Pigello[1] [Portinari] route is available any day; but from the 27th of February up to now, as I believe Your Magnificence well knows, I have not had any letters except this one, a reply to which I am now writing to Your Magnificence, reserving an answer to our lord until I have spoken with the Dauphin.

I see from our lord's letter that there is no great difference between what, I believe, is contained in my letters brought by Angelo Tani and what the Duke writes about the Dauphin. For since it seemed to me that the Dauphin always harped on one and the same string and since his testimony alone did not seem to me sufficient for getting at the truth, I came here to the Duke of Burgundy, where I found the windows open, as I wrote the Duke of Milan; and from then to this moment I have never in my conduct varied from what our lord now instructs me to do, so that I am happy to have approximated in my actions the judgment of our lord, whom I take as a model of the highest wisdom.

107·PROSPERO DA CAMOGLI *to*

CICCO SIMONETTA

Francia, cart. 525. Orig.

Io non so se deba cantar il Gloria in excelsis [au]t dir il Laudato Dio etc. de Don cavalero, essendo iuncto Martino qui heri et havendosi lui stesso portato le novelle de lui, doppoi ch'el partitte da me a 9 martio. Non dico me venessi esser mandato messi proprii, essendogli la via de Poggelo[1] quottidiana; nam dali 27 februario in qua, come credo ben sapia Vostra Magnificentia, io non ho havuto littere alcune, excepto questa, ale quale respondo ala Magnificentia Vostra per presenti, riservandomi de responder al Signore parlato che habbi cum el Delfin.

Vedo per quanto scrive la Signoria Sua non esser grande disformità da quello credo si contenga in mie littere portate per Angelo Tani a quello sente[a] el Signore del Delfin; nam parendomi non haver in la cura del Delfin salvo un medesmo ton, et non bastandomi ala vera information dele cose uno testimonio, venni qua dal Duca de Bergogna, unde trovai aperte le fenestre, come scripsi al Signore, et da lì in qua fui semper non allieno [sic] da quello scrive mò la Signoria Sua, siché me relegro approximarmi per pratica al parer del Signore, che ho per instructo de suma sapientia.

Magnifico Messer Cicco, quanto specta a quello tutto se conten in la littera dele excusatione da far in lo facto de D. Iacomo de Valperga

---

a. Ciphering error for "scrive" and it is so corrected in C. C.

Magnificent Messire Cicco, as regards everything in the letter about justifications [of the Duke's conduct] *in the Valperga affair,* etc., *I inform Your Magnificence that I have put forward and a thousand times repeated all these same arguments, even using the same words, and I have added to them others that seemed to me convincing. But—if all France will permit me to say so—such is the ostentation and egotism of the courtiers who surround the princes here that there is no reverence, humility, courtesy nor adoration in the world that they do not regard as their due; and Giacomo di Valperga is so pompous, that is, empty and full of nothing, that arguments are useless. Therefore, since in this case the gentle approach is the one to use in forwarding our lord's objectives, it has been and is necessary for me to temper the sour with the sweet.*

I was myself on the point of taking leave of the Duke of Burgundy when Martino arrived, and I have held up, in order to convey to the Duke what our lord bids me and to make a more ceremonious farewell than I would have done. Within three days, however, I will go to the Dauphin, God willing; and although, as regards the money [which the Duke of Milan offers], *it is truly very difficult to persuade a famished man that fasting is meritorious, nevertheless the instructions of our lord—namely to beg, supplicate, invoke magnanimity, generosity, lofty ideals and all the fine and efficacious prayers that are possible and licit for persuading the Dauphin to make the league—I will industriously follow, you need not fear. If I succeed, I will conclude the treaty on the agreed terms without exceeding them one iota. If I do not succeed, I will not end the negotiations but rather will use all the words that I have been instructed to use, and our lord and Your Magnificence will be informed of everything.*

On the subject of my returning speedily whether or not the treaty is concluded, seeing what our lord writes me in his last letter of April 17, about my going to England, etc., *I do not know what to say, since, as far as I am concerned, I do not think I should ever go beyond here. In opposition to this, there are two considerations: if I conclude with the Dauphin, I do not doubt that his lordship would want me to cross the*

etc., *adviso Vostra Magnificentia ho ditte et milleplicate tutte quelle medesme ragione, dico usque ad eadem verba, et hoglene iuncto de le altre che mi sonno parute rasonevole; ma, con supportation semper de tutta Franza, el l'hé tanto lo fasto et opinione d'essi proprii che han questi Principi de qua, che non hé reverentia, humilità, cortesia, né adoratione al mundo che non gli pia*[b] *devuta a loro; et D. Iacomo hé si ampuloso, hoc est sgompio et pieno de vacuità, che sonno irriti li argumenti; et per questo iuvando ali propositi del Signore li modi dolci, a me hé stato et hé necessario temperar lo agresto con lo zucharo.*

Io era proprio in procinto de prender commiato da questo Illustrissimo Signore, quando vene [sic] *Martino, et sum suprastato per explicar la substantia dele littere et far più gratioso adiosiati che non haria fatto. Siché fra tre dì me ne anderò dal Delfin, Deo duce, et quantumque a quello specta ali denari io vedo ch'el si può mal persuader al famelico che l'ieiunar*[c] *hé meritorio, pur a pié del Delfin quello che hé per conclusion del Signore, videlicet pregar, supplicar, invocar magnanimità, liberalità, sublimità et tutti quelli belli et efficaci preghi me seran possibili et liciti a persuader la Signoria Sua a liga, li userò studiosamenti, non dubitati. Profectando, concluderò in que* [sic] *termino sapite et* [non] *iota excedam; se nulla farò, non discluderò imo userò tutte quelle parole me sonno imposte et di tutto serà il Signore advisato et la Magnificentia Vostra. Nam del ritornarmene cossì presto rebus factis aut infectis, veduto quello me scrive el Signore per la ultima de 17 del andar mio in Anglia etc., io non so che affermare, cum ciò si che quanto a me non me par mai debba esser fuori de qua. Li oppositi rispecti sonno questi: se io concludo con el Delfin, non dubito vorrà la Signoria Sua che io passi là per augumento de sua reputation; similiter, se io* [non] *concludo, el serà in parte dele bone parole in che io lo vorria adulcir che io faci lo viagio. Preterea questo Duca de Bergogna mostra essergli per esser grato, et Monsignor lo Legato me ne instà, al qual io feci ala prima le obiecionette che scripsi al Signore, tutto per dar longa dulciter*

b. Read: paia.
c. Read: digiunar.

*Channel for the augmentation of his prestige; similarly, if I do not con-
clude the treaty, making the trip would help me to soften his lordship's
disappointment at my failure. In addition, the Duke of Burgundy
seems to favor the enterprise and the Legate urges me to undertake it.
To the latter I at first made the objections which I reported to our lord,
all of which were designed as a good excuse for delay so that I had time
to inform his lordship and await a reply—and, by the way, I marvel
that, with our lord writing that I should go to England, Your Magnificence has not sent me new letters of credence. I have urged the Legate
that he should also wait and see for a bit, all to the end above written,
especially since we now have some authentic information about England namely:*

*The Queen and her son, and the Duke of Somerset and his brother
have withdrawn to Scotland, and it is reported, but not certified, that
King Henry has been captured. It is affirmed, and indeed admitted,
that this withdrawal into Scotland is a fact and that they are treating
for a marriage between the sister[2] of the late King of Scotland and the
Queen's son, the Lancastrian Prince of Wales; and it is said that they
are annulling a certain homage that the English claim to be due from
the Scots and are making over to the Scots two towns[3] on the English-
Scots border, which have hitherto been occupied by the English to the
bitter indignation of the Scots, and in besieging one of which* [i.e. Ber-
wick] *the King of Scots was last year killed* [by the bursting of a can-
non].

*The Duke of Burgundy says that he has sent to dissuade the Scots'
Queen, a cousin[4] of his, from making this marriage. However, it is
feared, etc., and with a French fleet containing 20,000 men on the sea
and adding to that the ferocity of the Scots, it is to be feared that the
English are in for trouble; though the new King and the Earl of Warwick have indeed conquered all England, every last inch of it. On account of these uncertainties the Duke of Burgundy has not, up to now,
leagued himself with the new King and the Earl of Warwick, save for
favoring them in words, and he waits to see what will happen. The*

et haver spacio de advisar el Signore et aspectar resposta. Et maravi-
glomi, scrivendo el Signore che io vadi in Anglia, la Magnificenita
Vostra non m'habi mandato le littere nove. Io ho confortato al Legato
etiam lui stia al veder uno puocho, tutto ad finem suprascripto, maxime
che havemo iam tandem qualche verità de Anglia; silicet la Regina,[d] *el*
figlolo, el Duca de Sambrecet et suo fratello, esser retratti in Scocia et
se dice, sed non acerto, el Re de Anglia esser preiso. Se afferma et con-
fessa esser vera la dicta retratta in Scocia, et trattarsi parentato de una
sorella[2] *del condam Re de Scocia*[e] *in lo Principe de Gales, figlo dela*
Regina de Anglia; et se gli dice de quietar certa honoranza deli Scocesi
ad Anglesi et dar la iurisdicione privilegio de due terre[3] *che sonno li*
termini inter Scocia et Anglia, semper fin a qui essersele occupate per
Anglia cum grande dispecto de Scocesi, et ad una de quelle fu morto
lo anno passato lo Re de Scocia. El Duca de Bergogna dice havere
mandato a dissuader ala Regina de Scocia, chi hé sua cusina,[4] *questo*
facto. Pur se dubita etc., et essendo l'armata del Re de Franza con
homini vintimilia in mare, se segli adiungesse la ferocità de Scocesi, se
dubita inquietaria rancor ad Anglia; tamen el Re novo [et] el Conte de
Varuich la han conquistata tutta sine alio scrupulo. Per questi dubii el
Duca de Bergogna fin a qui non si hé ligato cum el Re novo et el Conte
de Varuich, salvo che li favorisse de parole et sta al veder. Dice ben
ch'el Re novo et el Conte de Varuich han l'armata de vele centocin-
quanta in mare contra a quella del Re de Franza, per il che la tempesta
che era in terra pare esser descendita in mare; et per questo io me sum
suprastato de passar et parendomi cose longhe. Tamen per non despiacer
el Duca de Bergogna, se cossì fussi el volesse, et per conpiacer al Delfin,
se cossì vorrà, et per conservar la voluntà del Legato, io ho preiso delib-
eration de attender resposta in Brugia; statim facto o non facto con el
Delfin me retrarò, pregando Vostra Magnificentia non prenda, excepto
in bona parte, questo mio retrar et mi dia preciso advisamento del
ritorno mio per esser excusato in supradictis.

---

d. C. C. incorrectly reads: el Re et Regina et suo fratello.
e. C. C. again incorrectly reads: Re de Anglia.

Duke says, however, that the new King and the Earl of Warwick have a fleet of 150 sail at sea to oppose the King of France. Therefore the tempest that shook the land seems to have descended on the water, and for this reason I have held off crossing, it being likely, I think, that the issue will be long drawn out.

Nevertheless in order not to displease the Duke of Burgundy, if he would wish me to cross, and in order to please the Dauphin if he would wish it also, and in order to keep the good will of the Legate, I have decided to await a reply at Bruges. [On receipt of this, I will go to Genappe to negotiate, but] *as soon as I have either succeeded or failed to conclude the treaty with the Dauphin, I will again withdraw. I beg Your Magnificence to take in good part this decision of mine about withdrawing and to give me precise directions about my return* [i.e. whether I should proceed to England or come back to Milan] *so that the Duke of Burgundy, the Dauphin, and the Legate will hold me excused for following orders.*

For the rest, *there came from the King of France to Bruges that Percivale Grillo, who remained at Bruges one day and then returned. He uttered a thousand nothings about the hopes of the King of France. He gives out the King to be well content with the nobles of Genoa and to blame himself for not having provided a different governor. Grillo says that the King is sending cavalry and has ordered 5,000 men from the Duke of Savoy and that in addition there will be Swiss and galleys and that the King has dipped into his coffers although there is little in them—and a thousand other things in the French manner. If a third were true, it would be sufficient to conquer Rome. I do not report these things because I fear them, but the going of these* [Genoese] *nobles to the King of France makes me suspicious, so much the more that they appear to have hope of discord in the government of Genoa.*

As to the Order of the Golden Fleece, according to information from a reliable source, they have not elected Count Galeazzo on account of the Duke of Orléans, especially for not having any certainty about the will of our lord regarding this matter.

Ceterum *el hé venuto dal Re de Franza a Brugs quello Princival Grillo, quale hé demorato a Brugs uno dì et se n'hé ritornato. Ha dicto mille per fumi de speranse del Re de Franza: dice el Re esser ben contento deli nobili de Zenoa, et haver culpa si medesmo per non havergli proveduto de altro governatore; dice che manda cavalli et ha comandato al Duca de Savoya homini cinquemilia, et ultra gli seran Suicii*[f]* et galee, et che ha el Re messo man al coffano, quantunque mantea* [sic]; *et mille cose ala gallica, se ne fusse lo tertio basteria per conquistar Roma. Io non digo queste cose perché io le tema, sed lo andar dal Re de Franza questi nobili mò mette suspecto, tanto più che monstran sperar in la discordia del Stato de Zenoa. Quanto del Ordine dela Tueson, secundo sum advisato per persona degna, non han electo lo Conte Galeazo per rispecto del Duca de Orliens, maxime per non haver certessa de* [la] *voluntà del Signore in questo facto. Siché de his omnibus piacia* [a Vostra Magnificentia] *advisar el Signore, ala cui Excelentia semper humiliter et ala* Magnificentia Vostra *me racomando.* Data ut in litteris.

---

f. Read: Sviceri or Svizeri.

Please inform our lord about all these things, to whose Excellency and to Your Magnificence as always humbly I recommend myself. Same date as in the letter.

HISTORICAL NOTES

1. Pigello di Folco d'Adoardo Portinari, manager of the Medici Bank at Milan, whose couriers to the branch at Bruges, where his brother, Tommaso, was assistant manager, often carried correspondence between Sforza and his ambassadors.

2. Actually, the infant daughter of the late King, James II, and sister of the reigning King, James III.

3. One town, Berwick-on-Tweed.

4. Mary of Guelders, the niece of the Duke, who had arranged her marriage to James II.

I am writing to Your Magnificence the enclosed, which you can signify to our lord as seems best to you. By Martino I received a letter of exchange. With heart and tongue I continually thank Your Magnificence. Owing more to Tommaso Portinari than the sum of the draft, I sent it to him to wipe out part of the debt.

I inform Your Magnificence that more is needed, though I do not expect to be believed; but, since I know how the wind is blowing, so that our lord may not be upset about me in these paltry matters do not take any trouble on my account to procure such things as would upset his excellency about me, for I do not merit it; and since I am, by nature and by misfortune, fated to fail, I will fail in silence. At least I thank God that I have to do with affairs of small moment, for, if they were of importance, I do not know that they might not, beyond of course the thoughts of doing well, give the servant some thoughts about the future.

I recommend myself to Your Magnificence. In great haste.

108 · PROSPERO DA CAMOGLI *to*

CICCO SIMONETTA

Francia, cart. 525. Orig.

Scrivo ala M. V. la inclusa, quale porrà V. M.tia significar al S.re come gli parerà. Per Martin hebbi una littera de cambio. Rengratio semper cum lo core et la lingua V. M.tia, et perché io era più in grosso obligato a Thomasio Portenaro, io ge la ho mandata per extinguer parte del debito. Adviso V. M.tia che altro se vole et io non ne voglo esser creduto; ma percioché io conosco lo vento, adcioch'el S.re non si turbi de me in rebus vilibus, baldamenti non prenda pena per me, la M. V., in procurar tale cose chi deban turbar la Ex.tia Sua verso di me, chi nol merito; et poiché io sum naturato et infortunato de semper crepar, crepirò da me stesso. Ben rengratio Dio che ho a far cose toccano puocho, nam se le cose fussero grande, non so se fussi ben ultra li pensieri del ben far, iunger al servitore pensamento de venir. Me racomando a V. M.tia. Raptissime.

Since I wrote to Your Lordship, things here have gone rather slowly, though, as usual, in favor of King Edward. So that Your Lordship may, in a few lines, understand the entire situation in these western regions—England, France, Scotland, and the Burgundian dominions—I am sending herein enclosed a copy of what I am writing to the Pope;[1] and so I remain waiting to learn what relish and savor affairs here have for those in the Curia, and we will proceed accordingly. I do not know how it will seem to others, but to me, who am right on top of affairs and have for a considerable time managed matters in these states, it seems that there is now offered a fine opportunity to do great and eminent things for the honor of God and of all Italy and of Your Lordship, if projects are understood and given support as they merit; and likewise will the opposite happen if they are neglected. I recommend myself always to Your Illustrious Lordship. Your ambassador left here some days ago and I believe he is near Bruges, and I will be in this neighborhood until it is time to cross the sea. Your Lordship will be informed of everything. Nevertheless I remind Your Excellency not to abandon the negotiation begun by your ambassador, because it matters much to your state—and so much the more am I pleased that I have put my hand to it and established a very good entrée to the Dauphin, which is also profitable for the Church, so that your cause and the Church's

109 · FRANCESCO COPPINI *to the*

DUKE OF MILAN

Inghilterra e Scozia, cart. 566. Orig.

Dapoi che scripsi ad V.S., le cose di qua vanno pur alquanto lente, benché al solito favore del Re Edwardo. Et accioché V. S. con pochi versi intenda tucto lo stato delle parti occidentali—Anglia, Francia, Scotia et di questo I.S.—mando inclusa una copia di quel che scrivo al S. Padre;[1] et così aspecto sentire che sapore o gusto hanno le cose di qua appresso della Corte, et secundo quello procederemo. Non so come parerà ad altri, ma ad me che sono sul facto et ho più tempo smaneggiati [sic] questi Stati, pare che se offerisca una bella occasione di far grandi et rilevate cose per honor di Dio et di tucta Italia et vostro, se sono intese et aiutate secundo che meritano et così l'opposito, se sono neglette. Raccomandomi sempre ad V.I.S. Lo vostro ambassadore si partì di qua più zorni fa et credo sia appresso Bruggia et io sarò in queste circumstantie, finché sarà tempo di passar il mare, et di tucto sarà V.I.S. advisata. Tuttavolta ricordo ad V.Ex. che non intralassi la pratica cominciata per lo dicto vostro ambassadore, perché importa assai ad lo Stato vostro, et tanto più mi piacerà quanto io ho messo le mani et facto assai bona intrata con quel S. etiam per lo Stato della Chiesa; siché l'una aiuterà l'altra,[2] et se Dio ne presta vita et le nostre opere siano acceptate, spero veder cose dignissime in poco tempo, le quali ad V.S. saranno ben grate. Valeat, Ex. V., cui me humiliter recomendo. Aspetto risposta delle cose di Roma de dì in dì.

will aid each other.[2] If God lends us life and our labors are accepted, I hope to see most noteworthy things in a short time, which will indeed be welcome to Your Lordship. Farewell, Your Excellency, to whom I humbly recommend myself. I await reply from day to day concerning the situation at Rome.

HISTORICAL NOTES

1. Coppini was seeking to secure the Dauphin's promise to revoke the Pragmatic Sanction of Bourges (1438) when he became King [Coppini to Pius II, Saint Omer, June 1, 1461, *Borgogna,* cart. 514; CSPM, I, 90–92].

2. This is the letter referred to in n. 1, above.

For the rest,[1] as I have many times, and lastly, written to Your Excellency from St. Omer, English affairs following the victory of King Edward are in this state.

King Henry, the Queen, [Edward] the Prince of Wales her son, the Duke of Somerset and his brother, and Lord Roos have withdrawn into Scotland. It is held for fact—but is not considered certain by those who have the best information—that a marriage is being negotiated between the sister of the late King of Scots[2] and the Prince of Wales, and it is said that King Henry has delivered up a castle called Berwick, the key to the English-Scots frontier, which castle, it is said, has been long claimed by the Scots but was of old occupied by the English by sheer force.

The French fleet of 20,000 men has left Normandy and sailed to England, among that force being, it is said, 5,000 men in the pay of [Charles] the Count of Maine. It is reported they have taken the outside route [to Scotland], around the [southern shores of the] island into the Gulf of Bristol [i.e. the Bristol Channel], in order, as it is thought, to test [the Lancastrian loyalties of] the people of Wales, who, it is indeed said, love the Queen. Nevertheless, Bristol is a strong city, and from there on, one can sail along the island northward to Scotland only in small coasting vessels, because of a tide that lasts six hours.[3] It is there-

110 · PROSPERO DA CAMOGLI *to the*

DUKE OF MILAN

Francia, cart. 525. Orig.

Ceterum,[1] come per altre più volte et ultimamenti ho scritto de verso Sancto Othomario [sic] a V. Ex.tia, le cose de Angliterra, poso la victoria del Re Edoardo, sonno in questi termini. Lo Re Henrico, la Regina, lo Principe de Gales, suo figlolo, lo Duca de Somesetrh et Monsignor de Ros, suo fratello, se sonno reducti in Scotia; et dicesi del parentato si tratta et se mette per facto, tamen non se ha per fermo da chi più ne intende, dela sorella del condam Re de Scotia[2] al Principe de Gales; et dicesi Re Henrico haver dato uno casello [sic], si domanda Barinch, chi hé inter quelle chiave de frontere da Anglia a Scotia, il qual castello se dice hé raxon antiqua de Scotia et antiquamenti occupato da Anglia per prepotentia.

La armata de Francesi, homini 20 milia, hé partita de Nortmandia et ita in Anglia, tra li quali homini se dice lo Conte de Humaine haverne pagato 5 milia. Se dice han priso la via de fuori dela insula in lo ghulpho de Bristolia, secundo se ha opinione, per anasar quelli populi de Gales, chi pur se dicono amar la Regina. Tutta volta Bristolia hé forte città et da lì in ultra, costesando la insula verso la Scotia, non se può ben navigar altre nave che navette del paese a transito per una marea, chi dura 6 hore.[3] Siché hé opinione non potran aproximarsi più ala Scotia de verso quella parte. De verso lo stretto de Dobla et Cales, quale hé migla 18, Varruich, se dice, havergli una armata, ma non

fore thought that the French will not be able to come closer to Scotland than the Bristol Channel.

Near the strait between Dover and Calais, which is eighteen miles wide, Warwick, it is said, has a fleet, not in order to oppose the French on the open sea but only in order to prevent their landing in England and to guard the strait.

Because of the Scots marriage and the support of Scotland and because of the goodly crew of Frenchmen [preparing to sail], it is feared here that there may be another battle, which, if it takes place, will certainly be the "coup de grâce" for that kingdom. Nevertheless King Edward and Warwick have complete control of the island and the realm and look to providing whatever is necessary. King Edward is now coming to London; I believe, to take measures for the security of the kingdom and to establish himself firmly against possible future dangers. It is true, my most illustrious lord, that these English have not the slightest form of political order, but if there is some authority in the country, it lies in King Edward and the Earl of Warwick.

The Dauphin and the Duke of Burgundy have sent to the Queen of Scotland to dissuade her [from agreeing to the Lancastrian marriage]. I do not know what they will accomplish. *Because of all these factors, some favoring the one side and some the other, the Duke of Burgundy is now taking great care not to reveal where he stands, except for what support he offers in words. Nonetheless, if King Edward comes to grief, it will be no laughing matter for the Duke.*

My lord of Croy told me when I left him that not until the government of King Edward is seen to be more firm and not until the outcome of the French naval attack is known, will the Duke of Burgundy be willing to reveal himself by making a league [with the Yorkists] *or giving any other demonstration of support; and if the King of France should agree to some sort of peace treaty between him and the Duke of Burgundy, I believe that, as the English situation got worse, the Burgundians would be the readier to accept such a treaty. This is the explanation, I believe, for the ambassadors who are being sent by the Duke of*

perciò da resister aperto mari ala gallica, sed solum apta a prohibirli il descender in la insula et guardar quello passo. Per lo parentato et favor de Scoti, et per questa bona chiera[a] de Francesi, hé qui dubita che non sia anchora qualche assalto et batagla, quale se serà, serà "il resto del grosso" [b] de certo a questo Regno de Anglia. Pur tuttavia lo Re Edoardo et Varruich han lo dominio tutto dela insula et lo Regno et tendino a quelli provedimenti sonno necessarii; et Re Edoardo ven al presente a Londres, credo, per dar et prendar li ordini al saldar lo Regno et fermarsi contra li periculi possono avenir. Hé vero, Ill.mo S.re mio, che questi Anglici non han una minima forma de regimento, ma pur se gle n'hé in capo alcuno, el n'hé in lo Re Edoardo e lo Conte de Varruich. *El Delfin et lo Duca de Bergogna* han mandato ala Regina de Scotia a dissuader. Non so quello farano.

Per tutte queste cose che sonno al presente da una parte et da un'altra, el Duca de Bergogna sta multo suspeso de non scoprirse, salvo in favorir de parole; et non dimanco, se el Re Edoardo fluit assilvi [sic], non se ne rideria. Monsignor de Crovi me disse in la partensa mia che finché non si veda lo Stato del Re Edoardo più fermo, et quello farà questa armata, el Duca de Bergogna non hé per scoprirse de la liga né de altra demonstratione; et se el Re de Franza se aquietassi a qualche compositione de pace inter lui et el Duca de Bergogna, io credo che come Anglia staesse peio, ne serian più contenti. Et questa credo sii la causa deli ambassatori che se adoperan da Duca de Bergogna al Re de Franza, et se dice esser per venir ambassatori del Re de Franza al Duca de Bergogna. Tamen non lo so de certo, et studierò de informarmene et haverò il modo ad intender la medula. Ben so che quando li ambassatori del Duca de Bergogna trattano la pace con el Re de Franza, gli hé interposta per parte del Re la dificultà del Delfin; quando quelli del Delfin sonno stati in pratica, gli hé similiter stata interposta la dificultà del Duca de Bergogna. Et se questa armata prospererà, credo serà il Re de Franza più superbo; sin autem et el Re Edoardo resti indubitato Rex

---

a. Read: schiera.
b. Quotation marks in the original.

Burgundy to the King of France, and French ambassadors are said to be coming to the Duke of Burgundy.

Nevertheless I do not know this for certain, and I will work to secure information about it and to find the means of better understanding the matter. However, I do know that when the ambassadors of the Duke of Burgundy treat for peace with the King of France, the French interpose the difficulty about the Dauphin; when the Dauphin's ambassadors have been in negotiations with the King, the French have, in the same way, interposed the difficulty about the Duke of Burgundy. And if this French fleet is successful, I believe that the King of France will be more haughty; if, on the other hand, King Edward remains indubitable King of England, I believe that the Dauphin and the Duke of Burgundy will be less ready to accept peace with the King of France. I therefore think that in the future the love and trust between the King of France and the Duke of Burgundy will be the same as it has been in the past. Of what I learned I will be entirely solicitous in continually informing Your Excellency, to whom I send, enclosed, a hasty sketch made by my rude hand only to represent to Your Excellency the form and shape of things presently impending there [i.e., in England].[4] I therefore beg Your Excellency to take it as a sign of my industriousness in giving you all information and not as a sign of my presuming to do something for which I have neither the manual nor the mental talent. I humbly recommend myself to you.

HISTORICAL NOTES

1. This dispatch evidently is part of another, now lost, probably written on June 1 [see doc. 113, n. 1, p. 397].

2. See doc. 107, n. 2, p. 372.

3. Prospero apparently had the curious idea that Scotland could be

de Anglia, io credo che el Delfin et el Duca de Bergogna seran più duri
ala pace del Re de Franza. Siché il futuro me par che serà tal fra el Re
de Franza et el Duca de Bergogna de amore et fede fra epsi, come hé
stato il passato; et de quello sentirò tutto serò sollicito in advisar con-
tinuamenti la Excellentia Vostra, ala qual mando qui alligato con queste
uno designo subitario fatto de mia ruda man solo per representar a V.
Ex.tia la forma et fation dele cose che impendono là al presente.[4] Siché
supplico a V. Ex. lo prenda in argumento del studio che ho in dar ogni
advisi a quella, et non in presumption che io habbi de far cose in che
né la man né lo ingenio mi basti; ala qual humiliter me racomando.

reached by sailing up the Severn River from the Bristol Channel; at least, the
tide he refers to is evidently the famous "Severn Bore."

4. The enclosure was apparently a map, as indicated in Prospero's dispatch of June 18 to the Duke, doc. 119, p. 425.

[. . . . .] and what I have written and what it will fall to me to write, take it in the good sense that I intended it, for so my loyalty merits, and I say this also about what I have written recently concerning my securing compensation from *Genoa,* for I remit all to what time, occasion, and what context will seem best to Your Magnificence. Therefore in regard to making provision for *money* here, as I formerly wrote to Your Magnificence, I would not want *our lord* to be upset for me about such paltry matters. Your Magnificence understands that if I wished for thousands here, I would have them; but I will wait and I would rather sell myself than do it, because these *Genoese* here are not friends of Caesar [i.e. of the Duke of Milan] and, for the honor of *our lord,* I refuse to have recourse to them. Indeed I can assure you, by God's truth, that whenever I have gone into debt *for a cloak, I have given one of my books* as security; and therefore I am prepared to behave patiently and endure everything rather than weary one whom I wish to please and serve as long as I live. I am therefore always content that Your Magnificence do what seems best to you in all and for all. I recommend myself to you.

I left the *Duke of Burgundy* because it seemed to me an excessive honor to support in a threadbare gown, in the same way that I left the

iii · PROSPERO DA CAMOGLI *to*

CICCO SIMONETTA

Francia, cart. 525. Orig.

[..........]ᵃ aliter non [...............] per questo [.......]
in bona parte [.........] in specialità mò me ne contento [........]
se per experiencia V. M.tia vole [.........] et esser apta a farmene,
quando si puotrà farne più questo che altra inante demonstratione,
siché [.....] et quello che ho scritto et quello mi accaderà scriver, lo
prenda in bona parte de me, perché cossì merita la fede mia; et questo
mi dico etiam su quello che ho scritto questi dì de quello mio refacimento da *Zenoa,* perché tutto remetto a quello tempo, quella occasione
et quella instantia parerà ala M. V. Quanto specta igitur a provedimento de *denari* qui io, come per altre scripsi a V. M.tia, non vorria
che el *Signore* se turbassi di me per tali minuterie. Intenda V. M.tia che
se io volessi qui miglara, io ne haria; ma me ne suprase[do] et più tosto
me venderia che farlo, perché questi de *Zenoa* qui non sunt amici Cesaris
et io per honor del *Signore* non ricurro a loro. Ben vi acerto, per Dio
vero, chi se io me ho debiuto [fare?] *un mantel de drapo, ho dato un
de mei libri*ᵇ per contra; et cossì sum apto a diportarmi patienter et
tutto suffrir più tosto che tediar a chi voglio piacer et servir [finché?]

---

a. A piece is torn off the top portion of this dispatch, and adjacent portions are badly
damaged and illegible even with the aid of ultraviolet light.
b. Chancery deciphering between the lines incorrectly reads: una geme et libri.

Dauphin because my discretion informed me that he cannot perform the miracles of Christ, namely, *of the five loaves and two fishes,* for I inform you that he has reached an extremity. So I am here, that is, neither at Cremona nor Piacenza—and I hope that, with the grace of God, I will secure some additional money before I am given leave to depart.

[. . . . . .] The honorable Master Guido [. . . . .] says that Ambrogio is responsible for this matter, and in the face on his pressing request I have not been able to withhold this letter although to the temperate mind of Your Magnificence it will, I am sure, seem to be too vehement, but I do not think honorable favors should be denied good and honest subjects and citizens. I recommend myself to Your Magnificence as always.

viva. Siché semper me contento de V. M.tia; facia quello gli pare in tutto, et in tutto et per tutto a quella me racomando.

Io me sum levato dal *Duca de Bergogna,* perché me pareva nimius honor in tenui toga; item dal *Delfin* perché ho inteso per discretion non può far miraculi de Cristo, ciohé *deli cinque pani et dui pesci,* advisandovi che hé una extremità la sua presente. Siché sum qui, hoc est né in Cremonese né in Placentina, et spero cum la gratia de Dio de tocar de aug[mento?] anzi che io sii spachiato.

[.......] gran che no[....................] voria pur[........ ....] del suo S.re esse[.........]serò sign[....] lo predi[.......] desider[.......] che havessero questa efficacia che la[........] di questi[................] che la causa del subdito suo ac[........] ch'el ha di[................] raveduto in Italia aut saltem per contemplatione de uno [............] la fa[....] render de novo instrumento [........]ra ben [............]ra per questo denaro di uno S. me et[........] et bo[.......] starà [.................] raxone [....] honesto re[..............]. Il Spectabile Maistro Guido No [.....] dice Ambrosio habia cura di questo, et ad sua instante rechiesta io non [ho] possuto denegar questa littera, quantunque ala modestia de V. M.tia sum certo parerà de troppo mia vehementia; ma ali honesti et boni subditi et citadini me par non si deba dinegar li honesti favori. Me racomando a V. M.tia semper. Data ut supra.

Some days ago I wrote from here to Your Excellency at great length concerning the situation in England and throughout the West. Since then, I have had letters from Your Excellency of May 16, by which I am informed that all my letters have arrived safely, and been forwarded to Rome as I desired. I am very much pleased to learn this, for the said letters were needed to comfort those minds which have been perhaps more gloomy than was necessary. I see that in your letters you have repeated your instructions to the Honorable Messer Prospero to have an understanding with me and follow my directions and urgings, especially about crossing to England. This likewise has given me great pleasure, particularly because after I received your letters there arrived here an ambassador of my lord of Warwick, who had dinner with me, Messer Prospero also being present. At the departure of this ambassador, in order to give some encouragement and information to His Majesty King Edward and the Earl of Warwick at this time when their government is not yet very stable—encouragement that would correspond to my former statements about Your Excellency and about your attitude—I wrote a letter concerning Messer Prospero's instructions and his commission to cross to England, and all this we, Prospero and I, told the ambassador, who was greatly pleased thereby.

Thus we have always been and are ready to cross as soon as oppor-

112 · FRANCESCO COPPINI *to the*

DUKE OF MILAN

Borgogna, cart. 514. Orig.

A dì passati scripsi di qui ad V. Ex. dello stato di Inghilterra et di tucto l'occidente copiosamente. Di poi ho lettere dalla prefata V. Ex. de dì sedici di maggio, per le quali sono advisato tucte le mie lettere essere arrivate assalvamento [sic] et mandate ad Roma, secondo il mio desiderio; di che ho havuto assai piacere, ché erano necessarie per conforto di quelli animi forsi più afflicti che non bisognava. Veggo appresso per decte lettere esser replicata la commissione allo Spectabile Messer Prospero dello intendersi con mi et seguitare i miei ricordi et conforti et maxime del passar in Anglia. Di che similmente ho ricevuto assai piacere et maxime perché da poi che ricevi [sic] le prime lettere, ritrovandosi qui uno ambasciadore di Mons. S. di Warwic et desinando con mi, dove anchora era dicto Messer Prospero, alla partita di decto ambasciadore, per dare qualche conforto et adviso ad la M.tà del Re Edwardo et ad Mons. S. di Warwic in questo tempo del loro Stato anchora non ben fermo, che corrispondesse ad quello che altre volte ho proposto et decto di V. Ex. et di sua dispositione, scripsi della commissione di decto Messer Prospero et del suo passare et così dicemo l'uno et l'altro al prefato ambasciadore, et quale ne prese grandissimo conforto. Et così semo sempre stati et stamo in punto al passar come ne venisse il destro, che credemo sarà alla ritornata del mio messo, che ho mandato in Anglia; et in questo mezo attendemo lettere opportune per lo passare di decto

tunity offers, which we believe will be on the return of my messenger whom I dispatched to England. In the meantime we await appropriate letters of credence for Messer Prospero's crossing, but even if they should not arrive in time, we will not hesitate to do what will seem most profitable and honorable for Your Lordship and your state, especially having written the letter I mentioned above. There is nothing else to write at present, except to recommend myself devotedly to Your Excellency, although by now this seems superfluous since Your Excellency knows that I am your creature and your instrument, not for mercenary reasons but out of long devotion and pure fidelity.

Messer Prospero, le quali se non arrivassino ad tempo, non staremo però di fare quello che ne parerà più utile et honore di V. S. et di suo Stato, et maxime havendo scripto come ho dicto di sopra. Altro non mi accade al presente, se non raccomandarmi devotamente ad V. Ex., quantunque horamai ne par essere superchio, sapendo essa che sono sua creatura et suo operatore non mercenario, ma de antiqua devotione et pura fede.

Having come here to send Martino the courier back to Your Excellency with what news there is up to now, I decided I should send him to St. Omer to *my lord of Croy* to see if my lord wishes to write anything more to Your Excellency and similarly to the Legate. While I was getting ready to dispatch Martino, there arrived letters from Your Excellency of May 16, to which I reply by this.

I was very happy to learn that Your Excellency has received all my letters up to that of April 28, for I was in a state of anxiety since the letters seem to me of importance to Your Excellency. With regard to the Duke of Burgundy, my lord [Charles, Count] of Charolais, the Duke of Clèves, my lord of Croy and his brother and with each of the lords of the Golden Fleece, and in describing the ceremonies of the Order, I have carried out Your Excellency's instructions, as you will see by my letters of May 9 from St. Omer. I have not sent you the names of the lords and knights of the Order because the *Duke of Burgundy's* household is so lacking in organization that not a secretary in it has been able to give me the names; but, God willing, I will myself make a list of the members by name and title.

I have been with the Legate and every day we write to each other. His excellency will come to stay in this town, where he will decide about his crossing to England and also about my crossing, as he will think best; for I will always be obedient to him since I defer to his

113 · PROSPERO DA CAMOGLI *to the*

DUKE OF MILAN

Francia, cart. 525. Orig.

Essendo venuto qui per expedir Martin cavalaro, et remandarlo a V. Ex.tia cum quello gli hé fin a qui, m'hé paruto debito mandarlo a Sancto Omer a *Mon.re de Crovi* a veder s'el voleva rescriver altro a V. Ex.tia, et similiter a Monsignor lo Legato; et interim spachiandolo, sonno supravenute littere de V. Ex.tia de 16 maii, ale quale per questa respondo.

Ho havuto grande consolatione de intender che V. Ex.tia habbi recevute tutte le mie littere fin a 28 aprilis perché pur ne stava in anxietà, parendomi pertenessero a V. Ex.tia. Cum lo Ill.mo S. Duca de Bergogna, Monsignor de Karloes, lo Ducha de Cleve, Monsignor de Crovi et suo fratello, et cum tutti singuli quelli S.ri Cavaleri dela Tueson, et in advisar come fu celebrata la solemnità, io satisfeci a quanto me scrive V. Ex.tia, come per littere de 9 maii dedi de verso Sancto Othomer, adviso a V. Ex.tia, ala qual non ho mandato li nomi deli Sig.ri et Cavaleri de dicto Ordine, perché in casa del *Duca de Bergogna* no' hé tanto ordine che gli sii secretario chi me li habbi sapiuti dare; ma, se a Dio piacerà, io li notarò mi proprio per nome et tituli.

Cum lo Reverendissimo Monsignor lo Legato fui et ogni dì si scriviamo; et venirà Sua Excellentia a star qui in questa terra, unde delibererà del suo passar in Anglia; et cossì de me quello che parerà a Sua Signoria, che semper gli serò ubediente, come me refero ala Signoria Sua. Solo se le cose andassero in longo, ho scritto per l'altra a Vostra

judgment. However, if matters are going to be drawn out, I have written to Your Excellency in a former letter about the information I need to clarify my mission. Concerning the main business with the Dauphin nothing else has happened here, as by mine of June 1[1] Your Excellency will be fully informed.

Concerning English affairs, letters of June 2 from London merchants report that the French fleet attacked the coast of Cornwall, doing some pillaging and burning, and has sailed back toward Normandy because it lacked eighteen Breton ships that up to then had not joined it.

Item: the letters report that King Edward is coming to London in order to be crowned and, as I note in former letters, to take appropriate measures for the governing of the kingdom, for the English Parliament has been summoned to meet on July 6 at London. This is what is known up to now. About whatever further news arrives, I will continually keep Your Excellency informed, to whom I humbly recommend myself.

Postscript: *Some of these Genoese merchants here have often asked me whether, should four or five thousand* [French] *foot-soldiers go to Genoa to succor the citadel, Your Excellency might take a hand in the matter. I answered that I was certain you would not, since Your Excellency is entirely aloof and has always remained aloof from Genoese affairs and, no matter what anyone says, has had of old and still has great reverence for the House of France. I was laughed at for saying this, the Genoese objecting that Cristoforo Panigarola and Biagio de Gradi[2] in the treaty of agreement between the Doge* [Prospero Adorno] *and the Archbishop* [Paolo Fregoso] *were denominated mediators and proxies in the name of Your Excellency. It would appear to me, then, that there is being prepared an attempt to succor the citadel by way of Savona and then on to Genoa. This I note for Your Excellency's information.*

Excellentia quello me par mi bisogni a più chiaressa mia. Dela causa principal cum el Delfin non accade qui altro, perché per la mia de uno presentis[1] *Vostra Excellentia intenderà il tutto.* Similiter sul facto de Angliterra, sul quale quale [sic] per littere de mercatanti de Londres de 2 presentis, se ha come la armata de Francesi ha ferito su la costa de Cornivagla et ha fatto alcuni damni de robaria et fuoco; et se ne hé renavigata verso Nortmandia, cum ciò sia che gli mancha 18 nave de Bertoni, che non eran fin a chi iuncte cum la armata. Item come lo Re Edoardo ven a Londres per incoronarsi et, come dico per le altre, per dar li modi opportuni al Regno; nam ali 6 de iulio hé ordinato de far parlamento generale in Londres. Questo hé quello habiamo fin a qui. Se altro gli serà, adviserò continuamenti V. Ex.tia, ala qual humiliter me racomando.

Post scripta. *Alcuni di questi mercatanti qui de Zenoa m'an intero-gato spesso se andassi a Zenoa quatro o cinque milia fanti per sucurer Castelleto, io creda che V. S. se ne impaciassi. Io gli ho resposto che sum certo de non più, cum ciò sia che de quelle cose V. S. omnino n'hé et semper stata aliena et ha havuto, et dica ha chi vogli, semper grande reverentia et ab antiquo ala casa del Re de Franza. Et se rideno de tal mio parlare, obiectando che Cristoforo Panigirola et Blasio da Gr[adi]*[2] *in lo contratto del acordio dal Duce al Arcivescovo sonno nominati mediatori, procuratori et procuratori o nomine de Vostra Excelentia. Et secundo me par, sonno per intentar lo sucurso per la via de Saona et inde a Zenoa; questo per adviso de Vostra Excelentia.* Ut supra.

HISTORICAL NOTES

1. This dispatch of June 1 has not been found.
2. Milanese agents sent to Genoa in May, 1461, to promote unity among the Genoese factions and aid the war effort against the French, as is attested by their numerous dispatches [*Genova*, cart. 414].

Concerning the arrival of courier Martino with the letter from the lord [i.e. Sforza]. He [Prospero] has taken leave of the Duke [of Burgundy] and those other lords etc. All have spoken with him with good will and made offers, and also those of the Order of the Golden Fleece. Because of the flattering treatment he received from members of the Order, he still hopes that they have elected Count Galeazzo [Sforza].

Lord Giacomo di Valperga came forth a mile to meet and greet him. Although Valperga conjectured that Prospero did not bring good news for him, because he knew that the Duke remained firm regarding his original position [about Valperga's inclusion in the treaty], he gave a good welcome to Prospero; for the rest, he remitted himself to the Dauphin.

The same thing was done to Prospero upon his arrival at Bruges. The Dauphin with great reluctance agreed to hear the extract from the letters of the lord, saying that he knew the contents etc. The Dauphin blames him because he did not put forward the reasons that moved the Dauphin to ask for a greater sum for lord Giacomo etc. and the Dauphin knew well how much he is obligated to the lord. Gaston is cast aside and wishes to leave, he and his brother, and the Dauphin is content that they depart—this because lord Giacomo blames them [i.e. for Sforza's attitude toward Valperga]. He [Prospero] has learned who

DUKE OF MILAN

Sommari, cart. 1560, fasc. 2. Minute[1]

Del giongere de Martin cavallaro con la littera del S. Che ha tolto licencia da Duca et quilli altri Signori etc. Che tuti l'ànno veduto volentiere et fattoli proferte et cossí quilli dela Tueson. Che per le careze fatteli per quilli dela Tueson ancor spera che habiano elletto [sic] el C. Galeazo.

Che D. Iacomo de Valperga gli vene incontra una lega et lo salutò; che licet suponia che non portava bone novelle per luy, perché sapeva el S. stare fermo sul primo proposto, fosse ben venuto; del resto se remetteva al Delfin.

El simile gli fo facto ad lo iungere a Bruge. Ch'el Delfin con gran fatica volse ascoltare l'extracto dele littere del S., dicendo che sapeva la continentia etc. Ch'el Delfin l'incolpa che non ha sposto [?] li respecti el movevano nel facto de D. Iacomo in maiore summa etc., et che sapeva ben quanto n'é obligato al S. Che Gascon é desmesso et vole partirse luy et lo fratello et el Delfin é contento che vadano; questo perché D. Iacomo l'incolpa. Che ha inteso chi fo cason dela scripta[2] terribile fece Gascon al S. Che se excusò col Delfin tanto honestamente quanto poté, biasimando chi diceva el S. non andare drito. Ch'el Delfin stete poy VI dì prima lo volesse intendere, facendoli dare de stranii moti. Poy mandò per luy et posta multa disse che D. Iacomo saria contento deli XII^m,[3] ma che voleva avisarne certi suoy parenti. Ch'el Delfin dice, se non fosse

was responsible for the terrible memorandum Gaston sent to the lord.[2] He excused himself to the Dauphin as honorably as he could, blaming the one who said the lord [i.e. Sforza] was not doing the right thing. The Dauphin then would not hear him for six days, having his people give very strange reasons. Then the Dauphin sent for him and, after many words, said the lord Giacomo would be content with 12,000,[3] but that he wanted to inform certain of his family. The Dauphin says, had it not been for the matter of lord Giacomo, he would never have spoken about money, but would have acted generously as he wrote. Prospero will proceed to amend the treaty and remove the clause relating to lord Giacomo. They are preparing the money, because, since lord Giacomo says, as the Dauphin affirms, that he will be content with the 12,000, the transaction can be carried out, and they do everything quickly. He [i.e. Prospero] will not disburse the money unless the treaty is properly amended and signed. He would like to be informed whether, should the Dauphin not wish the money, he should give it to lord Giacomo and what security he should require. He has been told by the Dauphin to write to the lord and the lady [i.e. Duchess Bianca] to urge them to offer a larger amount, given that the Dauphin is agreeing to a settlement out of regard for the lord.

As for news, he sent full information by Martino and in other letters. Lord Giacomo is informed from Milan about everything and it is from there that he receives information. Concerning the Marquess of Montferrat and [his brother] lord Guglielmo, he confirms what he wrote previously. The Dukes of Orléans and of Brittany are making great embassies. It is reported that the King of France is using threatening language. Divers schemes are on foot in France. He has read to the Dauphin the letter about his going to England; the Dauphin approved the project and thanked the lord etc. He would wait at Bruges to secure passage and, on securing it, would go to the Dauphin to consult about his journey.

Some say the King of Sicily [René], some say [Gaston,] the Count of Foix with 3,000 crossbowmen, is coming to succor [the French in the

stato el facto de D. Iacomo, may haria parlato de dinari, ma saria andato liberamente como scrisse. Che luy se reformarà el contracto et torà via le condicione de D. Iacomo. Che apparechiano li dinari, perché dicendo D. Iacomo como el Delfin afferma chi dirà essere contento ali XII^m, se possa exequire et fano presto tutto. Ch'el non darà li dinari s'el contracto non sarà sottoscripto et facto in bona forma. Che voria essere avisato che non volendo el Delfin li dinari, se li debbe [dare] a D. Iacomo, et che caucione debbe tore. Ch'é stato motegiato per parte del Delfin ch'el scriva al S. et ad Madona confortandoli a maiore summa, consyderato ch'esso Delfin vene ad questo per respecto del S.

De le novelle avisò per Martino a compimento et per altre littere. Che D. Iacomo é avisato da Milano d'ogni cosa et là dove ha li avisi. Del Marchese de Monferrato et S. Guilielmo afirma ciò scrisse per l'altre. Ch'el Duca de Orliens et de Bertagna fano gran messedata.[a] Se dice el Re de Franza dire dele male parole. Che in Franza se fanno diversi designi. Che ha lecto al Dalfin la littera del suo andare in Anglia, lo laudò et regratiò el S. etc. Che staresse ad aspectare passo in Bruges et che occurrendo andasse da luy per consultare questa soa andata.

Chi dice al secorso [sic] de Zeno[b] vene el Re de Sicilia, chi dice el Conte de Foys con III^m balistrieri. Che a sey de luglio se debe fare uno parlamento generale in Londres.

Ch'el Delfin gli ha dicto havere inteso che Guiotin é qui secreto mandato da Duchessa de Savoya, perché el Duca sta male et che essa Duchessa se butta in le braza del S. etc.

---

a. Read possibly: messaggiate.
b. Read: Zenoa.

citadel of] Genoa. On July 6 there is to be a meeting of Parliament in London.

The Dauphin says he has heard Guiotino [de Nores] has been sent here [i.e. to Milan] secretly by [Anne,] the Duchess of Savoy because the Duke is ill and she is putting herself in the arms of the lord etc.

HISTORICAL NOTES

1. Of this dispatch, only this summary made by the Chancery has been found. Its style of disconnected notations and incomplete sentences presents difficulties in interpretation and translation.

2. Gaston du Lyon's Memorandum to the Duke of Nov. 30, 1460 [doc. 57, pp. 27–37].

3. Prospero was unaware at this time that the Dauphin had sent to Milan an emissary [see doc. 120, p. 439], whose report apparently led him to issue on June 1, 1461, letters patent [see Appendix, doc. IV, p. 470] absolving Sforza from the execution of the Valperga clause in the Treaty of Genappe, and at the same time ratifying that treaty. The following day Louis issued another document acknowledging a debt of 18,000 Rhenish florins payable to the Duke six months from the date of the conclusion of their pending agreement or from his ascension to the throne, whichever came first [*Francia,* cart. 525; *Lettres,* I, 140, n. 1]. Also on June 2 the Dauphin accredited Charles Astars and Jean de Saubier for a mission to Sforza and recommended them to Cicco Simonetta [*Francia,* cart. 525; *Lettres,* I, 139–40].

Yesterday, upon my arrival at Antwerp, and Postscript.[1] Before being able to commit the present letters to a trusty messenger, I met the honorable knights, Count Lodovico Dallugo and the noble Zanone [Corio], emissaries of Your Excellency,[2] through whom I received letters of credence and learned of the prosperity both of Your Excellency and of your state and of your affection for me, all of which gave me very great pleasure and I continually thank Your Excellency, from whom I daily await information about the Roman situation. Since Count Lodovico and Zanone say, among other things, that they have commissions and letters from you for their crossing to England, and have not mentioned to me any commission for Messer Prospero nor reported anything about what the English lords formerly wrote to you and what I wrote and also about what I instructed Messer Antonio to say; and, on the other hand, since Messer Prospero, who is likewise here, says he has letters from Your Lordship ordering him, when he has fulfilled his principal commission, to return to Italy and says also that he does not have the letters he would need for crossing to England, though he awaits a final reply concerning his principal commission— and he seems to be quite perplexed—for these reasons I am also very displeased and so remain in a state of uncertainty. Therefore will Your Lordship please write and inform us what we should do. However, if

115·FRANCESCO COPPINI *to the*

DUKE OF MILAN

Inghilterra e Scozia, cart. 566. Orig.

Post scripta.[1] Essendo a dì nove venuto in Anversa, avanti che le presenti littere potessi commectere ad fidel messo, ho ritrovati lo Spectabile Cavalieri Conte Lodovico Dallugo et lo nobile Zenon,[2] messi di V.Ex., et per quelli ho ricevuto littere di credenza et inteso della prosperità di V.S. et di suo Stato et della affectione di quella verso di me, di che ho ricevuto assai piacere, regratiando sempre essa V. Ex., dalla quale attendo ogni giorno adviso delle cose di Roma. Et perché li prefati Conte Lodovico et Zenon intra l'altre cose dicono haver commissione et littere del passar in Anglia et non mi hanno facto mentione della commissione di Messer Prospero né delle cose altra volta scripte per quelli S. et per me et commesse etiam ad Messer Antonio, et da altro canto decto Messer Prospero, el quale similiter si ritruova qui, dice haver littere da V.S. che, spacciata la principal commissione, se ne ritorni in Italia né anchora havere le littere opportune per lo passare di Inghilterra, quantunque attende ad certa risposta sopra la decta principal commissione. Et parendomi essere alquanto perplexo ne ho preso anchora io alquanta displicentia et sto sospeso, pertanto harò piacere che V.S. scriva et ne dia adviso di quanto havemo ad fare. Tuctavolta se in questo mezo ne verrà il destro del passare, ne pigleremo quel partito che ne parerà più utile et honore di V.S. et maxime havendo scripto et significato ad la M.tà del Re et Mons. di Warwic quanto é decto di sopra, che non seguitando

in the meantime an opportunity to cross offers itself, we will embrace the course that appears the more profitable and honorable to Your Lordship, especially considering what we signified by letter, as mentioned above, to His Majesty the King and the Earl of Warwick, for our failure to follow up would cast a shadow on the minds of those lords. I can also certify to Your Excellency that that lord with whom it is Messer Prospero's principal commission to negotiate and with whom, it is hoped, there will be a favorable conclusion [i.e. the Dauphin], urges and very much desires our crossing to England.

If I merit some trust regarding matters here, and also taking into account my knowledge of Italian affairs and especially those of your state, I say that it will be useful and necessary for you continually to maintain an alert emissary between that realm [i.e. England] and these parts, and this, I believe, experience will demonstrate to you. My lord, you need not doubt that if, in your quarter, there is no lack of aid and encouragement for the beginnings and foundations we have established here, Your Lordship will see eminent accomplishment such as will gratify you highly. It remains now for Your Lordship to make the best provision you know how to and can make, and to let it be known where it counts particularly at this time since you lack neither power nor connections nor favor at the Curia, and I remind Your Lordship of the old proverb: who has the moment and yet continues to wait for it, loses it.

HISTORICAL NOTES

1. This postscript represents an addition to Coppini's dispatch of June 6, doc. 112, p. 391.

2. Count Lodovico Dallugo and Zanone Corio, and their secretary, Giovanni Pietro Cagnola, had been sent by Sforza to England apparently to con-

farebbe ombra nelle menti di que[i] S., et appresso certifico V. Ex. che quel S. della principal commissione del decto Messer Prospero, col quale si spera grata conclusione, loda et ha caro grandemente questo nostro proposito del passare. Et se ío merito qualche fede delle cose di qua colla notitia che ho delle cose di Italia et spetialiter di vostro Stato, dico che sarebbe utile et necessario sempre uno vostro messo acorto tra in quel Reame et in questi parti, et così credo vi dimostrerà la experientia, et non dubitate S.re che se di costà non ci mancha favore et caldo colli principii et fondamenti che havemo di qua, vedrà V.S. cose rilevate et da piacere sommamente. Resta hora che V.S. provegga ad quello che sa et può et faccilo intendere dove bisogna et maxime hora che non vi mancha potere né sapere né gratia appresso della Corte et ricordisi V.S. dell'antiquo proverbio: chi tempo ha et tempo aspecta, tempo perde.

gratulate Edward IV on his ascension to the throne. They arrived at Antwerp on June 3 [Zanone Corio to Sforza, Antwerp, June 7, 1461, *Borgogna*, cart. 514], but Corio did not cross the Channel with the others and returned to Milan [see doc. 120, p. 443].

On June 6 I dispatched Martino the courier directly to Your Excellency with a detailed explanation of what I have done in carrying out Your Excellency's instructions regarding my main mission with *the Dauphin* and, similarly, in carrying out the orders you sent me in your letter of May 16. This information I here repeat briefly so that if anything should happen to the courier—may nothing happen to him!—necessary advices will not be lacking to Your Excellency.

As for the mission I was charged to carry out with *the Dauphin,* the matter is reduced within the terms of Your Excellency's commission, and nothing lacks except the method of making payment[1] here in these parts. On the *Dauphin's* side, I do not know which was the deciding factor, good will or necessity or perhaps both; but on your side I know that your good guidance brought me success in the venture, for which I thank God. True it is that *the Dauphin* in many ways and by many circuitous words has indicated to me that he would have liked the amount to be larger, and he has given me much blame that it is not, saying he had been informed that this was not Your Excellency's doing but was owing solely to my malign reports on *Giacomo di Valperga.* Therefore since I was often requested to supplicate Your Excellency and the Duchess for something additional so that *the Dauphin* might reach the desired conclusion more out of good will than out of neces-

116 · PROSPERO DA CAMOGLI *to the*

DUKE OF MILAN

Francia, cart. 525. Orig.

Ali 6 di questo spachiai Martin cavalario da me diretto ala Ex.tia V. cum la expeditione distincta di quanto se hé facto per me in execution di quello me scripse V. Ex.tia per epso in la cura principal mia cum *el Delfin;* et similiter per littere di quella di 16 maii, il che replico qui summariamenti ad effecto che se altro accadessi a dicto cavalaro, quod absit, non manchi li advisi necessarii a V. Ex.tia. Per quello che io ho da curar de qua in servicii di quella, primum, cum *el Delfin* se hé redutto la cosa intra li termini dela commission de V. Ex.tia, et non mancha excepto ch'el si possi far lo pagamento[1] qui in queste parti. Non so dal canto del *Delfin* chi habbi fatto maior ioco o la bona voluntà o la necessità, forse l'uno et l'altro; ma so ben che dal canto de V. Ex.tia li boni adricii m'han fatto venturato, de che rengratio Dio. Vero hé che *el Delfin* per multe vie, in multa circuition de parole, me monstratte haria desyderato la summa fussi stata maiore; et m'ha dato multe culpe a me di questo, dicendo esser advisato questo non farsi per V. Ex.tia, solum per maligni riporti mei de *D. Iacomo de Valperga.* Siché, essendo io multo pregato de supplicar a V. Ex.tia et ala Ill.ma Madona de qualcosa più, adcioché *el Delfin* vegna più per bona voluntà che per necessità alo optato effecto, scripsi a V. Ex.tia il tutto, adcioché se gli paresse de farlo, lo possi fare et, parendogli de farlo, el se porria far in qualche presente de qualche gentileza per parte dela Ill.ma Madona ala

sity, I wrote all to Your Excellency so that if you think good to do it, you can do it; and if you do think good to do it, the additional amount might take the form of some charming present from my lady the Duchess to the *Dauphin's* wife. Nevertheless I remit all to Your Excellency, and it is sufficient for me that, obeying Your Excellency's commission, I have, thank God, brought the matter off, by means of your good guidance as I said above, and not because of any skill on my part.

Although *the Dauphin* has acted toward me as he thought best, I have nonetheless been patient at all times, practicing the humility that Your Excellency instructed me to observe; and, in addition, since I think your state to have been greatly bolstered by the alliance in this quarter, which indeed is a quarter that it was necessary to take into account, Your Excellency may be sure that, even if towers were placed on my shoulders, I am ready to suffer and endure all. I wrote thus, not trusting over much in the mental steadiness of the *French,* that is, in their constancy, etc., and I therefore beg Your Excellency quickly to arrange a method of payment here so that I can close the contract. This I will meanwhile put in order, changing the articles relating to *Giacomo* which were incompatible with the articles as restored since the treaty has force in perpetuity [whereas the Valperga clauses referred to a temporary matter]. This is the situation regarding my principal mission.

As for news, I reported how England has entirely submitted to King Edward. King Henry, the Queen, their son are in Scotland, expelled clear out of England without any remaining hope except in the Scots and the French fleet, according to word we have so far received.

Item: *the Duke of Burgundy* will not commit himself until it is seen what the Scots will decide about the proposed marriage between the Prince of Wales and the sister of the late King of Scots etc.[2]

Similarly, I reported, about my crossing to *England, how the Dauphin and the Duke of Burgundy,* to whom I gave notice of the matter, appeared to be greatly pleased about the advices Your Excellency has

dona del *Delfin*. Tamen di tutto me remetto a V. Ex.tia et basta a me che io, ubediendo la commissione de V. Ex.tia per li boni adricii di quella, ut supra, et non per altro che in me sia, ho sortito ventura dela cosa, del che rengratio Dio. Et quantumque se sii deportato *el Delfin* meco come gli hé paruto, io sum stato non di men patiente a tutto per la humilità me commette V. Ex.tia, et ultra che pur me pare el Stato di epsa receverne grande fermessa da questo canto de qua, che hé pur uno de quelli unde bisognava qualche riguardi; et per questo s'el me si nutrassi turre su le spalle, non dubiti V. Ex.tia che io sum apto a suffrir et patir tutto. Scripsi adunche non fidandomi troppo dela cervelitudine de *francesi,* hoc est dela constantia loro etc., pregando V. Ex.tia a dar presto il modo al pagamento di qua, adcioché io possi fermar lo contratto, quale metterò interim in ordine et mettarò [sic] dele particule de *D. Iacomo,* quale eran incongrue a quelle reciproce che sonno perpetue. Questo hé lo effecto dela cura principal.

De le novelle scripsi come la Anglia hé tutta supposta al Re Eduvard; Re Henrico, la Regina, lo figlolo esser in Scotia, scossi de Anglia netti sensa altra speransa; quanto per loro ymo non restargli altro che la speransa deli Scotti et dela armata de Francia, per quanto havemo fin a qui. Item come *el Duca de Bergogna* stava suspeso, finché si veda quello delibererà li Scotti per lo parentato si tratta dal Principe de Gales ala sorella de quondam Re de Scotia[2] etc. Scripsi similiter come del mio passar in *Anglia el Delfin et el Duca de Bergogna,* a chi io ne havia fatto noticia, monstravan haver grandementi grato lo adviso che ha havuto V. Ex.tia in questo, et me confortavano assai a lo andar et cossì lo R.mo Monsignor lo Legato; quale come predicator de V. Ex.tia, fin dal primo congresso nostro n'havia scritto in *Anglia* et attende reposta [sic], et io interim stava suspeso ad exemplo de *Duca de Bergogna,* maxime che fin a qui non ho littere de credentia ad ciò. Scripsi similiter come dele cerimonie de la Tueson et dele gratificatione me ne impone V. Ex.tia verso lo Ill.mo S. Duca et tutti quelli Principi et Cavaleri, io havia già fin da la partensa mia de S.to Othomaro senso quanto lo ingenio me havia servito. Questo hé lo effecto in summa de quello ho scritto a V.

had regarding the English situation, and strongly urged my making the journey, as did the Legate. After our first meeting the Legate, speaking for Your Excellency, wrote to *England* on the subject of my coming there and is awaiting reply; and I in the meanwhile have, following the example of the *Duke of Burgundy,* remained noncommittal, especially since up to now I have not had letters of credence for the purpose.

Similarly, I wrote about the ceremonies of the Golden Fleece and concerning the complimentary addresses Your Excellency instructed me to pay to the Duke and all the princes and knights of the Order, which mission I executed to the best of my ability before leaving St. Omer. This is the essence of what I wrote to Your Excellency by Martino, save that there should be added as further news that the swollen magnificence of *Gaston* [du Lyon] has been reduced, about which I will say nothing more because it would be boring to relate.

Then I learned, though not by letters from them, that there were here at Antwerp important ambassadors of Your Excellency. What with my solicitude for your affairs and the rarity of information from Milan and being in a state of mixed joy and anxiety to have some direct report about the well being of Your Excellency, my lady the Duchess, Count Galeazzo, and all the rest, I immediately took horse and came here, where I found Count Lodovico and Zanone.[3] They gave me letters of credence from Your Excellency in their behalf and told me of their desire to visit *the Dauphin and the Duke of Burgundy*. I gave them the mode of speaking that I thought would be most effective for them to employ, especially since, as I have many times written to Your Excellency, the relations between *the Dauphin and the Duke* require one to proceed adroitly. On their telling me that if *Giacomo* made any complaints to them they had a commission from Your Excellency to answer him, I took the responsibility of persuading them not to further exacerbate the matter, but to tread softly everywhere, since the whole affair was about to be settled. They should say only that they had no commission from Your Excellency, who regards all the *Dauphin's* peo-

Ex.tia per lo ditto Martin, salvo s'el se ha a iunger inter le novelle che la magnificentia de *Gascon* hé redutta in egregietà, del che per lo longo tedio che seria a narrar, me suprasedo qui.

Doppoi intesi, licet non per littere loro, esser qui ad Anvuers ambassatori solenni de V. Ex.tia; et subito in tanta solicitudine mia et rarità de advisi de là, come consolabundo et anxio de haver qualche viva noticia del bono esser dela Ex.tia V. et de la Ill.ma Madona, lo Illustre S. Conte Galeaz et tutti etc., montai a cavallo et venni qui unde trovai li Spectabili Conte Ludovico et Zenone;[3] quali me dedeno le littere de V. Ex.tia de credensa in loro et a quello me dissero del suo voler andar a visitar *el Delfin et el Duca de Bergogna*. Gli ho dato quello stampa de parlar che mi sii paruta più conveniente, maxime, Ill.mo S.re, che per quello ho scritto più volte ala Ex.tia V., inter *el Delfin et el Duca de Bergogna* bisogna dextrisia; et dicendomi loro se *D. Iacomo* obiectassi qualcosa etc., haver commission da V. Ex.tia de respondergli, me ho priso carrico de suaderli a non exasperare più la cosa, sed andar sul dulce a tutto, essendo la cosa in termini conducibili; et che di questo dican pur non haver commissione alcuna da la Ex.tia V., maxime chi reputa tutti quelli del *Delfin* per boni amici etc., et ha semper havuto dolor de li incommodi de *D. Iacomo* et semper gli faria piacer che si potessi; et qui confortatoli se ne referan pur a me chi sum di qua per ciò. Cum *el Duca de Bergogna* etiam gli ho ditto de quelli modi me paren necessarii, convenienti et utili; in summa in l'uno et l'altro a schifar li mali passi et andar su la bona, come sum certo per loro virtù et discretione saperan meglo far che io non gli ho ditto. Et ho havuto grande, ymo incredibile, consolatione de posser intender de V. Ex.tia quello che io desyderava; siché rengratio Dio, chi una volta m'ha consolato aliqualiter viva voce. Aspetto cum desyderio lo effecto di quanto ho scritto ala Ex.tia V. per Martino, et a quella semper humiliter me racomando.

ple as good friends and has always been sorry about *Giacomo's* troubles and would always do for him what you could—and here I urged them to take my word on this matter which I have been sent here specifically to deal with. I also told them what modes seemed to me necessary, fitting, and useful for them to employ in their visit to *the Duke of Burgundy*. In sum, in both cases I advised them to steer clear of the rapids and sail on smooth water, as I am certain that, with their high intelligence and discretion, they will know how to do better than I have told them. Finally, I have had the great, or rather the incredible, happiness of being able to learn what I hoped to learn about Your Excellency, and I thank God for it, who for once has consoled me with, as it were, a living voice.

I eagerly await the conclusion of what I have by Martino written to Your Excellency, to whom as always I humbly recommend myself.

HISTORICAL NOTES

1. See doc. 114, n. 3, p. 402.
2. See doc. 107, n. 2, p. 372.
3. See preceding doc. 115, n. 2, p. 406.

We have received all the letters you wrote, both to us and to Cicco our secretary, which were dated from St. Omer on the 9th of May; and from these we have learned about the ceremonies of the Order of the Golden Fleece and about your communications with the legate; and we have noted all the information you give and what you have accomplished up to that date. To answer briefly, we believe that by the time you receive this you will have concluded with the Dauphin the business for which you were sent and will have gone with the legate to England. If, however, you have not concluded, we wish to do everything possible so to conclude and should the Dauphin and the Duke of Burgundy and the legate think it best for you to depart, you will go whenever they think best and you will make every attempt to secure the good will of King Edward [IV] and the Earl of Warwick and all the other lords there and to gain a firm understanding of matters there; and, having done so, you will return to us.

We inform you that, Antoine delle Torre having arrived here on his way back from Rome to England, we have given him letters of credence addressed to King Edward, the Earl of Warwick, and other lords, as you will understand from him. In these letters we refer to what you will have said to him or will say on our behalf, so that these letters[1] are, in effect, credences for him and for you.

117 · *The* DUKE OF MILAN *to*

PROSPERO DA CAMOGLI

Francia, cart. 525. Minute

Havimo recevuto tutte le toe littere scritte cossì ad Nuy, como ad Cico, nostro secretario, date ad Sancto Thomero ad dì VIIII del passato et per quelle havimo inteso quello é seguito in lo facto de la Tueson; de quello havevi comunicato con Mon.re lo Legato, et tutti l'avisi ne day et quanto havevi fino alhora exequito. Breviter respondendo, dicimo che credemo alla recevuta de questa, haveray concluso con quello Ser.mo Mon.re Delfin quello perché tu sii là, et andato con lo prefato Mon.re Legato in Inglittera; et pur se non havessi concluso, volimo te sforza concludere, et concludendo, vadi como parerà ad esso Mon.re; et non possendo concludere et paresse ad la S. Soa et ad lo Duca de Bergogna et Mon.re Legato che vadi, andaray como parerà a loro Sig.rie et te incegnaray de farne benivolo quello Ser.mo S. Re Odoardo et Conte de Varoych et tutti quilli altri Signori dellà et intendere ben tute quelle cose dellà, quale intese, te ne retornaray da Nuy. Avisandote che, essendo gionto qui D. Antonio dala Torre, quale vene da Roma et retorna in là, gli havimo facte littere de credenza allo prefato Ser.mo S. Re Odoardo, Conte de Varoich et altri Sig.ri, como intenderay da luy; in le quale littere ne referimo ad quanto tu gli haveray dicto o diray per nostra parte, siché queste littere[1] vengano ad essere de credenza per luy et per ti. Faray adonche quanto havimo dicto et più presto te sia possibile et sforzate de retornare ben informato del tutto; et, havuta

You will then do as we have said, and as promptly as possible, and make all effort to return well informed about everything. As soon as you receive this, send word immediately about what you have accomplished with the Dauphin and about all other news you have that is worthy of notice. Here there is nothing new, save that King Ferrante's cause in the Kingdom of Naples is prospering. At Genoa things stand thus: the Doge is attending to the siege of the citadel and he has four bombards and blockading works surrounding it.

HISTORICAL NOTE

1. These letters, dated June 14, 1461, and addressed to Edward IV, Warwick, and other English lords, are in *Inghilterra e Scozia,* cart. 566; cf. CSPM, I, 96–97.

questa, avisane subito de quanto haveray fino a lì exequito con lo prefato Mon.re Delfin et de ogni altra cosa habii digna de aviso. De qua
non gl'é altro de novo, se non che le cose nel Regno vanno prospere per
la M.tà del Re Ferrando. De Zenoa le cose stanno pur cossì: el Duse
[sic] attende al assedio de Castelleto et gli ha quatro bombarde et
bucule[a] in circo.

---

a. Excavations around a besieged fortress to prevent supplies and reinforcements from reaching the garrison.

I do not doubt that from Martino and the messenger who left after him Your Magnificence has had, before receiving this, the advices about the situation here. This then will be brief.

Weighing within myself discretion on the one hand and purity of devotion on the other, I find that the latter conquers. Therefore I have thought good to write to Your Magnificence that, given the nature of affairs here and the dexterity required to tread the slippery path between *the Dauphin and the Duke of Burgundy* and given the wait-and-see attitude here regarding *English* affairs and matters impending in all directions, I do not know if it has been well to send *Count Lodovico and Zanone*—men of high rank for unimportant matters—since our remaining under cover for a little out of consideration for the hostility of the *King of France* seems to me the sound policy for the present. Nevertheless I am servant and not master and I am always content with everything, nor do I wish in any way not to support what seems best to the *Duke of Milan*.

Christendom is divided, not by parallels as Ptolemy did it but in another way which has been born as a result of their coming, namely, *the Pope, the Dauphin, the Duke of Burgundy, the Duke of Milan, King Edward, the Earl of Warwick, King Ferrante,* on one side; *the King of France, King Henry of England and his Queen, the King of*

118 · PROSPERO DA CAMOGLI *to*

CICCO SIMONETTA

Francia, cart. 525. Orig.

Non dubito che per Martin et lo messo doppoi partito de qua, V. M.tia habbi havuto, anti la recepiuta di questa, li advisi de quanto hé di qua; solo questa sub brevitate, cum ciò sia che concertando in me la discretion dal un canto, dal altro la purità et netisia de devotion, questa vence. Et m'hé paruto de scriver a la M. V. che, attento la natura de le cose de qua et la dextrisia bisogna inter *el Delfin et el Duca de Bergogna*; item attento la suspension in che hé anche qui *Anglia* et le cose que imminent undique, io non so se sii stato ben mandar *lo Conte Ludoico* [sic] *et Zenon,* nominibus magnis et rerum vacuis, cum ciò sia che star sutto coperta un puocho per rispecto del sdegno del *Re de Franza* me pareva sano per lo presente. Tuttavia io sum servitor, et non maistro, et sum semper contento de tutto né voglo in tutto non laudar quello pare al *Signore*. Et se divide la Cristianità non per parelelli come fece Ptholomeo, sed ad un altro modo, il qual hé nasciuto per la venuta predicta; videlicet, *il Papa, Delfin, Duca de Bergogna, Duca de Milano, Re Edoardo, Conte de Varruich, Re Ferrando* da una parte; *Re de Franza, Re Henrico, la Regina, Re de Sicilia, Duca de Savoia, Duca Iohanne, Duca de Modena* da un'altra.[1] Siché possiti intender le mensure cum quale se compassa il mondo de qua. Et dicesi pure che *dicti van in Anglia,* quod si est ex ordine *del Signore,* era condecente me havesti scritto, et similiter *al Legato,* revocando la commission mia de tal cosa,

Sicily [King René], *the Duke of Savoy, Duke John, the Duke of Modena* on the other.[1] Therefore you can understand the instruments by which the world is measured here.

And yet *Count Lodovico and Zanone,* it appears, *are going to England.* If they are doing so by order *of the Duke of Milan,* it would have been kind of you to let me know and also let the *Legate* know and to revoke my commission regarding such affairs, notwithstanding that for the reasons I have constantly pointed out in my letters I have not thought the journey to England to be safe for the one going or good for the *Duke of Milan.* And I am of this opinion now more than ever. Indeed, as I note above, to have people visit England without any real purpose will create more damaging suspicions than sending ambassadors there on a mission. I say this to you and I wish to have my opinion in writing, but I always defer to what the *Duke of Milan* and Your Magnificence have decided and will decide in the future. Hence I have not said, am not saying, and am not about to say anything contrary to what Count Lodovico and Zanone think is best, for I am certain that they know the governing principles of their mission, which perhaps I should not seek to fathom since not knowing more than it behooves me to know is the navigating chart for the likes of me.

For what else concerns Count Lodovico and Zanone, I refer you to their return from England.

I beg Your Magnificence to take in good part what I have written here and everything else and to make no more mention, or disclosure, of it than seems good to you and is in accordance with honor, for an honorable and worthy reason has moved me to write thus. Therefore I beg you to repute me not a giver of censure but a servant anxious to do good service.

non obstante che per li rispecti ho semper scritto fin a chi non m'hé paruto né sicuro per chi va né ben per *il Signore*. Et sum di questo apparer più che mai fin a chi. Rursus, come dico, far passar gente de là sensa altro a far, serà maior et più damnosa suspicione che preferevole andata. Io vi dico et voglio haver scritto il mio apparer semper remettendomene a quello ne habbi deliberato et deliberi in futurum *il Signore* et cossì V. M.tia, per il qual rispecto fin a chi non ho ditto a ditti né sum per dir in contrario de quello gli pare, perché sum certo habian la norma de quello han da far, che forse io non debbo cercare, cum non plus sapere quod oportet sapere, sia la carta del navigar de pari mei. Del resto de loro etc. me reporto a loro ritorno. Prego V. M.tia prenda et questo mio scriver et ogni altro in bene et non ne faci più mention, né pur aperta, de come gli pare et conven a la honestà, perché honesto et vale respecto me move; siché prego non mi reputiati censor, ma anxio servitor de ben servir.

HISTORICAL NOTE

1. Evidently Prospero means that as a result of Count Dallugo's and Corio's coming to the West, with the intention of going openly to Yorkist England, this alignment of European powers will become obvious [i.e. to the King of France].

I have written in detail to Your Excellency by Martino your courier, who left me on June 6, and I sent a summary of that letter by a messenger directed to *Pigello* [Portinari], who left Antwerp on June 11; and therefore I have little to write in this. Also I will say no more about the treaty with the *Dauphin,* which now entirely depends on what Your Excellency will commission me to do, and what provisions you will make concerning the execution of the treaty, the articles of which lie within the terms I was commissioned to offer, as by the aforementioned letters Your Excellency should be informed; and therefore there remains nothing for me to write here except news of the affairs and the state of these western regions, which almost up to this very moment are as follows.

I can confirm what I previously wrote about England: that it is entirely under the control of King Edward [IV]. King Henry, the Queen, the Prince of Wales, the Duke of Somerset and his brother, and Lord Roos, with some few others, of the remaining Lancastrians, who have loyally stayed with them, have withdrawn into Scotland, whence report comes that they are negotiating—though this is not formally confirmed—for a marriage of the Prince of Wales with the sister of the former King of Scots.[1] If the marriage should come about, it would be stipulated that the Scots actively aid King Henry to recover his realm

119 · PROSPERO DA CAMOGLI *to the*

DUKE OF MILAN

Francia, cart. 525. Orig.

Havendo scritto distinctamenti ala Ex.tia V. per Martino cavalario de quella chi partitte da me ali 6 del presente, et quello medesmo summariamenti per uno messo directo a *Pigello,* chi partitte da Anvers ali XI, resta per questa a scriver puocho; et suprasedendomi de le cose del *Delfin,* chi tutte sonno poste in quanto me ne commetterà et provederà V. Ex.tia, a proposito dil [sic] termine priso in quelle che hé inter le commissione de epsa, come per ditte vie debe esser advisata da me la prefata Ex.tia V., non mi resta qui scriver excepto novelle dele cose et stato de questo occidente, il quale al dì de hoggi quasi hé questo.

De la Anglia affermo quello ho scritto esser tutta in dition del Re Edoardo. Lo Re Henrico, la Regina, lo Principe de Gales, lo Ducha de Semesetrh, Monsignor de Ros, suo fratello, cum quello puocho del resto de sua banda, chi persevera cum loro, esser redutti in Scotia, unde hé fama habian pratica, che fin a chi non se afferma per conclusa, del parentato del Principe ala sorella del condam Re de Scotia;[1] et il qual parentato seguindo astipuleria che li Scoti dovessero far perforso [sic] a recuperar il Regno a Re Henrico etc., in favor del che la armata de Franciosi era in mare potentissima per assalir in Anglia, unde si fussi, cum grande speransa deli Henriceschi. Et mandai di questo il designo del paese e lo curso de la dicta armata et del assalto et ritorno di quella etc. Doppoi circa questo havemo de Anglia come in quello assalto fatto

etc. To the same end a very powerful French fleet took to the sea in order to make an attack upon England, an enterprise which gave great hope to the Lancastrians. Concerning this attack, I wrote about the geographical situation of England, the route taken by the fleet, its assault, and its return, etc.

We have since had word from England that in the attack made by the French fleet on the coast of Cornwall, which faces Spain, the French were repulsed and lost, some say 5,000, some say 2,000 men. The truth about England cannot be ascertained because of the inanity of those people and, if I may say so, because of the inept administration of *the Duke of Burgundy,* who is under the control of others, as formerly I wrote; and reports of such happenings and discussion of policy concerning them are based only on what news is had from merchants. Nevertheless we are informed for certain that the French fleet is being refitted in Normandy, which is a sign that they have had a repulse; and certainly, in my view, if they had gone into the Bristol Channel, as was thought they would by those who understand the political sympathies of the English [i.e. who know where Lancastrian sympathies are strongest] and as I thus signified by the map of the country which I sent to Your Excellency, the French would—I do not venture to say have achieved more—but at least would have better tested what favor and authority the memory of King Henry and the Queen could command, etc. We have since heard that though King Edward is coming to London for the opening of Convocation [i.e. the assembly of English ecclesiastics] and Parliament on July 6 in London, the Earl of Warwick has remained on the Scots frontier and has made arrangements in Ireland, a ferocious island country near Scotland, that if the Scots invade England as allies of King Henry, 20,000 Irish are to cross into Scotland to do what damage they can, which arrangement, in conjunction with the garrisons the Earl of Warwick has, is considered not only a good and sufficient but an auspicious provision against whatever wind fortune can send from Scotland. And as a result of the embassies and other efforts that are being employed—though not as solicitously as Your Ex-

per la armata in la costa de Cornivagla, quale hé opposita ala Hyspania, dicti Franciosi eran stati retusi et gle ne sia remasto chi dice 5 milia, chi dice 2 milia. Verità non se può haver de Anglia per la inanità de quelli homini et la puocha policitia de governo in questo cum supportation ha *el Duca de Bergogna,* il qual sta a goberno de altri, come alias ho scripto, et di tali accidenti si riporta et consigla secundo ne ha da mercatanti. Tamen havemo per certo che in Northmandia la armata si reforsa et hé signo che ha havuto rebuffo; et per certo, a mio veder, se fussero iti in lo gulpho de Briscoth, come estimava chi intende le vogle de Anglia et come per lo ditto designo significai a V. Ex.tia, hariano non ardisco de dir più profectato, sed al manco meglo experimentato quanto può la gratia et la auctorità del ricordo de Re Henrico et la Regina etc. Havemo doppoi come, venendo il Re Edoardo per far convento et parlamento ali 6 de iulio in Londres, lo Conte de Varruich era remasto ale frontere de Scotia et era ordinato in Hybernia, feroce paese et vicina insula a Scoti che, usiendo Scoti ali auxilii del Re Henrico in Anglia, dovessero de Hybernia passar XX^ti milia Hybernesi in Scotia a dannificarli; la qual cosa se reputa cum li presidii del Conte de Varruich bon et non solamenti sufficiente, ma favorevole provedimento a quanto vento fortunal possi buffar de Scotia; et cum le ambassiate et opere per ciò se fanno tuttavia al opposito, quamvis non cossì sollicitamenti come faria in tal caso V. Ex.tia, si reputa la Regina de Scotia se debba retrar da tal pensiero. Pur io non me despicio fin a chi che *el Duca de Bergogna* in quelle cose sta suspeso, quantumque han bella monstra, et sum de quelli a chi pare che sii bene per *la S. V.* far il simile et non ne fare altra desmonstratione [sic], finché non se ne veda più fermessa. Et per questo non ho ditto al *Legato* de passar et confortatolo lui etiam al suprastarsi, quantumque se ben io volesse andar, cum tutto che *V. S.* m'el comette, io non ho littere alcune de credensa et non mi par condecente far fundamenti de parole sensa pigno de littere. Questo hé circa Anglia fin a qui, et dico fin a qui, perché ogni dì et ogni hora si cambia conditione et stampa de fortuna in quelle cose.

Resta da *Re de Franza al Duca de Bergogna.* Ill.mo S. mio, hé tanto

cellency would act in such a case—in order to prevent a Lancastrian-Scots alliance, it is believed that the Queen of Scotland will abandon such thoughts.

However, I do not hold in disdain the fact that up to now the *Duke of Burgundy* takes no stand on these issues, although the outcome looks favorable, and I am of those who think indeed that it is well for *Your Excellency* to do the same and to make no further demonstration of your attitude until matters are seen to be better stabilized. It is on this account that I have not said to the *Legate* I would cross to England and have urged that he himself wait and see; yet even if I thought it good to go, I have no letters of credence, despite all that *Your Lordship* commissions me to do there, and I do not think it profitable to lay a foundation of words without the buttressing of letters.

Thus it is concerning England up to now, and I say up to now because every day and every hour conditions change and the impact of fortune on those conditions also changes.

There remain the relations between *the King of France and the Duke of Burgundy*. My lord, there is so much the greater difficulty in discerning the actual facts because the outward attitudes, by their effects, seem one thing and the inward truth, as reason finds it, seems another. *Hence it is that common folk are universally sure there will be war, while those who consider more profoundly the present nature of things here and in France, the disabilities of age, and the difficult and inauspicious disposition of affairs, are not led to think there will be war. The present situation is this: it is true that on both sides things appear to be disposed for war, and every day more so; but I weigh the one party and the other* as follows:

The King of France: It is true that he has on his side the crown of the realm and the great power and authority that goes with it. He is also leagued with the people of Liège, neighbors of the Duke of Burgundy who are always hostile to him. Liège is the most powerful city in all these parts—as I can affirm from having seen it—and at times the people of Liège have come down on the Duke's shoulders and chest

maior difficultà discerner da questo facto, quanto che le desmonstratione per li effecti pareno una cosa et lo intrinseco per la raxone pare
un'altra. *Et de qui nasce ch'el vulgo universaliter se acerta sula guerra,*
et chi considera più al fundo la natura dele cose presente de qua et de
là, et la età inhabile, le dispositione dele cose incomode et difficile, non
se adduce a pensare guerra. Li termini presenti sonno questi. El hé vero
che da l'un canto et dal altro pareno le cose esser desposte a guerra et
ogni dì più; puri io considero in l'una parte et l'altra ut infra.

El Re de Franza hé vero che ha dal canto suo la corona del Regno
et per consequente le forse et la auctorità che hé assai. Ha etiam Legeisi
ligate con essa, che sonno per sito vicini et ale spale del Duca de Ber-
gogna, città potentissima se ne hé in tutti questi peesi [sic], *del che af-*
fermo de veduta et aliquando han posto ale spale et lo pecto de cin-
quantamilia combatenti, quali non se scroloe [sic] *da dosso sensa sudore;*
et sonno populo infenso et infesto al Duca de Bergogna. Ha etiam la
necessità dele cose de Ingliterra, qualese fussero aspirate ala Regina, gli
pareva haver venciuto in breve quelle puncte cum el Duca de Bergogna,
che non ha possuto in longo tempo; et restando in Re Edoardo et Conte
de Varruich, gli pare debba seguir lo contrario.

Dala parte del Duca de Bergogna gli hé pur queste cose: primum
ch'el non hé uso de dar el suo sensa pagamento. Item, ha pur le forse
tante maiore quanto che stando in quello medesmo suspecto del con-
trario, se fussero subsequiti li designi de Ingliterra al Re de Franza, el
hé proveduto et ha in prompto mirabili presidii etc., *et inter cetera ha*
pur el Delfin, quale hé apto, come figlolo et futuro Re de Franza, a
subvertir tutta la casa del Re de Franza; et ultra tra el Delfin et el Duca
de Bergogna han dele oculte bone dispositione de Signori che sian in
Franza, et quanto per el Re se non hé il Conte de Humaine et lo Conte
de Fois, del resto de che se debba né fidar né aitar el Re, non se fa ex-
timo de qui. Preterea Parisio et tutta haverà Galia circumsita, et la
Northmania, la Britania et Gasconia, sonno suspecte al Re, che tutte se
meterian in garbuglo quando guerra fussi. Siché per queste ragione,
reputando io l'uno et l'altro ben che tolli de suoi governi, tamen pur

with some 50,000 soldiers, whom he has not shaken off his back without sweat. They are indeed an obnoxious and most troublesome people to the Duke. English affairs also inevitably affect the position of the King of France. If those affairs should turn out to be propitious for the Queen, he would appear to have taken in a short space a greater advantage over the Duke of Burgundy than he has been able to achieve in a long while. On the other hand, the King must think the reverse to be true if King Edward and the Earl of Warwick remain in control of England.

The Duke of Burgundy: His situation is thus. First, he is not accustomed to give of his own without receiving payment. Item: he has so much the greater power in that, although he is in the same uncertainty regarding England as is Charles VII, should the outcome there favor the King of France, the Duke is provided with, and has ready at hand, marvellous forces etc. Among other things, he also has the Dauphin, who is well situated, as heir and future King of France, to subvert the whole royal House. In addition, the Dauphin and the Duke between them have hidden affiliations among the French lords; and as for the King's strength, except for the Count of Maine and [Gaston] the Count of Foix, people here think little of the rest of his lords since they probably would neither aid nor be loyal to him. Furthermore, Paris and all region thereabouts, Normandy, Brittany, and Gascony are suspect to the King of France because all of them would foment disorders if there were war.

Therefore, considering particularly what can happen in the future, I am one of those who do not believe there will be war. It is true that there is one motive for war that would very much appear to outweigh everything else because it springs from the headstrong will of passionate men, namely: since those about the King of France know that His Majesty is old and feeble—for, truthfully he is not thought capable of riding ten leagues in armor etc.—and since they know that they are hated by the Dauphin, who, they think, would after his father's death be made King of France in despite of them and of whatever resistance

430

*assai consideratini in tanto caso de quello possi advenir, io sum de
quelli chi non credo de guerra. El hé vero che gli hé una ragion chi
pareria superchiar tutto perché hé posta in voluntà arbitraria de homini
passionati; videlicet che, considerando quelli chi sono intorno al Re de
Franza, la Sua Maiestà esser vechia et debile, che a non inganarsi el non
si reputa suficiente a caminar dece leghe in arme* etc.; *et vedendosi lo
odio del Delfin ale spale, il quale, quando altro fussi, extiman se faria
Re de Franza a loro despecto et sensa loro resistentia, forsi voluntieri
persuadeno al Re chi facia guerra per trovarsi loro sule arme, s'el acca-
desse tal caso dela morte del Re et a quello modo gli pareria posser far
boni pacti. Per il che, Illustrissimo Signor mio, io non so che iudicar né
sum sì temerario che vogli presumir de antiveder in tali nubili. Pur per
la fede et devotion ho ala Excellentia Vostra, volunteri scrivo a quella il
tutto de quello che io sento et non dimenticandomi, imo havendo semper, Illustrissimo Signor mio, il baticore dela puocha grassia*[a] *che hé dal
Delfin al Duca de Bergogna, et intendendo io che ogni dì più hé pericu-
losa da scoprirsi et dal canto del Delfin solo la necessità sua la ten
coperta, dal canto del Duca de Bergogna la opportunità se guerra fussi,*
ut supra. *Io prego Dio ogni dì che me dia gratia de posser presto et
dextro perficer la opera per che Vostra Excellentia me ha mandato, et
possermene ritornare.*

*Ceterum, in lo tempo che io sum di qua ho pur studiato cum uno
modo et un altro de atrarmi de quelli che io so opportuni a darme deli
advisi; et da persona degna de maior fede che questa, ho inteso ch'el
Vescovo Attrebatense, che sta in la Curia del Papa per el Duca de Bergogna,*[b] *ha scritto qui littere in carrico de Vostra Excellentia, chi habbi
scritto al Papa in desfavore de uno abbate de Sancto Ubertin designato dal Duca de Bergogna Vescovo de Tornai. La cosa hé questa: el
Duca de Bergogna ama questo abbate come factura de Mon.re de Crovi
et tutto el resto del mundo de qua lo ha in odio né credo gli sia più virtù
introductiva ala gratia del Duca de Bergogna, come che el Re de*

---

a. Read: gratia.
b. C. C. incorrectly reads: Delfin.

they can offer, they may perhaps be the more ready to persuade the King to make war so that, if the King should then die, they would have forces at their command and consequently would think themselves able to secure good terms. Therefore, my lord, I do not know what judgment to make nor am I so rash as to presume to foresee the future in such a cloudy situation. However, because of my loyalty and devotion to Your Excellency, I readily write everything to you that I have knowledge of—not forgetting, but rather having constant palpitations of the heart because of, the little love that is lost between the Dauphin and the Duke of Burgundy. I know that every day there is greater danger that this bad feeling will come into the open: on the Dauphin's part, only his necessity keeps it concealed; on the Duke's, the advantage of having the Dauphin should war come, as I wrote above.

I pray God every day to grant me the grace of being able quickly and adroitly to accomplish the mission that Your Excellency has given me and then of being able to make my return.

For the rest: in the time that I have been here, I have sought in one way and another to become acquainted with those whom I know to be well situated for giving me information; and, from a person worthy of greater trust than this, I have learned that the Bishop of Arras [Jean Jouffroy], now at the papal Curia on the Duke of Burgundy's behalf, has sent letters here charging Your Excellency with having written to the Pope unfavorably about an Abbot of St. Bertin [Guillaume Fillastre] who has been nominated by the Duke of Burgundy for the bishopric of Tournai. The matter is this. The Duke of Burgundy loves this abbot as a protégé of my lord of Croy, while the rest of the world here hates him—nor do I believe that a man can have a more effective entry to the Duke of Burgundy's favor than that, as in this case, the King of France cannot bear to hear him named. From the experience I have had of this abbot, he seems to me a man of little charity, and in addition, despite the favor and prestige Your Excellency enjoys here, he has small love for you. The Duke of Burgundy, to spite the King of France, nominated the abbot as Bishop of Tournai. The King of France, being ut-

Franza non vole audirlo nominar. Et ale experientie me ne hé accaduto fare, el me pare de puoca carità homo,[c] et ultra in tanta gratia et reputatione ha Vostra Excellentia de qua, puocho affecionato a quella. El Duca de Bergogna per dispecto del Re de Franza lo havia designato Vescovo de Tornai. Lo Re per nulla non lo vole, et per termine de medio se era pervenuto su uno figlolo del Duca de Borbon, nepote del Duca de Bergogna et cognato de D. Yharles,[2] figliolo del Duca de Bergogna,[d] del che pur el Duca de Bergogna sta duro. Monsignor de Yharles, per tor via da questo canto le contentione del Re de Franza, et per favor del cognato, et ultra che questo abbate hé odium gentium et de quelli che governan taliter qualiter el Duca de Bergogna, par habbia scritto in favor del cognato. Et in questo adstipula questo abbate ch'el dicto Monsignor de Arras habia scritto che la S. V. ha recomandato al Papa il fatto contrario a lui, et hé qui chi murmura et iudica de non bon proposito che Vostra Excellentia dele cose del Duca de Bergogna non senta cum la Signoria Sua. Hé vero che ho multi advisi che io ho [sic] delo dicto Monsignor de Arras concurreno che [non] sii troppo benivolo ala S. V.. Sum certo meser Otho facia tutto cum bona prudentia et de Vostra Excellentia non sii excepto mutto[e] bene et tutta iustificatione Pur la adviso voluntieri del tutto. El hé vero che quello chi m'ha dato lo adviso, chi hé bon servitor de V. S., multo me pregò a far che questo fussi a pié de V. S., adcioché quando el se resapesse, non gle ne venisse damno né carrico, chi gli potria esser grande per il suo afar che ha de qua. Et cossì per honestà ne suplico a Vostra Excellentia.

Item, li Luchesi de qui sparlano multo de Vostra Excelentia; et l'altro dì Iohanne Arnofino[3] me ne disse in qualità et quantità strania a proposito de certo loro citadino che dicono Vostra Excellentia havergli richesto, el qual loro han facto decapitar etc.. Io gli resposi che quando el parlasse de Vostra Excellentia cum la dignità se conven, che io gli

---

c. Read: homo de puoca carità.
d. The symbol used here for Charles of Burgundy is ".A." which does not appear in the key. Normally Prospero writes the name "Iarloes" with several symbols. We have followed C. C. in this case which also adds "figliolo del Duca de Bergogna."
e. Read: multo.

terly opposed to the nomination, has hit upon, as a rival candidate, a son [Louis] of the [late] Duke of Bourbon, who is therefore a nephew of the Duke of Burgundy and a brother-in-law of the Count of Charolais.[2] The Duke of Burgundy, however, remains obdurate.

Because the Count of Charolais favors his brother-in-law and because this abbot, universally hated, is one of those who govern—if it can be called governing—the Duke of Burgundy, Charolais has written, it appears, in support of Louis of Bourbon, in order to counteract the odium of Bourbon's being the choice of the King of France. The abbot now claims to have it from the Bishop of Arras that Your Lordship has made to the Pope a recommendation unfavorable to him; and there are here some who murmur and who judge that you have shown an unfriendly attitude, in that, in a matter of importance to the Duke of Burgundy, Your Excellency fails to act in unison with the Duke. It is true that the many advices I have about the Bishop of Arras agree that he is not too benevolent towards Your Lordship. I am sure that Messer Ottone has handled the matter prudently and that Your Excellency has every reason to act as you have done. However, I believe in sending you all information that comes to me. It is true that the one who gave me this intelligence, a man devoted to Your Lordship, has repeatedly begged me that the source of the information go no further than you, so that if the word leaks out, there will come no blame upon him, because it could greatly endanger what he has to do here. Therefore, out of honor, I make this supplication to Your Excellency.

Item: the merchants of Lucca here utter much malicious gossip about Your Excellency, and the other day Giovanni Arnolfini[3] made some very uncalled for remarks to me about a certain citizen of Lucca, whom the inhabitants of Lucca have had decapitated, they say, at Your Excellency's request, etc. I replied that when he spoke of Your Excellency with due courtesy I would give him a precise answer so that he would better understand the honorable attitude and the civilized manners a commonwealth should observe than he gave indication of understanding at present. I then made further remarks in the same vein. I

434

responderia ad partes per modo ch'el intenderia meglo che si sia honestà et tranquillità de ben viver per una republica che non mostrava de intender, et similia. Il che non per detrar ad alcuno, sed per altri advisi chi de là servissero ali propositi de Vostra Excellentia n'ho voluto far mio officio verso quella.

Scrivendo questa, sonno iuncte qui littere de Londres de 14 del presente, per le quale se dice lo Re Henrico haver recuperato Nevcastello [sic] *et lì dentro preso lo barba del Conte de Varruich, deputato Capitanio a quella guardia;*[4] *item, che Eboracum, id est Iorch, se era rebellato al Re Edoardo; et alcune altre cose de tal natura innovate, quale, quando fussero, serian grande suspicione che la armata de Franza supervenendo dovessi cum l'isoti*[t] *mover più le bracia che altri non extimava. Per il che sum pur de quello apparer,* ut supra, *de star de qua a tenir li panni a chi ioca ala lucta, finché si veda* etc.. Nichilominus [sic], in mandata paratissimus.

---

f. Read: l'insorti.

wanted thus to do my duty toward you, not to cast aspersions on any-one but to send you additional information which would serve your purposes there.

As I was writing this missive, there arrived letters from London of June 14, in which it is said that King Henry has recovered Newcastle and has captured within it the uncle of the Earl of Warwick who had been made captain of the town;[4] *item, that Eboracum—that is, York—had rebelled against King Edward; and that there had been other such reversals of fortune, which, if true, would lead one strongly to suspect that an attack on England by the French fleet aided by the rebels* [i.e. Lancastrians], *might have greater results than was thought. On this account I am indeed of the opinion expressed above about remaining here, that is, standing on the sidelines and holding the clothes of the rival players while they fight it out.* Nothing more; always prepared to serve you.

HISTORICAL NOTES

1. See doc. 107, n. 2, p. 372.

2. Philip the Good's sister, Agnes, had married Charles, Duke of Bourbon, deceased father of the reigning Duke, Jean, whose sister Isabelle was the wife of the Count of Charolais. At Charolais' request, Sforza had instructed Ottone del Carretto, his ambassador at the Curia, to recommend to Pius II that the Bishopric of Tournai be given to Charolais' brother-in-law Charles of Bourbon, Archbishop of Lyons. For unexplained reasons, however, the Pope refused to satisfy the request [Sforza to Ottone, Milan, Mar. 28, 1461 and Ottone to Sforza, Rome, Apr. 16, 1461, *Roma,* cart. 50].

3. Giovanni di Arrigo Arnolfini, virtual leader of the numerous and powerful Lucchese colony at Bruges, was financial agent for both the Dauphin and the Duke of Burgundy. His marriage at Bruges (1434) to Giovanna di Guglielmo Cenami, daughter of another rich merchant from Lucca, was immortalized in Jan van Eyck's famous painting [L. Mirot and E. Laz-

zareschi, "Un mercante di Lucca in Fiandra, Giovanni Arnolfini," *Bollettino storico lucchese,* XVIII (1940), 81–105]. The emnity between the Lucchese colony and Sforza was largely based on commercial rivalry with Milanese merchants, particularly with regard to the traffic in silk, the production of which was promoted by the Duke of Milan [M. Martens, "La correspondance de caractère économique échangée par Francesco Sforza, Duc de Milan, et Philippe le Bon, Duc de Bourgogne (1450–1466)," *Bulletin de l'Institut Historique Belge de Rome,* XXVII (1952), 229–34]. On July 4, 1461, Sforza wrote to the Duke of Burgundy recommending the Milanese merchant, Ambrogio Ruffino, who was involved in a dispute with Arnolfini, and instructed Prospero to intercede with the Duke on his behalf [*Reg. Missive* 52, fols. 6ov–6ir].

4. William Neville, Lord Fauconberg, created Earl of Kent shortly after Edward IV's coronation [June 28]; he was indeed Captain of New-castle, but the town was not recaptured by the Lancastrians.

Having returned on July 12 from Holland with the Legate [Francesco Coppini], *who had recently written to me here at Bruges that he had to confer with me, etc., I found at Antwerp, Messer Antonio della Torre*[1] *and from him I had a letter of Your Excellency's of June 14 containing, in sum, that Your Excellency believed I had some time ago concluded with the Dauphin and must have already gone to England; and that if I were not able to conclude with the Dauphin and if the Duke of Burgundy and the Legate approved, Your Excellency wants me to go to England, and to inform you immediately what I have done up to now.*

My most illustrious lord, of what I have done with the Dauphin I am certain Your Excellency will be fully informed from what I wrote by Martino the courier and from what afterward I sent by way of Antwerp. Also from that Antonio,[2] *the messenger that the Dauphin has sent from Genappe to Your Excellency, you will have been able to perceive the stability and constancy etc., since the Dauphin answers me in one way and then on the side sends off a message to you etc. Because I perceived something of this, I wrote with discretion to Your Lordship, by Martino, about the bad manners the Dauphin had shown me; but I willingly refrained from expatiating on this, for it is the end that counts and if the mission is a success, as far as I am concerned, I wanted to call*

120·PROSPERO DA CAMOGLI *to the*

DUKE OF MILAN

Francia, cart. 525. Orig.

Essendo ali 12 de questo ritornato de Olanda con Monsignor lo Legato, il qual questi dì me scripse qui a Brugs che haveva da conferir meco etc., trovai ad Anvers Messer Antonio dala Turre[1] et da lui hebbi une littere [sic] de Vostra Excellentia de 14 iunii continente, in suma, che Vostra Excellentia credeva che io havessi ogimai concluso con el Delfin, et fatto quello, che io dovesse ià esser ito in Anglia; et non possendo concluder con el Delfin, parendo al Duca de Bergogna et Monsignor lo Legato, V. S. vol che io vadi in Anglia et de quanto harò fatto fin a qui, subito io gli ne dii adviso.

Illustrissimo Signor mio, de quanto io habi fatto con el Delfin sum certo Vostra Excellentia, per quello gli scripsi per Martin cavalaro et doppoi per la via de Anvers, serà advisata a pleno; et etiam per quello Antonio,[2] messo che ha mandato de verso Genapio epso Delfin a Vostra Excellentia, harà poduto ben comprender dela saldessa et constantia etc., che a me se responda a uno modo et poi se mandi da canto etc.. Et perché io me avidi de qualcosa, scripsi a V. S. per epso Martino, a meza bucha, deli modi non boni havia tenuto el Delfin con mi; ma volunteri non li destendeva, come quello che spectava al fin et sucedendo lo effecto, quanto per me, voleva quittar tutto et prenderlo in bona parte. El che, Signor mio, tanti li reporti de che in tutto se refere el Delfin a D. Iacomo de Valperga, ch'el me par uno incanto; et rursus D. Iacomo

it quits and take all in good part. Such are the relationships here, with the Dauphin consulting Giacomo di Valperga about everything, that the whole thing seems to me an incantation; and, on the other hand, Valperga is, if I may say so, such a puffed up idiot that, by heaven, it is a purgatory to have to deal with him; and it is he who has brought it about that the Dauphin sent his own messenger to Your Lordship. However, I am happy that, here, I have at least remained in accord with them, and, there, Your Excellency is the one to whom the messenger is going and you will thus be able to come to a decision; and therefore, as long as all goes well, I am well content.

Indeed I keep thinking that there are in the Dauphin certain qualities that can justify his father ['s treatment of him], *but provided that in the future³ this little fire does no harm to us, all will be well. Having in mind that this mission is my main one and the others accessory, I have always concentrated on this, but because of these actions of the Dauphin I have had so much to do and say that I have not gone to England. And besides, as I also wrote to Your Lordship, the situation did not seem to me to be clear, or rather to be one more likely to cause trouble than be of value; and also the Legate had adopted a wait-and-see attitude. I therefore wrote recently, and sent my chancellor, to Count Lodovico and his companion, urging them not to cross to England until we were together or at least not to take the Legate's mission away from him since Your Lordship's honoring of the Pope* [i.e. in supporting the papal legate] *brings you great prestige in these parts, and what we cannot accomplish directly ourselves can be effected indirectly through the Pope. My chancellor found that Count Lodovico had decided to cross and Zanone to return; what the Legate, who is at Antwerp, thinks about the matter, Your Excellency will, I believe, learn from his letters, since my part is merely to support and commend what your emissaries do, who are, I know well, not lacking good instructions.*

Now that matters in England have turned out well, thank God, and the kingdom has become more peaceful and that therefore it would

hé tanto in tutto con suportation mato et vano che, per Dio, hé uno purgatorio haver a far con si. Et lui proprio hé stato il prometor de far che el Delfin mandassi altro messo a V.S.. Or io me alegro pur che al manco quanto de qua, io sum rimasto d'acordio, et de là, la Excellentia Vostra hé pur quella a chi se va et potrà deliberarsi; siché purché ben sia, io sum contento. Ben me par andar intendendo che in el Delfin sia pur qualche qualitate chi possono iustificar il padre, ma adciò ch'el non nocea in futurum,[3] questa candelletta serà bona. Et ricordandomi questa cura esser la principal et le altre accessorie, semper ho atteso a questa, in la qual, per li designativi movimenti del Delfin havendo havuto assai da fare et dir, non sum passato in Anglia. Et ultra etiam, come ho scritto a V. S., lo tempo non me pareva chiaro, imo più tosto in facia de carico che de utilitate; et cossì etiam se era suprastato Monsignor lo Legato. Et per questo scripsi questi dì proximi, et mandai lo mio cancellero al magnifico Conte Ludovico et lo compagno, confortando non passassero finché non fussemo insieme, aut saltem non prendessero il thema dal Legato, cum ciò sia che honorar il Papa hé grande favor de V. S. in questi paesi, et quello che noi de dirrecto non potressimo attentar, se potria far per lo indirrecto del Papa. Lo mio canceller venne, et trovò il Conte Ludovico in deliberation de passar et Zenon de ritornarsene del che, quello sentimento ne habbi havuto lo Legato, che hé ad Anvers, io credo Vostra Excellentia lo intenderà per sue littere; conciosia che a me non tocca, excepto laudar et comendar, quello che si faciano li messi de Vostra Excellentia, a quali so ben che non mancha bone instructione. Hora che le cose de Anglia sono, gratia a Dio, ridutte in bona et più pacifici termini, et che seria tempo opportuno, io me trovo sì sutto al attender de esser advisato da Vostra Excellentia de quanto harà fatto in la cosa dela liga cum lo messo del Delfin ho[a] de quanto me commetterà circa quello gli ho scripto per Martino etc., ch'el me par de suprastar qualche dì. Interim Monsignor lo Legato,

---

a. Read: o.

be a propitious time for me to cross, I find myself under the necessity of awaiting advices from Your Excellency about what action you will have taken, concerning the treaty, with the messenger of the Dauphin or about what you will commission me to do as a result of what I wrote you by Martino; and therefore I have thought it good to take no steps for some days. In the meanwhile, the Legate has been greatly pleased by the information Messire Antonio [della Tore] gave him about what Your Excellency has ordered regarding my going to England.

On coming here yesterday, I met the honorable Zanone on the road and I told him the news we have here about the behavior of the Dauphin and the insanities of Lord Giacomo, who is at Brussels and is having a suit of armor made, etc.

Item: about the criticisms that are uttered in the Dauphin's chamber regarding the courtesies that Your Lordship extends to the Dauphin's messengers—this on the subject of the falcon-keeper.[4] This man, on returning from Milan, made some inane remarks about the country and the people, and, in regard to Your Excellency, said that you had had him treated very well—these people here think that hospitality is all that counts—and he spoke of the presents you had ordered given to him; and, as I say, these criticisms were made in the Dauphin's presence.

Item: that the armor and other presents[5] Your Lordship gave to Gaston [du Lyon] are all being sold at Brussels, and I have seen them myself. The cloaks are in pawn, and I have made an arrangement with a friend of mine for purchasing them, even if I should have to obligate myself to the extent of 200 ducats in order to bring them back to Your Excellency.

Item: I told Zanone about the advices that a Master Charles [Astars], a secretary of the Dauphin, has given. He has been a long time in Savoy north of the Alps, where the Dauphin sent him when Your Excellency sent me here the first time [i.e. in Sept., 1460], the Dauphin thus banishing him from our negotiations because he is of the persuasion of my lord of Montauban, etc.[6] This Master Charles and

havuto lo adviso da Messer Antonio de quanto Vostra Excellentia havia ordinato del andata mia, n'ha havuto grande consolatione.

Venendo io heri qua, trovai il spectabile Zenon per camin, al quale ho ditto dele novelle havemo de qua deli deportamenti del Delfin et dele insanie de D. Iacomo, quale hé a Brocelle et se fa far una armatura etc.. Item, dele taxe che se mettono in la camera del Delfin ale cortesie che usa V. S. ali suoi messi, et questo fu al proposito del falconero.[4] Ritornato el qua, ha fatto quelle volatione gli hé paruto del paese et dela generatione, et al reguardo de Vostra Excellentia, dice che Vostra Excellentia gli ha fatto far bona chiera, in la qual costuma de questi consiste tutto lo bene de questoro; et del presente gli ha fatto far Vostra Excellentia; et qui, come dico, la taxa se hé fatta in presentia del Delfin. Item, come le arme et presenti[5] ha fatto V. S. a Gaston sonno tutti venduti in Brocelle, et holi vedute io stesso. Le iornee sonno in pegno, et ho suttomisso uno amico per comperarle, se io me dovesse inpignar de ducento ducati per reportarle a Vostra Excellentia. Item, gli ho ditto deli advisi che ha dato uno metre Charle, secretario del Delfin, chi hé stato longo tempo in Savoia de qua dali monti, unde el Delfin lo mandò fin dela prima volta che Vostra Excellentia me mandò de qua, et lo bannitte dal trattamento dela cosa nostra perché hé dela voluntà de Monsignor de Montaban,[6] etc.. Il qual metre Charle da uno canto, et D. Iacomo, sonno quelli chi han dato lo adviso del esser de Ghiotin secreto a Vostra Excellentia, et cossì ultimate del trattamento havia la Duchessa de Savoya con Vostra Excellentia. Et cossì, in conclusion, gli ho ditto quanto m'é paruto pertener, a che distinctamenti Vostra Excellentia sii advisata meglo che per littere. Vero hé che dele cose de Vostra Excellentia cum et Delfin da me, scilicet dela liga, el non ha havuto altro perché tutto gli ho ditto esser lo trattamento per aconsar le cose de D. Iacomo cum el Duca de Savoya. Ben acerto Vostra Excellentia che el Delfin non ten più secreto come fa uno canestro aqua. Supplico a Vostra Excellentia che non mi reputi temerario a dir cossì irreverentementi de uno Principe conciosia che, essendo questa cosa dela liga reguardosa a me, hé necessario advisar Vostra Excellentia del tutto. In

443

Lord Giacomo are the ones who have given the information about the secret relations between Guiottino [de Nores] *and Your Excellency and thus, ultimately, about the negotiations that the Duchess of Savoy is holding with Your Excellency.*

In conclusion, then, I told Zanone the things that seemed to me to be pertinent so that he can convey information to Your Excellency in greater detail than would be possible in a letter.

True it is that about the negotiations between Your Excellency and the Dauphin regarding the league, Zanone has not had anything else from me, for I told him that these negotiations were concerned only with arranging an accord between Giacomo di Valperga and the Duke of Savoy. Indeed I assure Your Excellency that the Dauphin no more keeps a secret than a wicker basket holds water. I beg Your Excellency not to consider me rash in speaking so irreverently about a prince, since this affair of the league is my responsibility and I must advise Your Excellency about everything. In addition, I have told Zanone how messengers ride frequently to the Dauphin regarding the illness of the King of France; and all the Dauphin's men are of the opinion that the King is not going to delude them this time as he has done other times and in other illnesses. There is no pilgrimage in these parts where there will not be found some of the Dauphin's men offering prayers regarding the King, etc.

At Brussels are the greater part of his courtiers, in order to furbish up their armor, and they do this openly as if they were about to go to Israel and Jerusalem. At Brussels I chanced to see, as I note above, Gaston's armor; I also saw Lord Giacomo, who says that the Dauphin has deputed to him 200 *horse and four secretaries and given him the mission of taking possession of all the cities,*[7] *and that the Dauphin, as of now, has distributed all the offices* [of the kingdom].

This is the second time that I, learning of this business, came to Brussels and sent my messenger to the Dauphin with a letter signifying to him that, since I thought it was close to the moment for having the reply from Your Lordship, I had drawn near in order not to lose time

super ho ditto al ditto Zenon come al Delfin frequentano li messi per la malatia del Re de Franza, et han tutti li suoi opinione che el Re non li deba più delezare a questa volta, come ha fatta[b] altri tempi et in altre malatie. Et non hé peregrinagio in questi paesi unde non sia de quelli del Delfin per tali preghi et oratione etc..

A Brocelle sonno le maior parte per metersi in puncto de arme, et caessi tutto ala palese, come se si dovesse andar in Israel et Ierusalem. Et lì me hé accaduto veder le armature de Gaston, ut supra, *et cossì D. Iacomo, qual dice che el Delfin gli ha deputato ducento cavalli et quatro secretarii per andar a prender la possession de tutte le citade;[7] et ha el Delfin iam ex nunc datto* [sic] *li officii tutti. Et hé questa la secunda volta io, sentendo questo, venni a Brocelle et mandato uno messo mio al Delfin con una littera significandogli che, parendomi esser presso al tempo de haver la resposta de V. S., io era aproximato per non perder tempo et veniria dala Excellentia Sua quando gli piacesi. Lecta la litera, la Excellentia Sua fece vista de grande consolatione, piacere del mio ritorno, et dissemi fusse parichiato lo logiamento. Doppoi domandò al mio messo se io avia novelle che castelleto fussi preiso et tutti quelli Galici taglatti a pecii* etc..[8] *Il qual gli resposi non saperlo, et lo tenne tre dì in suspeso per la resposta, et poi disse ch'el se reportava a D. Iacomo; per il che io non deliberai de conferir cum D. Iacomo, perché me pareria puoco honor de V. S. et con suportation puoca advertentia del Delfin de remeter le cose de Vostra Excellentia a D. Iacomo in tali casu, se ben in lo resto gli fusse discretion chi non gli hé né in questo né in altro. Et me sum venuto qui, unde attenderò li advisi et li comandi de V. S., quali serverò adunquuem* [sic]. *Io sum advisato che la Signoria Sua se ha avuto a mal de due cose di me: la una che io non ho mai voluto passar la suma* etc., *et iurato non haver commission de più, conciosia che ha advisatione de multo et multo più, ma percioché li Lombardi fan deli sacramenti quello che gli ne par, in questo el m'à per excusato; l'altra, che io habi scritto a Vostra Excellentia lo dubio che la*

---

b. Read: fatto.

and would come to his excellency if he wished me to. Upon reading the letter, the Dauphin gave the appearance of being greatly pleased with my return and sent word that lodgings were prepared for me. Then he asked my messenger if I had had the news that the citadel [of Genoa] was taken and the whole French garrison cut to pieces, etc.[8] The messenger answered that he did not know this. The Dauphin kept him waiting three days for a reply and then told him that he should refer to Lord Giacomo. However, I did not on that account decide to confer with Valperga because I think it small honor to Your Lordship and, if I may say so, little prudence on the part of the Dauphin for him to remit Your Excellency's affairs to Valperga in such a situation, even if otherwise Valperga had the discretion which indeed he does not have in this or in any other regard. And so I have come here where I will await the advices and commands of Your Lordship, which I will in every way follow.

I am informed that the Dauphin had two things against me: first, that I was unwilling to offer Valperga a larger sum of money and swore I had no commission to offer more, whereas he was informed that I could have offered much, much more—but since Lombards do with oaths what they please, he would excuse me on this score; second, that I had written to Your Excellency what the Dauphin had told me about his perplexity over how he should comport himself with Your Lordship if he should come to terms with the King of France. To the part about the oath I replied that I will be happy to have the truth seen by others. About what I reported to Your Excellency, I referred myself to what the Dauphin would have wished in such a case.

Through the arrival here of one of the Dauphin's messengers, I have found letters from London merchants who say that Count Lodovico[9] arrived in London and experienced as honorable a welcome as ever ambassador had, but that considering Your Excellency's renown, the Count's retinue seemed not good enough to send to such a King. Nevertheless, they say, these people have made a great thing of his coming, it appearing to them that the fame of their King's prowess

Signoria Sua me feci intender de come se ha [a] *comportarsi con V. S. acordandosi lui, Delfin, con el Re de Franza. Ala parte del sacramento ho resposto ch'el mi serà grato si veda per altri il vero. Del adviso, che io me ne riporto a quello haria voluto la Signoria Sua in tali casu.*

Da uno suo messo, iuncto qui, ho trovato litere de mercatanti de Londres, chi dicono come lo magnifico Conte Ludovico[9] *era iuncto in Londres, et veduto quanto honor adilmenti* [sic] *fussi mai ambassator; ma secundo lo nome de V. S., pareva mal acompagnato da mandar a tanto Rei. Tamen che quelli populi frequentementi ne han fatto grande festa, apparendo che la fama dela virtù del loro Rei sia già sì sparsa, che uno tal Principe lo mandi a salutar. Io haria caro cinque soldi ch'el Conte Ludovico havessi preiso da Monsignor lo Legato qualche stampa de deportamenti da tener in quello paese, et ultra etiam qualche introductione per favor de epso Legato, il qual hé tanto de Vostra Signoria quanto dir si possa et tanto predica per dritto et per traverso de quella, quanto per sua prudentia, che hé a mio iudicio multa, vede esser utile et ha adviso da me.*

Qui sonno littere de Franza in li mercatanti Florentini che dicono Vostra Excellentia haver fatto liga con el Re de Franza, et non solo havergli promettuto passo ale sue gente, ma etiam favore in tutte le cose che occuren al presente de là.[10] *Altre gente dicono non esser altri presidio ala oppugnation di castelletto salvo duomila soldati de V. S.. Io ne sum impressiato de multi, et ho resposo che cossì de l'una parte come del'altra me riporto ala verità, ben affermando che so Vostra Excellentia, et per natura et per servicii antiqui et merito dela Maiestà, portar grande reverentia ala corona de Franza. Altro di novello non hé di qua al presente, che io sapia.* Siché me racomando a V. Ex.tia, qual, prego Dio, conservi et feliciti in eternum. Brugs, die 20 iullii [sic] 1461.

Die 21, insero.

Post scripta. *Hoggi sonno littere de Roano qua, unde se dice che ala Curia del Re sonno adunati tutta la gentilisia dela Curia; et dicesi che la armata, chi doveva ritornar in Anglia, hé desarmata; et dela malatia*

must already be widely spread abroad since such a prince as you sent an emissary to greet him. I would certainly have been happier if Count Lodovico had taken from the Legate some advice on how he should behave in England, and also secured some letters of introduction from him, for the Legate is as devoted to Your Lordship as could be expressed, and right and left he says those things about you that in his shrewdness—which is in my judgment great—he sees to be useful and has been informed about by me.

Letters from France have arrived here among the Florentine merchants, who say that Your Excellency has made a league with the King of France and has promised him not only passage for French troops but also support in all that is happening at present there [in Genoa].[10] *Other folk say that the only troops besieging the Genoese citadel are 2,300 soldiers of Your Lordship. I have been pressed by many people to comment, and I have replied that in the case of both these reports I defer to the truth, affirming indeed that I know that Your Excellency, by your nature, by the services rendered of old to the House of France, and by the merit of His Majesty, has great reverence for the French crown. Otherwise, there is no other news here at present that I know of.* In conclusion, I recommend myself to Your Excellency, whom I pray God keep and bless forever. Bruges, July 20, 1461

July 21, enclosed.

Postscript. *Today letters arrived here from Rouen which report that all the court nobility has congregated at the royal court and that the fleet, which was supposed to launch another attack against England, has been disarmed. These letters make no mention of the illness of the King of France. However, someone who left the royal court on the ninth of July, and has come here, says that the King had suffered from a toothache but has recovered. The other day, at Brussels, I inquired about this from the Bishop of Tournai,* [Guillaume Fillastre] *who is the know-all of Burgundy, and he informed me that it was true that the King had suffered from a disease of the jaw and that it was said this*

del Re de Franza non si fa motto alcuno. Imo hé venuto qui persona propria, partitta ali novi del presente dala Curia, chi dice el Re haver havuto mal de denti et esser guarito. L'altro dì a Brocelle, domandandome io al Vescovo de Tornai, che hé il statutto[c] de Bergogna, el me disse che al vero el Re de Franza havia havuto una dogla [ad] una massilla, et che se diceva essergli apostemato le gengive da una masca. Questo hé quanto io ne sento; se altro ne di questo ne de altro sentirò, serò sollicito et fidelle [sic] in darne li debiti advisi a Vostra Excellentia, ala qual semper me racomando humiliter.

---

c. Read: satutto.

had caused an abscess on the gums. This is what I have heard; if I hear
further about this or other matters, I shall be solicitous and faithful in
sending appropriate notification to Your Excellency, to whom I always
humbly recommend myself.

HISTORICAL NOTES

1. An envoy of the Earl of Warwick, returning from a mission to the
Pope and to the Duke of Milan [see foregoing docs. *passim.*].

2. Following this emissary's mission, Astars and Saubier [see doc. 114, n.
3, p. 402] arrived in Milan some time before June 20 and left by this date
[Sforza to the Dauphin, Milan, June 29, 1461, *Francia,* cart. 525; *Reg. Mis-*
sive 52, fol. 81v–82r; *Lettres,* I, 352, incorrectly dated June 30], returning to
Milan on July 4 with the Dauphin's ratification of the new agreement as embodied in the letters patent of June 1, 1461 [Sforza to the Dauphin, Milan,
July 20, 1461, *Francia,* cart. 525; *Lettres,* I, 353–54; Sforza to Prospero, Milan,
Aug. 15 (Aug. 8 is crossed out), 1461, *Francia,* cart. 526]. In replying to the
present dispatch on Aug. 15 [cited above] Sforza informed Prospero of the
envoys' latest arrival and of the agreement reached, including his own ratification (July 24) of the Treaty of Genappe as amended [see Appendix, doc.
IV, p. 470–74], all of which had been concluded before the news of Charles
VII's death (July 22) reached Milan on Aug. 1. He also revealed that at the
insistence of the ambassadors he had increased the sum from 12,000 to 18,-
000 Rhenish florins, which he had decided to donate to Louis; had promised
to obtain a Church benefice for Valperga's son, Giovanni; and had issued
to Prospero new powers (dated Aug. 5, 1461 and identical to those of Aug.
26, 1460, but valid for one year and with the reservation for Charles VII elim-
inated) [*Trattati,* cart. 1528; BN, *Fonds Italien,* Cod. 1595, fol. 212r–212v,
and *Fonds Latin,* Cod. 10133, fol. 22r–22v]. Therefore, since the alliance had
now been ratified by both sides, Sforza ordered his ambassador to take leave
of the King and the Duke of Burgundy, and return to Milan as soon as possible because his report was needed by the envoys whom the Duke was about
to send to Louis.

3. Prospero's suspicions were quickly realized. On his way to Louis'

court, Astars met a royal emissary, a certain Gillet, bearing a letter in which the new King informed him that the recent accord with Sforza was not agreeable to Valperga, and instructed him therefore to interrupt the negotiations. If the agreement had already been concluded, Astars was ordered to request the mutual return of all letters and documents exchanged on this matter by Louis and the Duke. In communicating this news to Sforza, Astars announced that he was sending Gillet, on the King's orders, to Milan to arrange for the return of the documents [Astars to Sforza, Oriolet in Burgundy, Aug. 19, [1461], *Francia,* cart. 543]. The Duke expressed surprise and disbelief that such request could have been made by Louis, particularly in view of the fact that both Prospero and Coppini had sent nothing but good reports about the King's friendly disposition towards him. He hoped, therefore, that after Louis had heard the final report by Astars and Saubier and received his new ambassadors, who were soon to leave for the royal court, he would remain satisfied [Sforza to Astars, Milan, Sept. 5, 1461, *ibid.,* cart. 526].

4. In return for the falcon dispatched earlier by Sforza, the Dauphin sent the Duke three sparrowhawks carried to Milan by his falconer, Nicolas, Bastard de Lyère [The Dauphin to Sforza, Genappe, May 14, 1461, *Francia,* cart. 525; *Lettres,* I, 138]. Sforza thanked the Dauphin profusely for the gift [Sforza to the Dauphin, Milan, [June 27, 1461], *Francia,* cart. 525; cf. Sforza to Gaston du Lyon, Milan, June 27, 1461, *ibid.,* cart. 525].

5. i.e. the gifts given by the Duke of Milan to Gaston in May, 1460 [see doc. 57, n. 12, p. 39].

6. Montauban, though long a fugitive from Brittany, where he had been implicated in a political murder, apparently shared the Duke of Brittany's hostility to Sforza.

7. On Aug. 4 Valperga was made Chancellor of France by Louis XI, and held that post until Sept. 1 [Mandrot, I, 5, n. 2].

8. On July 17, 1461, a relief army of some 6,000 men under King René, sent by Charles VII to attack Genoa by land and sea and raise the siege of the *Castelletto,* met on the hills around the city a Genoese force stiffened by Milanese reinforcements. In the ensuing battle, the badly led French, overburdened by armor and the intense heat, were disastrously routed and hundreds captured. The number of Frenchmen who fell in battle, or drowned in an attempt to reach their ships, runs from 2500 [Simonetta, B. XXVIII, 446] to

4000 [Pius II, *Commentaries,* B. V, 370]. René and the remnants of his shat-
tered army repaired to Savona, still under French control, and thence returned to France. Three days later Sforza sent an account of the battle to
the Dauphin, pointing out that he had given access and supplies to the French
troops passing through the territory of his "adherents," but he carefully refrained from mentioning the crucial role his men had played in the defeat
of the French. [Sforza to the Dauphin, Milan, July 20, 1461, *Francia,* cart. 525;
Lettres, I, 354–56].

9. After being at first prevented by French ships from crossing the Channel from Calais [Cagnola to Sforza, Calais, July 5, 1461, BN, *Fonds Italien,*
Cod. 1589, fol. 16r], Count Dallugo and Cagnola finally crossed on July 6 and
arrived in London on the ninth [Cagnola to Sforza, London, July 9, 1461,
Inghilterra e Scozia, cart. 566].

10. See doc. 99, n. 1, p. 316.

APPENDICES

I·*Schema for a Treaty of Alliance*

between the DAUPHIN *and the*

DUKE OF MILAN

[Milan, August], 1460
Trattati, cart. 1528; Francia, cart. 525. Minutes[a]

IN NOMINE Domini nostri Yhesu Christi feliciter amen. Anno **a** nativitate eiusdem 1460 [die ************* mensis augusti] in [civitate Mediolani].

Notum sit omnibus et singulis presentibus et futuris quod, cum gratia Summi mentium humanarum Illuminatoris et Creatoris nostri, dudum fuisset orta cordialissima et singularissima affectio et benivolentia inter Ser.mum Principem et Excellentissimum D. D. Aluisium, Dalphinum Vienne, primogenitum Ser.mi et Christianissimi Principis D. D. Caroli presentis Regis Francorum parte una, et Ill.mum ac Ex.mum Principem D. D. Franciscum Sfortiam Vicecomitem, Ducem Mediolani etc., Papie Anglerieque Comitem ac Cremone Dominum parte altera. Cupientibus prefatis Principibus et Dominis hanc eorum cordialissimam et sincerissimam dilectionem notam esse, non tantum

---

a. Both minutes are in Prospero's hand. *Trattati,* cart. 1528 contains also three Italian versions of this schema. Another Italian text [*Francia,* cart. 525], has a number of variants—the most important of which are recorded below—that reflect an earlier stage of the negotiations before the decision to conclude the treaty at the Dauphin's court had been reached. Still another Italian version [*Trattati,* cart. 1529], shows changes in line with this decision.

modo inter ipsas partes, sed etiam inter ipsorum Dominorum filios, heredes et successores et quum memoria rerum humanarum labilis est, reduci in speciale documentum et declarationem per claram et publicam scripturam, quod quidem tanquam honestum, acceptabile ac rationabile, cupiens ipse Ser.mus D. D. Dalphinus non videri ingratus pro parte sui eius mutue et reciproce benivolentie et affectionis, que est inter Ex.am Suam ex una parte utsupra et ipsum prefatum Ill.mum D. D. Ducem Mediolani ex altera, et devotionis ac servitutis qua ipse Ill.mus D. D. Dux affectus est erga prefatum Ser.mum et Ex.mum D. D. Dalphinum etc., contentus fuit et contentatur ipse Ser.mus D. D. Dalphinus atque acceptavit et acceptat ac declaravit de mente sua ac sponte velle devenire ad intelligentiam et ligam cum ipso Ill.mo Principe D. D. Duce Mediolani supradicto[b] per medium atque interventum nobilis Prosperi Camulii, familiaris ac nuncii et legitimi procuratoris sui, prout apparet per mandatum et procuram in personam ipsius Prosperi factam, cuius tenor de verbo ad verbum, sequitur ut infra:

Franciscus Sfortia etc.[c]

Et pro executione huius earum partium optime mutue dispositionis, affectionis et voluntatis prefate partes pervenerunt ad intelligentiam et ligam insimul et vicissim sub capitulis, pactis et conventionibus ut infra, videlicet:

Quia in primis prefatus Ill.mus D. D. Dux Mediolani, sive prenominatus Prosper, eius nuncius et procurator ut supra agens, stipulans et

---

b. Cart. 525: medianti loro messi et procuratori, videlicet, per parte d'esso M.re Delfino, li magnifici et potenti Messer Iacomo di Conte de Valperga et de Maxino, cavalero et doctore de lege et Messer Guaschono de Leon, suo consigliero et primo scudero, etiam procuratore cum mandato speciale de cossì fare, como consta per sue littere patente del suo vero sigillo sigillate et per mano del [*****], suo secretario signate, el tenore dele quale de verbo ad verbum sequitur. Loys.

Per parte del prelibato Ill.mo Signore Ducha de Milano, li spectabili et magnifici Petro da Pusterla et Cicho [*****], similiter procuratori et messi suoy, como appare per publico instrumento rogato etc., el tenore del quale de verbo ad verbum sequitur. [It is to be noted that henceforth the procurators on both sides are mentioned at the appropriate places throughout this text.]

c. Only the first two words of Prospero's powers, dated Aug. 26, 1460, are given in the text [see doc. 54, n. 1, p. 6].

recipiens nomine Ex. Sue, dominorum filiorum, heredum et successorum suorum, vigore suprascripti mandati, promisit et seu promittit prefato Ser.mo et Ex.mo D. D. Dalphino, quod ut prosequatur id quod certissimum est mentis et dispositionis ipsius Ill.mi D. D. Ducis Mediolani supratacti versus prefatum Ser.mum et Ex.mum Principem D. D. Dalphinum, dominos eius filios, heredes et successores etc., hinc in antea habebit continue in singularem amorem, reverentiam et sinceram dilectionem atque adiuvabit, defendet et sustinebit Suam Ex.am eius statum, dominos filios, heredes et successores utsupra toto eius posse contra quem aut quosvis, qui ipsum offenderent aut offendere temptarent in persona, statu et bonis presentibus et futuris suis, dominorum filiorum, heredum et successorum suorum utsupra,[d] quemadmodum tenetur et facere debet quivis bonus, perfectus, sincerus et benivolus ac devotus servitor erga suum maiorem et affinem. Sed hoc non intelligantur contra suprascriptum Ser.mum et Christianissimum Principem D. D. Carolum, presentem Regem Francorum et genitorem ipsius prefati Ex.mi D. D. Dalphini[e] et ipso vivente.

Sed, adveniente casu, quem Deus avertat, quad prefatus Ser.mus et Christianissimus D. D. Carolus Rex Francorum, genitor prefati Ser.mi et Ex.mi D. D. Dalphini, ex presente vita discederet, tunc et eo casu intelligatur prefatum Ill.mum D. D. Ducem Mediolani teneri et obligatum esse versus prefatum Ser.mum D. D. Dalphinum, et sic promisit et promittit dictus Prosper, nomine Ex. Sue et vigore suprascripti mandati et procure sue, prefato Ser.mo D. D. Dalphino, seu eius nuncio et procuratori legitimo, presenti et acceptanti, quod ipse Ill.mus D. D. Dux Mediolani, in acquirendo in Francia Regnum Francie et Dalphinatum,[f] spectantis et pertinentis prefato Ser.mo D. D. Dalphino, tanquam regio

---

d. Cart. 525, crossed out: et evitare ogni danno, vergogna et inconveniente che al prefato Ser.mo Mon.re Delfino et suoy prefati figlioli, heredi et successori podesse accadere.

e. Cart. 525: perché ala Soa Maiestà ha portato et continuamente porta singularissimo amore et affectione, devotione et summa reverentia, et seria sempre in adiuto et difexa del honore, Stato et beni de la Soa Maiestà, perché per soa gratia, benignità et clementia se tenne essere singularmente amato da quella.

f. Cart. 525 omits: et Dalphinatum.

primogenito et ex constitutione regali, ipsum Ser.mum D. D. Dalphinum adiuvabit toto eius posse, atque illi favebit et serviet de suis gentibus armigeris, pedestribus et equestribus, et cum eius vexillo ac stendardo ducali[g] cum equitibus tribus milibus et peditibus mille; quorum peditum quarta pars sint balistrarii, quarta schioppeterii, quarta tarconarii et tarchettarii, reliqua quarta pars sint cum hastis, sive lanciis longis, quibus omnibus solutum sit ad expensas ipsius Ill.mi D. D. Ducis Mediolani pro tempore,[h] videlicet et termino anni unius, qui incipiat a die quo se ad iter posuerint suprascriptas gentes prodeundo ad auxilia et servicia predicta; et que copie, equitum et peditum, parate sint et esse debeant parte ipsius Ill.mi D. D. Ducis Mediolani supratacti in terminum mensium duorum post de ipsis requisitionem debitis modis factam per ipsum Ser.mum D. D. Dalphinum; et cui quidem Ser.mo D. D. Dalphino predicta acquisitione agenti, si opus fuerit dictis equitibus et peditibus ultra et preter tempus anni supra expressum, teneatur et obligatus sit ipse Ser.mus D. D. Dalphinus ipsis equitibus et peditibus subvenire et eis solvere suis propriis expensis quousque eos ad servicia sua retinebit, et hoc secundum ritum Francie,[i] videlicet pro singula lancia lumbarda scutos [****************] et pro singulo pedite scutos [***************] singulo mense.

Item, si quando dictus Ser.mus D. D. Dalphinus, futurus Rex Francorum, acquisiverit dictum Regnum in Francia, accidat Maiestatem Suam offendi ab aliqua persona in dicto suo Regno, per talem et ita notabilem offensionem et seu guerram motam, ut dignum et expediens videatur Maiestati Sue ipsum Ill.mum D. D. Ducem in auxilium et servicium suum requirere, tunc prefatus Ill.mus D. D. Dux, requisitus ab ipso Ser.mo D. D. Dalphino, tunc Rege, adiuvabit ad defendendum ipsum Ser.mum D. D. Dalphinum et serviet ipsi tunc Regi ad conservationem dicti sui Regni in Francia contra quamvis personam, que ipsum

---

g. Cart 525: cum mille lanze franzose che sonno sey milia cavalli et IIII[m] fanti a pede.
h. Cart. 525 omits: videlicet . . . . servicia predicta.
i. Cart. 525 omits: videlicet . . . . mense.

offenderet, aut molestaret utsupra, videlicet mittendo in Maiestatis et Regni sui predicti defensionem et servicium suprascriptum numerum equitum trium milium et peditum mille, aut vero illam quantitatem minorem ex eo numero, quam ipse Ser.mus D. D. Dalphinus, tunc Rex, censuerit requirendam et requiret,[j] quibus solvetur expensis et parte ipsius Ill.mi D. D. Ducis Mediolani utsupra per tempus anni unius; quod si dicta auxilia opportuna viderentur ipsi Ser.mo D. D. Dalphino, tunc Regi, pro tempore ulteriori dicti anni utsupra, liceat ipsi Ser.mo D. D. Dalphino, tunc Regi, dictos equites et pedites auxilia suprascripta retinere ad servicia Maiestatis et Regni sui predicti, aut alios equites et pedites, qui loco ipsorum auxiliorum similiter auxiliares missi fuissent aut mitterentur per ipsum Ill.mum D. D. Ducem Mediolani, atque eis uti et eos equites et pedites operam quantum et quandum eius Maiestati videbitur et placuerit durante illa guerra, cuius respectu missi fuissent, solvente videlicet ipso Ser.mo D. D. Dalphino, tunc Regi, talibus equitibus et peditibus auxiliariis propriis expensis Maiestatis Sue pro stipendio secundum ritum et consuetudinem Francie, videlicet scutorum [***** *************] pro qualibet lancia lumbarda in mense et scutorum [****************] pro quolibet pedite pro toto tempore quo ultra annum retinerentur.

Et si, finita dicta guerra et talibus auxiliariis equitibus et peditibus in Lumbardiam reversis, accideret postea aliud in Francia novum bellum, prefato Ser.mo D. D. Dalphino, tunc Regi Francorum utsupra teneatur similiter et obligatus sit prefatus Ill.mus D. D. Dux Mediolani denuo servire ipsi Ser.mo D. D. Dalphino, tunc Regi, et denuo auxiliares equites et pedites Maiestati Sue expedire et mittere ad omnem requisitionem prefati Ser.mi D. D. Dalphini, tunc Rgis, modo et forma suprascriptis et sic totiens quotiens accideret talis necessitas auxiliandi et eidem serviendi.

Et versa vice, prefatus Ser.mus D. D. Aluysius, Dalphinus Viennen-

---

j. Cart. 525 omits: quibus . . . . serviendi.

sis et futurus Rex Francorum, ut premittitur promisit ac tanquam Dalphinus nunc, et Rex in futurum promittit ipsi Ill.mo D. D. Duci Mediolani, sive predicto Prospero procuratori, agenti, stipulanti et recipienti nomine Ex. Sue, quod ipse Ser.mus D. D. Dalphinus ex nunc, et Rex succedente tempore, adiuvabit, fovebit, defendet, manutenebit et sustinebit ac proteget ipsum Ill.mum D. D. Franciscum Sfortiam Ducem Mediolani pretactum, eius Ill.mam D. D. Consortem Ducissam, dominos eius filios, heredes et successores suos in Ducatu Mediolani et in aliis eius et eorum dominiis, iuribus, iurisdictionibus et pertinentiis presentibus et futuris contra quamcunque personam et quamvis potentiam, que eum, aut suos utsupra, offenderet, aut offendere, molestare, inquietare, aut perturbare predictum Statum suum, aut suorum utsupra, modo aliquo, directo vel indirecto temptaret, aut moliretur; et hoc toto ipsius Ser.mi D. D., seu Dalphini, seu Regis posse. Et si prefato Ill.mo D. D. Duci, D. D. Ducisse, D. filiis, heredibus et successoribus suis opus fuerit auxiliis equitum et peditum, tunc prefatus Ser.mus D. D. Dalphinus, seu Rex, expediet ac mittet in tempus duorum mensium requisitionis reciproce utsupra, et ad omnem requisitionem de ipsis auxiliis mittendis pro tempore factam et quam fiet[k] equites quattuor mille et archerios duo mille, quibus de propria expensa ipsius prefati Ser.mi D. D. Dalphini aut Regis suprascripti solutum erit et solvi faciet ipse Ser.mus D. D. Dalphinus, sive Rex, utsupra, realiter et cum effectu de debito stipendio pro anno uno, incoando a die quo se se ad iter posuerint, utsupra; et hoc totiens quotiens et quandocunque occurret opus esse prefato Ill.mo D. D. Duci, sive ab Ex. Sue descendentibus, utsupra, et requisitio fiet aut facta fuerit per ipsum Ill.mum D. D. Ducem, aut suos utsupra, atque hoc sub modis, formis et temporibus que in precedenti reciproco capitulo continentur[l] et ad modum et stipendium solitum in Lombardia.

Hoc tamen acto et intellecto quod per presentia capitula, sive aliquod ipsorum non intelligatur preiudicatum, neque aliqualiter deroga-

---

k. Cart. 525: cavalli VI^m et arceri IIII^m.

l. Cart. 525 omits: et . . . . Lombardia.

tum capitulis Universalis Lige Italie, ymo illa intelligantur illesa remanere.[m]

Iurantibus etc.

Promittentibus etc.

Datum etc.

Presentibus etc.

---

m. Cart. 525: this paragraph is preceded by the following two: Et li presenti capituli, intelligentia et liga suprascripta se intendano cum reservatione et senza preiudicio de la Liga Universale de Italia et de li capituli d'essa.

Et perché in li capituli de la Liga Universale de Italia é uno capitulo del tenore infrascripto, videlicet: Item, guod facta conclusione presentis Lige, ulla partium predictarum devenire non possit ad aliquam intelligentiam seu ligam cum aliqua potentia italica, nisi de [communi] consensu et voluntate omnium partium predictarum, nisi illam fecerit sine preiudicio et cum reservatione capitulorum presentis Lige, cui nullo pacto liceat derogari. [Except for the bracketed addition, this is an exact quotation of article V of the Italian League as concluded at Venice on Aug. 30, 1454. G. Soranzo, *La Lega Italica (1454-1455)* (Milan, 1924), doc. 3, 193].

II · *Treaty between the* DAUPHIN *and the*

DUKE OF MILAN

Genappe [Genepii], October 6, 1460
Trattati, cart. 1528. Orig.

LUDOVICUS, Regis Francorum primogenitus, Dalphinus Viennensis Comesque Valentinensis et Diensis. Cum sit quod gratia Summi mentium humanarum Illuminatoris et Creatoris nostri, dudum fuisset orta cordialissima et singularissima affectio et benivolentia inter nos parte una, et Ill.mum et Ex.mum Principem avunculum nostrum carissimum, D. Franciscum Sfortiam Vicecomitem, Ducem Mediolani etc., Papie Anglerieque Comitem ac Cremone Dominum parte altera. Cupientibus nobis ambabus partibus hanc nostram cordialissimam et sincerissimam dilectionem notam esse, non tantum modo inter nos partes, sed etiam inter filios, heredes et successores nostros, et quoniam memoria rerum humanarum labilis est, reduci in speciale documentum et declarationem per claram et publicam scripturam, quod quidem tamquam honestum, acceptabile et rationabile cupimus specialiter nos, ne videamur ingrati pro parte nostra eius mutue et reciproce benivolentie et affectionis, que est inter nos ex una parte ut supra et ipsum prefatum Ill.mum avunculum nostrum carissimum D. Ducem Mediolani ex altera, et devotionis ac servitutis qua ipse Ill.mus D. Dux affectus est erga nos, idcirco contenti fuimus et contentamur atque acceptavimus et acceptamus ac declaramus de mente nostra ac sponte velle devenire et venimus ad intelligentiam et ligam cum ipso Ill.mo avunculo nostro carissimo D.

Duce Mediolani supradicto per medium atque interventu spectabilis viri Prosperi Camulii, oratoris et secretarii sui, et qui a prefato Ill.mo D. Duce Mediolani habet ad hec sufficiens mandatum manu propria ipsius Ill.mi D. Ducis suscriptum; et pro executione huius optime mutue utriusque nostrum dispositionis, affectionis et voluntatis pervenimus inter nos partes predictas ad intelligentiam et ligam insimul et vicissim sub capitulis, pactis et conventionibus ut infra, videlicet:

Quia in primis prenominatus Prosper, orator et secretarius ut supra, agens et stipulans nomine ipsius Ill.mi avunculi nostri carissimi D. Ducis Mediolani, heredum et successorum suorum utsupra, vigore dicti sui mandati, promisit et seu promittit nobis quod ut prosequatur id quod est certissimum mentis et dispositionis ipsius Ill.mi avunculi nostri carissimi supratacti D. Ducis Mediolani versus nos, filios, heredes et successores nostros, hinc in antea habebit continue in singularem amorem, reverentiam et sinceram dilectionem atque adiuvabit, defendet et substinebit nos, Statum, filios, heredes et successores nostros ut supra, toto eius posse, contra quem aut quosvis, qui not offenderent aut offendere temptarent in persona, Statu et bonis presentibus et futuris nostris, filiorum, heredum et successorum nostrorum ut supra.

Et versa vice nos Ludovicus prenominatus, Regis Francorum primogenitus, Dalphinus Viennensis, futurus Rex Francorum ex constitutione regali, promisimus, ac tamquam Dalphinus nunc et Rex in futurum, promictimus ipsi Ill.mo avunculo nostro carissimo D. Duci Mediolani pretacto, sive ipsi Prospero, oratori et secretario suo, agenti, stipulanti et recipienti nomine Ex.tie Sue, quod nos ex nunc et Rex succedente tempore adiuvabimus, fovebimus, defendemus, manutenebimus, substinebimus et protegemus ipsum Ill.mum avunculum nostrum carissimum D. Franciscum Sfortiam, Ducem Mediolani pretactum, eius Ill.mam D. Consortem Ducissam, eius filios, heredes et successores suos in Ducatu Mediolani et in aliis eius et eorum dominiis, iuribus, iuridicionibus et pertinentiis presentibus et futuris, contra quamcumque personam et quamvis potentiam, que eum aut suos ut supra offenderet aut offendere,

molestare, inquietare aut perturbare predictum Statum suum aut suorum ut supra, modo aliquo directo vel indirecto temptaret aut moliretur; et hoc toto nostri seu Dalphini seu Regis posse.

Item, si prefato Ill.mo Domino Duci, D. Ducisse, filiis, heredibus et successoribus suis opus fuerit auxiliis equitum et peditum, tunc nos Dalphinus nunc seu Rex in futurum, infra tempus mensium duorum requisitionis nobis parte ipsius Ill.mi D. Ducis aut suorum facte, et ad omnem requisitionem de ipsis auxiliis nostris ad se mittendis pro tempore factam et que fiet, expediemus et mittemus equites quatuor mille et archerios duo mille, quibus de propria expensa nostri tunc Regis, nos nunc Dalphinus et tunc Rex, solvi faciemus realiter et cum effectu de debito stipendio pro anno uno, incoando a die quo sese dicti equites et pedites ad iter posuerint, accedendo ad auxilia predicta; et hoc totiens quotiens et quandocunque occurret et videatur prefato Ill.mo avunculo nostro carissimo D. Duce sive Ex. Sue descendentibus opus esse, et parte ipsius aut suorum ut supra requisitio facta nobis fuerit de ipsis auxiliis aut parte eorum mittendis, et omnia alia pro ipso Ill.mo avunculo nostro carissimo D. Duce, eius Statu et suorum libentissime quidem et ex animo faciemus, que debet bonus et benivolus affinis ad talem maxime utilitatem cordiali vinculo, liga et intelligentia colligatus.

Hoc etiam intellecto quod per presentia capitula sive aliquod ipsorum non intelligatur preiudicatum neque aliqualiter derogatum capitulis Universalis Lige Italie, ymo illa illesa remanere intelligantur.

Demumque hinc inde inter nos tamquam Dalphinum nunc et succedente tempore futurum Regem Francorum ut supra pro nobis, heredibus et successoribus nostris ex una parte et ipsum Ill.mum avunculum nostrum carissimum D. Ducem Mediolani prenominatum, Ill.mam D. Ducissam, eius Consortem, filios, heredes et successores suos ut supra ex altera, deinceps sit et esse intelligatur, vigore suprascriptorum conventorum ut supra, cordialissima et sincerissima dilectio, liga et intelligentia perpetuo, ut dicitur inter nos partes, filios ac successores nostros ut supra dicitur valitura et duratura. In cuius signum et verum effectum, altera pars teneatur agere pro altera et eius conservatione,

464

utilitate et commodis et econtra quemadmodum pro se ipsa faceret et
hoc bona fide et pro posse. Et sic in executione premissorum habebun-
tur, fovebuntur, conservabuntur et tractabuntur pro posse officiales,
subditi, feudatarii, adherentes et recommandati ac servitores ipsarum
partium ut supra agentium inter sese, hinc inde advenientibus casibus,
et pura fide, ut dicitur, et nullo unquam in contrarium colore quesito.
Inter quos quidem certis rationibus iustis et debitis adducti, nos Dalphinus ut supra, non preiudicando aliis denominationibus talium hinc
inde inter nos partes pro tempore fiendis, annumeramus et nominamus
pro parte nostri spectabilem D. Iacobum de Valperga, dilectum consiliarium et cambellanum nostrum, et eius terras et bona, quamvis extra
iura nostra predicta posita sint, quem quidem D. Iacobum et terras ac
bona sua, que hoc tempore vexari licet iniuste videntur per Ill. D.
Ducem Sabaudie, ac eius bona ipse Ill.mus avunculus noster carissimus
D. Dux tueri et defendere ac conservare teneatur et in se tutelam eius
recipere debeat in eo statu saltem in quo erant die quarta septembris
proximi elapsi vel meliori et pacifico, si fieri poterit; et hoc non obstante
aliqua exceptione que vigore suprascriptorum allegari posset.

Ad que quidem omnia et singula suprascripta quantum pro parte
nostri servanda et adimplenda, nos tamquam Dalphinus nunc et Rex
Francorum futurus ut supra, promisimus eidem Prospero, nomine prefati Ill.mi avunculi nostri carissimi recipienti, et presentium tenore in
verbo legalis Principis promittimus pro nobis et heredibus ac successoribus nostris quod rata, grata et firma perpetuo habebimus et tenebimus
omnia et singula suprascripta atque ea plene servabimus et adimplebi-
mus, nec ullo unquam tempore eis aut alicui eorum aliquo modo, iure
vel causa nec aliquo quesito colore contraveniemus sub obligatione
honoris et fidei nostre; et sic tactis corporaliter Sacris Scripturis iuravimus presente ipso Prospero, et vigore dicti mandati sui talem promis-
sionem et iuramentum nostrum acceptante. Et ad eadem per ipsum
prefatum Ill.mum avunculum nostrum carissimum D. Ducem Mediolani ratificanda et per reciprocam scripturam et patentes litteras promit-
tenda et cum iuramentum et subscriptione propria reciproce cavenda

prout in presentibus litteris nostris pro parte nostri continetur, reservatum esse intelligatur arbitrium et tempus mensium duorum ipsi Ill.mo avunculo nostro carissimo D. Duci Mediolani; et ad dictum iuramentum super premissis reciproce ut dicitur faciendum et nostri nomine recipiendum, deputamus vigore presentium loco nostri nobilem Gastonum du Lion, consiliarium et scutiferum nostrum dilectum, suplentes ex plenitudine potestatis nostre in presentibus et precipue omnibus ac singulis particulis pro parte nostri ut supra specificatis omni solemnitati, tam iuris quam facti, que in presentibus servanda fuissent. In quorum testimonium presentes litteras fieri registrari ac nostro sigillo muniri iussimus manu propria nostra in maius robur subscriptas.

Datum Genepie in Brebantia, die sexta mensis octobris anno Domini millesimo CCCC^{mo} sexagesimo.

Loys

Bourré

III · *Ratification of the Treaty of Genappe by the*

DUKE OF MILAN

Milan [Mediolani], December 6, 1460
BN, Fonds Italien, Cod. 1588, fols. 343r–346r; Trattati, cart. 1528. Minutes

Franciscus SFORTIA VICECOMES, Dux Mediolani etc., Papie Anglerieque Comes ac Cremone Dominus. Certiores facti de conventionibus et capitulis initis et firmatis inter Ill.mum et Ex.mum Principem et Dominum D. Ludovicum, Ser.mi et Christianissimi D. D. Caroli Regis Francorum primogenitum, Dalphinum Viennensem Comitemque Valentinensem et Dyensem ex una parte, et insignem ac spectabilem secretarium nostrum Prosperum Camulium, oratorem et procuratorem nostrum, ad eius Ex.tia destinatum nomine nostro, ex altera, cum certis reservationibus prout in ipsis capitulis et conventionibus continetur, quas quidem conventiones cum ipsis capitulis in carta membrana et patentes litteras redactas et subscriptas manu propria prefati Ill.mi et Ex.mi D. D. Dalphini cum sigillo suo pendenti nobis presentatas per spectabilem virum Baldisonum Murinum, prefati Ill.mi et Ex.mi D. D. Dalphini secretarium, reverenter suscepimus, et gratissimo animo vidimus ac diligenter examinavimus et quarum tenor infra sequitur videlicet: [omitted].[a]

Et in primis prefato Ill.mo et Ex.mo Principi ingentes gratias agimus et habere debemus pro tanta caritate, benignitate et singulari humanitate, quibus nos, inclytam Consortem nostram, liberos, succes-

---

a. There follows the text of the Treaty of Genappe.

sores ac Statum nostrum tam gratiose amplectitur et in sua protectione recipere dignatur. Volentes igitur tanti Principis tam benigne voluntati et dispositioni pro parte nostri quo ad vires nostre suppetunt respondere et satisfacere omni modo iure, via et forma, quibus melius possumus et valemus, supradictas conventiones et capitula cum ea qua decet reverentia approbamus, ratificamus et acceptamus ac reciproce promittimus, cavemus et nos sub obligatione honoris et fidei nostre identidem obligamus.

Verumtamen quantum ad eam partem que magnificum D. Iacobum de Valperga in ipsis conventionibus nominatum eiusque terras et bona concernit, quoniam res ipse ab eodem statu et gradu, qui in dictis conventionibus requiritur alieno defectu delapse sunt post initas dictas conventiones, et ante quam de ipsis per dictum Prosperum ulla nobis noticia data fuerit et hoc absque ulla nostri culpa, prout[b] ex ipsa veritate et plerisque fidedignis de hoc informatis plenissime constat, non valentes propterea impresentiarum eam partem prout iacet approbare et ratificare. Ideo in supplementum eius quod aliter fieri non potest, ut Ex.ma D. Sua mentem et propositum nostrum ferventissimum intelligat et cognoscat et nos Sue Ex.tie, quo magis fieri possit complaceamus, remittimus ad Ex.tiam Suam predictum Prosperum, oratorem et procuratorem nostrum, de mente et voluntate nostra plenissime instructum, cui vice earum rerum quas in parte predicti D. Iacobi Sua Ex.tia fieri vult ad instaurandum id quod ad presens eo modo fieri non potest, quedam commisimus Sue Ex.tie nostro nomine explicanda, que sibi grata et rei illi commoda fore existimavimus pro quarum rerum observatione fidem et honorem nostrum etiam obligamus. Et sic tactis corporaliter Sacris Scripturis iuravimus presente ipso magnifico Gastono suprascripto, ad hoc pro ipso Ill.mo et Ex.mo D. D. Dalphino deputato, et qui ipsum sacramentum nostrum nomine quo supra acceptavit et acceptat [beneplacitum Ser.mi D. D. Dalphini pretacti nihilominus in

---

b. Crossed out in Cod. 1588 and included in cart. 1528: magnifico Gastono de Leone predicto eiusque fratri, consiliario et scutiferis ac fidis servitoribus prefati Ill.mi et Ex.mi D. D. Dalphini liquide constant et nobs retulerunt.

premissis reservando ad quod ratificandum et approbandum tempus duorum mensium proxime futurorum, incoandorum ad hodie prefato Ex.mo D. D. Dalphino reservatum fore intelligatur, et hoc attento suprascripto casu dicti D. Iacobi et suarum rerum ac exceptione superinde utsupra facta].ᶜ Eidem Ex.tie igitur supplicamus ut ipso Prospero iterum audito ea que nomine nostro promittet, que quidem sunt quantum a nobis salva honestate fieri possit grato animo acceptare et hec confirmare dignetur, et benigna mente suscipiat pro qua nos et filios ac successores nostros et Statum ac nostra omnia sibi et omnibus suis ad sua mandata iugiter observantissimos faciet et in eternum habebit.

[In quorum testimonium presentes litteras fieri et registrari ac sigilli nostri appensione muniri fecimus manu nostra propria in maius robur subscriptas.

Datum Mediolani, die sexta mensis decembris, anno a nativitate Domini nostri Yhesu Christi, millesimo CCCCº LXº, inditione nona].

---

c. This and the following bracketed passages are omitted in cart. 1528.

IV · *Confirmation and Ratification of the*

Treaty of Genappe, as Amended,

by the DUKE OF MILAN

Milan [Mediolani], July 24, 1461
BN, Fonds Latin, Cod. 10133, fols. 23r–25v and Fonds Italien, Cod. 1595, fols. 213r–216v; Francia, cart. 526. Copies

FRANCISCUS SFORTIA VICECOMES, Dux Mediolani etc., Papie Anglerieque Comes ac Cremone Dominus. Quanquam maiores nostri Ill.mi Principes Vicecomites, qui huius inclyte Civitatis Mediolani Principatum habuerunt ac Ill.mus Genitor noster et successive nos continuatis et vetustissimis temporibus summa fide, reverentia et devotione prosecuti fuerimus Serenissimam ac Christianissimam Regiam Domum Francorum; et viceversa Ser.mi Reges Domus ipsius, qui pro temporibus fuerunt, ipsos omnes maiores nostros singulari benivolentia, caritate atque clementia complexi et ultro citroque affinitatis vinculo sibi coniungere dignati sunt; nos tamen antique atque hereditarie devotionis non immemores, nedum res huiusmodi continuare, sed augere pro viribus semper conati fuerimus et preter eam quam erga Ser.mum atque Christianissimum Dominum Dominum Carolum, presentem Francorum Regem, gerimus tali ac tanta devotione et reverentia Ill.mo et Ser.mo Principi Domino Domino Lodovico, Delphino Viennensi eius primogenito et futuro Regi afficimur, ut si non factis certe ipsius saltem

animi effectu priscos omnes superare nobis persuadeamus eiusque sub-
limitati tantum debere fateamur, quantum persolvi humana ope vix
possit. Hic cum Ill.mus ac Ser.mus Princeps, ut cetera in nos collata
beneficia hoc loco pretereamus, ut animum nostrum re ipsa equaret, aut
potius superaret, ultra alia amicitie, caritatis, affinitatis et devotionis
vincula, nos ac Ill.mam Dominam Blancam Mariam, et liberos et successores nostros speciali gratia et clementia complecti dignatus est, et
lige, unionis ac indissolubilis amoris vinculum nobiscum contrahere,
patrocinium ac protectionem nostram in se suscipere, et ita Omnipoten-
tis Dei gratia factum est ut prelibatus Ill.mus et Ser. mus Dominus
Dominus Delphinus, futurus Rex, nos nostrosque omnes utsupra in
ligam, confederationem et intelligentiam puram, meram et sincerissimam acceptaverit, eamque inierit et confirmaverit, protectionemque
susceperit medio atque interventu spectabilis viri Prosperi Camulii,
oratoris et secretarii nostri, ac speciale mandatum habentis; quem
quidem Prosperum superioribus mensibus ad prelibatum Dominum
Dominum nunc Delphinum, et futurum Regem transmisimus, et quam
ligam, confederationem et protectionem ipse Dominus Dominus nunc
Delphinus, et futurus Rex geminatis publicis documentis et litteris
solemniter confirmare dignatus est; quorum, quarum tenor talis sub-
sequitur videlicet:

Lodovicus, Regis Francorum primogenitus, Delphinus Viennensis
Comesque Valentinensis et Diensis. Universis presentium serie fieri
volumus manifestum, quod cum inter Ill.mum et Ex.mum Principem,
Dominum Dominum Franciscum Sfortiam, Ducem Mediolani etc.,
avunculum nostrum honorandissimum, per medium atque interventum
spectabilis viri Prosperi Camulii, oratoris, procuratoris et secretarii ipsius
et ad hoc speciale mandatum habentis, ut constat litteris patentibus
ipsius avunculi nostri, datis Mediolani die XXVI mensis augusti
MCCCCLX, eius sigillo sigillatis ac ipsius propria manu subscriptis, ac
per magnificum virum Cichum de Calabria eius cancellarium signatis,
et nos Delphinum Viennensem antedictum inite et firmate essent certe

conventiones et capitula, tam pro nobis quam pro filiis, heredibusque, et successoribus et adherentibus nostris, cuius tenor sequitur et est talis. [omitted].[a]

Verum cum in ipsis capitulis inter cetera contineatur, quod ipse Ill.mus avunculus noster teneretur et deberet defendere et conservare, ac in suam tutelam recipere castra, terras, bona et loca magnifici militis, consiliarii et cambellarii nostri, Domini Iacobi de Valperga, que tunc vexabantur in statu in quo erant die quartra septembris proxime elapsi, aut meliori, et casu contigerit antequam ad notitiam prefati avunculi nostri honorandissimi devenerint dicte conventiones et capitula, castra, terras et loca predicti Domini Iacobi perdita et destructa fuerint, et ita sibi impossibile erat dictum capitulum adimplere; offerens tamen aliunde nobis et prefato Domino Iacobo rem convenientem facere, videbatur tamen eo respectu dictas conventiones et capitula amplius locum et effectum non habere, et quamlibet partium in suo primevo libero statu restare debere. Sed cum ipse prefatus avunculus noster nobis et prefato Domino Iacobo tantum fecerit, quod utrique nostrum satisfactum est et contenti remaneamus de ipso avunculo nostro; potissime considerantes actus per ipsum avunculum nostrum pro rerum dicti Domini Iacobi conservatione iam factos in subsidiis prestandis ac etiam capitulorum ignorantiam, singularemque dilectionem, quam ad nos gerit; ideo mentem et propositum nostrum declarantes, dicimus, intendimus, volumus, promittimus et declaramus, quod prefata liga, conventiones et capitula firma et efficacia permaneant, et eamdem obtineant roboris firmitatem ac alter nostrum alteri remaneat obligatus et astrictus, ac si ipse prefatus avunculus noster dicta castra, loca, terras et bona defensasset et in bono ac pacifico statu conservasset; et ideo omni modo, via, iure et forma, quibus melius possumus et valemus, supradictis non obstantibus premissis attentis ipsam ligam, conventiones et capitula iterato promittimus, laudamus, approbamus et confirmamus, ac in quantum opus sit de novo contrahimus et firmamus et volumus in sua roboris

---

a. There follows the text of the Treaty of Genappe.

firmitate permanere, et promittimus in verbo Principis et sub fide et sacramento corporis nostri, nostro subscripto notario et secretario ad opus prefati avunculi nostri stipulante dictam ligam, conventiones et capitula rata, grata et firma tenere, ac in futurum inviolabiliter observare, omni exceptione, que usque in hodiernum obiici posset non obstante. Et sic in manibus secretarii nostri subscripti iuravimus Sacrosanctis Scripturis tactis, ipsoque secretario, ut publica persona pro ipso avunculo nostro iuramentum acceptante, premissis attentis; supplentes ex plenitudine potestatis nostre in presentibus et precipue omnibus et singulis particulis supra specificatis, omni solemitati tam iuris quam facti, que in presentibus servanda fuisset: cum firmam spem geramus dictum avunculum nostrum, ipsum Dominum Iacobum et suos omnes in singulari gratia, protectione et beneficio nostri contemplatione suscepturum. In quorum testimonium presentes litteras fieri et registrari ac sigilli nostri munimine iussimus roborari, et propria manu subscripsimus. Datum Genepe in Barbantia, die primo Iunii anno Domini MCCCCLX primo. Signatum: Loys.[b]

Nos vero licet huiusmodi ligam, confederationem et intelligentiam, et predicta omnia et singula, quantum nostra interesset, ratificaverimus et approbaverimus, et ipsam protectionem subierimus, ut latius patet publicis litteris[1] superinde confectis et manu nostra propria subscriptis, quas ad prelibatum Ill.mum et Serenissimum Dominum Dominum nunc Delphinum, et futurum Regem superioribus mensibus transmisimus. Tamen volentes ex latere nostro omnia perficere, que ipsam ligam et confederationem, et omnia et singula supradicta perpetua atque eterna reddant; et agnoscentes optimam erga nos nostrosque omnes caritatem, liberalitatem, munificentiam et clementiam prelibati Principis, in primis Celsitudini Sue toto corde et spiritu, quas maiores animo concipere possumus, gratias agimus et nos nostrosque omnes perpetuo Serenitati Sue deditissimos atque devinctissimos fatemur. Deinde tenore presentium ex certa scientia, nullo iuris vel facti errore ducti ac alias omnibus modo,

---

b. An undated and incomplete copy of the Dauphin's letters patent is in BN, *Fonds Italien,* Cod. 1589, fols. 21r–24r.

iure, via, causa et forma, quibus melius, validius et efficacius fieri potuit et potest, intervenientibus etiam quibusvis solemnitatibus in similibus opportunis et necessariis, predictam ligam, confederationem et intelligentiam, et omnia et singula suprascripta debite et congrue referendo, libentissimo promptissimoque animo, et cum omni debita reverentia ipsam protectionem subimus, acceptavimus et acceptamus, et ratam, gratam et firmam, ac rata, grata et firma habuimus et habemus, nec non predictas conventiones, capitula, et omnia et singula in eis contenta acceptantes mutua stipulatione promittimus, cavemus, et nos sub obligatione honoris et fidei nostre, quantum ad nos attinet, pariter obligamus. Et sic tactis corporaliter Sacrosanctis Scripturis in manibus infrascripti secretarii nostri iuravimus, presentibus spectabilibus ac magnificis viris, Domino Carolo de Astarciis et Iohanne de Sabbies, prelibati Ill.mi et Serenissimi Domini Delphini et futuri Regis secretariis ac oratoribus, qui huiusmodi sacramentum nostrum et suprascripta omnia et singula utsupra Serenitatis Sue nomine acceptarunt et acceptant. Promittentes ex latere nostro utsupra predicta omnia et singula, semper et omni tempore rata, firma et grata habituros, et omni fide et sinceritate adimpleturos curaturosque et facturos pro viribus quicquid ope et facultate nostra fieri poterit, ut tanti Principis liberitati et clementie erga nos nostrosque omnes correspondere valeamus. In quorum fidem et testimonium presentes fieri iussimus et registrari nostrique sigilli appensione muniri, ac propria manu nostra subscripsimus. Datum in Civitate nostra Mediolani, die XXIIII Iulii MCCCCLXI.

Franciscus Sfortia Vicecomes manu propria subscripsit.

Signatum: Chichus

HISTORICAL NOTE

1. Dated Dec. 6, 1460 [see Appendix, doc. III, p. 467].

Index